The Emerald Handbook of Appearance in the Workplace

The Emerald Handbook of Appearance in the Workplace

EDITED BY

ADELINA BROADBRIDGE

University of Stirling, UK

United Kingdom – North America – Japan – India – Malaysia – China

Emerald Publishing Limited
Emerald Publishing, Floor 5, Northspring, 21-23 Wellington Street, Leeds LS1 4DL

First edition 2024

Reprints and permissions service
Contact: www.copyright.com

British Library Cataloguing in Publication Data
A catalogue record for this book is available from the British Library

ISBN: 978-1-80071-175-4 (Print)
ISBN: 978-1-80071-174-7 (Online)
ISBN: 978-1-80071-176-1 (Epub)

Printed and bound by CPI Group (UK) Ltd, Croydon, CR0 4YY

INVESTOR IN PEOPLE

Table of Contents

List of Figures and Tables   *ix*

About the Editor   *xiii*

About the Contributors   *xv*

Acknowledgements   *xxv*

Introduction   *1*
Adelina Broadbridge

Chapter 1   Appearance as Carnal Capital and Symbolic Violence: An Intersectional Approach   *19*
Mustafa F. Özbilgin, Marios Samdanis and Pelin Arsezen

Chapter 2   Is Curly Hair Viewed as Professional? Examining Hair Bias Against White Women With Curly Hair   *39*
Joy V. Peluchette and Katherine A. Karl

Chapter 3   Examining Hair Choices of Black Women in Academia   *57*
Katherine A. Karl, Joy V. Peluchette and Gail A. Dawson

Chapter 4   Body Weight Discrimination Against Women in Customer-Facing Roles: A Systematic Literature Review   *75*
Sharon Grant, Toby Mizzi and Elyse O'Loghlen

Chapter 5   Ageism, Sexism and Appearance: Navigating Workplace Discrimination in Later Life   *101*
Laura Hurd

Chapter 6   The Price of 'Extra Layers': British Muslim Women's Work and Career   *113*
Sajia Ferdous

Chapter 7   Dress Codes in a 'Singular They' World: Gender Nonbinary Identity and Expression and Employer Appearance Policies   *131*
Todd Brower

Chapter 8   Dressing to Be(come) a Business School Dean: Autoethnographic Accounts   *155*
Gina Grandy, Sharon Mavin and Elise Gagnon

Chapter 9   Appearance Matters: Appearance Management in Political Careers   *169*
Minita Sanghvi and Nancy Hodges

Chapter 10   Status Effects of Attractiveness at Work   *185*
Tonya K. Frevert, Tarya Bardwell and Lisa Slattery Walker

Chapter 11   Lookism Knows No Age: Aesthetic Labour in Women's Careers   *197*
Marjut Jyrkinen, Mira Karjalainen and Linda McKie

Chapter 12   Appearance Discrimination in Hiring: Challenges and Dilemmas for Managers in the United States   *213*
Bahaudin G. Mujtaba, Frank J. Cavico and Tipakorn Senathip

Chapter 13   Legislating Against Lookism in Australia   *233*
Chris Warhurst, Richard Hall and Diane van den Broek

Chapter 14   Appearance, Aesthetic Labour and Corporate Social Responsibility   *249*
Peter Waring

Chapter 15   Advising Clients on Appearance: Ethical Tensions and Positive Conversations   *273*
Julia Yates

Chapter 16   The Visibility of Invisibility: Exploring Criminal History Appearance and Implications to Careers   *287*
Nicole C. Jones Young and Kemi S. Anazodo

Chapter 17   The Impact of Workers' Tattoos and Piercings on Employment: Suggestions for Pragmatic Career Planning   *301*
Leonidas Efthymiou, Yianna Orphanidou and Achilleas Karayiannis

Chapter 18   A Tattooed Workforce – Still a Liability?   *317*
Beth Wood and Adelina Broadbridge

Chapter 19   Tattoos and the Social Psychology of Stigma: Implications for Career Development   *331*
Terence Chia and Andrew R. Timming

Conclusions   *343*
Adelina Broadbridge

Index   *361*

List of Figures and Tables

Chapter 1

Figure 1.   Carnal Capital and Forms of Embodiment.   27

Chapter 7

Figure 1.   Disaggregating Sex Assigned at Birth, Gender
             Identity, Gender Expression, and Sexual
             Orientation.   133

Chapter 15

Figure 1.   A Framework for Addressing Appearance in
             Career Conversations.   283

Chapter 2

Table 1.   Data Structure.   46

Table 2.   Means, Standard Deviations and MANOVA
             Results for Curly Versus Straight Hair.   50

Table 3.   Means, Standard Deviations and MANOVA
             Results for Long Brunette Versus
             Medium-Length Blond Hair.   51

Chapter 3

Table 1.   Percentage of Black Women in Higher
             Education With Afrocentric Hair by Category.   67

Chapter 4

Table 1.   Literature Search and Screening Procedure.   76

Table 2.   Data Extraction: Included Studies.   78

Chapter 9
Table 1.   Participant Information.   174

Chapter 17
Table 1.   Hotel Categories: Characteristics and
                Responses to Worker Body-Art.   308

Chapter 18
Table 1.   Different Job Categories.   323

For Ian. Love you.

About the Editor

Adelina Broadbridge, Stirling Management School, has spent a large part of her career teaching and researching HRM and diversity. A core theme of her research examines career development issues, with a specific focus on gender differences. She has authored over 50 peer reviewed articles, as well as a monograph, two other edited books, along with numerous book chapters and conference papers. She founded the globally recognised British Academy of Management's Gender in Management Special Interest Group. She has chaired tracks at various international conferences, and co-developed and facilitated several professional and personal development programmes for women in academia. In 2019, she was awarded the BAM Medal for Leadership. She led Stirling Management School's successful application for the Athena Swan Bronze Award. She is currently the Editor-in-Chief of *Gender in Management: An International Journal*.

About the Contributors

Kemi S. Anazodo, PhD, is an Assistant Professor at the Odette School of Business at the University of Windsor, in Ontario, Canada. Her research focuses on amplifying the voices of marginalised and stigmatised individuals as they navigate the employment landscape and employment processes. Dr Anazodo employs mixed methodologies to delve into social phenomena, such as identity, equity and stigma, shedding light on how individuals navigate the complexities of their employment experiences.

One of Dr Anazodo's key areas of investigation is the integration and reintegration of justice-involved individuals into the workforce. Her research examines the experiences and processes involved in successfully incorporating these individuals into employment. Through interdisciplinary collaborations, Dr Anazodo has collaborated with colleagues from diverse backgrounds, resulting in numerous conference presentations and published works. Her contributions to the field encompass the perspectives of both employers and individuals with a criminal history, spanning topics such as job search, employment selection and sustaining employment.

By delving into the intricacies of employment dynamics, Dr Anazodo strives to bring about positive change and create a more inclusive and equitable work environment for all individuals, regardless of their background or past experiences.

Pelin Arsezen is an Assistant Professor of Tourism Management at Mugla University, Turkey. She researches on management, human resources management, behavioural sciences and strategic management. Her studies focus on management in tourism industry. She has published over 30 papers on relationship between workaholic behaviours and job satisfaction of tourism industry employees, the relationship between paternalistic leadership and business performance in small tourism businesses, and mobbing, and on 5 star hotel chains. She has authored a book and book chapters such as post-modern organisations, voluntary tourism and social change, and conducted a study on the relationship between paternalism and emotional commitment to the organisation and job satisfaction in small-scale tourism enterprises. She has worked at EU projects and The Scientific and Technological Research Council of Turkey for Restructuring of Akdeniz University EU Documentation Centre, Tourism Cluster Competition and Performance Analysis. She has lectured on strategic management, career management, management and organisation.

Tarya Bardwell is a PhD student in the Organizational Science programme at the University of North Carolina, Charlotte. Her research interests include interpersonal interactions, stress and health in the workplace. She values a collaborative approach to research and works regularly with scholars in communication, sociology and psychology. She is pursuing an academic career in hopes of conducting research that informs efforts towards equity and well-being in the workplace.

Diane van den Broek, PhD, is an Honorary Associate Professor at the University of Sydney Business School, where she was previously an Associate Professor. Her work provides accessible creative analysis that seeks to reform policy settings that improve the material reality of vulnerable workers. She is a leading scholar in the field of labour migration and has received substantial competitive grants to undertake research into migrant work in the horticulture industry. Her role as Co-Convenor of the Migrants@Work Research Group led to annual events that facilitated interaction between policymakers, practitioners and academics on the issues of work and migration. Aside from issues related to migrant work, Diane's research has focused on workplace diversity and inclusion and aesthetics and identity.

Todd Brower is a Professor of Constitutional Law at Western State College of Law in California, USA, and teaches courses in Sexual Orientation, Gender Identity and Expression. He has an LL.M from Yale Law School, a J.D. from Stanford Law School, an A.B. *cum laude* from Princeton University and was a Fulbright Scholar in France. He was pro bono co-counsel in *Karahalios v. National Federation of Federal Employees, local 1263*, 489 US 527 (1989), argued before the US Supreme Court in the 1985–1986 Term.

Professor Brower is also the Judicial Education Director for the Williams Institute on Sexual Orientation, Gender Identity Law and Public Policy at the University of California – Los Angeles (UCLA) School of Law. He has held that position since 2006, although Professor Brower has been working in judicial education for a significant portion of his professional career since 1980. He has worked with the courts of several nations in Europe, in Africa, in North, Central and South America and with the judiciaries of most US states and federal agencies. He has taught for the National Judicial College since 2008 and worked with several international and national judicial and judicial education organisations. Professor Brower is the 2021–2022 President of the National Association of State Judicial Educators, the professional organisation for judicial and court employee education personnel.

Professor Brower's scholarly work involves courts and access to the judicial system. He is the author of various law review articles, book chapters, research studies and academic publications on the treatment of lesbian, gay, bisexual, transgender and queer (LGBTQ) persons in the courts. He co-edited two books on judicial education on sexual orientation and gender identity in Russian and Serbo-Croatian and was one of the Special Issue Editors for peer-reviewed academic journals in the United Kingdom and Italy. Professor Brower was the researcher and author of two reports on the treatment of LGBT court employees in the courts of England and Wales, and one of the main co-authors of a report on the treatment and experiences of court users and court employees in California. He served on the California Judicial Council – Access and Fairness Advisory Committee and was the Chair of its Subcommittee on Sexual Orientation Fairness and Co-Chair of its Subcommittee on Access for Persons with Disabilities.

Frank J. Cavico is a Professor Emeritus of Business Law and Ethics at the H. Wayne Huizenga School of Business and Entrepreneurship of Nova Southeastern University in Ft. Lauderdale, Florida. He has served as a faculty member at the school for 30 years. He has also taught Constitutional and Administrative Law at the doctoral level in the Huizenga School. Professor Cavico holds an LL.M degree from the University of San Diego, a J.D. from St Mary's University, a master's degree in Political Science from Drew University and a BA in Political Science from Gettysburg College.

Terence Chia is a registered Psychologist and an Adjunct Lecturer at Edith Cowan University's School of Business and Law. He received his PhD in Management and a master's degree in Industrial and Organisational Psychology from the University of Western Australia. He is passionate about research on leadership, culture and the organisational context, and investigates how these variables can reduce psychosocial risks and hazards, and positively influence employee well-being and team performance.

Gail A. Dawson is an Associate Professor of Management and Director of Diversity and Inclusion at the Rollins College of Business at the University of Tennessee at Chattanooga. Dr Dawson holds a PhD in Business Administration from the University of South Florida. She has taught a wide range of classes on the graduate and undergraduate level including human resource management, diversity and organisational behaviour.

Leonidas Efthymiou is an Associate Professor in Organisation, Tourism and Hospitality Studies at the University of Nicosia, and adjunct faculty at Unicaf University. He previously worked at Intercollege, Pearson Education and the University of Leicester. He has also taught online for Universities in Europe, Africa and the United States. He also travels frequently to Africa, in his capacity as Instructional Designer. He has co-edited and published several books, articles, media reports, policy papers, encyclopaedia articles and participates in EU-funded projects. His research output lies at the intersection of employment, digitisation and education. He has received a number of awards, including the best PhD Thesis award by the Academy of Management in 2011, Boston, Massachusetts. Prior to this, he trained at the universities of Leicester (PhD, MSc), Derby (BA) and the Higher Hotel Institute Cyprus (Dip. Hons).

Sajia Ferdous, Queen's University Belfast, UK. Sajia Ferdous is a Lecturer in Organisational Behaviour in Queen's University Management School, Queen's University Belfast. Her research mainly explores the intersections of gender, race/ ethnicity, age, religion and class within work and employment contexts. She has written about gender, ageing, intersectionality and migrants' integration issues with a particular focus on South Asian British Muslim diasporas in the United Kingdom.

Tonya K. Frevert is a semi-retired Adjunct Professor in the Department of Sociology at UNC Charlotte. She holds master's degrees in psychology (Northern Arizona University, 2012) and sociology (UNC, Charlotte, 2012) and a PhD in Organizational Science (UNC, Charlotte, 2015). Using an intersectional lens, her research critiques the reproduction of structural inequality in organisations and institutions. Her recent work focuses on removing equity gaps in STEM higher education.

Elise Gagnon is a graduate student pursuing Master's of Science in Organizational Studies with the Levene Graduate School of Business at the University of Regina located in Saskatchewan, Canada. Her research thus far has focused on employee engagement and recovery, and their effects on various facets of individual well-being.

Gina Grandy is a Professor and Dean with the Haskayne School of Business at the University of Calgary, Canada. Her research interests are in leadership, gender and women in leadership, identity, stigmatised work, competitive advantage and case writing. Her work has been published in such outlets as *Human Relations, Gender, Work & Organization, Organization, Management Learning, British Journal of Management* and *Journal of Business Ethics*. She co-edited the *Handbook of Qualitative Research in Business and Management* (2018) and *Stigma, Work and Organizations* (2017) and is past Editor of *Case Research Journal*.

Dr Sharon Grant is a Senior Lecturer in Psychology at Swinburne University of Technology in Melbourne, Australia. Sharon's research interests include organisational, social and health psychology, with a particular emphasis on weight stigma and related discrimination in obesity, and its negative effect on psychological/physical health and health behaviour. Sharon has conducted research on negative obesity stereotypes in Australia, weight-related discrimination in employment and the effect of imagery and messages in (mock) weight-related public health campaigns on anti-fat attitudes, perceived weight stigma and motivation and self-efficacy for healthy behaviour change. Sharon is an advocate for body size diversity, including the use of weight-inclusive (versus weight normative) images and messages in public health settings and the media.

Richard Hall, PhD, is a Professor and Deputy Dean of Leadership and Executive Education at Monash Business School at Monash University in Australia. Before joining Monash, Richard was the Professor of Work and Organisational Studies, and Associate Dean for Executive Management Education at the University of Sydney. His research interests focus on leadership, industrial relations and management education. He is the lead co-editor of the four-volume reference work *Leadership Development and Practice* (Sage, 2014).

Nancy Hodges, PhD, is the Burlington Industries Professor and Head of the Department of Consumer, Apparel, and Retail Studies at the University of North Carolina, Greensboro. Her research explores topics related to appearance and consumption and well as issues of women's education for and work in the global apparel industry. She has published multiple books and book chapters as well as more than 60 journal articles in such journals as the *Clothing and Textiles Research Journal*, the *Journal of Fashion Marketing and Management* and *Women's Studies International Forum*. She has received more than $1million in grant funding in support of her research.

Laura Hurd, MSW, PhD, is a Sociologist whose areas of expertise include the sociology of ageing, body image, embodiment and health. Her programme of qualitative research has been funded by the Social Sciences and Humanities Research Council of Canada and the Canadian Institutes for Health Research and has examined older men and women's experiences of ageism, physical changes, health, illness and social exclusion. She has published widely in journals such as *Ageing and Society, Journal of Aging Studies, Women and Aging, Canadian Journal on Aging, Qualitative Health Research, Health: An Interdisciplinary Journal for the Social Study of Health, Illness and Medicine* and *Sociology of Health and Illness.* Her book, *Facing Age: Women growing older in anti-aging culture*, was published by Rowman and Littlefield in 2011. Her current research is investigating the experiences and perspectives of gender and sexually diverse older adults.

Marjut Jyrkinen is a Professor in Working Life Equality and Gender Studies, University of Helsinki. She is Vice Director of the Gender, Society and Culture doctoral programme, and has a title of docent in administration and organisation studies at the University of Helsinki. She leads the consortium *En Route to Recovery: Diversity and Vulnerability in Care Work During and After the COVID-19 Pandemic* which is funded by the Trans-Atlantic Platform. Jyrkinen's research interests relate to gender and intersectionalities in society and working life as well as in the contexts of management and organisations. She has studied women manager's careers, gendered ageism and gendered violence, has been involved in many gender equality projects and acted in several international and national expert positions and tasks. Her research has been published, for instance, in *Gender, Work and Organization, Journal of Business Ethics, Gender in Management – An International Journal* and *Work, Employment and Society.*

Dr Achilleas Karayiannis is an Assistant Professor in Sustainability and Organizational Behaviour at Neapolis University in Paphos. Until recently, Achilleas was a Lecturer in Human Resources Management and Sustainability at Aston University in Birmingham.

Achilleas has done a BSc in "Business Administration and Management with Psychology" (2001–2004, Oxford Brookes university), an MA in "Organization

Studies" (2004–2005, Warwick university) and a PhD titled "Acting and Performing: An Organizational Approach" (2005–2009, Essex university).

Achilleas' research interests are focused on the exchange of roles at the intersection between everyday and professional life, on the pedagogical role of sustainability and the role of sustainability in the creation of sustainable competitive advantages for organisations and businesses. Achilleas authors articles in "Insider Cyprus" and "Forbes Cyprus" that are related to his research interests."

Mira Karjalainen is an Associate Professor (docent) in the Department of Cultures at the University of Helsinki and Jyväskylä University School of Business and Economics (JSBE). Her research on gender, organisations and management has focused on work–life balance, social sustainability of organisations, remote work and aesthetic labour, emotional and spiritual labour. Her current research project, funded by the Kone Foundation and carried out at the University of Helsinki, focuses on blurring boundaries of work, especially on friendships, networks and social labour. She has published in, for example, *Organization*, *Sociology Compass* and *Qualitative Research in Organizations and Management: An International Journal.*

Katherine A. Karl is the Henry Hart Professor of Management in the Rollins College of Business at UTC and holds a PhD in Organizational Behavior and Human Resource Management from Michigan State University. Dr Karl has taught a wide variety of courses including human resource management, employment law, labour relations, training and development, management skills, grievance and arbitration, organisational behaviour, principles of management and strategic management. Her research has focused on workplace polices related to employee attire and appearance, social media, workplace fun, workplace romance, employment termination, and also on generational differences, job values, performance feedback and the use of videotaped feedback in management education and development.

Sharon Mavin is a Professor of Leadership and Organisation Studies at Newcastle University following tenure as Director of Newcastle University Business School. Previously she held Dean, Director and Associate Dean Research roles at Roehampton and Northumbria Universities in the United Kingdom. Sharon is a Fellow of the Academy of Social Sciences, Royal Society of Arts and of the British Academy of Management (BAM). She was awarded the BAM Medal for Leadership in 2021 and added to the Northern Power Women Power List in 2022. Her recent research has been published in such journals as *Gender, Work and Organization, Management Learning, Human Relations* and *Gender in Management: An International Journal*. Sharon co-edited the Routledge *Handbook of Research Methods on Gender in Management* (2021).

Linda McKie joined the Faculty of Social Sciences and Public Policy at King's in January 2022. She was previously Dean/Head of School of the School of Social and Political Sciences, University of Edinburgh. Linda is currently Principal Investigator on the UKRI, Healthy Ageing Programme Grant on *Healthier*

Working Lives and Ageing for Workers in the Care Sector: Developing Careers, enhancing Continuity, Promoting Wellbeing (https://www.sps.ed.ac.uk/research/research-project/healthier-working-lives-care-workforce) and is also working with the *Advanced Care Research Centre* at the University of Edinburgh on transitions in care; www.ed.ac.uk/usher/advanced-care-research-centre. She is also a member of the Trans-Atlantic Platform project on care work during and after COVID-19 pandemic. In 2004, Linda was elected a Fellow of the Academy of Social Sciences (FAcSS) and has chaired grant award panels for a range of UK and EU funding bodies including the Academy of Finland, ESRC and EU COST.

Toby Mizzi is a registered Psychologist (counselling psychologist) and supervisor with over 10 years' experience working in mental health and disability. Toby previously worked at Swinburne University of Technology from 2008 to 2020 in a Lecturer/Tutor role in the psychology discipline. Toby has previously co-authored peer-reviewed papers investigating weight-based stereotypes and the impact of weight on hiring decisions.

Bahaudin G. Mujtaba is a Professor of Human Resources and International Management at the Huizenga College of Business and Entrepreneurship of Nova Southeastern University. Bahaudin is the author and co-author of books dealing with diversity, ethics and business management. During the past 30 years, he has had the pleasure of working with researchers, managers and human resource professionals in the United States, China, Japan, Brazil, India, Pakistan, Afghanistan, St Lucia, Grenada, Vietnam, Malaysia, Thailand, Bahamas, Jamaica, Morocco and others around the globe.

Elyse O'Loghlen is a PhD candidate and provisionally registered psychologist at Swinburne University of Technology, Melbourne, Australia. Elyse has received several awards for research excellence, including the Australian Psychological Society Prize (2019) and the Swinburne University Medal for the most outstanding undergraduate student in the Faculty of Health, Arts and Design (2019). Elyse's research interests include eating- and body image-related disorders and weight-related discrimination, and she is an advocate for the health at every size approach to public health. Elyse's PhD research explores personal and social factors that predict the severity and function of binge eating symptoms and she has published several peer-reviewed articles in this area.

Yianna Orphanidou is an Associate Lecturer in the field of Hospitality and Tourism at the University of Nicosia. She is a holder of a BA (HONS) in Hospitality Management and an MSc in Hospitality and Tourism Education from Surrey University (UK). She has an extensive practical and academic experience in the field of Tourism and Hospitality Management. She has participated in the technical and research teams of more than 20 funded European, International and National projects. She serves in a numerous Tourism and Hospitality professional organisations from the position of a board director. Her main research interest includes tourism sustainable development and hospitality human resources.

Mustafa F. Özbilgin is a Professor of Organisational Behaviour at Brunel Business School, London. He also holds two international positions: Co-Chaire Management et Diversité at Université Paris Dauphine and Visiting Professor of Management at Koç University in Istanbul. His research focuses on equality, diversity and inclusion at work from comparative and relational perspectives. He has conducted field studies in the United Kingdom and internationally and his work is empirically grounded. His research is supported by international as well as national grants. His work has a focus on changing policy and practice in equality and diversity at work. He is an engaged scholar, driven by values of workplace democracy, equality for all and humanisation of work.

Joy V. Peluchette is a Senior Professor of Management at Lindenwood University. She previously taught at the University of Wollongong (NSW Australia) and at the University of Southern Indiana. Dr Peluchette holds a D.B.A. in Organizational Behavior from Southern Illinois University at Carbondale. Dr Peluchette has taught a wide range of management courses at both the graduate and undergraduate levels, including organisational behaviour, principles of management, leadership skills, human resource management, business/government and society, diversity management and strategic management. Her recent research publications have focused on the human resource implications of workplace attire, workplace fun and use of social media, as well as issues related to the millennial generation such as helicopter parenting.

Marios Samdanis is a Senior Lecturer in Strategy, Entrepreneurship and International Management at Brunel Business School, Brunel University, London. His research interests revolve around creativity, new technologies, leadership and diversity. His published research includes themes, such as atypical leaders, creative leaders and inequalities in the artistic labour market. Prior to joining Brunel University London, Marios was a Lecturer in Art Business at Sotheby's Institute of Art and an Associate Lecturer in Digital Creativity and New Media Management at Birkbeck College, University of London.

Minita Sanghvi, PhD, is an Associate Professor in the Management and Business Department at Skidmore College. Her research focuses on gender and intersectionality in marketing and consumption. Her book *Gender and Political Marketing in the United States and the 2016 Presidential Election: An Analysis of Why She Lost* was published by Palgrave Macmillan in 2019. She has published articles in *Journal of Marketing Management and Journal of Business Research*. Taking her research beyond words, Dr Sanghvi co-curated an art exhibit titled: *Never done: 100 years of women in politics and beyond* at the Frances Young Tang Museum. And in 2021, she ran for election and was elected the first woman of colour and first LGBTQ commissioner in Saratoga Springs, New York.

Tipakorn Senathip earned a Master's of Public Administration degree from the faculty of political sciences at Ramkhamhaeng University (RU) in Bangkok, Thailand. She is now conducting doctoral research in public administration human resources and training practices at RU. She worked at the Institute of International Studies (IIS) of RU. As part of her administrative responsibilities at

IIS, she dealt with cross-cultural faculty members and students from all over the globe, including Thais. Her areas of research interests include human resources, training, sustainability and gender equality development.

Andrew R. Timming is a Professor of Human Resource Management at the Royal Melbourne Institute of Technology's College of Business. He holds a PhD in Economic Sociology from the University of Cambridge. His research centres around three main themes: employee selection decision-making, employee voice and occupational health and safety. He is an Associate Editor at *Human Resource Management Journal* and *International Journal of Human Resource Management* and sits on the Editorial Board of *Human Resource Management*. His Twitter handle is @timminglab.

Lisa Slattery Walker (formerly Rashotte) received her PhD in Sociology from the University of Arizona in 1998. Her research focuses on small group interaction, non-verbal behaviours, identity, emotions, gender and expectations. Her work has appeared in *Social Psychology Quarterly*, *Social Science Research*, *Social Forces*, *Sex Roles* and numerous other journals. Recently, she has conducted projects on altering the status meaning of gender and, with Murray Webster, on the effect of behaviours on inequality structures in small groups.

Chris Warhurst, PhD, FRSA, FAcSS is a Professor and Director of the Institute for Employment Research at the University of Warwick in the United Kingdom. His research focuses on aesthetic labour, job quality and skills. He is an Associate Research Fellow of SKOPE at the University of Oxford, a Fellow of the Royal Society and a member of the United Kingdom's Productivity Institute. He has been an expert advisor to the United Kingdom, Scottish and Australian Governments as well as to Eurofound, the OECD, Oxfam Scotland and the Scottish Living Wage campaign. He is the Co-Chair of ReWAGE, an ESRC-funded UK expert advisory group on building back better work and employment post-Covid. He has published 18 books, including *Aesthetic Labour* (Sage, 2020) and *Looking Good, Sounding Right* (Industrial Society, 2001).

Peter Waring is a Pro Vice Chancellor Transnational Education and also Singapore Dean for Murdoch University. As a qualified lawyer, Peter also holds degrees in Commerce and Management and a PhD in Industrial Relations. Peter is a graduate of the Australian Institute of Company Directors. Peter is the co-author of five books on employment relations. Overall he has published more than a 100 book chapters and articles in leading international and national journals. His research and teaching interests span the business and law fields of employment relations, human resource management, corporate governance, labour law and Higher Education Policy. He has lived in Singapore for the last 20 years.

Beth Wood is a graduate of the University of Stirling who is now pursuing a career in the financial sector as a Data Analytics Consultant. The quantitative data and research that she collated on the impact of tattoos on employability has led her to this data-driven and analytics role.

Julia Yates, City, University of London, UK. Julia Yates is an Associate Professor in the department of psychology at the City, University of London where she teaches on their MSc in Organisational Psychology. Her research interests are in career decision-making, the career development of those facing barriers at work and the impact of appearance on career paths. She has written a number of books on the topic of *career coaching*, most recently *The Career Coaching Toolkit*.

Nicole C. Jones Young, PhD, is an Associate Professor of Organizational Behavior at Franklin & Marshall College in Pennsylvania, US. Her research primarily focuses on the employment experiences of marginalised populations, such as individuals with a criminal history as well as organisational inclusion and anti-Black racism, both in academia and traditional workplace settings. She has collaborated with multiple management scholars, presented at various conferences and published a variety of work in academic journals on both of the aforementioned research areas. Dr Young also has a recent book on the topic of hiring individuals who possess a criminal history, currently titled *Now Hiring: A Manager's Guide to Employing Applicants With a Criminal History*.

Acknowledgements

I'd like to thank Dr Helen Beddow for her enthusiasm and commissioning this book in the first place. Thanks also to the Emerald team associated with this book and all the authors of the chapters. Without these people there would be no book.

I especially thank Shirley Warnock-Lowe for agreeing to feature on the front cover of this book, and also Rebecca Wilson for her skills in taking the photograph. These women work at Central Scotland School of Jewellery (founded by Jo Pudelko) and Central Scotland School of Craft (proprietor, Rebecca Wilson). Along with various other highly experienced and talented women artists, they provide unique workshops and classes where participants can grow their creative skills in a supportive and welcoming environment where sustainability is at the core of their practice. For more information about this wonderful endeavour see Central Scotland School of Jewellery – Central Scotland School of Jewellery (cssj.co.uk) and Classes & Workshops – An Artisan Craft School in Dunblane (scottishcraftschool.com).

I am indebted to a number of people throughout my academic career, many of whom have become treasured friends. My first venture in editing books was with Dr Sandra Fielden and I particularly thank her for her guidance, support and precious friendship. Other people who have been a joy to work with and are now cherished friends include Gail Clarkson, Ian Fillis, Karen Forrest, Lisa Haddow, Carol Marshall, Andrie Michaelides, Agneta Moulettes and Ian Spencer. I also am grateful to my colleagues from the British Academy of Management Gender in Management Special Interest Group who have provided much debate and stimulation of research activities. Finally, I am not forgetting 'help' from my four-legged family – Jamie and Cleo – who always make me smile.

I am lucky to have you all in my life.

Introduction

Adelina Broadbridge

Introduction

There has been considerable research looking at career management generally. However, a lot of this research ignores the prejudice that can occur in the process. Much of that which has done has highlighted the gendered nature of career management and shown how women struggle to overcome discrimination and prejudice at various stages within the workplace. Their careers are influenced by a range of micro, meso and macro factors (Broadbridge & Fielden, 2015, 2018; Kumra et al., 2014; Powell, 2018). The knowledge this work has produced has been critical in understanding the inequities of some people's career development. However, one area that has been relatively neglected academically is the effect that appearance might have on people's careers, and this too can be gendered. We live in a visual society and from a media perspective, hardly a day goes by without seeing reference to people's appearance, some of which is within the work context. This can have a profound effect on how people present themselves generally, and specifically at work. Yet, the impact of individual appearance on career success, either positive or negative, often remains unspoken or even unconscious within the world of work. Appearance in organisations is not a new phenomenon (Hopfl, 2000; Mills, 1951) and has been going on, in some instances, for hundreds of years. Nevertheless, it has been a relatively under-researched topic area in recent years. As Peluchette and Karl (2018) argue, styles change and so do people's definition of what is appropriate or inappropriate with regard to appearance in the workplace.

Appearance generally comprises part of our non-verbal communication to the world although aspects of verbal communication such as accents and demeanour may also constitute appearance. To many, a definition of appearance refers to the clothing that people wear, and certainly this has been the subject of numerous research in the field. Drawing on Stone (1995), clothing is an important social indicator to the identification of people, both for themselves and from the perspective of others. The approach adopted to appearance in this book was to encourage authors to adopt a broader interpretation of appearance should they wish to do so. Thus, the book also considers body capital (Brewis, 2017; Edmonds & Mears, 2017), demeanour and the way people look other than merely their clothing.

The Emerald Handbook of Appearance in the Workplace, 1–17
Copyright © 2024 by Emerald Publishing Limited
All rights of reproduction in any form reserved
doi:10.1108/978-1-80071-174-720230001

The physical body symbolises aspects of identity and the self (Haynes, 2008; Peluchette & Karl, 2007). Younger generations are increasingly identifying with more fluid and non-binary gender and sexual identities and are progressively expressing those identities in a more flexible and changing manner (Jones, 2018; Wilson & Meyer, 2021). Also, more people are showing their individualism and identity via alterations in their appearance, such as tattoos, piercings and cosmetic surgeries, but how might these impact on their experiences in the workplace? With the added intensification of the 'me too' campaign, and growing attention of the transgender and gender expansive agenda, now seems an apposite time to raise fresh academic awareness of some of the contemporary writing surrounding appearance at work.

The Importance of Appearance at Work

Appearance is regarded as very important in the workplace (Karl et al., 2013) and research shows how it can be an important component of the personal attributes required for employability (Carbery & Cross, 2015). Appearance can have a very real impact on how employees are perceived. However, it can be difficult to interpret because what is deemed 'appropriate' by one organisation may not be acceptable, and so regarded as 'inappropriate' in another. There is evidence that a person's dress and appearance can affect various aspects of the employment process right from the recruitment stage up to dismissal decisions (e.g. Baert & Decuypere, 2014; Crowder, 2010; Roehling et al., 2018). First impressions count and can be heavily influenced by attire (Howlett et al., 2013), and appearance and image has been shown to affect workplace promotions and salary decisions (Corbett, 2011; Peluchette et al., 2006), as well as career success (Peluchette & Karl, 2018; Yates et al., 2017).

Appearance at work may be to the individual's benefit or demise. From a positive point of view, it enables the employee to show their individualism. This might be particularly beneficial in certain types of occupations, say in the arts or creative industries. For example, Arndt et al. (2017) highlight the positive con-notations of tattoos for demonstrating creativity and freedom. Certain companies such as Apple embrace a degree of individualism from their employees, wanting them to be themselves and believing this will allow their creativity to flourish. Likewise, if a person is perceived to possess the 'correct credentials' for the organisation in which they are employed, they too might be better placed to reap the positive benefits associated with that employment. However, this might be more problematic to construe. What is meant by 'correct credentials' often is deeply connected with the culture and image the company wants to portray. Mead (1934) and Stone (1995) argued that the responses of others constitute and validate our sense of self. So, general appearance and bodily manipulations can have a significant effect on self-esteem when they are validated by the gaze of others. We can understand how this may play out in the work context.

Appearance Codes and Aesthetic Labour

McInnis and Medvedev (2021) contend that what one wears to work is important. They argue that proper dress is necessary in order to be seen and heard in one's profession, and they describe it as a 'language' that others will understand and associate with credibility and value. Organisational dress or appearance codes might on initial inspection be regarded as superficial and inconsequential. Yet, Brower (2013) maintained that they reflect on enshrined social stereotypes and expectations of women and men and how they look. Employee appearance, particularly in customer facing roles, has become increasingly important to numerous companies in their efforts to market the right image to their customers. The inclination of employers to hire, train, reward and promote employees based on their appearance is now mainstreamed and termed 'aesthetic labour' (Warhurst & Nickson, 2020). But this labour, also known as 'lookism', has the potential to create a new form of employment discrimination based on workers' appearance (Warhurst et al., 2009).

Aesthetic labour is a form of body capital where looks are translated into economic and symbolic rewards (Mears, 2014) and physical appearance is seen as the embodiment of individuals' capabilities. This creates the business linkage of the importance of appearance and work. It involves managing and self-control over appearance at work (Witz et al., 2003). Having the 'right' look and 'looking the part' is something that can be crucial to career success; people are judged by customers, recruiters, clients and the public (who may be considered prospective consumers) according to their attire and looks. Employee appearance therefore represents part of the overall brand reputation and image of the organisation. As a result, there has been numerous research on aesthetic labour, looking 'right' and the association with corporate image (e.g. Caven et al., 2013; Hall & van den Broek, 2012; Karl et al., 2013; Nickson & Baum, 2017; Pettinger, 2004; van den Berg & Arts, 2019; Warhurst & Nickson, 2020; Williams & Connell, 2010).

Companies want to create a certain corporate image in the eyes of their stakeholders and part of doing this is through having prescribed dress codes or customary practices. Both can potentially present problems for employees. On the one hand, prescribed codes may endorse a certain traditional and stereotyped look, while on the other hand, customary practices can be ambiguous. Some workplaces have strict dress codes; others have dress codes but these can be vague and bewildering, and open to interpretation. Other workplaces do not have policies regarding employee appearance; Middlemiss (2018) notes that smaller and medium sized organisations are less likely to have explicit dress codes than large organisations. This can lead to ambiguity, making it difficult for an individual to interpret how they should present themselves in various workplace situations. Often, unwritten rules about appearance in workplaces abound and these can result in both implicit and explicit bias and stereotyping occurring.

Concern for customer perceptions (Karl et al., 2013; Timming, 2015, 2017) and portraying a corporate brand image can be all important to some companies (Williams & Connell, 2010; Witz et al., 2003) in pursuit of economic gains. With this view, recruitment and selection allows for the filtering out of inappropriate people. Nickson et al. (2000) found job adverts encompassed various instances of appearance, speech and presentation, including some asking for photographs. This, they asserted, showed how organisations sought a particular look and disposition which might be even more important than the applicant's technical skills. They affirmed how some retailers controlled the appearance of their employees to the extent that an employee required management permission to cut or colour their own hair. Nickson and Baum (2017) contend that aesthetic labour has led to concerns about equality and fairness with regard to who can access entry level, frontline jobs. All of this confirms how organisations can create exclusionary practices, often right at the recruitment stage, in terms of who is deemed most appropriate to best represent a company's desired brand image (Caven et al., 2013; Nickson & Baum, 2017).

Research on customer perceptions of the retail service encounter has shown that customers seek reassurance in the service encounter, and this can be done by matching and mirroring the age and gender of customer facing staff with their expectations for who is credible and appropriate to deliver the service (Foster & Resnick, 2013). This clearly can have repercussions for the employment of certain categories of workers that might not face up to customer expectations. Often this can be those with protected characteristics. Although in the United Kingdom employers' dress code must not be discriminatory in respect of the protected characteristics in the Equality Act 2010, discriminatory dress codes remain widespread, especially in relation to women and transgender employees (Middlemiss, 2018). Some of the chapters of this handbook investigate aesthetic labour and also how people with protected characteristics nevertheless experience a form of discrimination in their appearance at work.

Making an Impression and Attracting the Attractive

Johnson et al. (2010) claim that job characteristics influence the relationship between physical attractiveness and ratings of employment suitability. Associated with aesthetic labour and lookism is evidence that has shown that 'attractive' people are regarded as more beneficial to and suitable in employment (Johnson et al., 2010; Hamermesh, 2011; Johnson et al., 2018; Langlois et al., 2000; Tartaglia et al., 2005). But what constitutes being 'attractive' and who determines whether employees are deemed 'attractive'? There is an association of beauty with positive characteristics (James, 2008; Lowman et al., 2019) and economic benefits for the organisation (Bruton, 2015). Other research substantiates that attractive employees have better jobs and earn better salaries than those deemed unattractive (e.g. Johnson et al., 2010; Hamermesh, 2011; Judge et al., 2009). Crowder (2010) argued how being attractive is more highly valued than being unattractive, and in career terms, associated with various positive qualities (higher productivity, intelligence and successful). Moreover, Madera and Hebl (2012) found job applicants with facial stigmas all to rate lower on hireability than non-stigmatised applicants. Bruton (2015) rejected arguments that hiring people based on their appearance (looks-based hiring or 'lookism') is not job relevant, concluding that this type of hiring is permissible for businesses where lookism produces clear economic benefits.

There are various signifiers that can hinder a person's career and experience in the workplace. When compared to an idealistic norm or subject to the scrutiny of others, it can affect some forms of employees far more than others. Certain categories of people might be more susceptible to appearance biases and stereotyping. Jones (2013) argued that all societies have dress/appearance codes to police the social significance of dress and appearance. The dress code message given, Jones argues, can include clues about the person's social status, income, occupation, ethnic and religious beliefs marital status, sexual availability, sexual orientation and self-identity. As such, certain research has looked at specific characteristics of people and provided insights about their 'suitability' regarding their employment. Gender is a noticeable characteristic that has drawn attention in prior literature (e.g. Fitzgerald, 2018; Haynes, 2012; Kuipers, 2015; Kukkonen & Sarpila, 2021; McInnis & Medvedev, 2021; Tsaousi, 2020), although less has been written about non-binary, gender expansive and transgender impacts (although see Hadjisolomou, 2021). Other characteristics that have been the subject to some research include age (Kumar, 2022; McInnis & Medvedev, 2021; Nickson & Baum, 2017), accents (Carlson & McHenry, 2006; Mai & Hoffman, 2014; Timming, 2017), race (Lee, 2020; Rosette & Dumas 2007), religion (Al-Waqfi & Forstenlechner, 2014; Hutchings et al., 2012; Metcalfe, 2010, 2011), size/weight (Crowder, 2010; Gruys, 2012; Haynes, 2012; Mujtaba & Cavico, 2016; Nickson et al., 2016; Powroznik, 2017; Roehling et al., 2018) and looks (e.g. Hosoda et al., 2003). Some of these are fixed while others are subject to manipulation to a certain extent. Moreover, various research has found people conform largely to western ideals of professionalism (Brower, 2013), or alter their appearance according to the situation (see Clarke & Turner, 2007; Rumens & Kerfoot, 2009). Brower (2013) contends that western dress appearance codes push men and women towards traditional gender presentation, which highlights the incongruity for women's professional roles.

There may be some aspects of appearance individuals have little control over, but there are other ways they can enhance their overall appearance by attire. Men often require little adjustments as they conform to a male standard code of dress, although they can use certain accessories such as ties to enhance their overall appearance. For women, this is more multifaceted. Peluchette and Karl (2018) argue that dress, accessories, make-up, hair colour, fragrance, nail colour can all be strategies that some women use to increase their physical attractiveness, in their attempt to help the management of the impression of others.

Moreover, Rhode (2010) outlined the obsession people now have with appearance, referring to the amount of money that is spent on cosmetics, hair care, plastic surgery and weight loss programmes nowadays. The growth of cosmetic surgeries has been enormous in the past decade, and Fortune Business Insights (2022) attribute this rising demand as being in response to the importance of aesthetics in our daily lives. Interesting to note is that in 2020 women accounted for 86% of the cosmetic procedures reported by Fortune Business

Insights (2022), which might not be surprising given the emphasis of women's appearance over men's. Nevertheless, we are witnessing the targeting of younger generations of men far more so than their previous counterparts.

Gender and Appearance

Much prior work has emphasised a gendered aspect to appearance issues in the workplace (Haynes, 2008) and so a brief mention about it is warranted in this introduction to set some context for some upcoming chapters. Women may be more sensitive to issues of dress and appearance, particularly as they need a greater legitimacy and acceptance in an organisation (Peluchette & Karl, 2018). Jyrkinen (2014) found women managers felt pressured about their appearance in order to be successful in their careers. Jones (2013) maintained that clothing is an important part of the gendered social structure and an aspect of human physical appearance, claiming that dress can be viewed as an overt display of femininity or masculinity. In most cases, the benchmark for defining 'correct credentials' is traditionally associated with a male standard or ideal. So particularly for women, and gender expansive or gender nonconforming persons, achieving the right look and being perceived as professional can be more complex than it can for men. How should women dress in order to be seen as appropriate for a professional role? We associate cis men in dark suits but dress for women can be far more varied and complicated and so they come under far more visibility and scrutiny.

The roles connected with women in management and the workplace often are incongruous to the stereotypical roles expected of women in society (Eagly & Karau, 2002; Heilman, 1983). Various researchers have explored links between leadership as a masculine construct and the disciplining of women's bodies, appearance and behaviours (Eagly & Karau, 2002; Haynes, 2008; Mavin & Grandy, 2012, 2013, 2016a, 2016b; Morley, 2013; Sinclair, 2005). These scholars assert that female leaders or managers experience negative evaluations because of a disconnect between the expectations of them as women and the expectations of them as leaders. Appearance in this sense can be extended beyond clothing to include behaviours. Social role expectations and role congruity theory mean that men are expected to possess agentic traits (i.e. those associated with leaders) while women are expected to possess communal traits (Eagly & Karau, 2002), and so women appear incongruous with the expectations of the leader role. This can present a double bind for women when it comes to promoted/ management jobs. Senior job requirements demand traditional masculine traits, yet when women display these qualities, they appear as gender atypical and inconsistent with their sex. This can result in them being denied a promoted post.

Despite pressures felt by women regarding appearance generally, their sexual appearance can cause problems in the workplace (Howlett et al., 2015). In some cases sexual labour can be a prerequisite for employment, with women employees being groomed and packaged into a corporate image to emphasise their aesthetic and sexual appeal to clients (Caven et al., 2013). While this brings economic benefits for the organisation, it also leads to women's objectification. Often, women's decisions on appropriate work dress involve considering the impact that sexuality has on competence and professionalism. This was also found to be the case for gay men (Rumens & Kerfoot, 2009). Sexual harassment creates problems for many women at work. In my own research on career development, several women directors spoke of the problems they had encountered in their careers because of sexual harassment, which in some cases led them to leave organisations or take a step back in their careers. This part of the research was not published for reasons of confidentiality as it concerned a particular industry where women were barely represented at such senior levels. However, several of the women spoke of how they felt objectified and how the industry norm was to seek striking looking women at this level. Johnson et al. (2018) also highlighted how attractive women may be objectified and subjected to greater sexual harassment. They argued that attractiveness can be a disadvantage for professional women (yet not men) in recruitment, promotion and compensation, and further noted how attractiveness can provoke greater same-sex competition, all of which can cause problems along the various stages of their careers. Kelan (2013) argued that being sexually attractive can also be regarded as unprofessional for women. Lizotte and Meggers-Wright (2019) outline how the media coverage of Sarah Palin's clothing and attractiveness during her political campaigning was at times objectifying, led to perceptions of her being unqualified for the role and generally provoked thoughts of incompetence and unintelligence in female candidates.

Inspiration Behind the Book

The idea for this book arose from a previous book on diversity in the workplace (Broadbridge & Fielden, 2018). That book was divided into eight sections, each examining one aspect regarding diversity and how this impacted those people's individual careers (e.g. age, gender, race, sexuality). One section we devoted to 'appearance,' and this contained chapters by some leading authors in the field. These chapters gave an insight into the sense of the enormity that one's appearance might have for one's progression in the workplace. For example, Nickson (2018) revealed how hiring on the basis of looks is a well-established strategy in a range of occupations and organisations. Roehling et al. (2018) showed how biases and negative stereotypes towards the obese can lead to discrimination in all phases of their employment. Peluchette and Karl (2018) highlighted the complexities of gendered behaviour and the double bind women can encounter for dressing femininely in a masculine world of work, and subsequently their perceived ability to perform their organisational roles. Johnson et al. (2018) revealed the hidden costs of attractiveness that can negatively influence career paths of professional women at different stages of their careers. The issues raised in these chapters underline how different facets of appearance can create issues for people and their workplace experiences and development. These issues demonstrated how appearance and 'looks' can have a crucial impact on the employment experience, yet may also provoke negative reactions. They advance understanding on how stereotypes are allowed to be perpetuated in the twenty-first century, and how appearance expectations align with dominant organisational cultures and norms. It seems, therefore, that how one looks might be regarded as equally, or even more, important than one's intellectual capabilities for the job (Inc, n.d.; Warhurst et al., 2000; Inc., n.d.). Exploring these issues further became the origin of this current book.

There are few laws to protect against discrimination based on appearance, which exposes some ethical implications of employers hiring on the basis of appearance (Nickson, 2018). Appearance discrimination is not a protected category but nevertheless is a real issue with regards to discrimination and has surfaced terms like 'lookism' (Cavico et al., 2012; Warhurst et al., 2012), 'looks based appearance' (Bruton, 2015), and 'aesthetic labour' (Nickson, 2018). Within the workplace, unfortunately there can exist more negative connotations associated with appearance, or contrasting words that show one feature as good and the opposite as bad (straight versus curly hair; fat versus thin; old versus young; white versus Black; abled versus disabled). Traditionally, the ideal would be regarded as white, male, young, slim and able bodied.

Approach to the Handbook

This handbook examines contemporary academic work on appearance the context of employment, covering an eclectic range of pertinent issues concerning appearance and the workplace. It draws on major authors in the field and examines different areas where appearance can have a significant impact on how employees are perceived and get on in their careers. As appearance is an aspect of an individual's self-identity in the workplace, and so it is important to examine its intersectionality with various protected characteristics such as gender, age, religion and sexual orientation at work. Aesthetic labour is a common part of corporate life, especially in customer facing roles. It can lead to employment discrimination based on physical appearance and have an impact on career progression. Accordingly, some authors have concentrated on the issue of aesthetic labour and lookism in the workplace. Three chapters of the book draw on the growing popularity of people expressing their self-identity via the form of body art, and how this can be presently perceived by employers and customers in organisations. Below is a synopsis of its content and authors.

Mustafa Özbilgin, Marios Samdanis and Pelin Arsezen point to the two aspects of appearance: physical qualities (e.g. height, weight, complexion and having a particular hair, eye and skin colour as well as choice and style of dress and attire) and the social dimension (how the physical qualities of a person are interpreted, rated and judged, and attributed varied meanings and values across different settings). They demonstrate how some people in the workplace may experience positive experiences while others negative, and take the reader through some underlying theories associated with appearance matters.

Joy Peluchette and Katherine Karl look at the differing experiences of professional women with regard to the appearance of their hair. They argue how hair can be part of one's identity and can lead to varying experiences in the workplace. They undertook a study looking at how curly haired white women fared in employment against their straight haired counterparts. Their empirical investigation showed straight-haired women to be rated significantly higher than curly-haired women on job characteristics that are fundamental to professional positions. An abundance of negative signifiers were used to describe curly hair in their chapter. Thus, they conclude that a bias against curly-haired women remains in the workplace.

In another chapter, Katherine Karl, Joy Peluchette and Gail Dawson highlight how negative stereotypes have been associated with Black women's Afrocentric hairstyles working in professional settings. This all leads to biases and stereotypes regarding competency and professionalism. Their work led them to choose a setting that is considered more genial, higher education, where they examined the influence of these biases. However, even in such a less formal sector, they found Black women employees tend to wear Eurocentric hairstyles in an effort to conform and be accepted.

Sharon Grant, Tobi Mizzi and Elyse O'Loghlen explain how discrimination against overweight employees persists in relation to hiring, job assignment, promotion, remuneration and work stability. Their chapter presents a systematic literature review of studies that have examined weight discrimination against heavier women in frontline customer-service role jobs. Negative stereotypes and prejudice mean that overweight people are stigmatised against their weight. This, they argue, predominantly affects women more than men, as heavier women as more likely to be judged as not conforming to society's body ideals.

In her chapter, Laura Hurd turns to the issue of age and appearance. She shows how age-based stereotypes and discrimination are gendered, resulting in differential impacts on older men and women seeking employment or already in employment. She specifies how the older body more generally, and appearance in particular are the focal points of ageist assumptions, norms and practices in the workplace. She concludes by reflecting on the implications and outcomes of age-based exclusion and discrimination on the lives of older female and male employees.

Sajia Ferdous examines the appearance of Muslim migrant women in western workplaces and the challenges they face. Their head wear clearly identifies their ethnic group or religion. She demonstrates how their appearance can impede the process of labour market integration, which limits their work choices and their longer term career progression. The chapter demonstrates how gendered and racialised practices in society can lead to social exclusion.

Todd Brower's chapter addresses the issues that arise when gender non-binary or gender non-conforming people are confronted with employer dress and appearance codes in the workplace. Using insights from queer theory, Brower explains how gender expansive employees serve to interrogate fundamental assumptions behind workplace dress policies and the formal and informal ways in which these policies are policed. The chapter explores this discordance and examines some possible employer responses.

Gina Grandy, Sharon Mavin and Elise Gagnon use reflexive accounts within academia to explore whether dress and appearance expectations have implications for women's career development and advancement. They adopt the position that women's bodies are abject and 'out of place' in organisations where the disciplining of women's bodies serve to regulate and silence women. Their work illustrates how hegemonic masculinity is both sustained and challenged through dress and appearance and how this might impact women's careers.

The chapter by Minita Sanghvi and Nancy Hodges investigates the importance of appearance for marketing politicians, and in particular female politicians. The chapter examines the innumerable issues women in politics face because of their appearance, and how women have successfully managed the issue of appearance at local, state and national levels.

Tonya Frevert, Tarya Bardwell and Lisa Slattery Walker outline the evidence regarding the status effects of physical attractiveness in the workplace. They argue that attractiveness serves as a social status that mostly provides benefits in the workplace, although they recognise that the results are not always positive. They analyse the effects across career development milestones in a worker's life including the selection and hiring process of employment, and the day-to-day interactions with colleagues and co-workers, as well as in leadership roles.

Marjut Jyrkinen, Mira Karjalainen and Linda McKie focus on aesthetic labour in their chapter. Their research examined interviews with women mid managers' knowledge workers in Finland and Scotland. They demonstrate how the various pressures placed on women regarding their appearance, and how these women felt the need to look good and sound right in their careers.

Bahaudin Mujtaba, Frank Cavico and Tipakorn Senathip discuss lookism from the perspective of appearance-based hiring practices in the United States. They emphasise how managers and employers often make hiring decisions based on the appearance and attractiveness of the job applicants. This is because outward appearance may be deemed to play a significant role in the hiring process and can determine which candidates eventually might get the job. They claim that physically attractive job applicants and candidates tend to benefit from an unearned privilege, which can be to the detriment of others who are equally qualified but considered less attractive for whatever reason. The authors affirm that preferring 'attractive' employees, and subsequently discriminating against those who are perceived as unattractive, can present legal and ethical challenges for employers and managers.

In their chapter, Chris Warhurst, Richard Hall and Diane van den Broek also discuss lookism, this time from the perspective of legislation. They note how this 'lookism' is not legislated for generally, and even where it is, not much is known about its effectiveness. Based on archival research, this chapter examines the procedures and operation of physical features inclusion in an Equal Opportunity Act in the state of Victoria in Australia where lookism is prohibited. They assess the efficacy of legal attempts to address employment discrimination based on employee appearance and highlight lessons about the legal challenge lookism presents.

Peter Waring explores the intersection of aesthetic labour, appearance-based discrimination, corporate diversity and inclusion strategies and corporate social responsibility (CSR). His assessment recognises genuine efforts to reject unethical forms of 'lookism' or 'appearance-based discrimination', but he also points to several contradictions. These include contradictions between the rhetoric of diversity and CSR and the continuation of aesthetic labour strategies for commercial advantage.

Julia Yates acknowledges how attractive, more aesthetically pleasing people have an advantage at all stages of the job application process, and throughout their careers. She indicates how this can present a dilemma to career advisers. Do they encourage people to improve their looks in the pursuit of a job, and thus perpetuate the stereotypes regarding appearance? She investigates some of the challenges this imposes, such as causing offence and perpetuating such an unfair and superficial value system to clients.

Nicole Young and Kemi Anazodo's chapter particularly shows how appearance and identity are interwoven and how this can play out for ex-offenders in their attempt to gain employment. Criminal history has been conceptualised as a socially stigmatised identity and their chapter presents an understanding into how the appearance of criminal history information may be left to interpretation and bias throughout the employment experience. They show how appearance-based inferences and information such as employment gaps can contribute to an array of unique career experiences and challenges as people with a criminal history seek to navigate their employment experience.

The chapter by Leonidas Efthymiou, Yianna Orphanidou and Achilleas Karayiannis examines managers' perceptions regarding body art and the impact this has on workers' tattoos and piercings in the hospitality sector. They find that body art may be forbidden, accepted or met with ambiguity. The authors surface how labour market conditions, along with managers' own dispositions can inflict challenges on employment and career planning.

A similar study by Beth Wood and Adelina Broadbridge investigates the issue of tattoos and examines whether the presence of visible tattoos still influences frontline workers' employment chances. They found that irrespective of a general societal shift towards greater tattoo acceptance and integration into modern society, some negative stereotypes about tattoos remain. Acceptance of tattoos in the workplace was dependent on the nature, size and location of the tattoo, as well as the occupation in question and individual customer characteristics. Employees with visible tattoos may still face stigma in the workplace. Their findings revealed that most people will cover up a tattoo during an interview out of fear of negative discrimination by the interviewer in the belief that this might affect their employment chances.

Terence Chia and Andrew Timming also concentrate their chapter on the implications for career development of people who have visible tattoos, questioning if they can face employment discrimination when looking for work or in progressing their career. They show how the appearance of employees is governed by managers' perceptions of consumers' preferences. They discuss how the creation of a marketing and brand proposition framework helps to build an organisational identity that can benefit consumers and the organisation. They also offer practical implications and strategies that organisations can consider to reduce such workplace discrimination.

Summary

This book tackles an area of employment where there is a limited appreciation of how appearance can impact on people's employment opportunities. The chapters represent a range of subject matter that falls under the overarching area of appearance in the workplace. Various chapters consider particular appearance characteristics possessed by people and how these impact on their job prospects. They show how appearance intersects with individual characteristics and how these might be to the benefit of some yet the detriment of others.

Other chapters concentrate on organisational prescriptive standards of aesthetic labour and lookism. They show how aesthetic labour is a common part of corporate life, especially in customer facing roles. These chapters reveal how aesthetic labour can lead to employment discrimination based on physical appearance and have considerable impact on employment chances if people do not conform to the organisational standards of expected appearance. The final chapters reveal how an individual's self-identity through body art may influence their employment. They consider how people with body art can be victimised and typecast in organisations. This might lead some of them to hide aspects of their self-identity, so they can better fit in with the culture and brand identity of the organisation.

This book was commissioned at the beginning of lockdown, and so there have been a few challenges along the way. The hard work and dedication of all the authors to the completion of this book is truly appreciated. Without them, there would be no book.

References

Al-Waqfi, M. A., & Forstenlechner, I. (2014). Barriers to Emiratisation: The role of policy and design and institutional environment in determining the effectiveness of Emiratisation. *International Journal of Human Resource Management*, *24*(2), 167–189.

Arndt, A. D., McCombs, G., Tolle, S. L., & Cox, C. (2017). Why are health care managers biased against hiring service providers with tattoos? *Services Marketing Quarterly*, *38*(2), 88–99.

Baert, S., & Decuypere, L. (2014). Better sexy than flexy? A lab experiment assessing the impact of perceived attractiveness and personality traits on hiring decisions. *Applied Economics Letters*, *21*(9), 597–601. https://doi.org/10.1080/13504851.2013.877564

Brewis, A. (2017). Introduction: Making sense of the new global body norms. In E. P. Anderson-Fye & A. Brewis (Eds.), *Fat planet: Obesity, culture, and symbolic body capital* (pp. 1–13). School for Advanced Research Press.

Broadbridge, A. M., & Fielden, S. L. (Eds.). (2018). *Research handbook of diversity and careers*. Edward Elgar.

Broadbridge, A. M., & Fielden, S. L. (Eds.). (2015). *Handbook of gendered careers in management: Getting in, getting on, getting out*. Edward Elgar. (30 chapters)

Brower, T. (2013). What's in the closet: Dress and appearance codes and lessons from sexual orientation. *Equality, Diversity and Inclusion: An International Journal*, *32*(5), 491–502. https://doi.org/10.1108/EDI-02-2013-0006

Bruton, S. (2015). Looks-based hiring and wrongful discrimination. *Business and Society Review*, *120*(4), 607–635.

Carbery, R., & Cross, C. (2015). *Human resource development*. Palgrave Macmillan.

Carlson, H. K., & McHenry, M. A. (2006). Effect of accent and dialect on employability. *Journal of Employment Counseling*, *43*(2), 70–81. https://doi.org/10.1002/j. 2161-1920.2006.tb00008.x

Caven, V., Lawley, S., & Baker, J. (2013). Performance, gender and sexualised work. Beyond management control, beyond legislation? A case study of work in a recruitment company. *Equality, Diversity and Inclusion: An International Journal*, *32*(5), 475–490.

Cavico, F. J., Muffler, S. C., & Mujtaba, B. G. (2012). Appearance discrimination, "lookism" and "lookphobia" in the work-place. *Journal of Applied Business Research (JABR)*, *28*(5), 791–802.

Clarke, V., & Turner, K. (2007). Clothes maketh the queer? Dress, appearance and the construction of lesbian, gay and bisexual identities. *Feminism & Psychology*, *17*(2), 267–276.

Corbett, W. R. (2011). Hotness discrimination: Appearance discrimination as a mirror for reflecting on the body of employment discrimination law. *Catholic University Law Review*, *60*, 615–652.

Crowder, C. L. (2010). Avoiding discrimination against overweight workers. *Employment Relations Today*, *36*(4), 39–44.

Eagly, A. H., & Karau, S. J. (2002). Role congruity theory of prejudice toward female leaders. *Psychological Review*, *109*(3), 573–598. https://doi.org/10.1037/0033-295x. 109.3.573

Edmonds, A., & Mears, A. (2017). Managing body capital in the fields of labor, sex, and health. In E. P. Anderson-Fye & A. Brewis (Eds.), *Fat planet: Obesity, culture, and symbolic body capital* (pp. 33–48). University of New Mexico Press.

Fitzgerald, T. (2018). Looking good and being good: Women leaders in Australian universities. *Education Sciences*, *8*(2), 54. https://doi.org/10.3390/educsci8020054

Fortune Business Insights. (2022). Cosmetic surgery market size, share, growth & trends [2029] (fortunebusinessinsights.com). https://www.fortunebusinessinsights.com/cosmetic-surgery-market-102628

Foster, C., & Resnick, S. (2013). Service worker appearance and the retail service encounter: The influence of gender and age. *The Services Industry Journal*, *33*(2), 236–247.

Gruys, K. (2012). Does this make me look fat? Aesthetic labor and fat talk as emotional labor in a women's plus-size clothing store. *Social Problems*, *59*(4), 481–500.

Hadjisolomou, A. (2021). Doing and negotiating transgender on the front line: Customer abuse, transphobia and stigma in the food retail sector. *Work, Employment and Society*, *35*(5), 979–988.

Hall, R., & van den Broek, D. (2012). Aestheticising retail workers: Orientations of aesthetic labour in Australian fashion retail. *Economic and Industrial Democracy*, *33*(1), 85–102.

Hamermesh, D. S. (2011). *Beauty pays: Why attractive people are more successful*. Princeton University Press.

Haynes, K. (2008). (Re)figuring accounting and maternal bodies: The gendered embodiment of accounting professionals. *Accounting, Organizations and Society*, *33*(4–5), 328–348.

Haynes, K. (2012). Body beautiful? Gender, identity and the body in professional services firms. *Gender, Work and Organization*, *19*(5), 489–507.

Heilman, M. E. (1983). Sex bias in work settings: The Lack of Fit model. *Research in Organizational Behavior*, *5*, 269–298.

Hopfl, H. (2000). Suaviter in modo, fortiter in re: Appearance, reality and the early Jesuits. In S. Linstead & H. Hopfl (Eds.), *The aesthetics of organization*. Sage.

Hosoda, M., Stone-Romero, E. F., & Coats, G. (2003). The effects of physical attractiveness on job-related outcomes: A meta-analysis of experimental studies. *Personnel Psychology*, *56*(2), 431–462. https://doi.org/10.1111/j.1744-6570.2003.tb00157.x

Howlett, N., Pine, K. J., Orakçıoğlu, I., & Fletcher, B. (2013). The influence of clothing on first impressions: Rapid and positive responses to minor changes in male attire. *Journal of Fashion Marketing and Management*, *17*(1), 38–48.

Howlett, N., Pine, K. J., Cahill, N., Orakçıoğlu, I., & Fletcher, B. (2015). Unbuttoned: The interaction between provocativeness of female work attire and occupational status. *Sex Roles*, *72*, 105–116. https://doi.org/10.1007/s11199-015-0450-8

Hutchings, K., Lirio, P., & Metcalfe, B. D. (2012). Gender, globalisation and development: A re-evaluation of the nature of women's global work. *The International Journal of Human Resource Management*, *23*(9), 1763–1787.

Inc. (n.d.). New research reveals why 'Appearance discrimination' is making workplaces even more toxic. https://www.inc.com/marcel-schwantes/are-your-colleagues-judging-you-based-on-your-appearance-new-research-reveals-how-far-discrimination-has-come-in-workplace.html#:~:text=In%20the%20workplace%2C%20the%20way%20you%20look%20can,don%27t%20fit%20into%20their%20idea%20of%20professional%20appearances

James, H. R. (2008, Winter). If you are attractive and you know it, please apply: Appearance based discrimination and employer discretion. *Valparaiso University Law Review*, *42*, 629–677.

Johnson, S. K., Keplinger, K., Kirk, J. F., & Chan, E. T. (2018). The perils of pretty: Effects of personal appearance on women's careers. In Broadbridge, A. M. & Fielden, S. L. (Eds.). *Research handbook of diversity and careers*. Edward Elgar, Chapter 8.

Johnson, S. K., Podratz, K. E., Dipboye, R. L., & Gibbons, E. (2010). Physical attractiveness biases in ratings of employment suitability: Tracking down the "beauty is beastly" effect. *The Journal of Social Psychology*, *150*(3), 301–318. https://doi.org/10.1080/00224540903365414

Jones, J. (2013). Trans dressing in the workplace. *Equality, Diversity and Inclusion*, *32*(5), 503–514.

Jones, E. M. (2018). The kids are queer: The rise of post-millennial American queer identification. In C. Stewart (Ed.), *Lesbian, gay, bisexual, and transgender Americans at risk: Problems and solutions*. Praeger.

Judge, T. A., Hurst, C., & Simon, L. S. (2009). Does it pay to be smart, attractive, or confident (or all three)? Relationships among general mental ability, physical attractiveness, core self-evaluations, and income. *Journal of Applied Psychology*, *94*(3), 742–755.

Jyrkinen, M. (2014). Women managers, careers and gendered ageism. *Scandinavian Journal of Management*, *30*(2), 175–185. https://doi.org/10.1016/j.scaman.2013.07.002

Karl, K., Hall, L. M., & Peluchette, J. (2013). City employee perceptions of the impact of dress and appearance: You are what you wear. *Public Personal Management*, *42*(3), 452–470.

Kelan, E. (2013). The becoming of business bodies: Gender, appearance and leadership development. *Management Learning*, *44*(1), 45–61.

Kuipers, G. (2015). Beauty and distinction? The evaluation of appearance and cultural capital in five European countries. *Poetics*, *53*, 38–51. https://doi.org/10.1016/j.poetic.2015.10.001

Kukkonen, I., & Sarpila, O. (2021). Gendered experiences of appearance-related perks and penalties in Finnish labor markets. *Nordic Journal of Working Life Studies*, *11*(S7). https://doi.org/10.18291/njwls.128715

Kumar, S. (2022). 'No country for old women': Female aging in Bollywood. *Indian Journal of Gender Studies*, *29*(3), 1–18.

Kumra, S., Simpson, R., & Burke, R. J. (Eds.). (2014). *The Oxford handbook of gender in organizations* (pp. 293–313). Oxford University Press.

Langlois, J. H., Kalakanis, L., Rubenstein, A. J., Larson, A., Hallam, M., & Smoot, M. (2000). Maxims or myths of beauty? A meta-analytic and theoretical review. *Psychological Bulletin*, *126*(3), 390–423.

Lee, S. (2020). Bias against natural hair limits opportunities for Black Women, study suggests. Verywell mind. https://www.verywellmind.com/bias-against-natural-hair-limits-opportunity-for-black-women-5077299

Lizotte, M., & Meggers-Wright, H. J. (2019). Negative effects of calling attention to female political candidates' attractiveness. *Journal of Political Marketing*, *18*(3), 240–266. https://doi.org/10.1080/15377857.2017.1411859

Lowman, G., Harris, P. D., & Mills, M. (2019). The influence of job candidates' physical appearance on interview evaluations: A prototype matching model. *Journal of Personnel Psychology*, *18*(2), 55–70. https://doi.org/10.1027/1866-5888/a000223

Madera, J. M., & Hebl, M. R. (2012). Discrimination against facially stigmatized applicants in interviews: An eye-tracking and face-to-face investigation. *Journal of Applied Psychology*, *97*(2), 317–330. https://doi.org/10.1037/a0025799

Mai, R., & Hoffman, S. (2014). Accents in Business Communication: An integrative model and propositions for future research, *Journal of Consumer Psychology*, *24*(1), 137–158.

Mavin, S., & Grandy, G. (2012), Doing gender well and differently in management. *Gender in Management: An International Journal*, *27*(4), 218–231.

Mavin, S., & Grandy, G. (2013). Doing gender well and differently in dirty work. *Gender, Work and Organization*, *20*(3), 232–251. https://doi.org/10.1111/j.1468-0432.2011.00567.x

Mavin, S., & Grandy, G. (2016a). A theory of abject appearance: Women elite leaders' intra-gender 'management' of bodies and appearance. *Human Relations*, *69*(5), 1095–1120. https://doi.org/10.1177/0018726715609107

Mavin, S., & Grandy, G. (2016b). Women elite leaders doing respectable business femininity: How privilege is conferred, contested and defended through the body. *Gender, Work and Organization, 23*(4), 379–396.

McInnis, A., & Medvedev, K. (2021). Sartorial appearance management strategies of creative professional women over age 50 in the fashion industry. *Fashion Practice, 13*(1), 25–47.

Mead, G. H. (1934). *Mind, body and society from the standpoint of a social behaviorist.* The University of Chicago Press.

Mears, A. (2014). Aesthetic labor for the sociologies of work, gender, and beauty. *Sociology Compass, 8*(12), 1330–1343.

Metcalfe, B. D. (2010). Reflections on difference: Women, Islamic feminism and development in the Middle East. *Managing Gender Diversity in Asia: A Research Companion,* 140–159.

Metcalfe, B. D. (2011). Women, empowerment and development in Arab Gulf States: A critical appraisal of governance, culture and national human resource development (hrd) frameworks. *Human Resource Development International, 14*(2), 131–148.

Middlemiss, S. (2018). Not what to wear? Employers' liability for dress codes? *International Journal of Discrimination and the Law, 18*(1), 40–51. https://doi.org/10.1177/1358229118757867

Mills, C. W. (1951). *White Collar.* Oxford University Press.

Morley, L. (2013). The rules of the game: Women and the leaderist turn in higher education. *Gender and Education, 25*(1), 116–131.

Mujtaba, B. G., & Cavico, F. J. (2016). Weight and appearance at work: Legal concerns related to race, ethnicity, and gender (Part I – Chapter 2). In M. F. Karsten (Ed.), *Gender, race and ethnicity in the workplace: Emerging issues and enduring challenges* (pp. 27–42). Praeger. ISBN-13: 978-1-4408-3369-4.

Nickson, D. (2018) The importance of how you look for getting in and getting on in the workplace. In A. M. Broadbridge & S. L. Fielden (Eds.), *Research handbook of diversity and careers.* Edward Elgar, Chapter 5.

Nickson, D., & Baum, T. (2017). Young at heart, but what about my body? Age and aesthetic labour in the hospitality and retail industries. In E. Parry & J. McCarthy (Eds.), *The Palgrave handbook of age diversity and work* (pp. 539–559). Palgrave Macmillan Ltd.

Peluchette, J. V., & Karl, K. (2007). The impact of workplace attire on employee self-perceptions. *Human Resource Development Quarterly, 18*(3), 345–360.

Peluchette, J., & Karl, K. (2018). 'She's got the look': Examining feminine and provocative dress in the workplace. In Broadbridge, A. M. & Fielden, S. L. (Eds.), *Research handbook of diversity and careers.* Edward Elgar.

Peluchette, J., Karl, K., & Rust, K. (2006). Dressing to impress: Beliefs and attitudes regarding workplace attire. *Journal of Business and Psychology, 21*(1), 45–63.

Petra Anyzova Raudenska petra. raudenska@soc.cas.cz emailed 13.05.21.

Pettinger, L. (2004). Brand culture and branded workers: Service work and aesthetic labour in fashion retail. *Consumption, Markets and Culture, 7*(2), 165–184.

Powell, G. N. (2018). *Women and men in management.* Sage.

Powroznik, K. M. (2017). Healthism and weight-based discrimination: The unintended consequences of health promotion in the workplace. *Work and Occupations, 44*(2), 139–170. https://doi.org/10.1177/0730888416682576

Rhode, D. (2010). *The beauty bias.* Oxford University Press.

Roehling, P. V., Roehling, M. V., & Elluru, A. (2018). Size does matter: The impact of size on career. In A. M. Broadbridge & S. L. Fielden (Eds.), *Research handbook of diversity and careers.* Edward Elgar, Chapter 6.

Rosette, A., & Dumas, T. (2007). The hair dilemma: Conform to mainstream expectations or emphasize racial identity. *Duke Journal of Gender Law & Policy, 14*(1), 407–421.

Rumens, N., & Kerfoot, D. (2009). Gay men at work: (Re)constructing the self as professional. *Human Relations, 62*(5), 763–786.

Sinclair, A. (2005). *Doing leadership differently: Gender, power and sexuality in a changing business culture.* Melbourne University Publishing.

Stone, G. (1995). Appearance and the self. In M. Roach-Higgins & J. Eicher (Eds.), *Dress and identity* (pp. 19–39). Fairchild.

Tartaglia, A., McHahon, B. T., West, S. L., & Belongia, L. (2005). Workplace discrimination and disfigurement: The national EEOC ADA research project. *Work: Journal of Prevention, Assessment & Rehabilitation, 25*(1), 57–65.

Timming, A. R. (2015). *Visible tattoos in the service sector: A new challenge to recruitment.*

Timming, A. R. (2017). *Body art as branded labour: At the intersection of employee selection.*

Tsaousi, C. (2020). That's funny … you don't look like a lecturer! dress and professional identity of female academics. *Studies in Higher Education, 45*(9), 1809–1820.

van den Berg, M., & Arts, J. (2019). The aesthetics of work-readiness: Aesthetic judgements and pedagogies for conditional welfare and post-Fordist labour markets. *Work, Employment and Society, 33*(2), 298–313. https://doi.org/10.1177/0950017018758196

Warhurst, C., & Nickson, D. (2020). *Aesthetic labour.* Sage.

Warhurst, C., Nickson, D., Witz, A., & Cullen, A. M. (2000). Aesthetic labour in interactive service work: Some case study evidence from the 'New' Glasgow. *The Service Industries Journal, 20*(3), 1–18.

Warhurst, C., van den Broek, D., Hall, R., & Nickson, D. (2009). Lookism: The new frontier of employment discrimination? *Journal of Industrial Relations, 51*(1), 131–136.

Warhurst, C., van den Broek, D., Nickson, D., & Hall, R. (2012). Great expectations: Gender, looks and lookism at work. *International Journal of Work, Organization and Emotion, 5*(1), 72–90.

Williams, C. L., & Connell, C. (2010). 'Looking good and sounding right': Aesthetic labor and social inequality in the retail industry. *Work and Occupations, 37*(3), 349–377. https://doi.org/10.1177/0730888410373744

Wilson, B. D. M., & Meyer, I. H. (2021). *Nonbinary LGBTQ Adults in the United States.* The Williams Institute. https://williamsinstitute.law.ucla.edu/wp-content/uploads/Nonbinary-LGBTQ-Adults-Jun-2021.pdf

Witz, A., Warhurst, C., & Nickson, D. (2003). The labour of aesthetics and the aesthetics of organization. *Organisation, 10*(1), 33–54.

Yates, J., Hooley, T., & Bagri, K. K. (2017). Good looks and good practice: The attitudes of career practitioners to attractiveness and appearance. *British Journal of Guidance and Counselling, 45*(5), 547–561.

Chapter 1

Appearance as Carnal Capital and Symbolic Violence: An Intersectional Approach

Mustafa F. Özbilgin, Marios Samdanis and Pelin Arsezen

Abstract

Appearance has two meanings. On the one hand, appearance is about the physical qualities of a person being of certain height, weight, complexion and having a particular hair, eye and skin colour as well as choice and style of dress and attire. On the other hand, appearance has a social dimension, as those physical qualities of a person are interpreted, rated and judged, and attributed varied meanings and values across different settings. Appearances can influence the experiences of individuals in the workplace in both positive and negative ways: Positive, when they are mobilised as a resource that increases the influence and advantage of individuals on others; and negative, when individuals are discriminated or disadvantaged on the basis of their appearance. Drawing on a Bourdieusian conceptual repertoire, this chapter delves into this duality of appearance and frames appearance both as a resource (a form of carnal capital) and a source of symbolic violence. As appearance is an aspect of an individual's self-identity in the workplace, this chapter explores appearance and intersectionality across gender, ethnicity, class and sexual orientation at work. Appearance is examined as a cross cutting category of diversity as both privilege (carnal capital) and disadvantage (symbolic violence).

Keywords: Appearances; carnal capital; Pierre Bourdieu; symbolic capital; intersectionality; diversity

Introduction

Appearance has been the subject of study across multiple disciplines and domains of research with a wide range of measures developed for capturing how objects

The Emerald Handbook of Appearance in the Workplace, 19–37
doi:10.1108/978-1-80071-174-720230002

look (Cash, 1990; Hunter & Harold, 1987). In the field of work and employment, appearance is often studied with a narrow focus on physical appearance, which is framed as a site of social and cultural advantage or disadvantage at work (Dellinger & Williams, 1997; Fisk, 2005). Appearance is defined in terms of the attractiveness, neatness, cleanliness and quality of dress of an individual (Stewart, 1985). Our perceptions on appearance are influenced by complex social and power relations, which on the one hand, empower the construction of 'self-identity' as 'the ability [of the person] to sustain a narrative about the self' (Giddens, 1991 in Barker, 2008, p. 217); and on the other hand, give rise to stereotypes and establish status beliefs (Ridgeway, 2011). Appearance also has a postcolonial aspect since individuals, especially the colonial subjects, have a tendency to internalise the beauty standards of institutionalised colonial discourses and practices which are constructed and presented as the embodiment of the absolute truth and, therefore, legitimise the cultural and ideological hegemony of perspectives from the Global North (Bağlama, 2019, pp. 86–87). Thus, discrimination based on appearance may not only take place because some individuals are seen as more or less attractive than others, but discrimination may also take place as appearance is politicised, gendered, ethnicised, racialised and sexualised.

In this chapter, we focus on physical appearance as a site of advantage and disadvantage at work as it intersects with categories of diversity and inclusion. Physical appearance has biological origins, referring to the physical and visible attributes of an individual's body. Yet, appearances are also socially constructed at least in two ways, as individuals curate their looks and others – consciously or not – engage in processes of interpretation of these visible features, attributing meanings, which can range from beautiful and attractive to ugly and unattractive. In the workplace, physical appearance may lead to privileging or stigmatisation of certain looks, while labelling of workers as professional, immaculate, hard working or lazy simply on the basis of their looks. Due to the influence of appearances, individuals spend a considerable amount of time in curating their physical appearance and making the sartorial choices to match or manage the expectations of a specific organisational or professional setting.

When organisational expectations of appearance are met, positive attributions are made regarding appearance. When organisational expectations are breached, negative attributions are made regarding physical appearance. Most organisational expectations of dress code and physical appearance are based on norms and professional standards, and as such, traditional sectors of work and employment often have narrowly defined dress codes and fail to offer inclusive sites which allow for varied expressions of physical appearance. Knowing the demands of their workplace, individuals usually comply with standards of appearance at work. For instance, interactive service jobs in sectors, such as retail and hospitality, rely significantly on aesthetic labour, requiring employees to possess soft skills and desired corporeal dispositions (Warhurst & Nickson, 2007).

In this chapter, by adopting an intersectional lens, we examine how appearance presents as a source of carnal capital and privilege as well as a source of discrimination, disadvantage and symbolic violence. We define carnal capital as a resource possessed by individuals, which allows them to construct and mobilise corporeal and embodied dispositions within a social space to achieve gains, such as influence and recognition. As such, carnal capital is connected with symbolic, cultural and social capital resources of an individual; and their habitus (Bourdieu, 1990). According to Bourdieu (1990), habitus influences the choices, actions and behaviours of individuals within a social space as they internalise objective dispositions and understand the 'rules of the game' within a social space like an organisation. Habitus is a form of sociality that is inscribed into the body, as social actors engage in embodied interactions with others as we participate in social life. Embodiment is constructed as individuals internalise objective dispositions such as, perceived needs, requirements of work and life, ideas of aesthetics, tradition and norms. Considering gender, ethnicity and class, appearance plays a significant role in the construction of self-identity. Hence, appearances shape the experiences of diverse individuals at work. For example, women and men are subjected to different dress codes. Similarly, ethnicity and class are often visible in physical appearance. In this way, the body becomes the site of social and political meaning, which can produce dual outcomes: For some, embodiment through the construction of appearance can be a source of advantage for individuals who have accumulated carnal capital, but for those who lack carnal capital, it can be a source of discrimination and symbolic violence.

Defining Appearance: Key Concepts and Disciplinary Perspectives

Appearance is defined in terms of inherent and outward physical attributes of individuals, such as their attractiveness; extrinsic qualities, such as neatness, cleanliness and quality of dress; and behavioural aspects including gestures, manners, taste, accent and speech (Bourdieu, 1984; Filkenstein, 2007; Ridgeway, 2014; Stewart, 1985). Studies on appearance originating from the field of social psychology, focus on the 'beauty bias' or the 'attraction-leniency effect', providing evidence of criminal defendants in courts, political campaigners, educators, and employees in organisations, according to which people who are perceived to be attractive tend to be rewarded more or punished less when compared with people who are considered to be less attractive (Rhode, 2010; Stewart, 1985). Literature in diversity management also stresses appearance as an implicit and unregulated form of discrimination, when individuals receive adverse treatment because of their looks (Cavico et al., 2013). Lookism is the construct which refers to discrimination based on physical appearance (Warhurst et al., 2009). Lookism was even condoned by law in some countries such as the United States, where people with disfigurement and diseases were barred from appearing in public (Schweik, 2009). Although 'ugly laws' have been abolished in the United States since the 1970s, there is still absence of legal protection against lookism discrimination in many countries including the United States, unless the particular kind of lookism could be considered as part of laws pertaining to other forms of discrimination, such as age or gender. In the absence of legal measures against lookism, this form of discrimination often remains unattended and unchallenged at in organisations.

Appearance is often perceived in terms of the familiarity with physiology of the body, which refers to the physical attractiveness of an individual, whether able bodied or with disability. Initially, perceptions about appearances are often influenced by the 'mere-exposure effect', according to which the more an individual is exposed to particular stimuli (e.g. facial characteristics), the more attractive they tend to value the stimuli (Bornstein & D'Agostino, 1994). Peskin and Newell (2004) verified this hypothesis in a series of experiments in which they identified familiarity and typicality as determinants for female face attractiveness. In other words, the more familiar we are with a particular appearance, and the more typical this appearance is within our cultural context, the more likely it is that we value it as attractive. Perceptual fluency, the cognitive ease to store and retrieve information about a stimulus, is considered to be the main factors that support the mere-exposure effect, which in turn can influence perceptions of attractiveness, empathy and taste (Bornstein & D'Agostino, 1994). The 'mere-exposure effect' in tandem with the 'attraction-leniency effect' can explain, for instance, the tendency of a white, upper-middle-class, able-bodied jury to demonstrate more empathy for the same charge towards a white, middle-class, able-bodied defendant than a non-white, working class or ghettoed defendant with a physical disfigurement or disability. Consider this in an employment situation between interview panellists and interview candidates.

The theme of appearance can also be approached from the viewpoint of aesthetics, which is a branch of philosophy that engages with questions of beauty and artistic taste. Immanuel Kant, one of the prominent figures in the philosophical study of aesthetics, argues that aesthetic or beauty requires judgement which in turn should be based on rules, canon or 'concept': A body of knowledge or standard against which objective assessments of aesthetic are based upon (Cohen, 2003). Judgements on aesthetics and beauty can be universal in terms of place and time, as long as the canon remains intact. Notoriously, the canon in aesthetics often refers to the rules of symmetry, known also as the 'golden ratio' phi $(\phi) = 1,61$, which is witnessed in nature, art, architecture, music and physical appearance of people; and punitively associated with our perceptions of beauty (Green, 1995). However, applying the idea of golden ratio as a canon to evaluate attractiveness and beauty of people can be problematic.

A review of research on facial attractiveness supports that 'people do generally agree on who is and who is not attractive' (Little et al., 2011, p. 1651). Yet, people do not seem to follow universally accepted aesthetic conventions, but their individual preferences which are influenced by factors, such as 'hormone levels and fertility, own attractiveness and personality, visual experience, familiarity and imprinting, and social learning' (Little et al., 2011, p. 1638). Averageness of a facial appearance ('how closely a face resembles the majority of other faces within a population') is also considered as a factor that increases attractiveness for genetic and social reasons (Little et al., 2011, p. 1640). It should be noted that these findings refer to facial appearances and not to all appearances which include clothing and manners. Little et al. (2011) discuss symmetry and averageness of facial appearances, justifying their arguments mainly on the basis that 'attractiveness is ingrained in our biology'. They also discuss sexually dimorphic shape cues (e.g. larger jaw bones in men as element of masculinity) and skin colour/ texture as elements of appearance which are socially constructed.

Biological and evolutionary factors seem to shape to an extent an individual's judgement on appearances, yet social factors play an important role too. For instance, Face Research Lab at the University of Glasgow Institute of Neuroscience and Psychology has created an algorithm which averages the facial characteristics of a sample population per gender, providing a version of typical male and female face for each country (Thorup et al., 2018; http://faceresearch.org). The study shows the variability of physical beauty across cultures. Undeniably, this project enhances our understanding of facial attractiveness on the basis of averageness across different cultures; but averageness is not the only aesthetic, especially in the age of pluralism and cosmopolitanism (Barker, 2008). The ways in which our societies become increasingly diverse may also influence people's perception on attractiveness and aesthetics. As such, we see two forms of aesthetics emerging today, one is locally embedded, which has connections with local history, culture and social norms and another that emerges as a result of globalisation, internationalisation and cosmopolitanism in general. In less ethnically diverse workplaces, attractive appearances could be determined based on the 'mere-exposure effect' and averageness. However, in more ethnically diverse organisations, cross-cultural attractiveness judgements are likely to depend on the exposure of each individual to diverse stimuli (Coetzee et al., 2014).

Appearances and beliefs associated with them have influenced evolution over the millennia through sexual selection (Wilson, 1978) and partner selection (Malakh-Pines, 2005). Sexual selection and attraction and romantic relationships in modern societies are influenced by norms, culture, social structures and power. For the most part of human history, and especially in pre-bureaucratic societies, personal identities used to be invisible from the realm of everyday life (Filkenstein, 2007). The history of the 'self' as a social construct has been driven by intellectual (e.g. Enlightenment, Liberalism), philosophical (e.g. Existentialism and the authentic self), cultural (e.g. Romanticism and Expressionism) and scientific (e.g. psychology as a discipline) developments over the past few centuries (Flynn, 2006; Freeden, 2015), creating a dual effect: The turn to individualism, on the one hand, which has liberated individuals to take command over their identity and appearance; and, on the other hand, the deceptive nature of appearances that reproduces status beliefs, stereotypes, and hegemonic relations in society. Consequently, the impact of appearances on careers and workplaces is a complex socially constructed issue which depends not only on averageness within a local context, but also on the construction and presentation of 'self' at work, and the perceptions and experiences of others who interact and consume these images. The empowering and emancipatory nature of appearances are analysed next focusing on the concepts of carnal capital and the discriminatory and disadvantage processes inherent in appearance are discussed through the lens of symbolic violence.

Carnal Capital and Symbolic Violence

Carnal sociology or theorising, i.e. deploying the body in order to theorise, is presented as a way to expand social science theorisation out of its contemporary confines (Nicolopoulous & Nicolopoulou 2015; Pitts-Taylor, 2015). The term 'carnal sociology' is attributed to Loïc Wacquant, student and collaborator of Pierre Bourdieu, and it is considered as an extension of Bourdieu's work on habitus (Pitts-Taylor, 2015). Research in social science vastly relies on data collection methods such as surveys, interviews and observations, which prioritise cognition, and the senses of hearing and seeing, over embodiment. Bourdieu and Wacquant suggest that the use of body as a method of data collection can expand social science research methods as the body has different ways of knowing than the mind alone. Bourdieu's (1990) concept of habitus can be considered as an early form of carnal theorising, and it is approach developed to study social reality closer to its nature, with the use of all the senses in the body.

Based on phenomenological epistemology, carnal theorising rejects the element of objectivity in research, as the body and the corporeal experience become a source of knowing (Moran, 2011; Pitts-Taylor, 2015). As a result, carnal as theorising and as a source of capital internalises and enacts social differences as corporeal engagement cannot be 'classless', 'ungendered' or 'unracial' (Pitts-Taylor, 2015; Young, 1990). Following the phenomenology tradition, the body for Bourdieu encompasses corporeal dispositions, including movements such as bending, greeting, dancing, kneeling, and some subtle bows and also distinctive linguistic and social practices that give meaning and purpose to bodily appearances. Bourdieu's notion of habitus (1990) expands Husserl's habit, by adding the element of practical knowledge or 'a feel for the game' which is not part of the conscious subjectivity (Moran, 2011; Robinson & Kerr, 2009). By bridging the physical, social and cultural domains of the body, Bourdieu approaches it as a political site on which power and status are negotiated, and habitus allows a reading of not only conscious subjectivity but also the internalised and unquestioned forms of inter-subjectivities, i.e. the embodied knowledge that often remains outside the scope of orthodox traditions of social scientific enquiry.

Habitus includes the cognition, emotions and corporeal dispositions of an individual within a social space, in which social actors compete and negotiate for stakes, gains and recognition (Bourdieu, 1990). Bourdieu (1990, p. 76) defines 'habitus' as 'a socially constructed system of cognitive and motivating structures' composed of an objective disposition, which usually refers to the 'rules of the game' and a subjective selection which is determined by the actions of agents within this social space. As Robinson and Kerr (2009, p. 881) explain: 'the capital an individual possesses partly defines how well they are accepted and integrated into a particular field and how they are able to position themselves within it. Thus, an agent whose habitus is perfectly adapted to the field possesses a *sens pratique*, defined as a 'feel for the game', to the extent that their habitus is 'invisible' to themselves. Through the use of concepts such as habitus, the field and the carnal theorising, it is possible to transcend the Cartesian duality of the mind and the body (Özbilgin & Bell, 2008) inviting scholars to consider the significance of the embodied knowledge in its embedded context.

Habitus, as a central theme in Bourdieu's sociology, derives – at least partially – from Husserl's phenomenological concept of habit as a form of conscious subjectivity which is used to analyse the ways in which people through their senses and embodiment construct meanings, emotions and identities in everyday encounters and situations, including the workplace (Moran, 2011). Habitus at a workplace context is often referred as 'professional habitus' (Srinivas, 2013). Prior research has appropriated professional habitus to explain how individuals develop their professional identity as a result of their inherited dispositions, including race, gender, social class; their cognition, motivations and embodied interactions at work.

Habitus within a professional setting or field depends on accumulated capital resources of individuals, including their social, symbolic and cultural capital, which in turn determine their agency, motivation and position within an organisation or professional field. Intentionally or not, habitus drives our choices, as we converge with or diverge from social conventions. Habitus does not necessitate compliance with dominant norms and expectations; as embodied dispositions often contradict or resist to them. More broadly, carnal theorisation does not only expand our methodological possibilities of social research, but it also allows us to consider the body as a site of social meaning, value and political contestation. Individuals deploy their carnal capital in order to improve their stakes in life, work, health and markets of labour, marriage, education and social standing. Carnal capital is an important capital resource that is used by individuals at work as form of influence based on appearances when interacting with others. Appearances that meet the expectations of the dominant group may suggest a high degree of carnal capital concentrated by an individual. Contrary, individuals from an ethnic minority background, for instance, may have to adjust their habitus and appearances at work in order to fit with the expectations of the dominant group. While carnal capital can be a source for advantage and influence for some individuals at work, it is a source for discrimination and oppression for others.

The concept of symbolic violence and the relevant concepts of symbolic power and cultural capital originate from the legitimisation of power by the state based on justification and belief (Bourdieu, 1996). Unlike hard power which is coercive, soft power is based on attractiveness and persuasion. Bourdieu uses the concept of symbolic violence to explain the domination of the upper social class over the working class not on the basis of coercion, but as a process of symbolic domination that takes place through the use of cultural capital acquired through their access to elite education (Bourdieu, 1984, 1996). Elite education as a form of credentialisation, is manifested in mannerisms, language, gestures, and taste, which are considered as instances of symbolic violence when projected to other social classes (Bourdieu, 1984). This process of social reproduction leads to the construction of taken-for-granted beliefs or doxa, such as the priority of elite educated, upper social class individuals to occupy highly rewarded positions of power. In this case, symbolic violence occurs between individuals which are legitimately rewarded and recognised and those which are legitimately excluded without necessarily lacking the skills and qualifications to perform particular roles and professions.

Our question here is whether and how do appearances create instances of symbolic violence in society. Symbolic violence is a concept which signifies hostility exercised upon a social agent or a social group through acts, performances and discourses that undermine their symbolic value (Bourdieu & Wacquant, 1992; Roumbanis, 2019). Symbolic violence is clearly based on the fact that power is always connected to identifiable social agents with distinct positions and dispositions in the field of hierarchical relations of power, in which symbolic value is distributed across agents, privileging some and violating the worth of others (Roumbanis, 2019).

Intersectionality, Carnal Capital and Symbolic Violence

Theory of intersectionality posits that individuals are often disadvantaged by multiple sources of oppression: their race, class, gender identity, sexual orientation, religion, and other identity markers (Crenshaw, 1990; McCall, 2008). An intersection denotes the crossing, juxtaposition, or meeting point, of two or more social categories. These categories include social identities (e.g. man, Indian), socio demographic categories (e.g. gender, ethnocultural), social processes (e.g. gendering, racialising), and social systems (patriarchy, racism). One of the challenges of intersectional analyses has been the fact that legal frameworks often are too blunt to tackle the complexity of appearance as it intersects with other categories of diversity and inclusion (Kamasak et al., 2020). In the absence of legal protection, initiatives taken by organisations are the main way for tackling appearance discrimination. Özbilgin and Tatli (2011) explain that effect in ensuring and promoting diversity and inclusion in organisations.

Carnal capital is the endowment that an individual will accrue by the virtue of how their body is built, structured, and how their body functions, operates, performs, how they shape, change and transform their bodies, and how their body is perceived, admired, liked or disliked, rewarded or punished by others. Therefore, we identify four distinct qualities that turn the body into capital. We argue that these four aspects are in a constant interplay, shaping the endowment of an individual's carnal capital (Fig. 1).

First, the biology and physiology of the body. Physiology referring to more or less symmetrical, impaired and non-impaired body, average and non-average characteristics (Little et al., 2011). As a form of carnal capital, these physiology characteristics generate assertions in the minds of people according to which outward appearance infers personality traits, such as being healthy, honest or fair (Little et al., 2011). As finely described by Filkenstein (2007, p. 123), this tendency has been the subject matter of physiognomy: 'Over the centuries links have been asserted between the shape of the head, or eyebrows, lips, ears and fingers, and the counterpart characteristics of intelligence, character, model rectitude, perversity and criminality. Some have argued that the shape of the nose signifies levels of

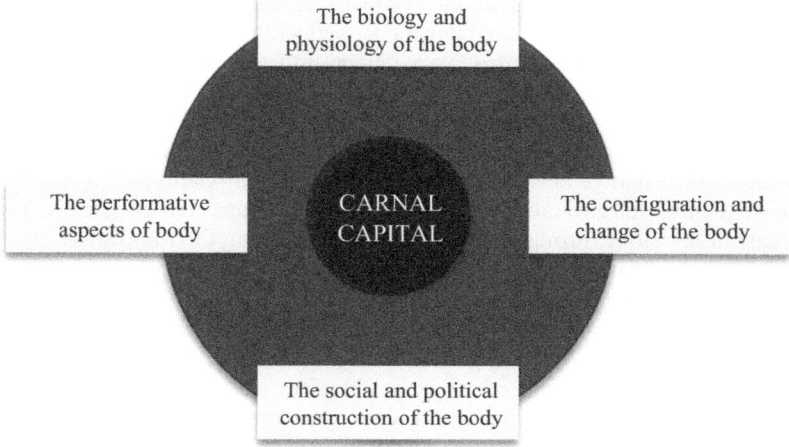

Fig. 1.   Carnal Capital and Forms of Embodiment. *Source:* The
authors.

cruelty, pugnacity and kindness, or that the ears demonstrate impulsiveness and
the capacity of memory'.

Although there is no clear evidence supporting the thesis of the physiognomy, a
similar technique known as Facial Action Coding System (FACS) has gained ground
since the late 1970s. FACS has been developed based on the work of Paul Ekman and
Wallace V. Friesen titled *What the Face Reveals* (1978), and it has evolved into a
system of taxonomising over ten thousand voluntary and involuntary facial
expressions which are then correlated with emotional states, such as anger, honesty,
modesty, fear (Ekman, 1997). FACS requires the use of technology – including
Artificial Intelligence (AI) more recently – to capture, analyse and compare these
facial expressions with the existing taxonomy. As such, FACS has been used as a tool
to evaluate the answers given by criminal defendants during interrogation or in court;
as well as conducting psychopathology and personality tests among others. By distinguishing voluntary from involuntary expressions, FACS research reveals that
facial expressions, and appearances, can only partially be manipulated and interpreted, as there is an aspect of appearance which is involuntary, spontaneous and
subliminal (Filkenstein, 2007).

AI-enabled applications are increasingly used in recruiting processes in organisations. While first impressions and physical appearances affect the perceptions of
interviewers during the recruiting process, the use of AI-enabled applications lessen
the impressional primacy effect, according to which 'people opt for evaluations that
confirm their existing beliefs' (Suen et al., 2019, p. 94). Although facial recognition
technologies can be used to analyse personality traits and attitudes of candidates in
interviews (van Esch et al., 2021), there are AI-enabled applications which are
designed to be 'appearance-blind', and thus unbiased. For instance, Tengai is an

interview software and conversational AI which can be used in the recruiting process, aiming to tackle discrimination relevant to gender, race, age, disability, sexual orientation and appearance (https://www.tengai-unbiased.com/).

Second, the performative aspects of the body. By highlighting the performative aspects of the body, appearances are approached as a social construct, being situational and ongoing as people enact their personal, social and/or professional identities. Performative acts stress the element of intentionality when individuals mobilise their carnal capital. Goffman (1959, p. 32) argues that people are trained to create impressions through staged performances using their appearances – and therefore, their carnal capital – 'before a particular set of observers' aiming to have 'some influence on the observers'.

Habitus, as practical knowledge of a situation, guide the corporeal dispositions and behaviour of an individual within the situation, including manners, gesture and posture, speech and use of language. Habitus enables individuals to make sense of a situation, internalising an objective structure. A simple example it is the typical behaviour of people in an interview situation or a corporate meeting, operating as actors following a script. The accumulation of carnal capital can determine the habitus of individuals within situations, when performing 'desired corporeal disposition' in order to achieve particular gains, such as status or influence (Bourdieu, 1990; Warhurst & Nickson, 2007).

Physical appearance intersects with all categories of diversity and inclusion in various ways. Intersectionality of gender and physical appearance is relatively well studied. In particular, women's physical appearance is subject to more scrutiny than men's appearance in organisational settings (Ford et al., 2017). With the male body being the dominant norm in many professional environments, the female body and its varied appearances and performances disturbs the normative order at work. The traditional workplaces such as financial service organisations in the United Kingdom have rigid forms of dress code for both women and men. Yet, men's choices of outfit have been set for a long time, women's attire and sartorial choices in an old sector like the financial services sector is still in a state of interpretation. One of the most successful women in finance in the United Kingdom, Helena Morrisey (2020) presents her work outfits in order to empower women and exchange views and ideas about sartorial choices for women across different work settings and functions such as meetings, workshops, talks and receptions. There is not a male equivalent of a similar thought leader in the United Kingdom who would advise men of varied clothes choices fit for different occasions. This example shows that women are under greater pressure and scrutiny to match their appearances to organisational and social expectations. Similarly, physical attractiveness has different meanings for women and men at work. While physical attractiveness may improve men's chances for leadership, physical attractiveness may also enhance women's chances in leadership, yet it may also expose women, unlike men, to unwanted attention and sexual harassment at work. Gender identity and politics has also an interesting intersection with appearance in terms of how the sartorial choices of a feminist, transvestite, transgender, and transsexual person may be received, perceived, allowed and disallowed in workplaces.

More broadly, performative acts are political acts within a social context, as not all individuals are equally entitled to perform. Traditionally, performative acts were reserved for the upper social classes. Thorstein Veblen (1899) coined the concept of conspicuous consumption to criticise the need of the emerging bourgeoisie in the United States to construct and perform class identity as differentiated from the working class through material consumption and leisure activities. Pierre Bourdieu (1984, 1993) analysed the tactics of cultural domination of the French bourgeoisie over the masses based on their accumulation of cultural capital, as manifested in manners, elaborate use of language, elite education and refined taste. Upper classes in industrial societies have retained their privilege in monopolising cultural attention through consumption and performed appearances that consolidate their class superiority and distinction (Bourdieu, 1984). As a result, appearances are product and producer of power relations in society, manifesting symbolic and material boundaries between social classes.

More recently, performativity is mobilised as a form of resistance to the status quo. Embodied performative acts can legitimise 'atypicality, as a process of constructing a self-identity that denies dominant norms within a social context' (Samdanis & Özbilgin, 2020, p. 109 emphasising Butler, 1993). For example, Nentwich et al. (2015) illustrate the way how Swiss women's right to vote movement mobilised performative acts by wearing traditional outfits to garner support from conservative women who resist women's right to vote.

Another example would be artists and subcultures, which have historically played an important role in terms of constructing images and performing appearances that aim to unsettle status beliefs (Ridgeway, 2014; Samdanis & Özbilgin, 2020). For instance, the pop artist Andy Warhol, the performance artist Marina Abramovic or the Young British Artist Tracey Emin are examples of artists who have pushed the boundaries of identity, gender and queer aesthetic through their embodied performances (Graw, 2009; O'Reilly, 2009). In addition, subcultures, such as the punks in the 1970s London, adopted and performed a radical and rebellious attitude which was manifested in clothing, make-up, music, dance and drugs; and in the ideology of anti-establishment and anti-consumerism, deeply rooted in the working-class struggle with the conservative British culture and national symbolism (Hebdige, 1979). In the context of punk subculture, the body as a generator of performance is a site of endowment with meanings and politics of contestation.

Thus, appearance is also performative as it involves performances of the body in order to comply or renegotiate the norms and legitimacy of performative appearances in a specific cultural or social milieu with a certain value system.

Third, the configuration and change of the body. The change of body can be classified in three broad categories: Natural, involuntary and voluntary. Natural change occurs obviously with the passage of time, altering potentially the ways in which individuals mobilise carnal capital at different stages of life. The existence of age discrimination and negative age stereotypes in organisations against younger or older employees can be interpreted in terms of their restricted access to carnal capital (Kunze et al., 2011, 2013). This dimension also introduces the element of time in terms of accumulating carnal capital, which in theory, peaks at some point, due to the experience of individuals to mobilise it successfully. Carnal capital is also context-specific and related to existing expectations and stereotypes associated with particular professions. For instance, artists and musicians are likely to mobilise carnal capital from a relatively young age; in contrast to a young pilot, who might be perceived as inexperienced because of their age.

Involuntary change is often associated with impairment. Paterson and Hughes (1999, p. 608) note 'unlike the non-impaired body which is customarily "unaware" of itself until it is confronted by pain, the impaired body is permanently stunned into its own recognition as a consequence of the disablism which permeates everyday life'. Disablism as a form of discrimination can be attributed the stereotypical views that associate carnal capital with non-impaired individuals, as well as constituting impairment as a form of Otherness. Exploring the carnal politics of disability, Paterson and Hughes (1999) note that disability complicates the simple formulations of Cartesian dualism between body and mind, where the agency of the person with disability in the context of their disability needs to be reconsidered. In fact, disability scholarship has been at the centre stage of discussion of appearance discrimination. Disability scholars and activists have fought against appearance discrimination such as the ugly laws of the pre-1970s United States in order to win rights for people with disfigurement and illness to join public life.

Voluntary change of the body occurs when individuals decide or require a configuration of their body. Transgender individuals experience configuration of the body through a period of transition. Change of the body is also experienced in the cases of plastic surgery (i.e. cosmetic or after an accident), as well as when individuals reconfigure their appearance through tattoos, piercing or changing hairstyles. Appearance and ethnicity also intersect in surprising ways. Ethnicity is an important identity construct that shapes not only people's beliefs, cultural repertoires, linguistic resources but also it also distinguishes people in terms of their appearance. Many aspects of ethnic identity are visible through attire. For example, how hair is cut or kept, covered or revealed, whether facial hair is grown or groomed, what colours or choices of outfit and accessories are used. As such what appears to be an innocuous choice by workplaces to demand certain appearances such as a dress code would be imbued with ethnic markers. In the case of the United Kingdom, work outfits and dress codes are highly ethnicised to fit with the white anglo saxon norms. Some organisations have taken on the challenge of Black, Asian and Minority Ethnic (BAME) inclusion, by allowing a wider repertoire of attire based on ethnic differences. One remarkable example at the intersection of gender, ethnicity and appearance is the politics of braiding and rasta hair styles which are ethnically marked with African and Caribbean cultural heritage.

Recently, a case of race discrimination relevant to hair style has captured the attention of media in the United Kingdom (Young, 2020). Social activists, young Black organisers and organisations, such as the Halo Collective and the Advocacy Academy have responded to this form of racial discrimination by exposing malpractices at schools and workplaces. The Halo Collective shares a story of appearance-related racial discrimination experienced by a Black woman who sought employment at the London-based department store Harrods: 'In 2017, a Black woman claimed she was told by an external agency to chemically straighten her hair if she wanted a job at the high-end department store Harrods. Speaking in an evidence session for the Petitions and Women and Equalities Select Committees in Parliament, she said: 'I have worked in retail before, notably at Harrods. They are really quite bad and I ended up leaving as a result of that' (https://halocollective.co.uk/halo-workplace/).

In many African tribes, hairstyle is a signifier of identity, social status, origin and religion. When Africans migrate to European countries, they are often subjected to Eurocentric aesthetics which is disconnected from their traditions. These encounters often force Africans to change, adapt to or resist the European aesthetics. For European aesthetics perception, Afro hair is not historically and culturally construed as beautiful, despite some changes with cosmopolitan aesthetics. Because of this old negative perception, African migrants were exposed to European culture and aesthetics without much reciprocity. Yet there are changes today. For example, Araba Sam (2018) studied Ghanaian women's perception of hair and found that they are now at peace with their hair. Yet the struggle of women from African diaspora in Europe for recognition of their aesthetics may not be at the same level of ease.

More specifically, Black people in the United Kingdom have experienced discrimination because of their afro-textured hair which is not straightened with the use of chemicals. As Dabiri (2020, n.p.) reported for the Guardian 'across the country black and mixed-black pupils are being excluded [from school] because their hair is too short, too long, too big or too full. Pupils have been excluded for fades, locs, braids, natural afros and more – in effect every single style and necessary protective method for the maintenance and upkeep of afro hair has been penalised, often in the harshest possible ways'; adding that 'with the advent of the natural hair movement people of African descent have been rejecting the standard that insists we must straighten our hair to fit in'. Configuration is generally received as empowering individuals to develop a desired personal identity, can also be dictated by the dominant culture in terms of demanding from people to comply, implicitly or explicitly, with the appearances of the dominant group. For more on the appearance of hair see Chapters 2 and 3.

Fourth, the social and political construction of the body. This is a case in which individuals mobilise and manipulate appearances in order to achieve personal gains or defuse negative consequences associated with their appearance. Performativity in tandem with discursive acts often advocate political action of resistance against the dominant norms and status beliefs within an organisation (Butler, 1993; Ridgeway, 2011).

The liberal view on the social and political construction of the body would place the progressive individual as commander of meaning and identity. Often, the political construction of the body takes place within cultural industries, such as the fashion industry which is global industry of creating visuality and meaning especially in terms of liberating the female body (Graw, 2009). The French fashion designer Gabrielle Bonheur 'Coco' Chanel (1883–1971) is considered as one of the leading figures in the fashion industry who has successfully politicised the female body. In the early 1920s, Chanel popularised the 'causal chic' as a feminine style, liberating women from the 'corseted silhouette' (Loschek, 2009). In the post-World War I era, the designs created by Chanel, such as the creation of the androgynous image, echoed the struggle for the reduction of gender inequality and the 'portended greater freedoms for women following the war – a category that covered everything from smoking cigarettes and drinking cocktails in public to driving cars and piloting airplanes' (Davis, 2006, pp. 433–34). These social changes reveal gender as a socially constructed identity, which is negotiated in tandem with the evolving meaning of appearances: 'When – in the late 1950s – women were becoming increasingly independent and forcing their way into the world of work, Coco Chanel offered an uncomplicated tailored suit, suitable for any occasion' (Loschek, 2009, p. 105). Nevertheless, appearances in the fashion industry are influenced by commercial dynamics which shape the ways in which we 'imagining our existence are inserted into the mind's eye of the other' (Filkenstein, 2007, p. 197). Driven by advertising and the industrial society, we are trained to construct, interpret, consume and appreciate appearances (Adorno, 1991; Crane, 2000; Klein, 2000) supported by conspicuous consumption and luxury, aiming to maintain class boundaries.

In another study, Ford et al. (2017) report that both male and female leaders in organisations consider first impressions to be important. Nevertheless, female leaders appeared to be more prepared or obliged to 'strip all signifiers of femininity' and wear clothes that promote an androgynous, non-sexualised or neutral identity at work. Although this situation of intended neutrality indicates compliance with the norms of male domination, it often represents an act deliberately performed by female leaders to avoid the backlash associated with the stereotypes and social expectations that stem from their salient identity (Ridgeway, 2011), and enable them to construct an identity based on collective and inclusive values. These embodied experiences of inequality and hostility trigger habitus, and the need of female leaders to construct a new type of leadership based on values instead of appearances and impressions (Kelly, 2014).

Autonomy and independence in choosing appearances are still racialised and gendered, and therefore, persisting views on appearances can establish symbolic violence within organisations. People in organisations engage with processes of self-portrayal which are often aligned with the 'external standards of professional competence' (Roberts, 2005, p. 700). While the appearances of men at work go largely unnoticed, appearances of women seem to oscillate between two extreme positions: The feminised appearance which is often perceived as a corporeal disposition; and the neutral appearance which aim to 'strip all signifiers of femininity' (Ford et al., 2017). Especially for female employees, 'being-themselves-at work' is much more challenging proposition than for their male counterparts. Yamak et al. (2016) show that gender is both a form of carnal capital and a system of symbolic violence that resists change among corporate elites, despite changes in social mores and institutional mechanisms for gender equality. Their study illustrates how gender order is retained not only by men but also by women who subscribe to and benefit from the patriarchal dividend associated with the uneven and exploitative nature of the gender order.

Bourdieu and Wacquant (1992, p. 170) consider gender as a social construction and a 'paradigmatic form of symbolic violence'. This view is in agreement with earlier views which identified the female gender as quintessentially 'Other' (de Beauvoir, 1989 [1949]); a condition which does not seem to have changed significantly in the modern workplace despite the emergence of new norms and ethos of 'be-yourself-at work' (Fleming & Sturdy, 2011). 'Be-yourself-at work' ethos is based on the premise that individuals feel empowered when expressing their authentic self and identity at work, especially in their interactions with colleagues (Fleming & Sturdy, 2009). Although 'fun' informal interactions between colleagues can provide opportunities for people in organisations to express their 'true' self, sexuality and identity, still these behaviours take place within an organisational context which is overarched by norms. According to Fleming and Sturdy (2009), 'be-yourself-at work' and be 'fun' at work are new norms which are used for both empowering and controlling people in organisations. These organisational contexts tend to favour employees who can manifest 'difference' through their appearance and they are willing to participate in collective 'fun'.

Exploring carnal theorising could help us understand symbolic valuing and devaluing of the body. For example, erotic desire as part of carnal capital can confer status in social settings. Abubakar et al. (2019) examine the way possession of erotic capital may influence managerial attitudes in the hospitality industry. They found that erotic capital may have both positive outcomes such as improved corporate image and negative outcomes such as absenteeism. They argue that effective management of erotic capital is required for organisations to combat negative consequences and accrue its unique benefits.

Requena (2017) studied the relationship between subjective well-being and erotic capital, drawing on Hakim's (2010) conception of erotic capital. They tested four hypotheses regarding the importance of erotic capital compared to other types of capital and analysed how an individual's degree of subjective well-being is affected by erotic capital. Their results showed the importance of erotic capital as a generator of subjective well-being and a better predictor of it than other types of capital. They found beauty significantly affected subjective well-being for both men and women. In addition, their findings showed that beauty had equal importance in the subjective well-being of men and women. They highlighted that erotic capital was in reality the most important factor but people tended to believe that education or social connections could be more important. There is a difference between what people believe to be important and what was important. According to Requena (2017) above-average attractiveness was more rewarding for men than for women.

Conclusion

Overall, appearance intersects with all diversity categories in intricate ways. As there are no laws to protect individuals from appearance discrimination generally in the United Kingdom today, it is important to study how appearance discrimination manifests across categories of diversity as outlined above. Appearance is a cross cutting category of diversity. Yet appearance has not been studied extensively within the frame of diversity and inclusion. Appearance is examined as a cross cutting category of diversity as both privilege (carnal capital) and disadvantage (symbolic violence). There is limited insight into the implications of carnal capital for individuals at work. Carnal capital is central for understanding organisational politics, including the ways in which gains and discrimination, privilege and disadvantage, likes and dislikes emerge. People, intentionally or not, internalise these beliefs which become part of their habitus. If an individual is in a position to take advantage of their appearance, they may mobilise their carnal capital in order to achieve individual gains. As in the case of other forms of biases, raising awareness about the impact of appearances on our perceptions and decisions may help to mitigate or lift stereotypes and status beliefs associated with particular groups and appearances in society. Yet, it is also absolutely essential to consider the significance of a legal framework. As we know from other categories of equality, diversity and inclusion that if a category of difference is not protected by coercive legal arrangements, it is likely to get overlooked (Jonsen et al., 2013).

References

Abubakar, A. M., Anasori, E., & Laisis, T. T. (2019). Physical attractiveness and managerial favoritism in the hotel industry: The light and dark side of erotic capital. *Journal of Hospitality and Tourism Management, 38*, 16–26.

Adorno, T. W. (1991). The schema of mass culture. In J. M. Bernstein (Ed.), *The culture industry* (pp. 53–84). Routledge.

Araba Sam, R. (2018). *Cultural globalisation and its implications for the African woman's hair: The case of Ghana.* Unpublished doctoral dissertation. University of Ghana.

Bağlama, S. H. (2019). Zadie Smith's white teeth: The interpellation of the colonial subject in multicultural Britain. *Journal of Language, Literature and Culture, 66*(2), 77–90.

Barker, C. (2008). *Cultural studies: Theory and practice* (3rd ed.). SAGE.

de Beauvoir, S. (1989 [1949]). *The second sex.* Knopf.

Bornstein, R. F., & D'Agostino, P. R. (1994). The attribution and discounting of perceptual fluency: Preliminary tests of a perceptual fluency/attributional model of the mere exposure effect. *Social Cognition, 12*(2), 103–128.

Bourdieu, P. (1984). *Distinction: A social critique on the judgment of taste.* Harvard University Press.

Bourdieu, P. (1990). *The logic of practice.* Polity Press.

Bourdieu, P. (1993). *The field of cultural production.* Polity.

Bourdieu. (1996). *The state nobility: Elite school in the field of power.* Stanford University Press.

Bourdieu, P., & Wacquant, L. J. D. (1992). *An invitation to reflexive sociology.* University of Chicago Press.

Butler, J. (1993). *Bodies that matter.* Routledge.

Cash, T. F. (1990). The psychology of physical appearance: Aesthetics, attributes, and images. In T. F. Cash & T. Pruzinsky (Eds.), *Body images: Development, deviance, and change* (pp. 51–79). Guilford Press.

Cavico, F. J., Muffler, S. C., & Mujtaba, B. G. (2013). Appearance discrimination in employment. *Equality, Diversity and Inclusion: An International Journal, 32*(1), 83–119.

Coetzee, V., Greeff, J. M., Stephen, I. D., & Perrett, D. I. (2014). Cross-cultural agreement in facial attractiveness preferences: The role of ethnicity and gender. *PLoS One, 9*(7), e99629. https://doi.org/10.1371/journal.pone.0099629

Cohen, T. (2003). The inexplicable: Some thoughts after Kant. In B. Gaut & P. Livingston (Eds.), *The creation of art: New essays in philosophical aesthetics* (pp. 138–147). Cambridge University Press.

Crane, D. (2000). *Fashion and its social agendas: Class, gender, and identity in clothing.* University of Chicago Press.

Crenshaw, K. (1990). Mapping the margins: Intersectionality, identity politics, and violence against women of color. *Stanford Law Review, 43*, 1241–1299.

Dabiri, E. (2020, February 25). Black pupils are being wrongly excluded over their hair. I'm trying to end this discrimination. *The Guardian.* https://www.theguardian. com/commentisfree/2020/feb/25/black-pupils-excluded-hair-discrimination-equality-act. Accessed on March 2020.

Davis, M. (2006). Chanel, Stravinsky, and musical chic. *Fashion Theory, 10*(4), 431–460.

Dellinger, K., & Williams, C. L. (1997). Makeup at work: Negotiating appearance rules in the workplace. *Gender & Society, 11*(2), 151–177.

Ekman, R. (1997). *What the face reveals: Basic and applied studies of spontaneous expression using the facial action coding system (FACS).* Oxford University Press.

van Esch, P., Black, J. S., & Arli, D. (2021). Job candidates' reactions to AI-enabled job application processes. *AI and Ethics, 1*(2), 119–130.

Filkenstein, J. (2007). *The art of self invention: Image and identity in popular visual culture.* I.B. Tauris.

Fisk, C. L. (2005). Privacy, power, and humiliation at work: Re-examining appearance regulation as an invasion of privacy. *Louisiana Law Review, 66*, 1111.

Fleming, P., & Sturdy, A. (2009). "Just be yourself!": Towards neo-normative control in organisations? *Employee Relations, 31*(6), 569–583.

Fleming, P., & Sturdy, A. (2011). 'Being yourself' in the electronic sweatshop: New forms of normative control. *Human Relations, 64*(2), 177–200.

Flynn, T. R. (2006). *Existentialism: A very short introduction.* Oxford University Press.

Ford, J., Harding, N. H., Gilmore, S., & Richardson, S. (2017). Becoming the leader: Leadership as material presence. *Organization Studies, 38*(11), 1553–1571.

Freeden, M. (2015). *Liberalism: A very short introduction.* Oxford University Press.

Goffman, E. (1959). *The presentation of self in everyday life.* Penguin Books.

Graw, I. (2009). *High price: Art between the market and celebrity culture.* Sternberg Press.

Green, C. D. (1995). All that glitters: A review of psychological research on the aesthetics of the golden section. *Perception, 24*(8), 937–968.

Hakim, C. (2010). Erotic capital. *European Sociological Review, 26*(5), 499–518.

Hebdige, D. (1979). *Subculture: The meaning of style.* Routledge.

Hunter, R. S., & Harold, R. W. (1987). *The measurement of appearance.* John Wiley & Sons.

Jonsen, K., Tatli, A., Özbilgin, M. F., & Bell, M. P. (2013). The tragedy of the uncommons: Reframing workforce diversity. *Human Relations, 66*(2), 271–294.

Kamasak, R., Özbilgin, M., & Yavuz, M. (2020). Understanding intersectional analyses. In E. King, Q. Roberson, & M. Hebl (Eds.), *Research on social issues in management on pushing understanding of diversity in organizations* (pp. 91–113). Information Age Publishing.

Kelly, S. (2014). Towards a negative ontology of leadership. *Human Relations, 67*(8), 905–922.

Klein, N. (2000). *No Logo.* Flamingo.

Kunze, F., Boehm, S. A., & Bruch, H. (2011). Age diversity, age discrimination climate and performance consequences–a cross organizational study. *Journal of Organizational Behavior, 32*(2), 264–290.

Kunze, F., Boehm, S., & Bruch, H. (2013). Organizational performance consequences of age diversity: Inspecting the role of diversity-friendly HR policies and top managers' negative age stereotypes. *Journal of Management Studies, 50*(3), 413–442.

Little, A. C., Jones, B. C., & DeBruine, L. M. (2011). Facial attractiveness: Evolutionary based research. *Philosophical Transactions of the Royal Society B: Biological Sciences, 366*(1571), 1638–1659.

Loschek, I. (2009). *When clothes become fashion: Design and innovation systems.* Berg.

Malakh-Pines, A. (2005). *Falling in love: Why we choose the lovers we choose.* Taylor & Francis.

McCall, L. (2008). The complexity of intersectionality. In *Intersectionality and beyond* (pp. 65–92). Routledge-Cavendish.

Moran, D. (2011). Edmund Husserl's phenomenology of habituality and habitus. *Journal of the British Society for Phenomenology, 42*(1), 53–77.

Morrisey, H. (2020). Personal Instagram page. https://instagram.com/helena morrissey?igshid=yq76n6mxp8ua

Nentwich, J. C., Özbilgin, M. F., & Tatli, A. (2015). Change agency as performance and embeddedness: Exploring the possibilities and limits of Butler and Bourdieu. *Culture and Organization, 21*(3), 235–250.

Nikolopoulos, K. P., & Nicolopoulou, K. (2015). Bourdieu's 'carnal theorising' in organisations and management: Bridging disembodiment and other old dichotomies. In *Pierre Bourdieu, organization, and management* (pp. 81–95). Routledge.

O'Reilly, S. (2009). *The body in contemporary art.* Thames & Hudson.

Özbilgin, M. F., & Bell, M. P. (2008). The rise of Cartesian dualism and marketization in academia. In D. Barry & H. Hansen (Eds.), *The SAGE handbook of new approaches in management and organization* (p. 268). Sage.

Özbilgin, M., & Tatli, A. (2011). Mapping out the field of equality and diversity: Rise of individualism and voluntarism. *Human Relations, 64*(9), 1229–1253.

Paterson, K., & Hughes, B. (1999). Disability studies and phenomenology: The carnal politics of everyday life. *Disability & Society, 14*(5), 597–610.

Peskin, M., & Newell, F. N. (2004). Familiarity breeds attraction: Effects of exposure on the attractiveness of typical and distinctive faces. *Perception, 33*(2), 147–157.

Pitts-Taylor, V. (2015). A feminist carnal sociology?: Embodiment in sociology, feminism, and naturalized philosophy. *Qualitative Sociology, 38*(1), 19–25.

Requena, F. (2017). Erotic capital and subjective well-being. *Research in Social Stratification and Mobility, 50*, 13–18.

Rhode, D. L. (2010). *The beauty bias: The injustice of appearance in life and law.* Oxford University Press.

Ridgeway, C. L. (2011). *Framed by gender*. Oxford University Press.

Ridgeway, C. L. (2014). Why status matters for inequality. *American Sociological Review, 79*(1), 1–16.

Roberts, M. L. (2005). Changing faces: Professional image construction in diverse organizational settings. *Academy of Management Review, 30*(4), 685–711.

Robinson, S. K., & Kerr, R. (2009). The symbolic violence of leadership: A critical hermeneutic study of leadership and succession in a British organization in the post-Soviet context. *Human Relations, 62*(6), 875–903.

Roumbanis, L. (2019). Symbolic violence in academic life: A study on how junior scholars are educated in the art of getting funded. *Minerva, 57*, 197–218.

Samdanis, M., & Özbilgin, M. (2020). The duality of an atypical leader in diversity management: The legitimization and delegitimization of diversity beliefs in organizations. *International Journal of Management Reviews, 22*, 101–119.

Schweik, S. M. (2009). *The ugly laws: Disability in public*. New York University Press.

Srinivas, N. (2013). Could a subaltern manage? Identity work and habitus in a colonial workplace. *Organization Studies, 34*(11), 1655–1674.

Stewart, J. E. (1985). Appearance and punishment: The attraction-leniency effect in the courtroom. *The Journal of Social Psychology, 125*(3), 373–378.

Suen, H. Y., Chen, M. Y. C., & Lu, S. H. (2019). Does the use of synchrony and artificial intelligence in video interviews affect interview ratings and applicant attitudes? *Computers in Human Behavior, 98*, 93–101.

Thorup, B., Crookes, K., Chang, P. P., Burton, N., Pond, S., Li, T. K., Hsiao, J., & Rhodes, G. (2018). Perceptual experience shapes our ability to categorize faces by national origin: A new other-race effect. *British Journal of Psychology, 109*(3), 583–603.

Veblen (1899 [1993]). *The theory of the leisure class*. Dover Publications.

Warhurst, C., & Nickson, D. (2007). Employee experience of aesthetic labour in retail and hospitality. *Work, Employment & Society, 21*(1), 103–120.

Warhurst, C., Van den Broek, D., Hall, R., & Nickson, D. (2009). Lookism: The new frontier of employment discrimination? *Journal of Industrial Relations, 51*(1), 131–136.

Wilson, E. O. (1978). *On human nature*. Harvard University Press.

Yamak, S., Ergur, A., Özbilgin, M. F., & Alakavuklar, O. N. (2016). Gender as symbolic capital and violence: The case of corporate elites in Turkey. *Gender, Work and Organization, 23*(2), 125–146.

Young, I. M. (1990). *Throwing like a girl: And other essays in feminist philosophy and social theory*. Indiana University Press.

Young, S. (2020). New code launched to protect employees and students against hair discrimination. *Independent*. https://www.independent.co.uk/life-style/afro-code-hair-discrimination-halo-unilver-b1768543.html. Accessed on September 26, 2020.

Chapter 2

Is Curly Hair Viewed as Professional? Examining Hair Bias Against White Women With Curly Hair

Joy V. Peluchette and Katherine A. Karl

Abstract

While there is some evidence of bias against curly hair, this chapter provides a more comprehensive analysis by examining comments made by women about their hair experience, how it affects their identity, their experiences in the workplace and the challenges it presents to them in their decision to straighten their hair or leave it naturally curly. Utilising a qualitative inductive approach, we identify themes in the comments that could be tied to relevant theories and provide a framework for future research. This chapter also includes an empirical examination of individual beliefs regarding the impact of female hair texture (curly vs. straight hair) on others' perceptions of her and her workplace outcomes. Responses from 235 participants show that straight-haired women were rated significantly higher than curly haired women on job characteristics that are important to professional positions. Thus, a bias against curly haired women appears to exist in the workplace.

Keywords: Curly hair; hair bias; women; conformity; labelling; hair straightening

While statistics show that one in three women in the United States has naturally curly hair, many of them are frustrated, having grown up feeling marginalised in a world where long, straight and sleek hair has been upheld as the ideal (Johnson, 2021; Mendleson, 2010; Neff, 2015). According to Michelle Breyer, co-founder of naturallycurly.com, she recalls being called all kinds of nicknames – Brillo pad, Bozo, big hair, Medusa, poodle head and fuzz – when growing up with a head of curly hair. Even though she feels that people's views have broadened, it is clear to her that curly hair is not considered to be a standard of beauty (Smith, 2011). For

The Emerald Handbook of Appearance in the Workplace, 39–56
Copyright © 2024 by Emerald Publishing Limited
All rights of reproduction in any form reserved
doi:10.1108/978-1-80071-174-720230003

decades, the popular press has relayed such stories of curly haired women lamenting about what they perceive as a bias associated with their hair and the pressure to conform to societal expectations of what is viewed as attractive.

Much of this bias has been influenced by the media and advertisers. In her *New York Times* column in 'The Mirror', Judith Newman provides an example of Ms. Stanger, host of Bravo's 'Millionaire Matchmaker', who tells women she is auditioning for the show to lose their curls, arguing 'I just know that to be a dream girl you need straight, long, silky, humidity-resistant hair. Also, I think curly hair reminds men of . . . a pterodactyl nest' (Newman, 2011, p. 2). Likewise, Cools (2017) argues, 'In any movie where the main character is an ugly duckling in need of a makeover [she] usually has curly hair and they get it straightened and suddenly they are beautiful. The most memorable example I can think of is Mia from the *Princess Diaries*' (p. 2).

Hair salons and companies that produce hair products have also reinforced this mindset about curly hair. Lorraine Massey, a Manhattan-based stylist who ironed her own curls for many years, says, 'Our whole training is based on making it go away. It's all about imposing upon it, making it change' (Mendleson, 2010, p. 3). Similarly, curly haired writer Newman (2011) states:

> . . . one gets the sense that curly hair is the consolation prize. Products from Ouidad and Devachan, both specializing in curlies, seem to be patting us on the back and saying 'Listen, we know what you want. We know. But be proud. If you can't have straight hair without massive amounts of time and effort, at least we'll help you look like you didn't stick your finger in an electric socket'.
>
> (Newman, 2011, p. 1)

In recent years, there has also been the widespread popularity of dry-bar salons offering blowouts for an affordable price and targeting curly haired women in their advertising.

Evidence shows that curly haired women find that this stigma carries over to how they feel or are treated in the workplace. Gretchen Heber, co-founder of naturallycurly.com, states, 'Many of our readers have said that they weren't treated favourably in job interviews when they wore their hair curly as when they straightened it. Many straighten their hair for a more "professional look"' (Levenson, 2003, p. 21). Similarly, Jessica Kupferman, who was interviewed as part of a *Business Insider* story on 'Does Having Curly Hair Hurt Your Career?', states,

> I have had curly hair all of my life and I can tell you, many of us curly haired gals straighten when we go on a job interview so that we don't seem to[o] 'crazy' or wild-minded. I know I often do. In my more corporate days, when I wanted to be taken seriously, I would straighten my hair – and it was much longer and took me an hour. I'm not sure WHY there's that mindset – almost as if curls

are created by insanity brainwaves and therefore can't be trusted –
but even women with curly hair will tell you, we act accordingly.
And men never seem to have this problem. I've never met a man
interest[ed] in straightening his hair, ever.

(Lepore, 2012, p. 2)

Hoda Kotb of the *Today Show* developed an interview series with several curly
haired women and found that physical therapist Karen Hall, who regularly wears
her hair curly, tried a straight hairstyle for three days (What's in a Hairstyle?
Women Test Reactions to Straight vs. Curly Dos, 2015). Karen Hall's notes from
Day 2 said, 'I have been called "Doctor" more today than I have since I started
here. All of a sudden straight hair made me official. One physician told me that he
likes my hair straight and that it makes me look more professional, more serious,
and older. What? What is that supposed to mean? Am I not professional or
serious with curly hair?' (p. 4).

Evidence also suggests that curly haired women experience dissonance
regarding their hair and how to manage their professional identity. By conforming to societal pressure and straightening one's hair, they gain the benefit of
fitting in but struggle with inauthenticity and challenges associated with maintaining that look. For example, Newman (2011) states, 'For most of my life,
changing my curls seemed disrespectful of my ethnicity, my family. I might as well
have moved to Greenwich, Connecticut and started wearing pearls'. (p. 1). With
the recent onset of the natural hair movement by Black women, many white
women are beginning to question why they should not also be embracing their
natural curls, tired of the time and heat damage involved in straightening their
hair and wanting to feel good about their 'natural beautiful self' (Breslaw, 2014;
Cools, 2017; Ferreira, 2018, 2019; Weiner, 2017).

While the academic literature has given little attention to examining social
perceptions of hair, there are a few recent studies that have examined others'
perceptions of curly hair or hair with texture. A study by Gonzalez et al. (2016)
investigated the extent to which hair characteristics influence hiring decisions and
found that blonds and brunettes fare better with straight hair, as opposed to curly,
and those with short hair relative to long hair. Another study looked at how
manipulations of hair diameter, density and style in computer-generated pictures
impacted perceptions of women's age, health and attractiveness (Fink et al.,
2016). Findings showed that women with straight hair were perceived as
younger, healthier and more attractive than those with wavy hair. A more recent
study by Koval and Rosette (2021), which also examined hair bias in recruitment,
found no evidence of bias as white women with curly hair and straight hair
received comparable ratings on professionalism, competence and likelihood to
select for an interview. Because these studies provide evidence of somewhat
limited and inconsistent findings, we believe that the question of bias against curly
hair warrants further investigation.

The purpose of this chapter is to provide a more comprehensive analysis of
curly hair bias by examining comments made by women about their hair experience, how it affects their identity, their experiences in the workplace and the

challenges it presents to them in their decision to alter their hair or leave it naturally curly. Utilising a qualitative inductive approach, we analyse the comments, look for themes that can be tied to relevant theories and provide a framework for future research. Thus, while relevant theories are described below, these were identified after common themes were discovered and labelled in our examination of the qualitative data. In addition, this chapter includes an empirical examination of individual beliefs regarding the impact of female hair texture (curly vs. straight hair) on others' perceptions of her and her workplace outcomes.

Theoretical Framework

In this section, we provide a review of the relevant theoretical work tied to this issue, focusing on labelling and conformity.

Labelling Theory

The concept of labelling seems to influence all aspects of hair bias. When viewed as a social construct, Becker (1963) argues that social groups label what is right and wrong or deviant based on the social norm of the majority. Characteristics and behaviours viewed as different from this norm are given negative labels, and people associated with these labels are stigmatised and viewed as outsiders. Similarly, Goffman (1963) used the word 'stigma' to refer to 'an attribute that is deeply discrediting' (p. 3) and sets one apart from others. Kitsuse (1980, p. 2) expanded on the notion of stigma to include 'genetic stigmata' that can impact marginalised people, such as body type, left-handedness and hair colour. In their examination of the stigmatisation of red hair, Heckert and Best (1997) made the argument that stigmatisation could also be extended to include hair texture.

The stigmatisation of curly hair has existed throughout history, with Western civilisation depicting curly hair as sensuous or appearing to have 'a mind of its own' as reflected in early art and literature. According to Jolly (2004), artists often depict Eve with sinuous curls, alluding to the idea that Eve seduced Adam to sin. Similarly, Botticelli's and Titian nudes show females with wild flowing hair (Newman, 2011). In the book *Jane Eyre*, Mr Brocklehurst spots a girl in Lowood School with curly hair and says that the curls are to be cut off because they are in defiance of God (Levenson, 2003). In more recent times, female comedians with curly hair (e.g. Phyllis Diller, Lucille Ball, Gilda Radner) have extended the stereotype that curly haired women cannot be taken seriously (Newman, 2011). The outcome of this stigmatisation for women with curly hair is unhappiness, low self-esteem and self-hate. Research sponsored by DoveHair found that only 40% of girls describe their curly hair as beautiful, and many wish they could change their hair to be straight. These feelings do not appear to change with age, as this study also found that only one in 10 adult women like their curly hair (Allam, 2015; Neff, 2015).

Facades of Conformity

Many white women with curly hair opt to straighten their hair to minimise the perception that they are different from others or because they see it as an economic necessity for employability and/or career growth. This phenomenon reflects what Hewlin (2003) refers to as 'facades of conformity'. In the workplace, when personal and organisational values conflict, some employees may feel the need to behave in ways that are consistent with the organisation, thereby masking their true self. These facades often result in situations where conforming is seen as a necessity to be successful in the organisation and viable alternatives do not exist. According to Hewlin (2003), conforming is more likely to exist in situations where individuals perceive greater subjectivity in how decisions are made, particularly regarding factors related to success (e.g. promotions, recognition, raises). The results for individuals who create these facades are feelings of hypocrisy and dissonance. Curly haired writer Zoe Weiner states,

> When I got a job as a fashion assistant in New York after my college graduation, straight hair seemed like the only way to go. The few times I showed up rocking my natural curls I felt 'sloppy' and 'unkempt', and it seemed like everyone in the office was judging me for not spending more time 'perfecting' my appearance. ...This 'put together' version of me was 'winning at life' – I was on the 'right' career path, had the 'right' wardrobe and lived in the 'right' neighborhood in the 'right' city – but deep down I was really unhappy.
>
> (Weiner, 2017, p. 3)

Clearly, the inauthenticity associated with conforming to the accepted beauty standard takes an emotional toll on individuals, resulting in frustration and resentment. Thus, the following research questions are driving this chapter:

RQ1. What are some common themes that describe the experiences of curly haired women in the workplace, and what existing theories fit these themes?

RQ2. To what extent does female hair texture (curly vs. straight) impact others' perceptions of a woman and her workplace outcomes?

Method

Study 1

Data Collection
The data for our study were collected from four websites (i.e. blogs) that were identified by performing a Google search using the search terms 'curly hair', 'perceptions' and 'workplace'. We also included the word 'comments' in our Google search to help ensure that we would find sites in which readers had left comments related to the topic of curly hair. This Google search produced 420,000

results. The first four websites with 10 or more reader comments were selected. We used saturation as the criteria in determining the number of websites (Glaser & Strauss, 1967). That is, additional sites we examined beyond the original four provided more examples of the same themes or topics but no new information. The four websites used were www.naturallycurly.com, www.mumsnet.com, www.hairromance.com and www.reddit.com and the discussion topics were 'Is curly hair professional?', 'Perceptions of curly hair', 'Is straight hair more professional?' and 'Difficult to be taken seriously with curly hair?'. All posts (i.e. reader comments) made on these four websites ($N = 191$) were cut and pasted into an Excel spreadsheet and included in the analysis.

Data Analysis
First, we reviewed the data and combined comments that were made by the same person. This resulted in a total of 131 contributors. Next, we eliminated comments that did not directly address curly hair. After eliminating 14 comments that were deemed irrelevant, we arrived at our final sample ($N = 117$). We conducted our analysis using a grounded theory approach, which requires researchers to suspend any pre-existing theoretical expectations or biases before data analysis and let the data dictate the formulation of the theory (Glaser & Strauss, 1967; Strauss & Corbin, 2008). We began with open coding, where we were 'open' to and actively seeking new concepts relevant to hair bias (Strauss & Corbin, 2008). Specifically, we read through all the comments and identified initial concepts, grouping them into categories. Whenever possible, we used in vivo codes for each category where 'in vivo coding is a form of qualitative data analysis that places emphasis on the actual spoken words of the participants' (Manning, 2017, p. 1). This process resulted in 14 categories. Next, we engaged in axial coding, which involved searching for relationships among the categories and identifying higher order themes (Strauss & Corbin, 2008).

Study 2

Data Collection
A total of 235 participants were recruited from undergraduate management courses (Principles of Management, Organizational Behaviour) at two medium-sized universities, one located in the Midwest and the other located in the southeastern part of the United States. Participation was voluntary although participants were given some minimal course credit for doing so. All students in each class agreed to participate. The demographics of the participants were as follows: 52% were male ($N = 123$), 81% were white ($N = 190$), 8% were Black ($N = 19$), 5% were Asian ($N = 12$), 2% were Hispanic/Latino ($N = 4$) and the remaining 5% ($N = 10$) indicated either 'Other' or did not indicate their ethnicity. The average age was 21.81 (sd = 3.18).

Design and Procedure
Questionnaires were administered to and collected from the 235 students during class time. Survey questionnaires contained the following sections: demographics, photo of a woman with either straight or curly hair and a measure of participants' beliefs regarding the impact of hair on workplace outcomes.

Hair Manipulation. Each participant was randomly assigned a photo of one of two women: a long-haired brunette and a medium-length haired blond. While neither hair length nor hair colour was the focus of this study, we used two different women to determine if there was curly hair bias for two different women. Thus, there was a total of four photos: a woman with long straight brunette hair, a woman with long curly brunette hair, a woman with medium-length curly blond hair or a woman with straight medium length blond hair. Above each photo was the statement, 'Assume this is a recruiter for one of the companies at which you have applied'.

Workplace Outcomes Measure. Participants' beliefs regarding the impact of hair on workplace outcomes was measured using a modified version of the scale developed by Peluchette et al. (2006). Using a five-point Likert scale (1 = strongly disagree, 5 = strongly agree), participants were asked their level of agreement or disagreement as to whether the recruiter's appearance would have a favourable impact on six outcomes: her ability to carry out her job effectively, her career success, her pay/compensation, her co-workers' views of her, her supervisor's views of her and applicant's views of her. Next, participants used a 5-point Likert scale (1 = very poor, 5 = excellent) to answer the following questions, 'Based on your first impression, how would you rate her on each of the characteristics listed below?' This was followed by a list of eight characteristics: professionalism, credibility, friendliness, competence, agreeableness, conscientiousness, attention to detail, ability to influence others.

Results

Study 1

Our qualitative analysis resulted in the identification of 14 first-order concepts and three higher order themes as shown in Table 1. These three higher order themes included: (1) labelling (i.e. stigma associated with curly hair); (2) conformity and (3) no curly hair bias. Below, we provide a discussion of the themes shown in Table 1.

Labelling
Consistent with labelling theory, several commenters noted that others tend to label them when they wear their hair in a curly style. Examples include: 'you must be the crazy one, huh?', 'another adjective is "lazy"', 'people are always like "Oh, you didn't feel like doing your hair today?"', 'it is virtually impossible to cut the "honestly I am a professional" mustard ... Curly girls are common, matronly, or sexy. They aren't professional' and 'I think people take you more seriously when

Table 1. Data Structure.

Second-order Themes	First-order Concepts	Sample Comments
Labelling	1. Curly hair is wild, less discrete	The issue with curly hair is that it looks bulkier than straight hair, and in a corporate environment, you are expected to look as discrete as possible because any attention derived to your looks influences the communication process.
	2. Not taken seriously	I have wavy/curly hair and am always taken more seriously (which is reflected in how much money I earn) if my hair is straight.
	3. Unprofessional	It's really sad, but I think straight hair is an easy way to look more professional, especially in a corporate environment. The problem is that curly hair, when it's not styled properly, looks wild and sometimes messy, more so than unstyled straight hair. A person's whole look (clothes, makeup, hair, nails) is a reflection of their personality and perceived capabilities and getting that promotion is so much about what other people think.
	4. Lazy	I also feel that curly hair (on women) is less favoured because of the 'try' factor. To the uninitiated, all-natural hair means no diffuser, woke up like this, lazy hair.
	5. Curly hair is less attractive	I often get comments about how people 'would love to see

		my hair straight'. Those comments always make me feel that they don't think my long curly hair (past my shoulders and black) is good enough.
	6. Lookism in general	Women are always judged more on their appearance than men; I agree it should be more about looking neat than curls vs straight.
Conformity	1. Straighten for interview	As someone who's been in the job-hunting market for a while, I will say that when I go on a job interview, I will straighten my hair. And I HATE to straighten my hair. But my experience has been that I am not taken seriously as a professional woman who knows her field of expertise (and I have 13 years of experience in my profession and am pretty good at what I do) in an interview situation otherwise.
	2. Depends on where you work	It probably depends on where you work and on how conservative the company is.
	3. Curly hair takes time and work to tame	Having perfectly straight blown out healthy hair is expensive to maintain. It takes me an hour to straighten my hair.
	4. If employer has bias against curly hair, I wouldn't want to work there	If someone doesn't want to hire me because of my hair, then it's probably not a place I want to work at, you know?
No curly hair bias	5. There is no bias against curly hair	I've never had the impression that anyone has discounted me because of my hair.

(Continued)

Table 1. *(Continued)*

Second-order Themes	First-order Concepts	Sample Comments
	6. Straight haired women who wish they had curly	I have straight hair and have always envied women with curly hair. I think if curly hair is well groomed it looks gorgeous.
	7. Embrace the curls	I spent years trying to blow dry my wavy hair but eventually decided to embrace the curls.
	8. Hair perceptions are more about condition and cut	Curly hair can definitely look groomed and well-behaved with the right cut and treatment.

your hair is "in control." It's like some people assume that messy hair = messy, disorganised person'. One woman commented that her friend was told by her boss that her curly hair would look 'too wild' for the customers.

The labelling process also causes some women to internalise the 'beautiful hair is straight hair' ideal. For example, sample comments include: '[I] straighten my curls for work … [I] prefer my curly look to be honest but [I] think it makes me look a bit mad', 'I always straighten it for interviews or big meetings why?? Cause I feel it looks like I'm more in control??' and 'It's really sad, but I think straight hair is an easy way to look more professional, especially in a corporate environment'. One woman commented that, although she wears her curly hair naturally at work, she always has some hair pins stashed in her desk in case she senses that others are perceiving her curls as too messy or 'edging into crazy lady territory'. Thus, the above comments provide evidence that labelling theory is relevant as theoretical support for understanding curly hair bias.

Conformity

Consistent with Hewlin's (2003) 'facades of conformity theory', many women felt pressure to conform to expected standards of appearance. For example, comments included 'I'm often told that I look like I'm "too much" and need to "tone it down"', 'a senior colleague once warned me that I'd never be taken seriously unless I straightened my hair', '[people say] "you look so good with straight hair, you should straighten it all the time"', 'I straighten my hair every day for work. I once left it curly (its natural state) and my boss said something about my holiday hair!' and 'As someone who's been in the job-hunting market for a while, I will say that when I go on a job interview, I will straighten my hair. And I HATE to straighten my hair. But my experience has been that I am not taken seriously as a professional woman who knows her field of expertise (and I have 13 years of experience in my profession and am pretty good at what I do) in an interview situation otherwise'. Several others commented on the time and cost required to achieve straight hair, and there were a number who expressed resentment for having to conform. For example, one commenter stated, 'I find myself trying to make my hair pin-straight and neat for job interviews or other "serious" events . . . It's a shame that we have to think about what our hair is saying about us and our abilities!'

Some noted that the pressure to conform depended on the type of job or nature of the workplace. For example, one woman stated, 'It probably depends on where you work and on how conservative the company is. A friend of mine with really gorgeous curly hair works at an airport and her boss told her, that if she wanted to wear her hair open, she'd have to straighten it'. Others stated, 'I work in sales and I think everyone straightens their hair' and 'I am a stay at home Mum for now and have been for the last few years. . . . Pop me back into corporate land and I'd have to straighten, straighten, straighten because it gives a PREDICTABLE result'. Others indicated feeling significantly less pressure to conform, with comments like 'I see and wear my hair curly quite often for work (it's straight as a board naturally). . . but, I work with nonprofits so we generally do what we want' and 'I work in IT where people somehow expect you to look a little different. Nobody ever cared about my hair whether I wear it curly or straight or about my clothes as long as I look clean, healthy and presentable. And I'm very glad for that'. However, some took a stronger position, indicating that, if an employer pressured them to alter their curly hair, they would not want to work there.

No Curly Hair Bias
While most commenters voiced opinions that supported the existence of hair bias, several disagreed. Sample comments include: 'I have curly hair and have never felt I needed to straighten it to feel professional' and 'I think curly hair looks lovely and have envied people with natural curls ever since I was little'. Others believed that negative perceptions about curly hair were more related to hair condition and cut, rather than hair texture. For example, one woman commented, 'I think curly hair can look professional as long as it's not dried out or fried looking'. Another stated, 'I believe that hair does impact drastically on your "professional image" however I think it has less to do with whether it's curly or straight and more to do with how you wear it and the condition that it's in'.

Still others exhibited lack of conformity by embracing their curls, 'I'm curly and never straighten it, I feel it's part of me and wild suits me. Don't really care if others don't agree' and 'I've never even honestly given any thought about straightening my hair for work to seem more "professional." I am curly hair, and they can love it or leave it'. These comments provide evidence that some curly haired women feel comfortable with their curls and discount the negative perceptions associated with such a hair style. It is possible that some women feel a sense of job security, depending on their occupation or career stage, and are willing to risk the consequences of bias about their appearance. However, others did acknowledge some concern about the impact of their hair on their career success. For example, a woman commented, 'I have long curly hair so it can be distracting when it's all down. I wear it down sometimes at work after I've been there for a little while but usually end up pulling it back loosely off and on since it's in the way. ... Maybe at the start of my career, I would straighten if I had shorter hair (when I had less experience to back me up). Unfortunately, people view straight hair as more professional and looks matter'.

Study 2

Tables 2 and 3 contain the mean ratings and standard deviations for each of the workplace outcome measures. Because of the large number of dependent variables, a MANOVA was conducted first to minimise the Type I error rate. The multivariate tests revealed significant main effects for both hair texture (curly versus straight [F (14, 218) = 2.35, $p < 0.01$]) and hair colour (blond versus brunette [F (14, 218) = 4.34, $p < 0.000$]). The multivariate test for the interaction between hair texture and hair colour was not significant [F (14, 218) = 1.55, $p = 0.10$]. The results of the univariate tests revealed that straight haired women were

Table 2. Means, Standard Deviations and MANOVA Results for Curly Versus Straight Hair.

Dependent Variables	Straight		Curly		
	M	SD	M	SD	*F* (1, 231)
Professionalism	3.81	0.75	3.31	0.92	12.93***
Credibility	3.42	0.78	3.26	0.73	0.37
Friendliness	4.00	0.93	3.61	0.96	3.94*
Competence	3.53	0.78	3.36	0.76	1.36
Agreeableness	3.65	0.78	3.36	0.89	3.68
Conscientiousness	3.59	0.75	3.32	0.77	3.74
Attention to detail	3.58	0.84	3.09	0.98	9.74**
Ability to influence others	3.77	0.93	3.36	1.01	6.55*
Her ability to carry out her job effectively	3.00	1.11	2.98	0.95	0.00
Her career success	3.41	0.89	3.20	0.86	2.15
Her pay/compensation	3.16	0.88	2.99	0.94	0.81
Her co-workers' views of her	3.85	0.83	3.52	0.92	7.13**
Her supervisor's view of her	3.82	0.80	3.50	0.92	5.06*
Applicants' views of her	3.86	0.89	3.50	0.94	6.32*

*$p < 0.05$, **$p < 0.01$, ***$p < 0.001$.

Table 3. Means, Standard Deviations and MANOVA Results for Long Brunette Versus Medium-Length Blond Hair.

Dependent Variables	Brunette		Blond		
	M	SD	*M*	SD	*F* (1,211)
Professionalism	3.28	0.76	3.86	0.87	21.87***
Credibility	3.11	0.69	3.58	0.74	22.08***
Friendliness	3.44	0.92	4.19	0.85	34.77***
Competence	3.34	0.71	3.56	0.82	3.46
Agreeableness	3.32	0.80	3.70	0.84	9.04**
Conscientiousness	3.26	0.67	3.67	0.81	13.57***
Attention to detail	3.03	0.92	3.67	0.86	22.81***
Ability to influence others	3.37	0.93	3.79	0.99	7.10**
Her ability to carry out her job effectively	2.94	1.03	3.04	1.04	0.55
Her career success	3.21	0.88	3.42	0.87	1.99
Her pay/compensation	2.95	0.92	3.21	0.90	4.46*
Her co-workers' views of her	3.62	0.91	3.76	0.86	0.35
Her supervisor's view of her	3.50	0.88	3.83	0.83	5.47*
Applicants' views of her	3.55	0.91	3.83	0.92	3.20

*$p < 0.05$, **$p < 0.01$, ***$p < 0.001$.

rated significantly higher than the curly haired women on professionalism, friendliness, attention to detail, ability to influence others, her co-workers' views of her, her supervisor's view of her and applicants' views of her. In addition, the blond woman (regardless of whether it was curly or straight) with medium length hair was rated significantly higher than the long-haired brunette on professionalism, credibility, friendliness, agreeableness, conscientiousness, attention to detail, ability to influence others, her pay/compensation and her supervisor's view of her.

Discussion

When examining the website comments posted about curly hair in Study 1, we found that how women think and feel about their hair is largely influenced by the labelling process. Comments indicated that hair, which is viewed as different from the norm of 'smooth and straight', is stigmatised by others as wild, unprofessional and less attractive. Another source of individuals' feelings about their hair stems from pressures that they experienced to conform to expectations about what is viewed as appropriate. Often, individuals indicated that these pressures started when they were young but then continued into adulthood and the workplace. The emotional toll that conformity had on those who were altering their hair to meet job or organisational expectations was reflected in the comments as resentment and/or feeling inauthentic. This supports previous research that aesthetic or appearance labour can result in cognitive dissonance, stress and unhappiness (Peluchette et al., 2006; Witz et al., 2003). In addition, we observed comments by those who do not think that there is a bias against curly hair or rallied against feeling that they had to alter their hair to conform to expectations. Overall, these feelings about their hair influence curly haired women's choice of hair style and their decision to conform (or not) to others' expectations, all of which have implications for the workplace.

Our findings for Study 2 demonstrate that a bias against curly haired women appears to exist in the workplace. Straight-haired women were rated significantly higher than curly haired women on job characteristics that are important for professional positions. Specifically, perceptions of professionalism, friendliness, attention to detail and ability to influence others were all significantly influenced by hair texture. It is interesting to note that hair texture (curly vs. straight) not only impacted our respondents' view of the female recruiter but also their perceptions of how she would be viewed by others, both within and outside the firm (e.g. co-workers, her supervisor and applicants to the firm). These findings have important implications for the workplace. Because straight-haired women were viewed more positively than curly haired women on key performance related characteristics, they could be given preferential treatment by supervisors in terms of special job assignments, high-profile projects and other opportunities such as networking and mentoring programmes that are important for career advancement. This may be even more likely in cases where these opportunities involve interfacing with key stakeholders or parties who are critical to the success of the organisation. In addition, supervisors may evaluate straight-haired women more favourably on performance reviews, creating a negative effect on compensation and promotional opportunities for curly haired women.

It is important to note that our findings confirm the existence and validity of a 'what-is-beautiful-is-good stereotype' (e.g. Eagly et al., 1991; Jackson et al., 1995) which is based on implicit personality theory. Although appearance norms and attractiveness are culturally based, hair is a significant part of our appearance and has been shown to influence what others deem as attractive (Cavico et al., 2012; Dechter, 2015; Kwan & Trautner, 2009; Warhurst et al., 2012; Weitz, 2001). Research shows that attractiveness matters as much for men as for women, that attractiveness bias does not change based on the amount of job-related information provided, and that attractiveness is an asset in employment decisions related to hiring, performance reviews and promotion (Hosoda et al., 2003). Given the potential impact of this hair bias on curly haired women's treatment in the workplace, one can see why some feel the need to conform to expectations and alter/straighten their hair.

Limitations and Directions for Future Research

Both Study 1 and Study 2 are not without limitations. Participants in Study 1 were self-selected. It is possible that those who choose to respond to the online discussion boards may not be representative of the general population. Future research should focus on targeting broader samples of working curly haired women. The generalisability of our findings is also limited by the self-report nature of the data and the possibility of social desirability bias; however, the overall intent of Study 1 was to identify existing theories that would provide directions for future research on hair bias in the workplace, not to test existing theory.

In Study 2, our participants examined photos rather than interacting with real people and then provided self-reports of how they thought the woman's appearance might affect workplace outcomes. While this indicates the power that photos can have on influencing perceptions (e.g. photos on resumes), future research involving real women and outcomes would be helpful in gaining a better understanding of the degree of bias that exists in the workplace. Also, while we reported the results of our comparison between participants' ratings of the blond versus the brunette, it should be noted that we did not control for length of hair or facial expression. The superior ratings received by the blond woman could be because she had a friendly smile, whereas the brunette had a slight closed-mouth smile. The blond and brunette also differed in terms of hair length so hair length and other aspects of appearance should be controlled in future research.

Building on the theories presented earlier, we see opportunities for future research on hair bias in the workplace. While we collected comments posted by women about their hair, more in-depth research is needed to examine the self-perceptions of women with curly hair and how it is impacting them in the workplace. Although we found evidence in the comments to support labelling theory and facades of conformity, it is important to investigate whether there are other theories that could be applied to explain the experience of curly haired women in the workplace.

Future research should also examine the self-perceptions of those who wear their hair naturally curly versus those who straighten/alter their hair. For those who feel the need to conform or alter their hair, it is important to examine factors related to individuals' identity that may influence how they respond to the pressure to conform. For example, previous research shows that individuation and social anxiety are relevant aspects of self-concept that are tied to conformity (Santee & Maslach, 1982). Similarly, stability (a higher order factor of the Big Five including emotional stability, agreeableness and conscientiousness) positively predicts conformity, whereas plasticity (extraversion and openness) is a negative predictor (DeYoung et al., 2002). It is likely that these factors would influence how women with curly hair present themselves in the workplace.

In addition, future studies should examine whether factors such as generational group, career stage and organisational type/culture impact one's response to the pressure of conformity. For example, the Millennial generation has been found to be more independent than previous generations (Twenge & Campbell, 2008) and those in Generation Z place a high value authenticity and sincerity (Burke, 2019). Thus, curly haired women in either of these generational groups may be less likely respond to the pressure to conform, as compared to women in older generational groups. It is also possible that career stage can have an impact on responses to pressures to conform. Those early in their career and at mid-career stage may feel more vulnerable to expectations of 'fitting in' to advance within their organisation. It is also important to examine the type of work, the industry that one works in and the organisational culture. These factors may impact the intensity of the pressure to conform (e.g. TV/broadcasting jobs versus working in a research lab) and the amount of flexibility/discretion that is provided to individuals, with some workplace environments allowing for more freedom of expression than others (Quinn & Rorbaugh, 1983).

Finally, building on labelling theory, it is important to more thoroughly examine the impact that curly hair has on others' perceptions of one's competence, professionalism and other workplace outcomes. If the observer has curly hair, how does that influence their perception of others with curly hair in the workplace? Do they more negatively judge the target for failure to conform or see the target as 'selling out' by not wearing their hair naturally curly? How does the gender and age of both the observer and the target impact the observer's perceptions of competence and professionalism? Clearly, the result of these perceptions can have significant implications for an individual's compensation, promotional opportunities and career mobility.

References

Allam, N. (2015, January 21). 'Love your curls' is the message behind Dove's latest ad campaign. https://fustany.com/en/beauty/hair/love-your-curls-is-the-message-behind-doves-latest-ad-campaign. Accessed on June 30, 2022.

Becker, H. (1963). *Outsiders*. The Free Press of Glencoe.

Breslaw, A. (2014, December 14). Is there a stigma against curly hair? https://www.cosmopolitan.com/style-beauty/news/a33862/curly-hair-stigma-workplace. Accessed on June 30, 2022.

Burke, F. (2019, February 26). Gen Z is all about authenticity. https://medium.com/clyde-group/gen-z-is-all-about-authenticity-59d863b0bdcf. Accessed on June 29, 2022.

Cavico, F., Muffler, S., & Mujtaba, B. (2012). Appearance discrimination, "lookism" and "lookphobia" in the workplace. *Journal of Applied Business Research*, *28*(5), 791–802.

Cools, J. (2017, November 6). Let's talk about racism and the natural hair movement. https://medium.com/jmcools/lets-talk-about-racism-and-the-natural-hair-movement-dcec15857592. Accessed on June 29, 2022.

Dechter, E. K. (2015). Physical appearance and earnings, hair color matters. *Labour Economics*, *32*, 15–26. https://doi.org/10.1016/j.labeco.2015.11.002

DeYoung, C., Peterson, J., & Higgins, D. (2002). Higher-order factors of the Big Five predict conformity: Are there neuroses of health? *Personality and Individual Differences*, *33*(4), 533–552. https://doi.org/10.1016/S0191-8869(01)00171-4

Eagly, A. H., Ashmore, R. D., Makhijani, M. G., & Longo, L. C. (1991). What is beautiful is good, but...: A meta-analytic review of research on the physical attractiveness stereotype. *Psychological Bulletin*, *110*(1), 109–128. https://psycnet.apa.org/doi/10.1037/0033-2909.110.1.109

Ferreira, J. (2018, July 17). Is there room for white women in the natural hair movement? https://hiplatina.com/white-women-natural-hair-movement/. Accessed on June 29, 2022.

Ferreira, J. (2019, February 1). Why the curly and natural hair movement is so important. https://hiplatina.com/importance-curly-hair-movement/. Accessed on June 29, 2022.

Fink, B., Hufschmidt, C., Hirn, T., Will, S., McKelvey, G., & Lankhof, J. (2016). Age, health, and attractiveness perception of virtual (rendered) human hair. *Frontiers in Psychology*, 7, 1–12. https://doi.org/10.3389/fpsyg.2016.01893

Glaser, B., & Strauss, A. (1967). *The discovery of grounded theory*. Aldine.

Goffman, E. (1963). *The presentation of self in everyday life*. Doubleday.

Gonzalez, K., Mercado, B., & Dilchert, S. (2016). Does hair hurt career marketability? Investigating the influence of hairstyle on hiring decisions. *Academy of Management Annual Meeting Proceedings*. https://doi.org/10.5465/ambpp.2016.14301abstract

Heckert, D., & Best, A. (1997). Ugly duckling to swan: Labelling theory and stigmatization of red hair. *Symbolic Interaction*, *20*(4), 365–384.

Hewlin, P. (2003). And the award for best actor goes to. . .: Facades of conformity in organizational settings. *Academy of Management Review*, *28*(4),633–642. https://doi.org/10.5465/amr.2003.10899442

Hosoda, M., Stone-Romero, E., & Coats, G. (2003). The effects of physical attractiveness on job-related outcomes: A meta-analysis of experimental studies. *Personnel Psychology*, *56*(2), 431–462. https://doi.org/10.1111/j.1744-6570.2003.tb00157.x

Jackson, L. A., Hunter, J. E., & Hodge, C. N. (1995). Physical attractiveness and intellectual competence: A meta-analytic review. *Social Psychology Quarterly*, *58*(2), 108–122. https://doi.org/10.1111/j.1744-6570.2003.tb00157.x

Johnson, J. (2021, December 22). Dove and academy award-winning filmmaker Matthew A. Cherry partner to inspire kids with curly hair. https://www.blackenterprise.com/dove-and-academy-award-winning-filmmaker-matthew-a-cherry-partner-to-inspire-kids-with-curly-hair/. Accessed on June 30, 2022.

Jolly, P. H. (2004). Hair: Untangling a social history. *Art History Faculty Scholarship*, 8. https://creativematter.skidmore.edu/art_his_fac_schol/8. Accessed on June 29, 2022.

Kitsuse, J. (1980). Coming out all over: Deviants and the politics of social problems. *Social Problems*, *28*(1), 1–13. https://doi.org/10.2307/800377

Koval, C. Z., & Rosette, A. S. (2021). The natural hair bias in job recruitment. *Social Psychological and Personality Science*, *12*(5), 741–750. https://doi.org/10.1177%2F1948550620937937

Kwan, S., & Trautner, M. (2009). Beauty work: Individual and institutional rewards, the reproduction of gender, and questions of agency. *Sociology Compass*, *3*(1), 49–71. https://doi.org/10.1111/j.1751-9020.2008.00179.x

Lepore, M. (2012, July 31). Does having curly hair hurt your career? https://www.businessinsider.com/does-having-curly-hair-hurt-your-career-2012-7. Accessed on June 29, 2022.

Levenson, E. (2003). A curly minority enjoys liberation. *New Statesman*, *132*(4643), 18–21.

Manning. (2017). In vivo coding. In J. Matthes, C. S. Davis, & R. F. Potter (Eds.), *The international encyclopaedia of communication research methods* (pp. 1–2). https://doi.org/10.1002/9781118901731.iecrm0270. Accessed on June 29, 2022.

Mendleson, R. (2010, March 22). The lost art of curl maintenance. https://www.macleans.ca/culture/the-host-art-of-maintenance/. Accessed on June 30, 2022.

Neff, J. (2015). Curly cues: Dove add emojis. *Advertising Age, 86*(21), 1.

Newman, J. (2011, August 7). Making waves, with no apology. *New York Times, 1*(L). Business Insights: Global. http://bi.gale.com/global/article/GALE%7CA2635 92650/4bd87c974c5f6b0d26f5212355370ca4?u=sain20269

Peluchette, J., Karl, K., & Rust, K. (2006). Dressing to impress: Beliefs and attitudes regarding workplace attire. *Journal of Business and Psychology, 21*(1), 45–63. https://doi.org/10.1007/s10869-005-9022-1

Quinn, R., & Rorbaugh, J. (1983). A spatial model of effectiveness criteria: Towards a competing values approach to organizational analysis. *Management Science, 29*(3), 363–377. https://doi.org/10.1287/mnsc.29.3.363

Santee, R., & Maslach, C. (1982). To agree or not to agree: Personal dissent amid social pressure to conform. *Journal of Personality and Social Psychology, 42*(4), 690–700. https://psycnet.apa.org/doi/10.1037/0022-3514.42.4.690

Smith, D. (2011). Curlies unite! https://mospace.umsystem.edu/xmlui/bitstream/handle/10355/81765/MIZZOUMag-CurliesUnite.pdf?sequence=1. Accessed on June 30, 2022.

Strauss, A., & Corbin, J. (2008). *Basics of qualitative research: Techniques and procedures for developing grounded theory* (3rd ed.). Sage.

Twenge, J., & Campbell, S. (2008). Generational differences in psychological traits and their impact in the workplace. *Journal of Managerial Psychology, 23*(8), 862–877. https://doi.org/10.1108/02683940810904367

Warhurst, C., van den Broek, D., Hall, R., & Nickson, D. (2012). Great expectations: Gender, looks, and lookism at work. *International Journal of Organisation and Emotion, 5*(1), 72–90. https://doi.org/10.1504/IJWOE.2012.048593

Weiner, Z. (2017, October 11). I stopped straightening my curls – Here's what happened. https://www.allure.com/story/i-stopped-straightening-my-curls/. Accessed on June 29, 2022.

Weitz, R. (2001). Women and their hair: Seeking power through resistance and accommodation. *Gender & Society, 15*(5), 667–686. https://doi.org/10.1177%2F089124301015005003

What's in a hairstyle? Women test reactions to straight vs. curly 'dos. (2015, January 20). https://www.today.com/style/curlpower-women-switchcurly-straight-hairstyles-test-reactions-1D80436614. Accessed on June 29, 2022.

Witz, A., Warhurst, C., & Nickson, D. (2003). The labour of aesthetics and the aesthetics of organization. *Organization, 10*(1), 33–54. https://doi.org/10.1177%2F1350508403010001375

Chapter 3

Examining Hair Choices of Black Women in Academia

Katherine A. Karl, Joy V. Peluchette and Gail A. Dawson

Abstract

Based on literature providing evidence that Afrocentric hairstyles (e.g. afros, braids, dreadlocks) of Black women working in professional settings are often associated with negative stereotypes and biases regarding competency and professionalism, this chapter examines the extent to which these biases may be influencing the hairstyle choices of Black women employed in higher education. While academic workplaces tend to be more flexible and informal than non-academic settings, we found many Black women in higher education are, nonetheless, choosing to wear Eurocentric hairstyles. However, choice of hairstyle was influenced by academic discipline, type of institution and level in the university hierarchy.

Keywords: Afrocentric hairstyles; Black women; bias; impression management; academia; professional

Every day around the world, Black women encounter bias if their hair is worn in its natural state (Maynard & Jules, 2021; Morgan, 2020; Omotoso, 2018; Oyedemi, 2016). As indicated in a recent *USA Today* article, 'Black people young, old and in-between have been rejected for jobs, schools and other public places because of the texture and style of their hair' (Ellis & Jones, 2019). Many have attributed this bias to stereotypes that associate natural Black hair with sloppiness, unruliness or even militance (Rosette & Dumas, 2007; Wu, 2019). As a result, California and New York were the first states in the United States to enact laws in 2019 to prevent discrimination against people of colour for wearing natural hairstyles and since then, 14 other states have followed suit and at least 10 other states are proposing such laws (Tannenbaum, 2022; Wright, 2022). Legislation is also currently being considered at the federal level in the United States with the Creating a Respectful and Open World for Natural Hair (CROWN) Act

The Emerald Handbook of Appearance in the Workplace, 57–74

Copyright © 2024 by Emerald Publishing Limited

All rights of reproduction in any form reserved

doi:10.1108/978-1-80071-174-720230004

and if passed, its protection would automatically apply to all 50 states (Tannenbaum, 2022). Similar initiatives are occurring in the United Kingdom with the development of the Halo Code in 2020 which guarantees Black people protection from discrimination when wearing natural hairstyles in both schools and workplaces (Coates, 2020). So far, Unilever UK and several top law firms have adopted the code as part of their commitment to diversity (Lock, 2021; Macfarlane, 2020).

Academic literature focused on natural hair bias provides evidence that Afrocentric hairstyles (e.g. afros, braids, twists, dreadlocks) of Black women working in professional settings are often associated with negative stereotypes and biases regarding competency and professionalism (Davis Tribble et al., 2019; Donahoo, 2019; Ellis-Hervey et al., 2016; Hudson et al., 2017; Opie & Phillips, 2015; Patton, 2006; Randle, 2015). Such bias is reflected in the following statements by participants in a qualitative study by Dawson et al. (2019) 'I was just hired a week ago and was told that my hair was offensive to some people. I was like wow. I just got told that the hair that grows straight out of my head is offensive' (p. 394).

Similar evidence of bias has been found in empirical studies. Opie and Phillips (2015) found that employment candidates with Afrocentric hair were evaluated as less professional and less likely to succeed than those with Eurocentric hairstyles. Additionally, Afrocentric hairstyles were rated as less professional than straightened hair, regardless of evaluator race. Likewise, a study by Johnson et al. (2017) of the Perception Institute found that participants rated naturally textured Black hair as less beautiful, less attractive and less professional than smooth, straightened hair. Their findings also suggest that Black women feel they will not be accepted in corporate America unless they conform to Eurocentric hairstyles, where Eurocentric hairstyles (with reference to Black women) are defined as those that require straightening hair (either chemically or thermally) or otherwise altering hair, in texture and/or length to give it a more Caucasian or Eurocentric appearance. For example, 20% of the Black women who participated in this study expressed that they feel social pressure to straighten their hair for work. Further evidence of conformity was found in a study examining the hairstyle choices of Black female executives where only 23 (14.7%) out of the 156 Black women executives examined in the study wore Afrocentric hairstyles (Dawson & Karl, 2018).

Theoretical Framework and Relevant Literature

In this section, we discuss our theoretical framework. Like Dawson and Karl (2018), this study uses a social identity–based impression management framework (Roberts, 2005) to make predictions. Research demonstrates that individuals invest a considerable amount of energy into constructing professional images that will be perceived favourably by others including coworkers, supervisors and clients (Goffman, 1959; Rafaeli et al., 1997; Rafaeli & Pratt, 1993). For example, studies show that clothing style and grooming influence others' perceptions of the wearer including intelligence, competence and professionalism (Sanghvi & Hodges, 2015); chances of getting hired (Forsythe, 1990; Hurley-Hanson & Giannantonio, 2006; Koval & Rosette, 2021); customers' perceptions of her ability to provide quality service (Karl et al., 2013; Kim et al., 2009; Yan et al., 2011); performance reviews (Easterling et al., 1992); and the likelihood that someone will offer her help (Danzis & Stone-Romero, 2009).

Roberts (2005) asserts that social identity group membership adds a layer of complexity to professional image construction in that what is commonly considered professional is culturally biased and associated with being white/ Anglo, masculine, heterosexual, middle class and well educated (Britton, 2000). For example, Gray (2017) recounts her own experience in applying for jobs and notes that the preparation process for Black women involves a 'multi-layered checklist'. According to Gray (2017, p. 7), 'In every single item on my list, I remembered how I would try to account for the stereotypes of my Blackness'. In addition to typical issues, her checklist included issues unique to Black women such as voice ('try not to sound like an angry Black woman'), timely arrival ('no coloured people time, arrive half an hour early') and hair ('perfectly combed, tamed, neat and professional').

Similarly, social identity–based impression management (SIM) is the process of strategically influencing others' perceptions of one's own social identity to form a desired professional image. Roberts (2005) identifies two categories of SIM strategies used in professional image construction: (1) social recategorisation, where individuals use self-presentation behaviours to attempt to change the social categories to which they are assigned and (2) positive distinctiveness strategies that are aimed at communicating that difference is valuable and involve creating a positive social meaning for one's social identity. The social recategorisation strategy of assimilation is particularly relevant to hairstyle choices of Black women. Assimilation involves reducing the salience of one's own social identity by 'emphasising similarities with members of more positively regarded social identity groups' (p. 696). Recognising that some organisational decision-makers view natural Black hair as inappropriate in the workplace, many Black women wear Eurocentric hairstyles to minimise the perception that they are different from their colleagues or because they see it as an economic necessity for employability (Donaldson, 2012; Rosette & Dumas, 2007; Thompson, 2009). As stated by a participant in the Dawson et al. (2019) study:

> I do have to 'press out' my hair to impress the interviewers of my future profession. I don't like it, but, until I get the job, I'll choose the road less resistant to my natural beauty. (p. 397)

Positive distinctiveness strategies are also reflected in Black women's hairstyle choices. Rather than reducing the salience of their identity group, some women have integrated natural hairstyles into their professional image. For example, in another qualitative study, one Black woman stated 'I have to be confident in who I am and walk into a room for [an] interview or something with a White man and say well you're going to respect me. You're going to take me seriously. I think going natural has made me more confident in who I am' (Davis Tribble et al., 2019, p. 390).

Integration can involve challenging others' simplistic or negative stereotypes (Roberts, 2005). An example is a Black female university administrator who after being told her dreadlocks were unprofessional by a colleague, wore a suit for three weeks. She then went up to the person and said, 'Do I really look less professional to you? Not that I need to prove anything to you, but I wanted you to understand that how I wear my hair has nothing to do with my level of professionalism' (Crews, 2007, p. 76). Likewise, Gray (2017) noted that when Black women's natural hairstyles were questioned or criticised, some women responded by educating their white colleagues on the challenges of Black hair and the need for convenient options.

The purpose of the current study is to extend past research by examining the hairstyle choices of Black women employed in higher education. We chose to examine Black women in academic environments because appearance norms tend to be less rigid in academia than those of other organisations. For example, Tsaousi (2020) noted that in higher education, the environment tends to be more loose or flexible in terms of appearance than other environments. Likewise, Rafaeli and Pratt (1993) noted that academic institutions, which endorse values such as creativity or innovation, tend to have dress norms that are low in consistency and conspicuousness, where conspicuousness refers to the extent that the organisation's members can be specifically identified based on their dress (e.g. uniforms). We suggest that this low level of consistency and conspicuousness will be reflected in the hairstyle choices of Black women working in academia. That is, we expect there may be more variety of hairstyles in an academic environment than a business environment. In addition, the current study examines three potential situational variables that may influence Black women's hairstyle choices: level in the organisational hierarchy, type of university (Historically Black College or University [HBCU] versus a Predominantly White Institution [PWI]) and academic discipline.

Level in the Organisational Hierarchy

Research shows that Black women are underrepresented in higher education, both in faculty positions and administrative positions (McChesney, 2018). Some have attributed this underrepresentation to the multiple 'isms' faced by Black women including racism, sexism, classism, tokenism and colourism (Perkins, 2014; Wallace et al., 2014). In addition, retention of Black women in academia is influenced by daily microaggressions or communications, whether intentional or unintentional, that conveys hostile and derogatory messages to the target person because of her membership in a stigmatised group. For example, many Black women described incidents in which it was assumed by others that they must be a low-level coordinator, that they worked in a cafeteria or cleaning position on campus or that they were not the supervisor of their department or office (Perkins, 2014). Backhanded compliments are another example, such as 'You don't act like a typical Black person' (p. 8), or 'It's like they're surprised that you are capable of doing something, it's not just like, you did a good job, it's like, "oh you did great, I wasn't expecting that from you"' (p. 123).

This study investigates the hairstyle choices of Black women at four levels within the academy: faculty, department chairs, deans/directors and provosts or presidents. Existing research examining Black women in academia suggests that women at all levels have experienced hair bias and the common sentiment of those interviewed was that Black hair was supposed to look like white hair (Donahoo, 2019; Farley, 2016; Gray, 2017; Perkins, 2014). For example, Bright (2010) interviewed Black female senior-level administrators (dean, provost, vice president) in traditionally white community colleges and found many had been criticised for their natural hair choices. For example, a short Afro was described by a white colleague as 'a little severe' and another was told by the college president, 'I don't think you look professional with your hair like that [a natural hairstyle]'. Townsend (2019) also found that Black female administrators felt they had to avoid Afrocentric hairstyles. One woman was confronted by her supervisor regarding her hairstyle, questioning her ability to demonstrate professionalism when wearing that hairstyle. Many of the Black female Student Affairs professionals interviewed by Perkins (2014) feared that their hair might disqualify them from professional advancement. Likewise, many of the Black women administrators (at the director level or above) interviewed by Farley (2016) felt 'they had to make a conscious effort for their intelligence and skills to be the focus point and not their hair' (p. 50). Black female faculty had similar views. Pittman (2012) found female Black faculty experienced microaggressions from both colleagues and students when wearing a natural (Afrocentric) hairstyle. One indicated that white colleagues chided her on an almost daily basis about her natural hair or ethnic clothing and another received similar comments from her white students such as 'You can't possibly be the professor because your hair looks like this [i.e. natural African American hair]' (p. 88). Likewise, a participant interviewed by Gray (2017) believed that Black women faculty were expected 'to be very pressed and permed and made up' (p. 118).

While existing research suggests there is natural Black hair bias at all levels in colleges or universities, we expect there to be more bias at higher levels than lower levels. More specifically, we expect that faculty will feel less pressure to conform to Eurocentric hairstyles than administrators. This is in part, because past research shows that appearance norms are dependent on one's position (Fitzgerald, 2018; Lipton, 2020; Tsaousi, 2020). For example, university administrative employees who worked with faculty and students felt it was appropriate to dress more casually than those who interacted more with other administrative offices on campus or members of the business community (Rafaeli et al., 1997). Because faculty interact mostly with students and other faculty, it is likely that faculty will feel less pressure to conform to Eurocentric hairstyles.

In addition, there is evidence suggesting that some faculty feel the need to wear a natural (Afrocentric) hairstyle to serve as role models for their students. Thus, these women adopt SIM strategies of positive distinctiveness as opposed to assimilation. For example, one of the participants interviewed by Gray (2017) said she wanted Black female students to feel there is someone that 'they can connect with, that they can identify with, who understands the tensions, and struggles, and barriers that they experience being on a predominantly White campus' (p. 129). According to Gray (2017), 'this woman recognized that her hair was a marker of race that students related to and she used it as a tool to build her relationships with her students' (p. 130). The study participant further stated, "I want to make [it] easier for the next Black female that comes around with natural hair. They'll say, 'Look at her. Okay. She's going to be a phenomenal person to work with because the last lady we had that looked like her with that type of hair turned out to be really, really good'" (p. 130).

Additionally, research demonstrates that people are likely to engage in impression management when interacting with high-status and powerful people, given their dependence on these individuals for valued resources and outcomes (Leary & Kowalski, 1990; Pandey, 1986; Schlenker, 1980). This finding has been found to extend to hairstyle choices of Black female executives (Dawson & Karl, 2018). Specifically, their study found that founders and co-founders of their own companies were more likely to have Afrocentric hairstyles (31.6%) than non-founders (9%). Given that upper-level administrators are more dependent than faculty on high-status and powerful people for outcomes and rewards, it is more likely they will engage in impression management strategies such as altering their hair. Therefore, we predict:

H1. Eurocentric hairstyles will be more common among upper-level administrators than faculty.

Type of University

Given that Blacks are less of a minority at HBCUs than they are at PWIs, one might assume that Black women would feel more comfortable choosing to wear Afrocentric hairstyles at HCBUs. However, a closer examination of the history and culture of HBCUs suggests the opposite may be true. HBCUs are defined as those that were established prior to 1964 for the purpose of addressing the educational needs of Black people who, for the most part, did not have access to traditional colleges and universities (Gasman & Abiola, 2016). Although a few HBCUs existed prior to the Civil War, the majority were established shortly after and were focused on providing educational opportunities for newly freed slaves (Albritton, 2012). Deeply rooted in the Black community's commitment to uplift and empower its people and largely funded through church and religious organisations, HBCUs emerged as highly conservative schools (Albritton, 2012; Commodore, 2019; Harper & Gasman, 2008).

In addition to providing basic educational needs, HBCUs sought to create a degree of 'respectability' to help Black people integrate into white society in a way that they would be viewed as less threatening and worthy of civil and political rights. Higginbotham (1992) refers to the 'politics of "respectability"' as an attempt to combat negative stereotypes and lessen the discrimination and prejudice experienced at the hands of those who characterised Blacks as inferior. Creating an image of respectability often involved conformity to white middle-class standards and repression of Afrocentric cultural expression in the forms of dress, speech patterns, leisure activity and music among other things. As a result, many HBCUs created environments that were highly conservative with restrictive rules stipulating strict dress codes and behaviour reflecting higher cultural and moral standards than those of other universities. While HCBUs have been praised for providing supportive environments and fostering success despite the challenges of inadequate preparation and disadvantaged socioeconomic backgrounds that often plague their students, they are often criticised for being overly conservative, restrictive environments where divergence from normative standards for hair, dress and general conduct are viewed as unacceptable (Ball, 2013; Harper & Gasman, 2008; Njoku & Patton, 2017; Patton, 2014).

It should also be noted that Black women at HBCUs not only face negative stereotypes associated with being female and Black but also face negative perceptions and judgements associated with being employed at an HBCU versus a PWI. Thus, based on having an additional layer of stereotype threat, one could expect Black women at HBCUs to be more likely to avoid Afrocentric hairstyles to mitigate negative perceptions often associated with hair (unattractive, unprofessional or threatening). In support, Pronin et al. (2004) found that, when faced with a stereotype threat, individuals engage in identity bifurcation. That is, they selectively disidentify with aspects of their social identify group that are viewed as threatening. Therefore, we predict:

H2. Eurocentric hairstyles will be more common among Black women at HBCUs than at PWIs.

Academic Discipline

Even though higher education tends to be more flexible than other working environments in terms of appearance standards (Tsaousi, 2020), there is considerable variation in terms of what is viewed as appropriate for faculty members. To be successful, faculty members want to be viewed as credible and, because of concerns for tenure and promotion, they tend to adopt the norms of their department and institution (Dowling, 2008; Knight & Yorke, 2004; Lavin et al., 2010). Additionally, most faculty see themselves as role models and career mentors to students in preparing them for employability in specific professions and occupations. Thus, appearance standards are influenced, in part, by academic discipline (Jones, 2009).

Evidence that appearance norms vary across academic disciplines was found in a Louisiana State University website 'What They Wore: A history of fashion at LSU' in a paper by Annison et al. (2017) indicating that professors from different disciplines dress in different attire tailored to their own needs. Faculty in business were viewed as dressing more formally than other faculty, with women in dresses and heels and men in sports coats. Those interviewed indicated that it was important to set an example for what their students would expect in the corporate sector. In the disciplines of Math and the Sciences, faculty felt that it is better to dress comfortably and safely than professionally. Because these disciplines often involve working in a lab with protective wear, faculty tended to wear business casual (khakis and button-down shirts) or dress more informally if they were going out into the field. In the disciplines of Humanities and the Social Sciences, faculty were the most casual in their style of dress, ranging from untucked shirts and khakis for men and sweaters/blouses for women. Shoe choices ranged from formal wear (dress shoes, leather loafers) to sneakers. When interviewed, faculty indicated that they wanted to be comfortable but also be more approachable to students. In Engineering, the faculty dressed similarly to those in the Math and Sciences disciplines, but a key difference was an attention to professionalism in their clothing and grooming (haircut, facial hair). Just like the faculty in Business, Engineering faculty were concerned with setting an example of professionalism for their students.

Similar comments regarding attire differences by academic discipline were posted in comments to the Quora.com website 'Why do some Professors Dress More Formally than Others?'. Faculty posted comments such as 'Business and law profs tend to dress more formally. It could be a holdover from their days in the corporate world', 'I teach business students and it is true, our norms are for more dressed up', 'It depends heavily on the field, I don't think I've ever seen a law professor or econ professor walk around in shorts but I am in Engineering and we have quite a bit of flexibility here so I wear shorts probably 60% of the year', 'I teach Math and usually wear a shirt, pair of jeans, and normal decent shoes', 'Engineering and science disciplines are more informal in clothing styles', 'I teach in the Social Sciences and I wear black jeans, decent shoes, and a rotation of nice sweaters or shirts'. While these are anecdotal comments, they clearly reflect appearance norms by disciplines which exist across higher education.

Given the above evidence regarding appearance norms and attire in various academic disciplines, it is likely that similar norms exist related to hairstyle. In support, Gray (2017) noted that some of the Black women faculty in her study believed that expectations for Black hair expression in the academy were dependent upon the programme or department in which the faculty taught. Likewise, a participant in another qualitative study stated, 'I'm just going to go based on what the College of Business does … we have these posters of students and even though we have gotten better at focusing on the fact that we have different minorities, once again, all of them have one type of hairstyle [Euro-centric]' (Donahoo, 2019, p. 86).

We suggest that discipline-based attire norms will be like norms associated with hairstyle such that academic disciplines with formal appearance norms will be associated with Eurocentric hairstyle expectations and those with more informal norms will allow for greater freedom of expression and be accepting of Afrocentric hairstyles. It is important to note that academic disciplines associated with professional programs (such as Business, Health Professions, Education, Law) have more formality in appearance standards to meet expectations of the profession. Thus, consistent with the social recategorisation strategy of assimilation, we would expect Black females in these academic disciplines to wear Eurocentric styles to reduce the salience of their own social identity. In academic disciplines with less formal appearance standards (such as Humanities and Arts), we would expect Afrocentric hairstyles to be more popular. These academic disciplines are focused more on creativity and allow for more variation in appearance norms. Therefore, we predict:

H3. Eurocentric hairstyles will be more common among Black women in academic disciplines with more formal appearance norms (e.g. Business, Health Professions, Law) as opposed to those with more informal norms (e.g. Arts and Humanities).

Method

Like the methodologies used in previous studies (Dawson & Karl, 2018; Takeda et al., 2005), we collected our sample online from the 'Appointments' section of the *Journal of Blacks in Higher Education* website (jbhe.com/appointments/). All faculty and administrator photos posted on the 'Appointments' page from 2018 and January through March of 2019 were included in the sample. However, because this yielded only 53 deans, we extended our search for deans through August of 2019. The final sample included 414 Black women working in academia comprised of 110 faculty, 127 department chairs or directors, 71 deans and 106 presidents or provosts. Presidents are the chief executive of the university, whereas the provost is the chief academic officer of the university, providing administrative leadership and evaluation of all academic activities and faculty affairs. Using the background information provided, we determined that 102 were employed at HBCUs, while 312 were employed at PWIs. Because a wide variety of academic disciplines were represented, the authors grouped similar disciplines together into 10 categories before making comparisons based on discipline. These 10 categories included: (1) Communication, Media, PR, Journalism ($N = 18$), (2) Health Professions ($N = 27$), (3) Public Administration and related fields ($N = 23$), (4) Business/Economics ($N = 45$), (5) Social Sciences ($N = 50$), (6) Education/Higher Education ($N = 78$), (7) Law ($N = 38$), (8) Science, Technology, Engineering and Math (STEM) disciplines ($N = 38$), (9) Humanities (not including Arts, $N = 55$) and (10) Arts ($N = 20$). There were 22 that were not included in any discipline because either no information was provided on discipline, or there were less than five women in that discipline (e.g. disciplines excluded were agriculture and forestry, sport management and library science).

Next, each author independently coded the hair in the photos of all 414 women as being either Afrocentric or Eurocentric. A few photos resulted in disagreement mainly due to the photos having been cropped too small to determine hairstyle. In that case, further research was done to discover larger photos on the individual's university website and once obtained, there was 100% agreement.

Results

A total of 194 (46.9%) women in our sample chose Afrocentric hairstyles demonstrating that women in academic environments are more likely to wear natural hairstyles than those in corporate business environments. In comparison, only 15% of the women executives and entrepreneurs in the Dawson and Karl (2018) study chose to wear Afrocentric hairstyles. Regarding level in the university, faculty were most likely to wear Afrocentric hairstyles (56.4%), followed by Directors, Managers or Chairs (52%), then Deans (49.3%), and Presidents or Provosts (29.2%). The results of a Chi-square analysis showed the difference was significant [X^2 (3, $N = 414$) $= 18.40$, $p < 0.000$]. The results of a mean comparison using ANOVA was also significant [F (3, 410) $= 6.46$, $p < 0.000$]. A comparison of means using a Bonferonni correction revealed that those in the position of president or provost were significantly more likely than all other groups to wear Eurocentric hairstyles. No other comparisons were significant. This finding lends partial support for *H1* in which we predicted that Eurocentric hairstyles would be more common among upper-level administrators than faculty.

Regarding a comparison of HBCUs and PWIs, we found Black women at HBCUs were significantly more likely to wear Eurocentric hairstyles than those at PWIs [X^2 (1, $N = 414$) $= 8.56$, $p < 0.01$]. Thus, *H2* was supported. Finally, we examined whether hairstyle choice was related to one's discipline and a Chi-square analysis showed a significant difference [X^2 (9, $N = 392$) $= 41.88$, $p < 0.000$]. The results of a mean comparison using ANOVA was also significant [F (9, 382) $= 5.08$, $p < 0.000$]. A comparison of means using a Bonferonni correction revealed that those in the arts were significantly more likely to choose Afrocentric hairstyles than those in any other discipline except for humanities. In addition, those in humanities were more likely to choose Afrocentric hairstyles than those in health professions ($p < 0.05$), public administration and related fields ($p < 0.05$), or communication, media, public relations or journalism ($p < 0.05$). No other comparisons were significant. This finding provides partial support for *H3* (Table 1).

Discussion

Negative stereotypes and bias against Afrocentric hairstyles (e.g. braids, dreadlocks, afros) have received considerable attention in both the academic literature and popular press (Dawson et al., 2019). This study expanded on existing literature by examining the hairstyle choices of Black women in higher education. In support of past research suggesting academic settings have more liberal standards regarding dress and appearance, we found more women in higher education wore Afrocentric hairstyles than what has previously been reported in business settings (Dawson & Karl, 2018).

Utilising a social identity–based impression management framework (Roberts, 2005), we also found support for our hypotheses predicting that the hairstyle choices of Black women in higher education would be influenced by position level

Table 1. Percentage of Black Women in Higher Education With Afrocentric Hair by Category.

	N	Percentage	Chi-Square
Level			18.70***
President or Provost	106	29.2%	
Dean	71	49.3%	
Director, Manager, Chair	127	52.0%	
Faculty	110	56.4%	
HBCU			8.56**
Yes	102	34.3%	
No	312	51%	
Discipline			41.88***
Communication, Media, PR, Journalism	18	22.2%	
Health Professions	27	25.9%	
Pub Admin and Related	23	26.1%	
Business/Economics	45	40.0%	
Social Science	50	42.0%	
Education/Higher Education	78	42.3%	
Law	38	47.4%	
STEM	38	52.6%	
Humanities (no Arts)	55	65.5%	
Arts	20	95.0%	

**$p < 0.01$, ***$p < 0.001$.

in the university, type of university and academic discipline. For example, we found Black women in the position of President or Provost were significantly more likely to wear Eurocentric hairstyles than those at lower levels. Given previous research demonstrating that Afrocentric hairstyles are associated with the angry Black woman stereotype or militance (Dawson et al., 2019; Rosette & Dumas, 2007), and that these traits are unlikely to lead to positive attributions regarding the leadership potential of such women (Rosette et al., 2016), it is not surprising that Black women at upper levels of university administration feel more pressure to engage in SIM via assimilation. That is, they conform to Eurocentric norms to minimise the negative stereotypes associated with natural hairstyles. It is also likely that many Black women in leadership positions, like those described earlier, have experienced either overt comments that their natural hair was considered unprofessional or covert hints such as disapproving 'looks' from others. Likewise, we found that women at HBCUs are more likely to choose

Eurocentric hairstyles than those at PWIs, supporting the literature describing the history and culture of HBCUs as being highly conservative and repressive of Afrocentric cultural expression. We also found that Black women in the academic disciplines of Arts and Humanities are more likely to wear Afrocentric hairstyles than those associated with professional programmes (e.g. Business, Law, Education, Health Professions). These findings are consistent with the informality of appearance norms associated with the Arts and Humanities disciplines.

Limitations and Directions for Future Research

The sample used for this study was a convenience sample drawn from an online source which included Black men and women appointed to new positions in higher education. Due to the limited amount of information provided, we were not able to determine either the length of service at the university or the tenure status of our sample. Thus, it is possible that the sample was not an accurate representation of all Black females in higher education. In addition, the number of women per discipline varied widely. Future research using a larger sample drawn from specific academic disciplines, controlling for length of service and or tenure, would allow for a better test of the impact of academic discipline on hairstyle choices. Another limitation is that, while our findings are consistent with a SIM theoretical framework, we did not specifically examine why Black women in higher education make the hairstyle choices that they do. Future research examining the question of 'why' would provide a better understanding of the Afrocentric hair bias phenomenon.

Conclusion

While hair bias is only one of the many hurdles or deterrents that Black women face in pursuing academic careers (Hill, 2019; Townsend, 2019), it is nonetheless an important one. This is evident, not only due to the large number of studies indicating its prevalence, but because hair is a significant part of one's identity and often linked to self-esteem, especially for Black women (Ellis-Hervey et al., 2016). In fact, Randle (2015) suggests 'one might even insist [Black] women are defined by their hair' (p. 3). Yet, the results of this study suggest that many Black women in academia do not feel comfortable in presenting their natural hair and instead feel pressured to conform to Eurocentric standards of what is deemed professional. Such conformity tends to cement the status quo whereby straightened or chemically treated hair becomes the norm and appearance standard for those entering academia.

The unfortunate consequences of this are that Black women could potentially be discouraged from pursuing academic careers, further perpetuating their gross underrepresentation at all levels of academia (Daut, 2019; Whitford, 2020). With few Black women visible in senior positions in academia and even fewer with natural hairstyles, Black female students may decide that an academic career is not an attractive path for them. This is reflected in a comment from a student interviewed by Donahoo (2019) who lamented 'I was kind of upset when I saw [a Black female professor] straightening her hair because someone told her to ... for someone to tell her, a woman with a PhD, that something was wrong with her hair was disheartening to me' (p. 87). In addition, Black female faculty may feel the extra cost to conform to Eurocentric standards (in terms of time, money and even health including chemical burns, damage to hair follicles, higher risk of uterine fibroids) may not be worth the effort and therefore opt not to pursue higher-level administrative positions in academia (Bowen & O'Brien-Richardson, 2017; Haskin & Aguh, 2016). As a result, Black female faculty would have fewer role models to offer support and mentorship, limiting their ability to be successful. Until society accepts that hair texture has nothing to do with professionalism, this vicious cycle is likely to continue. Recent increases in the number of Black women wearing natural hairstyles on television may indicate existing views are changing (Griffin, 2019). Perhaps similar changes will occur in academia such that hair will no longer be an issue for the career success of Black women.

References

Albritton, T. J. (2012). Educating our own: The historical legacy of HBCUs and their relevance for educating a new generation of leaders. *The Urban Review, 44,* 311–331. https://doi.org/10.1007/s11256-012-0202-9

Annison, D., Jackson, R., Gagliano, H., & Daste, B. (2017, December 4). *What they wore: A history of fashion at LSU.* Faculty fashion. https://fashionlouisianastate universityhistory.wordpress.com/2017/12/04/faculty-fashion. Accessed on July 6, 2022.

Ball, C. (2013, October 11). *Dress codes, Black respectability, and what's keeping HBCUs from moving forward.* https://madamenoire.com/311477/dress-codes-black-respectability-two-keeps-hbcus-moving-ahead/. Accessed on June 29, 2022.

Bowen, F., & O'Brien-Richardson, P. (2017). Cultural hair practices, physical activity, and obesity among urban African American girls. *Journal of the American Association of Nurse Practitioners, 29,* 754–762. https://doi.org/10.1002/2327-6924.12513

Bright, D. A. (2010). *Pioneering Women: Black women as senior leaders in traditionally white community colleges* (Unpublished doctoral dissertation) ERIC ED514630. George Washington University.

Britton, D. (2000). The epistemology of the gendered organization. *Gender & Society, 14*(3), 418–434.

Coates, H. (2020, December 14). *The Halo Code is here to help percent hair discrimination in the UK.* https://www.vogue.co.uk/beaty/article/the-halo-code. Accessed on July 7, 2022.

Commodore, F. (2019). Losing herself to save herself: Perspectives on conservatism and concepts of self for Black women aspiring to the HBCU presidency. *Hypatia, 34*(3), 441–463. https://doi:10.1111/hypa.12480

Crews, L. C. (2007). *The experiences of African American administrators at predominantly white two-year and four-year institutions.* ProQuest Dissertations Publishing, 3354476. Wayne State University.

Danzis, D. A., & Stone-Romero, E. (2009). Effects of helper sex, recipient attractiveness, and recipient femininity on helping behavior in organizations. *Journal of Managerial Psychology*, *24*(8), 722–737. https://doi.org/10.1108/026839409 10996761

Daut, M. L. (2019, July 28). *Becoming full professor while Black*. https://www.chronicle.com/article/becoming-full-professor-while-black/. Accessed on June 29, 2022.

Davis Tribble, B. L., Allen, S. H., Hart, J. R., Francois, T. S., & Smith-Bynum, M. (2019). "No [right] way to be a black woman": Exploring gendered racial socialization among black women. *Psychology of Women Quarterly*, *43*(3), 381–397. https://doi.org/10.1177/0361684318825439

Dawson, G., & Karl, K. (2018). I am not my hair, or am I? Examining hair choices of Black female executives. *Journal of Business Diversity*, *18*, 46–56.

Dawson, G. A., Karl, K. A., & Peluchette, J. V. (2019). Hair matters: Toward understanding natural Black hair bias in the workplace. *Journal of Leadership & Organizational Studies*, *26*(3), 389–401. https//:doi.org/10.1177/1548051819848998

Donahoo, S. (2019). Owning Black hair: The pursuit of identity and authenticity in higher education. In T. Thomas (Ed.), *Navigating micro-aggressions toward women in higher education* (pp. 73–95). IGI Global.

Donaldson, C. (2012). Hair alteration practices amongst Black women and the assumption of self- hatred. *Applied Psychology Opus*, *3*(Fall), 29–32. https://issuu.com/nyu_applied_psych_opus/docs/fall2012. Accessed on June 29, 2022.

Dowling, W. (2008). The impact of faculty apparel in the classroom. *College Teaching Methods & Styles Journal*, *4*(1), 1–11. https://doi.org/10.19030/ctms.v4i1.5042

Easterling, C. R., Leslie, J. E., & Jones, M. A. (1992). Perceived importance and usage of dress codes among organizations that market professional services. *Public Personnel Management*, *21*(2), 211–219. https://doi.org/10.1177%2F0091026 09202100208

Ellis-Hervey, N., Doss, A., Davis, D., Nicks, R., & Araiza, P. (2016). African American personal presentation: Psychology of hair and self-perception. *Journal of Black Studies*, *47*(8), 869–882. https://doi.org/10.1177%2F0021934716653350

Ellis, N. T., & Jones, C. (2019, October 14). Hairstyle discrimination is getting another look. https://www.usatoday.com/story/news/nation/2019/10/14/black-hair-laws-passed-stop-natural-hair-discrimination-across-us/3850402002/. Accessed on June 29, 2022.

Farley, Y. O. (2016). *An exploration of the identity and career development of African American women in higher education leadership: Does hair style make a difference?* Doctor of Philosophy (PhD), dissertation, Educational Foundations & Leadership. Old Dominion University. https://doi.org/10.25777/h4rk-6d59.

Fitzgerald, T. (2018). Looking good and being good: Women leaders in Australian universities. *Education Sciences*, *8*(2), 54. https://doi.org/10.3390/educsci8020054

Forsythe, S. M. (1990). Effect of applicant's clothing on interviewer's decision to hire. *Journal of Applied Social Psychology*, *20*(19), 1579–1595. https://doi.org/10.1111/j.1559-1816.1990.tb01494.x

Gasman, M., & Abiola, U. (2016). Colorism within the historically Black colleges and universities (HBCUs). *Theory into Practice*, *55*(1), 39–45. https://doi.org/10.1080/00405841.2016.1119018

Goffman, E. (1959). *The presentation of self in everyday life*. Doubleday.

Gray, S. (2017). *To curl up or relax? That is the question: Tenured black female faculty navigation of black hair expression in academia* (Unpublished doctoral dissertation). Southern Illinois University. ERIC. (2011268807; ED578001).

Griffin, C. (2019, February 28). TV is in the midst of a Black hair revolution we can't ignore. https://www.tvguide.com/news/features/black-hair-natural-hairstyles-tv-blackish-this-is-us-insecure/. Accessed on June 29, 2022.

Harper, S. R., & Gasman, M. (2008). Consequences of conservatism: Black male undergraduates and the politics of historically Black colleges and universities. *The Journal of Negro Education*, 77(4), 336–351. https://www.jstor.org/stable/25608703

Haskin, A., & Aguh, C. (2016). All hairstyles are not created equal: What the dermatologist needs to know about black hairstyling practices and the risk of traction alopecia (TA). *Journal of the American Academy of Dermatology*, 75(3), 606–611. https://doi.org/10.1016/j.jaad.2016.02.1162

Higginbotham, E. B. (1992). African American women's history and the meta-language of race. *Signs: Journal of Women in Culture and Society*, 17(2), 251–274. https://www.jstor.org/stable/3174464

Hill, R. F. (2019). The danger of an untold story: Excerpts from my life as a Black academic. *Journal of Education for Library & Information Science*, 60(3), 208–214. https://doi.org/10.3138/jelis.2019-0008

Hudson, M. L., Hunter, K. O., & Rogers, P. C. (2017). Hair and outrospection in the nonprofit and public sectors. *Qualitative Research Journal*, 17(2), 124–139. https://doi.org/10.1108/QRJ-08-2016-0049

Hurley-Hanson, A., & Giannantonio, C. (2006). Recruiters' perceptions of appearance: The stigma of image norms. *Equal Opportunities International*, 25(6), 450–463. https://doi.org/10.1108/02610150610713755

Johnson, A., Godsil, R., MacFarlane, J., Tropp, L. R., & Goff, P. A. (2017, February). Explicit and implicit attitudes toward Black women's hair. https://perception.org/wp-content/uploads/2017/01/TheGood-HairStudyFindingsReport.pdf. Accessed on June 29, 2022.

Jones, J. (2009, December 1). The academic wardrobe: Habitude. *The Chronicle of Higher Education*. http://www.chronicle.com/blogs/profhacker/the-academic-wardrobe-habitude/22857. Accessed on June 29, 2022.

Karl, K., Hall, L. M., & Peluchette, J. (2013). City employee perceptions of the impact of dress and appearance: You are what you wear. *Public Personnel Management*, 42(3), 452–470. https://doi.org/10.1177%2F0091026013495772

Kim, J., Ju, H. W., & Johnson, K. K. P. (2009). Sales associate's appearance: Links to consumers' emotions, store image, and purchases. *Journal of Retailing and Consumer Services*, 16(5), 407–413. https://doi.org/10.1016/j.jretconser.2009.06.001

Knight, P., & Yorke, M. (2004). *Learning, curriculum, and employability in higher education*. Routledge Falmer.

Koval, C. Z., & Rosette, A. S. (2021). The natural hair bias in job recruitment. *Social Psychological and Personality Science*, 12(5), 741–750. https://doi.org/10.1177%2F1948550620937937

Lavin, A., Davies, T., & Carr, D. (2010). The impact of instructor attire on student perceptions of faculty credibility and their own resultant behavior. *American Journal of Business Education*, 3(6), 51–62. https://doi.org/10.19030/ajbe.v3i6.442

Leary, M. R., & Kowalski, R. M. (1990). Impression management: A literature review and two- component model. *Psychological Bulletin*, *107*(1), 34–47. https://psycnet.apa.org/doi/10.1037/0033-2909.107.1.34

Lipton, B. (2020). Academics' dress: Gender and aesthetic labour in the Australian university. *Higher Education Research and Development*, *40*(4), 767–780. https://doi.org/10.1080/07294360.2020.1773767

Lock, S. (2021, March 24). Several UK firms sign up to code tackling afro hair discrimination. https://www.law.com/international-edition/2021/03/24/several-uk-firms-sign-up-to-code-tackling-afro-hair-discrimination/#:~:text=Eversheds%20Sutherland%2C%20Pinsent%20Masons%20and,Top%20100%20firm%20Fletcher%20Day. Accessed on July 6, 2022.

Macfarlane, J. (2020, December 11). What is the halo code? New UK guidelines to protect black people with afro textured hair explained. https://www.scotsman.com/news/people/what-halo-code-new-uk-guidelines-protect-black-people-afro-textured-hair-explained-3064873. Accessed on July 7, 2022.

Maynard, D.-M. B., & Jules, M. A. (2021). Exploring her roots: Black Caribbean hair identity and going natural using social media networks. *Journal of Black Psychology*, *47*(1), 3–30. https://doi:10.1177/0095798420971892

McChesney, J. (2018, May). *Representation and pay of women of color in the higher education workforce* (Research report). CUPA-HR. https://www.cupahr.org/wp-content/uploads/CUPA-HR-Brief-Women-Of-Color-1.pdf. Accessed on June 29, 2022.

Morgan, J. (2020, February 28). These Black women's stories prove hair discrimination happens here daily. https://www.refinery29.com/en-gb/hair-discrimination-uk-workplace. Accessed on July 6, 2022.

Njoku, N. R., & Patton, L. D. (2017). Explorations of respectability and resistance in constructions of Black womanhood at HBCUs. In L. D. Patton & N. N. Croom (Eds.), *Critical perspectives on Black women and college success* (pp. 31–43). Routledge.

Omotoso, S. A. (2018). Human hair: Intrigues and complications. *Journal of Pan African Studies*, *12*(8), 1–4. https://www.jpanafrican.org/vol12no8.htm. Accessed on July 6, 2022.

Opie, T. R., & Phillips, K. W. (2015). Hair penalties: The negative influence of Afrocentric hair on ratings of Black women's dominance and professionalism. *Frontiers in Psychology*, *6*(1311), 1–16. https://doi.org/10.3389/fpsyg.2015.01311

Oyedemi, T. (2016). Beauty as violence: 'Beautiful' hair and the cultural violence of identity erasure. *Social Identities*, *22*(5), 537–553. https://doi.org/10.1080/13504630.2016.1157465

Pandey, J. (1986). Sociocultural perspectives on ingratiation. In B. Maher (Ed.), *Progress in experimental personality research* (Vol. 14, pp. 205–229). Academic Press.

Patton, T. O. (2006). Hey girl, am I more than my hair? African American women and their struggles with beauty, body image, and hair. *National Women's Studies Association Journal*, *18*(2), 24–51. https://www.jstor.org/stable/4317206

Patton, L. D. (2014). Preserving respectability or blatant disrespect? A critical discourse analysis of the Morehouse Appropriate Attire Policy and implications for intersectional approaches to examining campus policies. *International Journal of Qualitative Studies in Education*, *27*(6), 724–746. https://doi.org/10.1080/09518398.2014.901576

Perkins, R. M. (2014). *The influence of colorism and hair texture bias on the professional and social lives of Black women student affairs professionals.* LSU Doctoral Dissertations 2510. https://digitalcommons.lsu.edu/gradschool_dissertations/2510

Pittman, C. T. (2012). Racial micro-aggressions: The narratives of African American faculty at a predominately White university. *The Journal of Negro Education, 81*(1), 82–92. https://muse.jhu.edu/article/842955

Pronin, E., Steele, C. M., & Ross, L. (2004). Identity bifurcation in response to stereotype threat: Women and mathematics. *Journal of Experimental Social Psychology, 40*(2), 152–168. https://doi.org/10.1016/S0022-1031(03)00088-X

Rafaeli, A., Dutton, J., Harquail, C. V., & Mackie-Lewis, S. (1997). Navigating by attire: The use of dress by administrative employees. *Academy of Management Journal, 40*(1), 19–45. https://doi.org/10.5465/257019

Rafaeli, A., & Pratt, M. (1993). Tailored meanings: On the meaning and impact of organizational dress. *Academy of Management Review, 18*(1), 32–55. https://doi.org/10.5465/amr.1993.3997506

Randle, B. A. (2015). I am not my hair; African American women and their struggles with embracing natural hair. *Race, Gender & Class, 22*(1–2), 114–121. https://www.jstor.org/stable/26505328

Roberts, L. M. (2005). Changing faces: Professional image construction in diverse organizational settings. *Academy of Management Review, 30*(4), 685–711. https://doi.org/10.5465/amr.2005.18378873

Rosette, A., & Dumas, T. (2007). The hair dilemma: Conform to mainstream expectations or emphasize racial identity. *Duke Journal of Gender Law & Policy, 14*(1), 407–421.

Rosette, A. S., Koval, C. Z., Ma, A., & Livingston, R. (2016). Race matters for women leaders: Intersectional effects on agentic deficiencies and penalties. *The Leadership Quarterly, 27*(3), 429–445. https://doi.org/10.1016/j.leaqua.2016.01.008

Sanghvi, M., & Hodges, N. (2015). Marketing the female politician: An exploration of gender and appearance. *Journal of Marketing Management, 31*(15–16), 1676–1694. https://doi.org/10.1016/j.leaqua.2016.01.008

Schlenker, B. R. (1980). *Impression management: The self-concept, social identity, and interpersonal relations.* Brooks/Cole.

Takeda, M. B., Helms, M. M., Klintworth, P., & Sompayrac, J. (2005). Hair colour stereotyping and CEO selection: Can you name any blonde CEOs? *Equal Opportunities International, 24*(1), 1–13. https://doi.org/10.1108/02610150510787917

Tannenbaum, E. (2022, June 9). *Here's every state that has passed the Crown Act.* https://www.glamour.story/the-crown-act-banning-hair-discrimination. Accessed on June 29, 2022.

Thompson, C. (2009). Black women, beauty, and hair as a matter of being. *Women's Studies, 38*(8), 831–856. https://doi.org/10.1080/00497870903238463

Townsend, C. V. (2019). *Advancing African American women in public higher education: A phenomenological study of recruitment, retention, and career ascension* (Unpublished doctoral dissertation). Northwest Nazarene University.

Tsaousi, C. (2020). That's funny...you don't look like a lecturer! Dress and professional identity of female academics. *Studies in Higher Education, 45*(9), 1809–1820. https://doi.org/10.1080/03075079.2019.1637839

Wallace, S. L., Moore, S. F., & Curtis, C. M. (2014). Black women as scholars and social agents: Standing in the gap. *The Negro Educational Review, 65*(1–4), 44–62.

Whitford, E. (2020, October 28). There are so few that have made their way. https://www.insidehighered.com/news/2020/10/28/black-administrators-are-too-rare-top-ranks-higher-education-it%E2%80%99s-not-just-pipeline. Accessed on June 29, 2022.

Why do some professors dress more formally than others? (n.d.). https://www.quora.com/Why-do-some-professors-dress-more-formally-than-others. Accessed on July 6, 2022.

Wright, A. (2022, March 31). More states consider bills to prohibit discrimination against black hair. https://www.pewtrusts.org/en/research-and-analysis/blogs/stateline/2022/03/31/more-states-consider-bills-to-prohibit-discrimination-against-black-hair. Accessed on June 29, 2022.

Wu, F. (2019, July 12). Victory for natural black hair benefits all of us. https://diverseeducation.com/article/149645. Accessed on June 29, 2022.

Yan, R.-N., Yurchisin, J., & Watchravesringkan, K. (2011). Does formality matter: Effects of employee clothing formality on consumers' service quality expectations and store image perceptions. *International Journal of Retail & Distribution Management*, *39*(5), 346–362. https://doi.org/10.1108/09590551111130775

Chapter 4

Body Weight Discrimination Against Women in Customer-Facing Roles: A Systematic Literature Review

Sharon Grant, Toby Mizzi and Elyse O'Loghlen

Abstract

The thin feminine body ideal in Western society has persisted, despite becoming less representative of the female population, with obesity rates consistently rising since the 1980s. Recently, the COVID-19 pandemic has exacerbated obesity rates, due to curtailed interventions, restricted mobility/ enforced physical inactivity and increased reliance on processed food with a longer shelf life due to social isolation (World Obesity Foundation, n.d.). Individuals with obesity report weight discrimination in a broad range of settings, including employment, where researchers have documented weight discrimination in relation to hiring, job assignment, promotion, remuneration and work stability. Weight discrimination may be worse for jobs involving public interaction, particularly for women, because heavier women do not conform to societal body ideals, leading to weight stigmatisation such as anti-fat attitudes and beliefs (e.g. negative stereotypes) and prejudice. This chapter presents a systematic literature review of studies that have examined weight discrimination against women with obesity in jobs involving public interaction, i.e. 'customer-facing roles'.

Keywords: Obesity; women; weight discrimination; employment; customer-facing roles; customer service

Introduction

Several years ago, the first author (SG) was on an interview panel for a research job that involved public interaction. After interviewing several applicants who were unsuitably qualified, skilled or experienced relative to key selection criteria, the panel interviewed an applicant whose credentials were an excellent match. The

The Emerald Handbook of Appearance in the Workplace, 75–100
doi:10.1108/978-1-80071-174-720230005

applicant performed very well in the interview and SG was confident that the panel had found the successful applicant. After the applicant left the room, SG turned to a colleague and said enthusiastically, 'So, what do you think?' He turned to her and replied, 'But she's fat'. SG was stunned. Not only had she not noticed the applicant's weight but also it was irrelevant. The applicant was suitable for the position and was subsequently hired after SG vehemently rejected the notion that the weight of the applicant was relevant in any way, shape or form (no pun intended).

As an academic working in organisational psychology, this experience raised SG's intellectual curiosity about weight discrimination in the workplace. When an opportunity later arose to work with a colleague who was an obesity researcher, weight stigma and discrimination was the logical choice. In the years that followed, SG undertook several studies on the topic. In 2014, the first and second authors examined explanatory mechanisms in the relationship between women's body weight and discrimination in hiring decisions, with a focus on job visibility as a moderating variable. This chapter expands on this work by presenting a systematic literature review on weight discrimination against women in 'customer-facing roles', defined as jobs that involve public interaction as a primary function, e.g. service and sales roles.

Literature Search and Screening Procedure

We searched six relevant electronic databases using a search string designed to capture a broad range of literature relating to weight discrimination in employment settings (see Table 1). We chose to focus on women as they are more likely to be negatively stereotyped in job settings (Pascal & Kurpius, 2012), which may lead to related discrimination (Grant & Mizzi, 2014). Our Research Questions (RQ) were:

RQ1. What is the evidence for weight discrimination against overweight/obese women in customer-facing roles?

Table 1. Literature Search and Screening Procedure.

Database	Inclusion Criteria	Exclusion Criteria
Business Source Complete PsycINFO PubMed	Literature addressing weight discrimination: (a) among overweight or obese women and (b) in employment settings and (c) in customer-facing roles	Literature that does not address all three of the following: Discrimination (a) among overweight/obese women, (b) in employment settings and (c) in customer-facing roles
Scopus SocIndex	Peer-reviewed/refereed book chapters and journal articles	Not peer-reviewed, including grey literature
Web of Science	Qualitative and quantitative studies, mixed-methods studies and review papers (e.g. meta-analyses)	Legal literature, e.g. anti-discrimination law (or similar), case law analysis
	Full-text available in English	Full-text not available in English

RQ2. Does overweight/obesity adversely affect women more than men in customer-facing roles?

We included both overweight and obesity in our search to capture a broader range of studies on the influence of larger body sizes on employment discrimination in customer-facing roles. Among adults, overweight and obesity for both sexes and all ages is commonly classified using a weight-for-height index, Body Mass Index (BMI), calculated as kilograms/metres^2 (World Health Organization [WHO], 2021). As a rough index, a BMI greater than or equal to 25 is categorised as 'overweight' and a BMI greater than or equal to 30 is categorised as 'obese' (WHO, 2021). However, it is important to note that this simple index may neither reflect the same degree of fatness across individuals due to factors such as muscle mass (WHO, 2021) nor is it necessarily used to operationalise overweight and obese targets in weight discrimination studies (see Table 2). Many studies that use the descriptors 'overweight' or 'obese' likely do so on the assumption that many individuals equate these terms with 'abnormal or excessive fat accumulation that may impair health' as well as BMI (WHO, 2021).

The search string was employment or employee or 'customer service' AND discriminat* or bias* AND weight or obes* or overweight or 'over weight', with some variation depending on the database, e.g. some databases require the researcher to populate multiple search lines and then combine these lines. The literature search was completed on 18/11/2019 and returned 1,790 articles. Authors 1 and 2 completed literature screening. In the first step, they independently screened Titles and Abstracts for relevance, based on predetermined inclusion/exclusion criteria (see Table 1). This resulted in 1,584 excluded articles. In the second step, they independently screened the full text of the remaining 206 articles for eligibility and resolved disagreements (minimal) through discussion.

Theory and Concepts

Authors 1 and 2 initially retained 28 articles for inclusion. They also screened review articles identified in the search and subsequently included one additional article. However, there was a clear qualitative divide among the articles. Some examined the association between body weight and occupational attainment and/ or wages in large, secondary (e.g. population) datasets (see Baum & Ford, 2004; DeBeaumont, 2009; Han & Kim, 2017; Han et al., 2011; Han et al., 2009; Harper, 2000; Haskins & Ransford, 1999; Lee et al., 2019). Others, mostly experiments, used direct measures/observations of discrimination (see Table 2). Given the scope of the literature, we elected to focus on studies that manipulated or measured body weight, and to examine evaluative (or perceived/self-reported) workplace outcomes (c.f., Rudolph et al., 2009). There were also two qualitative studies. One (Harris & Small, 2013) analysed online promotional videos of major hotels in Sydney, Australia, with reference to the perceived size of tourism workers' bodies; this study was excluded on the basis that it did not examine discrimination directly. The other, a fieldwork study (Gruys, 2012) of frontline workers in a plus-sized women's clothing store, specifically addressed discrimination and was

Table 2. Data Extraction: Included Studies.

Authors and Year	Aims	Participants	Design/Variables	Manipulates Sex of Candidate	Manipulates Job Type	Analyses	Evidence of Weight Discrimination (Women, Customer-Facing Roles)	Quality Rating
Research question 1: What is the evidence for weight discrimination against overweight/obese women in customer-facing roles?								
Finkelstein et al. (2007)	Investigates the impact of job candidate weight (average or overweight) on job-related ratings, and moderators/ mediators of the applicant weight-obesity discrimination relationship.	Convenience sample of 751 (60% female) introductory psychology students aged 18–20 years at a mid-western, US university (15% had hiring experience).	*Laboratory experiment.* IVs: *Applicant weight* (average, overweight) and *race* in video-taped interviews. *Level of qualifications.* *Job type* (public – receptionist, private contact – data entry keyer). CVs: *Rater race. Negative affect.* DVs: Hireability, adaptability and interpersonal skills ratings.	Female targets only.	Yes.	ANOVA. Mediation analyses were not pursued.	Yes. For the public job, when the applicant was Caucasian, the overweight applicant was rated significantly lower than the average weight applicant for adaptability. In addition, for the public job, when the applicant was Caucasian, the overweight applicant was rated marginally lower than the average weight applicant for interpersonal skills. However, for the private job, the overweight applicant was rated marginally higher on interpersonal skills than the average weight applicant.	20%

Study	Aim	Sample	Design and Variables	Target sex		Analysis	Conclusion	%
Grant and Mizzi (2014)	Investigates the effect of applicant weight on employability ratings with five alternative explanations of weight discrimination: Perceived lack of fit based on job type, obesity stereotypes, physical attractiveness stereotypes, perceived organisational costs, and rational bias.	Convenience sample of final year psychology undergraduate students (151 women, 52 men) from a university in Melbourne, Australia. Mean age: 24.31 years (SD = 7.36). Approximately 20% had previous recruitment/selection experience.	*Laboratory experiment.* *IVs: Applicant weight* (overweight, average weight). *Job type* (visible; face-to-face sales of gym memberships versus non-visible; telephone sales of gym memberships). *Mediators:* Obesity stereotypes, physical attractiveness stereotypes, perceived organisational costs, rational bias. *CVs: Participant sex. Motivation to control prejudiced reactions.* *DVs: Employability ratings.*	Female targets only.	Yes.	ANOVA. Mediated regression analysis.	No. There was no interaction between applicant weight and job type.	60%
Klesges et al. (1990)	Evaluates the impact of health status (normal, obese, diabetic) and qualification level on hiring decisions.	Convenience sample of graduate or upper level undergraduate business students (124 women, 157 men, 14 missing) in the United States	*Laboratory experiment.* *IVs/Predictors: Employee/candidate health status* (normal, obese, diabetic). *Employee/candidate qualifications* (highly qualified versus marginally qualified). Confederates appeared in videos.	Female targets only.	No. The position was a clerk-receptionist in a midsized wholesale company	ANOVA	Yes. The obese applicant was rated as significantly less likely to be hired compared to the normal-weight applicant.	20%

Table 2. *(Continued)*

Authors and Year	Aims	Participants	Design/Variables	Manipulates Sex of Candidate	Manipulates Job Type	Analyses	Evidence of Weight Discrimination (Women, Customer-Facing Roles)	Quality Rating
			DVs: Hiring recommendation. Ratings on work habits, likelihood of medical absenteeism, non-medical absenteeism/reliability and interpersonal skills and problems.					
Merritt et al. (2018)	Examines the effects of imagined intergroup contact on anti-fat bias in the context of job interviews.	Convenience sample of 154 (79.2% female) undergraduate students from the psychology subject pool at a medium-sized, mid-western, US university. Mean age: 23.95 years.	*Laboratory experiment.* *IVs: Candidate weight* (normal weight, obese) in a video (seated). *Intervention* (control or intergroup conflict). *CVs: Motivation to control prejudice.* *DVs: Competence and warmth ratings. Hiring recommendation.*	Female targets only.	No. The position was: Sporting goods salesperson.	Moderated mediation analyses.	Yes. The obese candidate received lower ratings of competence than the thinner candidate; however, this was not seen in the intergroup contact condition (ICC). The ICC intervention reduced anti-fat bias in hiring recommendation by alleviating biased perceptions of candidate competence.	20%

Study	Aim	Sample	Design	Targets	Job position	Analysis	Results	Response rate
O'Brien et al. (2008)	Investigates discrimination against obese candidates, and whether explicit and implicit anti-fat attitudes predict discrimination.	Convenience sample of university students (77 women, 76 men) from New Zealand who participated for course credit. Mean age: 40 years (SD = 5.04). Mean BMI: 23.	*Laboratory experiment.* *IVs: Candidate weight (pre- and post-bariatric surgery photographs).* *CVs: Explicit anti-fat attitudes.* *Automatic obesity bias.* *DV: Rankings of six applicants on characteristics.*	Female targets only.	No. The position was a mid-level manager in a large department store chain (included on the basis that most jobs in sales and service occupational categories require regular customer contact; c.f. DeBeaumont, 2009).	ANOVA. Paired sample t-tests. Pearson correlations. Multiple regression.	Yes. Obese targets were rated lower than non-obese targets across all characteristics: *Leadership potential, predicted success, likelihood to select and recommended salary.*	40%
O'Brien et al. (2013)	Tests whether prejudicial attitudes, personal ideologies, personality, and physical appearance are related to obesity-based employment discrimination.	Convenience sample of 102 (80% female) undergraduate students who participated as part of a course requirement. Mean age: 20.17 years (SD = 4.63). Geographic location not specified.	*Laboratory experiment.* *IVs: Candidate weight (pre- and post-bariatric surgery photographs).* *Anti-fat prejudice.* *Authoritarianism.* *Social Dominance Orientation.* *Physical appearance evaluation and investment.* *CVs: Participant sex.* *BMI.* *DVs: Ratings for leadership potential, predicted success,*	Female targets only.	No (see above study).	*T-tests.* Pearson's correlation coefficients. Hierarchical regression.	Yes. Obese targets were rated significantly lower than non-obese targets across all criteria: *Leadership potential, predicted success, likelihood to select and salary.*	40%

Table 2. *(Continued)*

Authors and Year	Aims	Participants	Design/Variables	Manipulates Sex of Candidate	Manipulates Job Type	Analyses	Evidence of Weight Discrimination (Women, Customer-Facing Roles)	Quality Rating
			likelihood to select and salary, combined to form *a 'total employment rating'. Candidate quality rankings.*					
Swami, Chan, Wong, Furnham, and Tovée (2008)	*Study 1* examines weight discrimination in occupational hiring using vignettes.	Convenience sample of 30, British male undergraduate students who participated on a voluntary basis. Mean age: 24.90 years (SD = 9.40).	*Laboratory experiment. IV:* Applicant BMI (photographs of 10 women drawn from each of the five BMI categories: Emaciated, underweight, normal, overweight, obese). Photographs obscured heads, so facial attributes would not influence ratings. *DVs:* Participants were asked how likely they were to hire an applicant for the	Female targets only.	No. Scenarios related to a sales management role that required public interaction.	ANOVA. Multiple regression analysis.	Yes. The optimal BMI for hiring likelihood was in the underweight range; applicants on either side of this peak were less likely to be hired. Applicant BMI category explained 84.8% of the variance.	40%

Study	Aim	Sample	Method/Design			Analysis	Findings	%
Swami et al. (2010)	Investigates the extent of weight bias in occupational decisions including associations with attitudes towards obese individuals.	Convenience and snowball sample of general population (520 women, 504 men) in the southern German-speaking area of Central Europe (mainly Austria). Mean age: 28.33 years (SD = 10.94)	*Laboratory experiment.* *IVs: Vignette condition.* Participants were presented with 10 female images from the Photographic Figure Rating Scale (Swami et al., 2008) followed by scenarios: Hiring, promotion and job termination. *Attitudes towards obese individuals.* *CVs:* BMI. *DVs:* Participants rated the figures whom they were most likely and least likely to hire, promote or terminate.	Female targets only.	No, see above study.	Percentages (figure most likely to be selected) ANCOVA. Partial correlational and regression analysis.	Yes. Overweight and obese women were less likely than normal weight women to be hired or promoted and more likely to be terminated. However, emaciated women were more likely to be terminated than obese women.	20%
Research Question 2: Does overweight/obesity adversely affect women more than men in customer-facing roles?								
Agerström and Rooth (2011)	Investigates whether automatic obesity biases related to work productivity predict likelihood of inviting obese versus normal	Hiring managers (77 women, 76 men) from Rooth (2009) who (1) handled the entire hiring process alone, (2) invited either normal weight or obese applicants to an	*Field experiment.* *IVs: Applicant weight* (facial photograph; normal weight versus obese) and *sex.* *Job type* (computer professionals, business sales assistants, preschool teachers, accountants,	Yes.	Yes.	Sign tests.	No. Differences in call back rates did not correspond to a public interaction versus no public interaction dimension.	80%

position, trainee in sales management.

Table 2. (*Continued*)

Authors and Year	Aims	Participants	Design/Variables	Manipulates Sex of Candidate	Manipulates Job Type	Analyses	Evidence of Weight Discrimination (Women, Customer-Facing Roles)	Quality Rating
	weight applicants to job interviews.	interview for a large number of cases and (3) produced meaningful IAT data. Mean age: 40 years (SD = 10.41).	nurses, restaurant workers and shop sales assistants). *DVs:* Call back rates, i.e. difference in how many normal weight versus obese applicants were invited to the job interview by email/ telephone.					
Bartels and Nordstrom (2013)	Examines the impact of applicant weight and sex, job type and employer attitudes on employee screening decisions.	An online sample of 452 US participants (52.9% female, 40.9% male, 6.2% no response) were recruited via Mechanical Turk. Nearly half had hiring experience.	*Online experiment. IVs: Applicant weight and sex.* Applicant, photographed from the waist up. *Note.* Researchers used ratings of the applicant's weight rather than the manipulated variable in order to obtain a continuous weight variable. *Level of job visibility and level of job*	Yes.	Yes.	Hierarchical regression analyses (one per job type). Step 1: Applicant age and sex of typical worker for job. Step 2: Applicant weight, sex and their interaction. Step 3: Anti-fat	Yes. For the high visibility and high physical demands job, female applicants who were overweight had the lowest mean suitability ratings compared to all other applicant groups.	60%

			physical demands: Restaurant server: High visibility/high physical demands. Concierge: High visibility/low physical demands. Banquet set up worker: Low visibility/high physical demands. Guest service agent: Low visibility/low physical demands. *CVs: Applicant age. Sex of typical worker for job. Anti-fat attitudes.* *DVs: Job suitability ratings.*	attitudes, three-way interaction between applicant weight, applicant sex and participant anti-fat attitudes.	Yes.	
Bellizzi and Hasty (1998)	Examines the effect of obesity and gender on employee job assignments and performance evaluation.	Participants drawn from a commercial mailing list of 10,400 sales managers representing various US industries/firms; 741 research packets were returned/useable for the assignment hypotheses and	*Field experiment.* Sales scenarios and role playing with practising sales managers. *IVs: Applicant weight.* The 'voluntary' section of the application indicated either that the applicant needs special accommodations for	ANOVA, MANOVA.	Yes.	60%

No. Weight discrimination was evident, but women were not more adversely affected by weight than men.

Table 2. (*Continued*)

Authors and Year	Aims	Participants	Design/Variables	Manipulates Sex of Candidate	Manipulates Job Type	Analyses	Evidence of Weight Discrimination (Women, Customer-Facing Roles)	Quality Rating
		755 for the discipline hypotheses.	obesity (likely to be classified as a legitimate disability covered by the ADA) OR that the applicant was very athletic (based on leisure activities) and not overweight. *Applicant sex.* *Job type* (face-to-face sales, telephone sales) *Product type* (exercise equipment and clothing [image sensitive] or construction fastening equipment [non-image sensitive]). *DVs: Territory fit assignment decision* (challenging, non-challenging). *Supervisory discipline for poor performance* (appropriateness of five graded alternatives).					

	Aim	Sample	Method/Design			Analysis	Findings	
Bellizzi and Hasty (2000)	Examines the effect of obesity and gender on job assignment in the context of a traditionally masculine occupation, and whether or not successful prior work experience can overcome negative stereotyping associated with overweight women.	See above study; 797 research packets were returned but only 388 responses were used.	*Field experiment.* See above study. Face-to-face contact was emphasised in conjunction with description of the position: Sales representative level 1. *IVs: Applicant weight* (see above study) and *sex. Job type* (more challenging or less challenging sales territory). *CVs: Applicant experience.* *DV: Territory assignment decision. Job-person fit assessment* for the two territories (within-subjects factor).	Yes.	Yes.	Repeated measures MANOVA.	No. Weight discrimination was evident, but women were not more adversely affected by weight than men.	60%
Flint et al. (2015)	Seeks to identify whether individuals with obesity are discriminated against when applying for employment in active compared	Convenience sample of employees (74 women, 107 men) with previous recruitment experience from workplaces varying in	*Field experiment.* *IVs: Candidate weight* (obese photograph, normal weight photograph, unknown/no photograph) *Candidate sex. Workplace physical*	Yes.	Yes. However, based on physical activity level. One job (retail salesperson) is customer-facing.	Repeated Measures ANOVA.	Yes. The female, obese candidate was rated as the least suitable for employment across all four workplaces (suitability scores decrease as activity level increases).	60%

Table 2. (*Continued*)

Authors and Year	Aims	Participants	Design/Variables	Manipulates Sex of Candidate	Manipulates Job Type	Analyses	Evidence of Weight Discrimination (Women, Customer-Facing Roles)	Quality Rating
	to non-active work environments. *Note.* One of the job types included was a retail salesperson.	physical demand (sedentary, standing, manual work and heavy manual work) in Czech Republic, Slovenia and the UK Mean age: 38.25 years (SD = 8.99).	*activity level (sedentary – administrative assistant, standing – university lecturer, manual – retail salesperson, heavy manual – labourer).* *DVs:* Ratings for *teamwork ability, social competence, job efficiency, intelligence, motivation and leadership skills.* One question directly asked whether the candidate was suitable for the job. A composite score was calculated across all items. Each participant rated the suitability of all six					

candidates for all job types.

Study	Aim	Sample	Method	Sexes considered	Analysis	Discrimination found	%
Gruys (2012)	Examines how a body-accepting corporate branding ideology impacts inequality among frontline, plus-sized service workers.	10 months of fieldwork conducted by a paid sales associate (female) in the United States	Participant observation.	No. The study was undertaken at one outpost of a women's plus-sized clothing store with a corporate chain of over 800 stores.	Qualitative analysis. Yes. Considers employees of both sexes.	Yes. Employees were segregated into jobs and tasks according to sex and body size.	80%
Jasper and Klassen (1990)	Examines social perceptions and attitudes about non-obese and obese salespeople, specifically desire to work with non-obese/obese salespeople, and evaluations of the effectiveness of these salespersons' job performance.	Randomly selected undergraduate students (67 women, 67 men). No further information provided.	*Laboratory experiment. IVs: Salesperson's size* (obese, non-obese). *Salesperson's sex. CVs: Participant sex. DVs: Desire to work with salesperson. Expected effectiveness of salesperson.*	No. The study focused on employees described as 'salespeople'.	ANOVA. Yes.	Yes. For *desire to work with salesperson,* men indicated significantly less desire than women to work with an obese woman, but men's and women's responses were the same for desire to work with an obese man.	20%
Nickson et al. (2016)	Examines whether the negative effect of a subtle increase in	Stratified random sample of 120 valid responses (60 women, 60 men) from a	*Laboratory experiment. IVs: Facial image type* (original versus heavier versions [four	Yes	ANOVA. Yes.	Yes. Women were evaluated more negatively for customer-facing roles than	60%

Table 2. (*Continued*)

Authors and Year	Aims	Participants	Design/Variables	Manipulates Sex of Candidate	Manipulates Job Type	Analyses	Evidence of Weight Discrimination (Women, Customer-Facing Roles)	Quality Rating
	fatness for female applicants is stronger in customer-facing roles than in non-customer-facing roles.	convenience sample of 182 visitors to university in Scotland who participated in the research. Mean age: 25.67 years (SD = 10.47).	faces, low and high BMI manipulations). *Job type.* Customer-facing (e.g. waiter/waitress, receptionist, sales assistant, etc.) versus non-customer-facing (e.g. chef, kitchen porter, stock assistant, etc.). *Sex of face.* *CVs: Sex of participant.* *DVs: Hiring likelihood.*				non-customer-facing roles but there were no differences across job type for men.	
Pingitore et al. (1994)	Examines whether job type moderates weight-related discrimination in an employment decision.	Convenience sample of introductory psychology students (221 women, 99 men) from a university in Chicago, US, who participated on a voluntary basis for course credit.	*Laboratory experiment.* *IVs: Applicant weight* (video-type condition; overweight, normal weight) and *sex.* *Job type* (systems analyst, sales representative). *Rater's sex and body schema* (low, high).	Yes.	Yes	ANOVA.	No. There was no significant interaction between applicant weight and job type.	20%

Study	Aim	Sample	Variables			Analysis	Findings	
Rooth (2009)	Examines whether there is differential treatment in the hiring of obese individuals in the labour market.	Fictitious applications (1970) were sent to 985 Swedish (Stockholm) firms/ recruiters in high demand occupations that varied in skill requirement and degree of customer contact needed: Computer professionals, business sales assistants, preschool teachers, accountants, nurses, restaurant workers (mostly waiters) and shop sales assistants.	*DVs: Hiring decision.* *Field experiment.* *IVs: Applicant weight* (manipulated photo) *and sex.* *Skill level of occupation.* *Degree of customer contact in occupation.* *CV: Attractiveness rating.* *DVs:* Relative call back rates for interviews received via telephone (voicemail) or email for obese versus normal weight applicants and the difference in call back rates for men and women.	Yes.	Yes.	Probit regression. Aggregated groupings were constructed for the sales occupations business sales assistants, shop sales assistants and restaurant workers.	Yes. Weight-related differences in call back responses for sales jobs (aggregated) was larger for women than for men.	100%
Ruggs et al. (2015)	Study 2 was relevant and examines clientele's evaluations of and behavioural intentions towards heavy retail personnel and how such evaluations and intentions may	Convenience sample of students from the psychology research pool of a private university in Southern US. There were 298 useable responses from 347 (64% female, 55% male; 1% no response).	*Laboratory experiment.* *IVs: Employee weight* (control versus heavy, with the latter wearing obesity prostheses) *and sex.* *DVs:* Stereotypes, evaluations of employees, evaluations of the	Yes.	No. Confederates appeared in videos marketing a series of products to promote the launch of a fictitious retailer's website.	MANOVA. Multiple mediation analyses (not reported as these do not include drill down data for men and women).	Yes. Overall, women were more adversely affected by weight than men.	40%

Table 2. (*Continued*)

Authors and Year	Aims	Participants	Design/Variables	Manipulates Sex of Candidate	Manipulates Job Type	Analyses	Evidence of Weight Discrimination (Women, Customer-Facing Roles)	Quality Rating
			organisation, evaluations of products, future intentions to support the company.					
Vallejo-Torres et al. (2018)	Examines perceived work discrimination due to weight bias for workers in customer-facing and non-customer-facing jobs.	Secondary data (European Health Interview Survey 2009–2010), focussing on 4,576 women and 5,319 men who were employed at the time of the survey which was distributed to individuals aged 16 years and over in Spain.	*Survey.* *Predictors:* *Respondent BMI category* (obesity = BMI greater than or equal to 30) and *sex.* *CVs:* *Sociodemographic variables* (see article for full list). *Occupation type.* Models stratified by occupation type were defined by whether individuals worked in customer-facing roles. *Health indicators.* *DVs: Perceived work discrimination (binary)*	Yes (survey question)	Yes (survey question)	Logistic regression.	Yes. Obesity increased perceived work discrimination in customer-facing roles for women but not for men.	60%

Research Question 1 and 2

| Sartore and Cunningham (2007) | *Study 1* examines attitudes, perceptions and preferences towards female applicants, varying in body weight and qualifications *(RQ1).*

Study 3 has similar aims but varies applicant sex *(RQ2).* | *Study 1* Convenience sample of 138 (51.4% female, 48.6% male) health and kinesiology students at a large university in Texas, US. Mean age: 20.2 years (SD = 1.8).

Study 3 As per Study 1, except 99 university students (66.7% female, 33.3% male). Mean age: 22 years (SD = 2.40). | *Laboratory experiments.* *Study 1* *IVs: Female applicant weight* (thin versus overweight photograph of face and upper body). *Qualification level* (high, low).

CVs: Applicant attractiveness. Similarity to the self.

DVs: Trait attributions. Person-job fit. Hiring recommendation.

Study 3 as per Study 1 except that the sex of the applicant was added as an IV. | *Study 1* female targets only. Study 2 yes. | No. Study 1 was based on the job 'group fitness instructor' and Study 3 'personal trainer'. | MANCOVA. | Study 1: Yes. The unqualified thin applicant was perceived as a better fit for the job and as more hireable than the qualified overweight applicant. When applicants possessed high qualifications, all three DVs were higher for the thin applicant than the overweight applicant.

Study 3: No. Women were not more adversely affected by weight than men. | 60% |

thus included. The final review includes 21 articles, as summarised in Table 2. Within articles, we report only on individual studies and findings that address our research questions.

A quality assessment of the 21 articles was conducted independently by authors 1 and 3 using the Mixed-Method Appraisal Tool (MMAT; Hong et al., 2018), with disagreements (moderate) resolved through discussion. The MMAT is designed to critically appraise the methodological quality of articles that use a range of research designs. The MMAT is considered an efficient quality appraisal tool with good inter-rater reliability (Pace et al., 2012). The MMAT checklist comprises five criteria questions, with a total quality rating score for each study calculated as a percentage of 'yes' responses divided by the five criteria items. Studies were rated as high (scores of 80% and 100%), moderate (scores of 40% and 60%) or low quality (scores of 0% and 20%). MMAT scores are presented in Table 2. Results showed that most studies were of adequate quality: three studies (14%) were of high quality, 13 studies (62%) were of moderate quality and five studies (24%) were of low quality. The most common methodological problems were among experimental studies, where authors did not adequately explain how randomisation was performed or whether groups were comparable at baseline, and where outcome assessors were not blinded to interventions. Inter-rater reliability for the total quality score, calculated using a two-way mixed model intraclass-correlation coefficient, was 0.69, indicating good agreement between assessors (Cicchetti, 1994).

The bulk of studies (10) were US studies, although Europe and the United Kingdom were also well-represented (7). Two studies were Australasian (Australia, New Zealand) and two did not specify location. There was little variation in methods, with almost all studies being experimental (including five field experiments) that manipulated weight using stimulus materials such as photographs/images, videos or vignettes. The two non-experimental studies used participant observation or surveys. However, there was considerable variation in study design. Seven studies focused exclusively on women in customer-facing roles (i.e. did not manipulate applicant sex or job type), and two studies focused exclusively on women but manipulated job type; we used these nine studies to address *RQ1*. Four studies focused exclusively on customer-facing roles but manipulated applicant sex, and nine studies manipulated/considered both applicant sex and job type; we used these 13 studies to address *RQ2*. Note there are '22 studies' here as one article included two studies that manipulated different independent variables (IVs). We outline the findings below.

What Is the Evidence for Weight Discrimination Against Overweight Women in Customer-Facing Roles?

All seven of the studies that focused exclusively on women in customer-facing roles found evidence of weight discrimination. In two of these studies, there was also evidence of weight discrimination towards emaciated women. However, these studies provide the least amount of information to answer our research question, as it is not possible to conclude whether women with obesity face more discrimination in customer-facing roles than in non-customer facing roles.

The two studies that focused exclusively on women, but manipulated job type, produced conflicting findings. One study found no evidence of an interaction between applicant weight and job type (gym membership sales in person versus via telephone) on perceived employability. The other study found that applicant race, included as an additional IV (independent variable), moderated this inter-action: Caucasian, overweight women were rated less favourably for a customer-facing receptionist role, but more favourably on interpersonal skills for a non-customer-facing receptionist role. Notably, the customer-facing roles used in these two studies varied (gym membership sales versus receptionist), suggesting that role type rather than public interaction could have influenced the findings. Information about weight may be judged as salient with regard to gym mem-bership sales regardless of whether the role is customer-facing or not. Negative obesity stereotypes (e.g. lazy and unfit; Grant et al., 2016) may undermine perceived ability to sell the benefits of regular exercise to others. Thus, obesity stereotypes may restrict the range of industries in which women who are over-weight can secure employment, or limit the range of opportunities for career progression within such industries.

Does Obesity Adversely Affect Women More Than Men in Customer-Facing Roles?

Three of four studies that compared men and women within customer-facing roles only found evidence that heavier women were more adversely affected by discrimination than heavier men. All of these studies focused on sales roles. The fourth study, which produced unexpected results, included 'personal trainer' as the role. As discussed above, negative obesity stereotypes concerning physical fitness could have attenuated the effects of other IVs, including applicant sex, in this study. Furthermore, this set of studies provides a weak assessment of our research question because it is not possible to determine whether heavier women are more adversely affected than heavier men in customer-facing compared to non-customer-facing roles.

This brings us to the final set of nine studies that manipulated both applicant sex and job type. These studies offer mixed results. Of the four studies that did not find the expected effect (heavier women are more adversely affected), Pingitore et al. (1994) failed to find an interaction between applicant weight and job type and thus did not explore the moderating effect of applicant sex. The absence of an interaction between weight and job type in this study was possibly due to the types of jobs used (i.e. systems analyst and sales representative; the difference in customer interaction between these two jobs was not clearly communicated to participants). Bellizzi and Hasty's (1998, 2000) studies both used data based on the same field experiment, in which the obesity manipulation uniquely involved a voluntary statement from 'the applicant' indicating either that they needed special accommodations for obesity *or* that they were very fit and not overweight. Weight discrimination was present for both men and women. Given that weight discrimination towards women could reflect lookism – whereby thinness is perceived as attractive and receives a premium, and fatness is perceived as unattractive and receives a penalty – the non-aesthetic nature of this manipulation (special accommodations required versus none) might have negated sex differences. Alternatively, alerting an employer to potential health problems might have elicited discrimination based on perceived organisational costs, irrespective of applicant sex.

Of the five studies that supported a more adverse effect for heavier women, two manipulated the physical activity level involved in the job. In one study (Flint et al., 2015), participants rated the suitability of candidates for a range of jobs, which included graded physical activity levels. Although heavier women fared worse in a retail role relative to administrative assistant and university lecturer roles, sex differences were largest for the labourer role, suggesting that physical fitness was a more important predictor of discrimination than public interaction. Similarly, Bartels and Nordstrom (2013) found that the expected interaction been applicant weight and applicant sex was only present for a job where high levels of visibility and physical activity were both present. In Nickson et al. (2016), the three-way interaction between applicant weight, job type and applicant sex was only marginally significant, suggesting a need for further research. Rooth (2009) examined *call back rates* for interviews, rather than evaluative ratings per se, for occupations that varied in skill requirements and degree of customer contact. Obesity-related differences in call back rates for sales occupations (aggregated) were larger for women compared to men. The study by Vallejo-Torres et al. (2018) is the only survey study included in the review; the finding that obesity increased *perceived work discrimination* for women (but not men) in customer-facing roles suggests further research regarding the personal experiences of individuals with obesity in these roles may be informative to our research questions.

Practical Implications and Recommendations

This review does not resolve whether or not weight discrimination is unique to customer-facing roles, or indeed to women. For instance, our findings suggest that factors such as race, industry (e.g. fitness) or health-related organisational costs may moderate the relationships among applicant weight, applicant sex, job type and discrimination. We recommend that future experiments utilise designs which, at a minimum, manipulate both applicant body weight and applicant sex in conjunction with different dimensions of job type (public interaction, physical activity and industry) to provide a robust test of sex differences in weight discrimination for different types of jobs. In addition, we recommend research in real-world settings, including studies that examine the lived experiences of heavier individuals in customer-facing roles, to increase understanding of discrimination in this setting. Furthermore, the reasons for weight discrimination differences in customer-facing roles between the sexes remain under-researched, thus the question of *why* – e.g. negative obesity stereotyping, lookism, customer discrimination/rational bias – warrants attention in future research. A goal should be to help eliminate weight- and sex-based inequality in work settings through appropriate interventions. Such interventions might include: workplace harassment training to challenge negative obesity stereotypes; education about the complex aetiology of obesity; skill development (e.g. respectful language and sensitivity training in relation to people with obesity); reporting weight-related discrimination in the workplace and reviewing related policies; and using structured interviews to increase consistent, objective evaluation and decrease subjectivity which may lead to weight-related discrimination (see, e.g. Bartels, 2016; Ruggs et al., 2013). In addition, the inclusion of photographs in job applications should be avoided unless justified, given that images may lead to implicit or explicit weight-related biases that override essential information such as experience and skills. Photographs may be justified where recruiters are interviewing several candidates over a short interval or keeping applications on file for the longer term, as photographs enable recruiters to match resumes with faces to facilitate recall and their candidate preferences. Where employers do require photographs, the specifications should be standardised, e.g. professionally taken, front facing portrait photo (passport style), neutral facial expression and professional attire. A potential issue, however, is the public accessibility of social media accounts, which provide ready accessibility to additional visual information about job applicants, with evidence suggesting that many employers are using this information, a practice known as 'cybervetting' (Gruzd et al., 2020). Of course, there are also professional concerns, such as maintaining separate personal and work social media accounts and understanding privacy settings, which all job applicants and employees should consider.

This chapter began with one example of a situation where a female job applicant was evaluated not on her merit, but on a factor unrelated to job performance – overweight. Our findings from the literature search confirm that heavier women experience discrimination relative to other women on evaluative workplace outcomes such as call back rates, perceived competence/job fit, suitability ratings, hiring likelihood, job/task assignment, perceived potential/success, promotion and termination and perceived discrimination. A caveat is that women who are very underweight may also fare worse than others on some outcomes.

References

Agerström, J., & Rooth, D. O. (2011). The role of automatic obesity stereotypes in real hiring discrimination. *Journal of Applied Psychology, 96*(4), 790–805.

Bartels, L. K. (2016). Fat women need not apply: Employment weight discrimination against women. In M. L. Connerley & J. Wu (Eds.), *Handbook on well-being of working women* (pp. 33–46). Springer.

Bartels, L. K., & Nordstrom, C. R. (2013). Too big to hire: Factors impacting weight discrimination. *Management Research Review, 36*(9), 868–881.

Baum, C. L., & Ford, W. F. (2004). The wage effects of obesity: A longitudinal study. *Health Economics, 13*(9), 885–899.

Bellizzi, J. A., & Hasty, R. W. (1998). Territory assignment decisions and supervising unethical selling behavior: The effects of obesity and gender as moderated by job-related factors. *Journal of Personal Selling and Sales Management, 18*(2), 35–49.

Bellizzi, J. A., & Hasty, R. W. (2000). Does successful work experience mitigate weight-and gender-based employment discrimination in face-to-face industrial selling? *Journal of Business & Industrial Marketing, 15*(6), 384–398.

Cicchetti, D. V. (1994). Guidelines, criteria, and rules of thumb for evaluating normed and standardized assessment instruments in psychology. *Psychological Assessment, 6*(4), 284.

DeBeaumont, R. (2009). Occupational differences in the wage penalty for obese women. *The Journal of Socio-Economics, 38*(2), 344–349.

Finkelstein, L. M., Frautschy Demuth, R. L., & Sweeney, D. L. (2007). Bias against overweight job applicants: Further explorations of when and why. *Human Resource Management: Published in Cooperation with the School of Business Administration, The University of Michigan and in Alliance with the Society of Human Resources Management, 46*(2), 203–222.

Flint, S., Codreanu, S., Ilic, V., Zomer, C., Cadik, M., Gomalou, A., & Watson, P. (2015). "Obesity discrimination in the workplace:" You're hired. *Journal of European Psychology Students, 6*(2), 64–69.

Grant, S., & Mizzi, T. (2014). Body weight bias in hiring decisions: Identifying explanatory mechanisms. *Social Behavior and Personality: International Journal, 42*(3), 353–370.

Grant, S. L., Mizzi, T., & Anglim, J. (2016). 'Fat, four-eyed and female' 30 years later: A replication of Harris, Harris, and Bochner's (1982) early study of obesity stereotypes. *Australian Journal of Psychology, 68*(4), 290–300.

Gruys, K. (2012). Does this make me look fat? Aesthetic labor and fat talk as emotional labor in a women's plus-size clothing store. *Social Problems, 59*(4), 481–500.

Gruzd, A., Jacobson, J., & Dubois, E. (2020). Cybervetting and the public life of social media data. *Social Media & Society, 6*(2), 1–13.

Han, E., & Kim, T. H. (2017). Body mass index and self-employment in South Korea. *Journal of Biosocial Science, 49*(4), 463–477.

Han, E., Norton, E. C., & Powell, L. M. (2011). Direct and indirect effects of body weight on adult wages. *Economics and Human Biology, 9*(4), 381–392.

Han, E., Norton, E. C., & Stearns, S. C. (2009). Weight and wages: Fat versus lean paychecks. *Health Economics, 18*(5), 535–548.

Harper, B. (2000). Beauty, stature and the labour market: A British cohort study. *Oxford Bulletin of Economics & Statistics, 62*, 771–800.

Harris, C., & Small, J. (2013). Obesity and hotel staffing: Are hotels guilty of 'lookism'. *Hospitality & Society, 3*(2), 111–127.

Haskins, K. M., & Ransford, H. E. (1999). The relationship between weight and career payoffs among women. *Sociological Forum, 14*(2), 295–318.

Hong, Q. N., Fàbregues, S., Bartlett, G., Boardman, F., Cargo, M., Dagenais, P., … Pluye, P. (2018). The Mixed Methods Appraisal Tool (MMAT) version 2018 for information professionals and researchers. *Education for Information, 34*(4), 285–291.

Jasper, C. R., & Klassen, M. L. (1990). Perceptions of salespersons' appearance and evaluation of job performance. *Perceptual and Motor Skills, 71*(2), 563–566.

Klesges, R. C., Klem, M. L., Hanson, C. L., Eck, L. H., Ernst, J., O'Laughlin, D., . . . Rife, R. (1990). The effects of applicant's health status and qualifications on simulated hiring decisions. *International Journal of Obesity, 14*(6), 527–535.

Lee, H., Ahn, R., Kim, T. H., & Han, E. (2019). Impact of obesity on employment and wages among young adults: Observational study with panel data. *International Journal of Environmental Research and Public Health, 16*(1), 139–151.

Merritt, S., Gardner, C., Huber, K., Wexler, B., Banister, C., & Staley, A. (2018). Imagine Me and You, I Do: Effects of imagined intergroup contact on anti-fat bias in the context of job interviews. *Journal of Applied Social Psychology, 48*(2), 80–89.

Nickson, D., Timming, A. R., Re, D., & Perrett, D. I. (2016). Subtle increases in BMI within a healthy weight range still reduce women's employment chances in the service sector. *PLoS One, 11*(9), 1–14.

O'Brien, K. S., Latner, J. D., Ebneter, D., & Hunter, J. A. (2013). Obesity discrimination: The role of physical appearance, personal ideology, and anti-fat prejudice. *International Journal of Obesity, 37*(3), 455–461.

O'Brien, K. S., Latner, J. D., Halberstadt, J., Hunter, J. A., Anderson, J., & Caputi, P. (2008). Do antifat attitudes predict antifat behaviors? *Obesity, 16*(S2), S87–S92.

Pace, R., Pluye, P., Bartlett, G., Macaulay, A. C., Salsberg, J., Jagosh, J., & Seller, R. (2012). Testing the reliability and efficiency of the pilot Mixed Methods Appraisal Tool (MMAT) for systematic mixed studies review. *International Journal of Nursing Studies, 49*(1), 47–53.

Pascal, B., & Kurpius, S. E. R. (2012). Perceptions of clients: Influences of client weight and job status. *Professional Psychology: Research and Practice, 43*, 349–355.

Pingitore, R., Dugoni, B. L., Tindale, R. S., & Spring, B. (1994). Bias against overweight job applicants in a simulated employment interview. *Journal of Applied Psychology, 79*(6), 909–917.

Rooth, D. O. (2009). Obesity, attractiveness, and differential treatment in hiring. *Journal of Human Resources, 44*, 710–735.

Rudolph, C. W., Wells, C. L., Weller, M. D., & Baltes, B. B. (2009). A meta-analysis of empirical studies of weight-based bias in the workplace. *Journal of Vocational Behavior, 74*(1), 1–10.

Ruggs, E. N., Hebl, M. R., Law, C., Cox, C. B., Roehling, M. V., & Wiener, R. L. (2013). Gone fishing: I–O psychologists' missed opportunities to understand marginalized employees' experiences with discrimination. *Industrial and Organizational Psychology, 6*(1), 39–60.

Ruggs, E. N., Hebl, M. R., & Williams, A. (2015). Weight isn't selling: The insidious effects of weight stigmatization in retail settings. *Journal of Applied Psychology, 100*(5), 1483–1496.

Sartore, M. L., & Cunningham, G. B. (2007). Weight discrimination, hiring recommendations, person–job fit, and attributions: Fitness-industry implications. *Journal of Sport Management, 21*(2), 172–193.

Swami, V., Chan, F., Wong, V., Furnham, A., & Tovée, M. J. (2008). Weight-based discrimination in occupational hiring and helping behavior. *Journal of Applied Social Psychology, 38*(4), 968–981.

Swami, V., Pietschnig, J., Stieger, S., Tovee, M. J., & Voracek, M. (2010). An investigation of weight bias against women and its associations with individual difference factors. *Body Image, 7*(3), 194–199.

Vallejo-Torres, L., Morris, S., & Lopez-Valcarcel, B. G. (2018). Obesity and perceived work discrimination in Spain. *Applied Economics, 50*(36), 3870–3884.

World Health Organization. (2021, June 9). *Obesity and overweight.* https://www.who.int/news-room/fact-sheets/detail/obesity-and-overweight

World Obesity Foundation. (n.d.). *Coronavirus* (COVID-19) & Obesity. https://www.worldobesity.org/news/statement-coronavirus-covid-19-obesity

Chapter 5

Ageism, Sexism and Appearance: Navigating Workplace Discrimination in Later Life

Laura Hurd

Abstract

Ageism refers to the systematic, cultural devaluation of agedness and concomitant discrimination against older adults that is endemic to Western industrialised societies. Age-based discrimination is expressed through the numerous, taken-for-granted, negative stereotypes that equate oldness with frailty, senility, asexuality, obsolescence and loss of attractiveness. It is also evident in the institutional policies and everyday practices that both subtly and overtly exclude older adults from full and meaningful access to resources and opportunities in various organisational settings, including the workplace. This chapter explores the ways that ageism shapes and constrains the experiences and prospects of older workers as they endeavour to obtain or retain employment and/or access to training and promotions. I will discuss how age-based stereotypes and discrimination are gendered, resulting in differential impacts on older men and women seeking employment or those who are currently employed. I will further consider how the older body more generally and appearance in particular are the focal points of ageist assumptions, norms and practices in the workplace. I will conclude by reflecting on the implications and outcomes of age-based exclusion and discrimination on the lives of older male and female employees.

Keywords: Ageism; age-based discrimination; appearance; lookism; older adults; sexism

Introduction

There are numerous adages used in everyday conversations that highlight the social perils of being old. Such expressions as 'you look good for your age' or

The Emerald Handbook of Appearance in the Workplace, 101–112
Copyright © 2024 by Emerald Publishing Limited
All rights of reproduction in any form reserved
doi:10.1108/978-1-80071-174-720230006

'I am young at heart' reflect the assumptions that looking or behaving old are undesirable, if not culturally reviled. Older adults, especially women, are also cautioned against appearing as though they are 'mutton dressed as lamb' by improperly adopting fashions that are only considered suitable for the young. Older women who overtly express their sexuality and seek younger partners are further maligned as 'cougars' while ageing men who engage in sexual relationships with younger individuals are either lauded or viewed pityingly and with suspicion. The cultural space between being praised for having a youthful appearance or demeanour and being ridiculed for behaving in age-inappropriate ways is fraught with ageist stereotypes and discrimination that underpin the lives of older adults. Nowhere are the deleterious consequences of age-based policies and practices more evident than in the workplace where social norms and body ideals concerning age, gender and appearance collide in ways that increasingly penalise older adults, especially older women. Critically exploring these intersections, in this chapter, I will consider the research and theorising concerning ageism, gender and the workplace, with a particular focus on how appearance is a focal point for age-based exclusion and discrimination. Thus, I will examine how older men and women's workplace experiences and prospects are linked to and delimited by their abilities to approximate gendered appearance and body ideals that privilege youthfulness as a proxy for attractiveness, health, potential and productivity. Additionally, I will consider how older individuals strive to navigate as well as mitigate the physical and social changes that typically accompany growing older by using various gendered, behavioural and appearance management strategies. Finally, I will discuss how ageism in the workplace impacts older adults' sense of identity and well-being and offer some practical implications and recommendations.

Ageing, Gender and the Older Body

In Western society, later life is assumed to be a time of inevitable and progressive decline and decay marked by increasing poor health, dependence, senility, sexual dysfunction, lethargy, social disengagement, obsolescence and loss of attractiveness (Nelson, 2002; Palmore, 1999). In contrast, youth and middle age are thought to be the epitome of creativity, health, vibrant sexuality, energy, strength, innovation, productivity and physical appeal. The socially constructed polarisation of 'old' and 'bad' versus 'young' and 'good' is reflective of and reinforced by ageism or 'the systematic stereotyping and discrimination against older adults because they are old' (Butler, 1975, p. 12). Age-based discrimination entails 'the use of chronological age to mark out classes of people who are systematically denied resources and opportunities that others enjoy, and who suffer the consequences of such denigration, ranging from well-meaning patronage to unambiguous vilification' (Bytheway, 1995, p. 14). Often unchallenged and unrecognised, ageism is both explicitly and implicitly expressed and reinforced in social policies and practices, as well as everyday interactions (Levy, 2017).

Historically, one came to be labelled and thought of as old upon turning 65 and subsequently transitioning into retirement (Costa, 1998). However, our social landscape has changed considerably as fixed retirement ages have largely disappeared and labour laws have been established that prohibit employers from asking potential employees their ages (Malatestinic, 2018). In lieu of chronological age, appearance has been used as the primary way that people are marked as old in organisational settings (Hurd, 2021). The complexities associated with using looks as a metric for age have escalated amidst the proliferation of consumer products and services that can be used to alter one's body and obfuscate one's age. In our youth and appearance-obsessed world, men and women face intensifying pressure to purchase everything from clothing, diets and exercise regimens to cosmetics, non-surgical cosmetic procedures and surgeries to achieve and maintain a desirable, youthful appearance and thereby fight against the negative social consequences associated with looking and being seen as old (Hurd Clarke, 2011).

At the same time, older men and women's appearances are ascribed meanings and perceived differently. Indeed, age-based discrimination in social and organisational settings reflects and is reinforced by gendered body norms and ideals. For example, exalted masculinity is associated with youthfulness, athleticism, health, strength, productivity, hypersexuality and self-reliance (King et al., 2021; Thompson & Langendoerfer, 2016). Esteemed male bodies are active ones that are valued as vehicles for accomplishment, action and the expression and assertion of political, economic, physical and social power. In contrast, idealised femininity is equated with fertility, caregiving and, most especially, beauty, which is primarily associated with youthfulness, fitness, health, slimness and voluptuousness (Bordo, 2003; Tiggemann & Zaccardo, 2016). Preferred female bodies are valued for their nurturing and aesthetic qualities as well as their ability to garner the interests of heterosexual men (Hakim, 2011). Given the emphasis on youthfulness and health within gendered body ideals, ageing invariably poses a problem for both men and women who progressively lose social status and recognition as their appearances, physical abilities and health statuses change over time.

Similarly, there is a double standard such that ageing has a more negative impact on older women's social standing and perceived femininity as compared to older men and their presumed masculinity (Sontag, 1997). For men, growing older may, at least temporarily, enhance their masculine status as distinguished, experienced, sexy and influential leaders, particularly those who are wealthy and politically powerful (Calasanti & Slevin, 2001; Hurd Clarke et al., 2014; McGann et al., 2016). Thus, men may continue to accrue and maintain social currency with age as a result of their accumulating knowledge, expertise and resources. In contrast, as women lose their perceived attractiveness relative to ageist beauty ideals, they are progressively robbed of their cultural visibility, perceived sexual desirability and social status (Hurd Clarke, 2011; Sontag, 1997). In this way, the bodies and appearances of ageing men and women are read differently, with concomitant distinctions in their locations in age and gender hierarchies.

Ageism, Appearance and the Workplace

There is a wealth of research that has documented how ageism impacts the opportunities and prospects of older workers. It is well known that after age 50, individuals are more likely to be unemployed for longer periods of time and to subsequently re-enter the workforce in lower paying, deskilled jobs (Berger, 2021; Harris et al., 2018). In much of the existing research, appearance is indirectly implicated as employers have been found to internalise ageist stereotypes and consequently be disinclined to hire, retain or promote individuals who they perceive to be older and thus less suitable and desirable as compared to their younger counterparts (Cheung et al., 2011; James et al., 2013; Karpinska et al., 2013; Posthuma & Campion, 2009). In particular, employers often erroneously assume that older workers are less competent and productive (Krings et al., 2011; Shiu et al., 2015), less capable of adopting and effectively using new technology (Sharit et al., 2009; Van Dalen et al., 2010), less deserving, willing or able to receive training and learn new skills (Fleischmann & Koster, 2018; Fuertes et al., 2013; Kluge & Krings, 2008), less flexible and adaptable (Gringart et al., 2012; Henkens, 2005; Loretto & White, 2006) and less physically robust and able to engage in manual labour (Bowman et al., 2017; Egdell et al., 2018).

There is a growing body of research that has examined how appearance is directly linked to employers' hiring, opportunity allocation and retention decisions. A few studies have found that older adults may experience looking older to be an asset in the workplace. For example, in their qualitative interviews with male pharmacy sales representatives, aged 45–86, Foweraker and Cutcher (2015) found that the men were able to successfully construct masculine identities as their ageing appearances were perceived as indicators of their expertise and experience. Similarly, in their interviews with 15 key informants and 22 employers, Egdell et al. (2019) found that older workers in law and health care were valued and perceived to have 'an advantage, as age was equated with experience' (p. 453). In contrast, the vast majority of the research has found that employers tend to view looking old as a deficit. In particular, employers perceive that older workers possess less aesthetic capital (Anderson et al., 2010), or particular physical attributes that can be 'utilised in economic and social exchange' (Sarpila et al., 2020, p. 1), as compared to their younger counterparts. Consequently, older workers are assumed to be less capable of successfully performing aesthetic labour, as they lack 'particular embodied capacities and attributes that appeal to the senses of customers' (Warhurst & Nickson, 2007, p. 103). The emphasis on having a youthful, attractive appearance as a prerequisite for employment has been found to be especially important for those seeking or holding public or client-facing jobs, such as receptionists, flight attendants, restaurant servers, sales representatives, television broadcasters, actors and fitness industry workers (Bowman et al., 2017; Hurd Clarke & Griffin, 2008; McGann et al., 2016; Moore, 2009; Rowson & Gonzalez-White, 2019; Spedale et al., 2014). In these positions, employees' appearances are simultaneously assumed to be important for enticing consumers but also for projecting a marketable and appealing image for their companies as a whole (Johansson et al., 2017).

However, 'lookism' (Granleese & Sayer, 2006, p. 508), or discrimination linked to appearance, is not universally experienced. Indeed, older women are more likely than their younger and male counterparts to face stereotyping, discrimination and exclusion in the workplace that is directly linked to their appearances (Bowman et al., 2017; Duncan & Loretto, 2004; Raisborough et al., 2021; Spedale et al., 2014). Examining the differential impacts of looking and being older on male and female workers, Itzin and Phillipson (1993) introduced the term 'gendered ageism' as they argued that within organisational culture, 'ageism is significantly gendered and…sexism operates always with a dimension of ageism' (Itzin & Phillipson, 1995, p. 92). Gendered ageism is not only prevalent in customer service, fitness, media and sales professions, which have put a well-documented emphasis on employees' appearances. Rather, research has found that older women face discrimination linked to how they look in a variety of sectors. For example, in their study of higher education, Granleese and Sayer (2006) found that female professors' experiences of misogyny and gendered ageism were related to others' assessments of and responses to their ageing appearances. Similarly, in their survey of financial sector employees, Duncan and Loretto (2004) found that 'many of the accounts of ageism provided by women contained a sexualised element' (p. 107) as attacks on the older female workers' characters and competencies were framed in terms of their perceived loss of femininity over time. Jyrkinen (2014) interviewed 15 Finnish women in senior management positions who described various forms of gendered ageism including a discounting of their accumulated experience and decreased access to promotions relative to their male counterparts at all stages of their careers, which they themselves attributed to their age, gender and appearances. Finally, Walker et al. (2007) interviewed 12 women, aged 50 to 65, who reported that those working in professional jobs tended to be more concerned about the way they looked because maintaining youthful attractiveness was thought to be important for women's occupational advancement. Consistent across all these studies are the findings that, relative to men, women are considered to be old at younger ages and are devalued, excluded and/or side-lined in their careers because of their perceived increasing deviation from feminine beauty ideals, with resultant long-term, negative financial and social consequences (Duncan & Loretto, 2004; Jyrkinen, 2014; Jyrkinen & McKie, 2012).

Older Workers' Experiences of and Responses to Ageism in the Workplace

Older adults are well aware of the cultural devaluation of those deemed old, and often report having personally experienced negative attitudes or overt discrimination in their everyday lives, including in the workplace (Handy & Davy, 2007; Hurd Clarke & Griffin, 2008; Minichiello et al., 2000). Older workers frequently describe feeling less valued, welcome and visible and at heightened risk of either being laid-off or unable to secure new employment as they age and their appearances change (Bowman et al., 2017; Hurd Clarke & Griffin, 2008; Hurd

Clarke & Korotchenko, 2016; Rahn et al., 2021; SigurĐardóttir & Snorradóttir, 2020). Moreover, studies have found that ageism undermines the confidence, self-esteem and well-being of older adults (Åberg et al., 2020; Hassell & Perrewe, 1993) and leads to decreased employee satisfaction and commitment (Macdonald & Levy, 2016).

Consequently, older workers may actively try to mitigate the impact of ageism on both their sense of self as well as their career prospects. To begin, they may distance themselves from or even overtly reject the label of old as they argue that their appearances and behaviours are a testimony to their inherent youthfulness (Hurd, 1999; Minichiello et al., 2000; Slevin, 2006). Alternatively, older adults may differentiate between their chronological and felt ages, as they suggest that they feel younger than their actual ages (Choi et al., 2014; Weiss & Lang, 2012). Additionally, older adults may actively strive to construct and perform a youthful identity and thereby conceal their chronological ages. For example, in her study of the employment seeking experiences of 30 individuals, aged 45–65, Berger (2009) found that her participants modified their resumes and avoided conversational topics or vocabularies during job interviews that might inadvertently reveal their chronological ages and thereby diminish their chances of successfully obtaining employment.

Older workers, especially women, also often engage in appearance management strategies designed to make them look more youthful. Older women have been found to choose clothing that masks or compensates for the bodily changes that accompany ageing, such as wrinkles, sagging or flabby skin, increased weight and altered body shapes (Francis, 2011; Hurd Clarke et al., 2009; Steffan, 2021). Likewise, older women often report dressing in a way that reduces their hypervisibility and allows them to 'fit in' (Lövgren, 2016, p. 382). Thus, they use fashion to appear more youthful and thereby align themselves with the norms of 'young organisational culture' (Berger, 2009, p. 327). However, older women also frequently emphasise the importance of being demure (Lövgren, 2016; Twigg, 2015). For example, even as they felt pressure to dress youthfully, older female workers in the fashion industry were careful to present a modest, professional, age-appropriate image by not wearing overly revealing clothing (McInnis & Medvedev, 2021).

Hair care is another focus of appearance-management for older employees. Given that having grey hair is often considered a hallmark of oldness (Hurd Clarke & Korotchenko, 2010; Ward & Holland, 2011), older adults, especially ageing women, frequently dye their hair in advance of job interviews (Berger, 2009; Bowman et al., 2017). In their interviews with women aged 50–7, McInnis and Medvedev (2021) found that most of their participants felt that having dyed hair was 'an economic necessity' (p. 38) in order to both obtain and retain employment. Similarly, the older women who were surveyed by Cecil et al. (2022) perceived that it was important to colour their hair to avoid losing credibility as competent workers.

Finally, some studies have found that older adults may turn to cosmetic surgeries and non-surgical cosmetic procedures in an effort to enhance or shore up their aesthetic capital. In particular, older individuals often describe feeling compelled to use non-surgical cosmetic procedures like Botox and injectable fillers or surgical procedures like facelifts and tummy tucks to make themselves appear more youthful and appealing to others, including potential employers (Berkowitz, 2017; Hurd Clarke & Griffin, 2008; Hurd Clarke et al., 2007; Slevin, 2009). Once again, these studies highlight the underlying gendered ageism that shapes and constrains the experiences of older workers as women report greater pressure to alter and manage their ageing appearances as compared to older men. Collectively, the research points to the ways that workplace culture and the societal valuation of youthfulness and young-looking appearances more broadly shape older adults' sense of identity and perceived need to modify and manage the way they look so as to optimise their workplace chances and experiences.

Practical Implications and Recommendations

In this chapter, I have explored how social norms and ideals concerning age, gender and appearance combine to influence the employment prospects and experiences of older workers. The research concerning ageism in the workplace reveals that older workers are less likely to secure employment or be treated equitably on the job. Moreover, the extant literature indicates that age-based discrimination is often linked to appearance and gendered body ideals, to the particular detriment of ageing women. Even as both men and women experience progressive exclusion as they deviate from youthful standards of physical attractiveness, older female workers are especially vulnerable to 'lookism' or the negative attitudes and resultant discrimination linked to their ageing appearances. The consequences of appearance-based discrimination in the workplace are far-reaching for older women, as they are more likely to experience financial insecurity and lack of access to pensions in later life (Barnum et al., 1995; Berger, 2021; Falkingham & Rake, 1999; Harnois, 2015).

While there is some evidence that employer attitudes towards older workers in general are improving (Kluge & Krings, 2008), appearance-based ageism in the workplace continues to be deeply engrained. There is an urgent need for education about the subtle and overt ways that gendered ageism is internalised and operationalised in the workplace. In particular, employers need to better understand and thereby confront the ways that their, often unconscious, bias towards younger workers influences their hiring, retention, promotion and resource provision decisions. Additionally, labour laws need to more clearly define and respond to age-based discrimination, especially as it relates to appearances and gendered body ideals. Ultimately, workplace culture needs to be overhauled so that, similar to sexism, racism and homophobia, it becomes socially unacceptable, if not unthinkable, to treat people inequitably on the basis of their appearances and perceived chronological ages. In an era of population ageing, where the numbers of available younger workers relative to their more experienced older counterparts is shrinking, there is a pressing economic need to rethink employment policies and practices. Given that ageism is a form of exclusion that we will all potentially face even if we cannot presently imagine such a future, it behoves us all to confront and ameliorate the deeply ingrained prejudice against ageing and older people that underlies the social construction of culture in the workplace and beyond.

References

Åberg, E., Kukkonen, I., & Sarpila, O. (2020). From double to triple standards of ageing. Perceptions of physical appearance at the intersections of age, gender and class. *Journal of Aging Studies*, *55*, 100876.

Anderson, T. L., Grunert, C., Katz, A., & Lovascio, S. (2010). Aesthetic capital: A research review on beauty perks and penalties. *Sociology Compass*, *4*(8), 564–575.

Barnum, P., Liden, R. C., & Ditomaso, N. (1995). Double jeopardy for women and minorities: Pay differences with age. *Academy of Management Journal*, *38*(3), 863–880.

Berger, E. D. (2021). *Ageism at work: Deconstructing age and gender in the discriminating labour market*. University of Toronto Press.

Berger, E. D. (2009). Managing age discrimination: An examination of the techniques used when seeking employment. *The Gerontologist*, *49*(3), 317–332.

Berkowitz, D. (2017). *Botox nation: Changing the face of America*. NYU Press.

Bordo, S. (2003). *Unbearable weight: Feminism, western culture, and the body* (10th anniversary ed.). University of California Press.

Bowman, D., McGann, M., Kimberley, H., & Biggs, S. (2017). Rusty, invisible and threatening: Ageing, capital and employability. *Work, Employment & Society*, *31*(3), 465–482.

Butler, R. N. (1975). *Why survive? Being old in America*. Harper & Row.

Bytheway, B. (1995). *Ageism*. Open University Press.

Calasanti, T. M., & Slevin, K. (2001). *Gender, social inequalities, and aging*. AltaMira Press.

Cecil, V., Pendry, L. F., Salvatore, J., Mycroft, H., & Kurz, T. (2022). Gendered ageism and gray hair: Must older women choose between feeling authentic and looking competent? *Journal of Women & Aging*, *34*(2), 210–225.

Cheung, C., Kam, P. K., & Ngan, R. M. (2011). Age discrimination in the labour market from the perspectives of employers and older workers. *International Social Work*, *54*(1), 118–136.

Choi, N. G., DiNitto, D. M., & Kim, J. (2014). Discrepancy between chronological age and felt age: Age group difference in objective and subjective health as correlates. *Journal of Aging and Health*, *26*(3), 458–473.

Costa, D. L. (1998). *The evolution of retirement: An American economic history 1880–1990*. University of Chicago Press.

Duncan, C., & Loretto, W. (2004). Never the right age? Gender and age-based discrimination in employment. *Gender, Work and Organization*, *11*(1), 95–115.

Egdell, V., Fuertes, V., Tjandra, N. C., & Chen, T. (2019). Employer policy and practice toward older workers in Hong Kong: The role of shifting intergenerational dynamics. *Journal of Aging & Social Policy*, *31*(5), 445–466.

Egdell, V., Maclean, G., Raeside, R., & Chen, T. (2018). Age management in the workplace: Manager and older worker accounts of policy and practice. *Ageing and Society*, *40*(4), 784–804.

Falkingham, J., & Rake, K. (1999). Partnership in pensions: Delivering a secure retirement for women. *Benefits, 26*, 11–16.

Fleischmann, M., & Koster, F. (2018). Older workers and employer-provided training in the Netherlands: A vignette study. *Ageing and Society, 38*(10), 1995–2018.

Foweraker, B., & Cutcher, L. (2015). Work, age and other drugs: Exploring the intersection of age and masculinity in a pharmaceutical organization. *Gender, Work and Organization, 22*(5), 459–473.

Francis, D. (2011). Daily rituals of dress: Women re-creating themselves over time. *Journal of the American Society on Aging, 35*(3), 64–70.

Fuertes, V., Egdell, V., & McQuaid, R. (2013). Extending working lives: Age management in SMEs. *Employee Relations, 35*(3), 272–293.

Granleese, J., & Sayer, G. (2006). Gendered ageism and 'lookism': A triple jeopardy for female academics. *Women in Management Review, 21*(6), 500–517.

Gringart, E., Jones, B., Helmes, E., Jansz, J., Monterosso, L., & Edwards, M. (2012). Negative stereotyping of older nurses despite contact and mere exposure: The case of nursing recruiters in Western Australia. *Journal of Aging & Social Policy, 24*(4), 400–416.

Hakim, C. (2011). *Honey money: The power of erotic capital*. Allen Lane Press.

Handy, J., & Davy, D. (2007). Gendered ageism: Older women's experiences of employment agency practices. *Asia Pacific Journal of Human Resources, 45*(1), 85–99.

Harnois, C. E. (2015). Age and gender discrimination: Intersecting inequalities across the lifecourse. *Advances in Gender Research, 20*, 85–109.

Harris, K., Krygsman, S., Waschenko, J., & Laliberte Rudman, D. (2018). Ageism and the older worker: A scoping review. *The Gerontologist, 58*(2), e1–e14.

Hassell, B. L., & Perrewe, P. L. (1993). An examination of the relationship between older workers' perceptions of age discrimination and employee psychological states. *Journal of Managerial Issues, 5*(1), 109–120.

Henkens, K. (2005). Stereotyping of older workers and retirement: The managers' point of view. *Canadian Journal on Aging, 24*(4), 353–366.

Hurd, L. (1999). "We're not old!": Older women's negotiation of aging and oldness. *Journal of Aging Studies, 13*(4), 419–439.

Hurd, L. (2021). The politics of looking old: Older adults and the aging body. In M. Craig (Ed.), *The Routledge companion to beauty politics* (pp. 357–364). Routledge.

Hurd Clarke, L. (2011). *Facing age: Women growing older in anti-aging culture*. Rowman and Littlefield.

Hurd Clarke, L., Bennett, E. V., & Liu, C. (2014). Aging and masculinity: Portrayals in men's magazines. *Journal of Aging Studies, 31*, 26–33.

Hurd Clarke, L., & Griffin, M. (2008). Visible and invisible ageing: Beauty work as a response to ageism. *Ageing and Society, 28*(5), 653–674.

Hurd Clarke, L., Griffin, M., & Maliha, K. (2009). Bat wings, bunions, and turkey wattles: Body transgressions and older women's strategic clothing choices. *Ageing and Society, 29*(5), 709–726.

Hurd Clarke, L., & Korotchenko, A. (2010). Shades of grey: To dye or not to dye one's hair in later life. *Ageing and Society, 30*(6), 1011–1026.

Hurd Clarke, L., & Korotchenko, A. (2016). 'I know it exists...but I haven't experienced it personally': Older Canadian men's perceptions of ageism as a distant social problem. *Ageing and Society*, *36*(8), 1757–1773.

Hurd Clarke, L., Repta, R., & Griffin, M. (2007). Non-surgical cosmetic procedures: Older women's perceptions and experiences. *Journal of Women & Aging*, *19*(3/4), 69–87.

Itzin, C., & Phillipson, C. (1993). *Age barriers at work*. METRA.

Itzin, C., & Phillipson, C. (1995). Gendered ageism: A double jeopardy for women in organizations. In C. Itzin & C. Phillipson (Eds.), *Gender, culture and organizational change. Putting theory into practice* (pp. 84–94). Routledge.

James, J. B., McKechnie, S., Swanberg, J., & Besen, E. (2013). Exploring the workplace impact of intentional/unintentional age discrimination. *Journal of Managerial Psychology*, *28*(7/8), 907–927.

Johansson, J., Tienari, J., & Valtonen, A. (2017). The body, identity and gender in managerial athleticism. *Human Relations*, *70*(9), 1141–1167.

Jyrkinen, M. (2014). Women managers, careers, and gendered ageism. *Scandinavian Journal of Management*, *30*(2), 175–185.

Jyrkinen, M., & McKie, L. (2012). Gender, age and ageism: Experiences of women managers in Finland and Scotland. *Work, Employment & Society*, *26*(1), 61–77.

Karpinska, K., Henkens, K., & Schippers, J. (2013). Retention of older workers: Impact of managers' age norms and stereotypes. *European Sociological Review*, *29*(6), 1323–1335.

King, N., Calasanti, T., Pietilä, I., & Ojala, H. (2021). The hegemony in masculinity. *Men and Masculinities*, *24*(3), 432–450.

Kluge, A., & Krings, F. (2008). Attitudes toward older workers and human resource practices. *Swiss Journal of Psychology*, *67*(1), 61–64.

Krings, F., Sczesny, S., & Kluge, A. (2011). Stereotypical inferences as mediators of age discrimination: The role of competence and warmth. *British Journal of Management*, *22*(2), 187–201.

Levy, B. R. (2017). Age-stereotype paradox: Opportunity for social change. *The Gerontologist*, *57*(S2), S118–S126.

Loretto, W., & White, P. (2006). Employers' attitudes, practices and policies towards older workers. *Human Resources Management Journal*, *16*(3), 313–330.

Lövgren, K. (2016). Comfortable and leisurely: Old women on style and dress. *Journal of Women & Aging*, *28*(5), 372–385.

Macdonald, J. L., & Levy, S. R. (2016). Ageism in the workplace: The role of psychosocial factors in predicting job satisfaction, commitment, and engagement. *Journal of Social Issues*, *72*(1), 169–190.

Malatestinic, E. (2018). From inappropriate to illegal: Interview questions to avoid. *Indianapolis Business Journal*, *39*(19), 8–10.

McGann, M., Ong, R., Bowman, D., Duncan, A., Kimberley, H., & Biggs, S. (2016). Gendered ageism in Australia: Changing perceptions of age discrimination among older men and women. *Economic Papers*, *35*(4), 375–388.

McInnis, A., & Medvedev, K. (2021). Sartorial appearance management strategies of creative professional women over age 50 in the fashion industry. *Fashion Practice*, *13*(1), 25–47.

Minichiello, V., Browne, J., & Kendig, H. (2000). Perceptions and consequences of ageism: Views of older people. *Ageing and Society*, *20*(3), 253–278.

Moore, S. (2009). 'No matter what I did I would still end up in the same position': Age as a factor defining older women's experience of labour market participation. *Work, Employment & Society*, *23*(4), 655–671.

Nelson, T. D. (2002). *Ageism: Stereotypes and prejudice against older persons*. MIT Press.

Palmore, E. B. (1999). *Ageism: Negative and positive* (2nd ed.). Springer.

Posthuma, R. A., & Campion, M. A. (2009). Age stereotypes in the workplace: Common stereotypes, moderators, and future research directions? *Journal of Management*, *35*(1), 158–188.

Rahn, G., Martiny, S. E., & Nikitin, J. (2021). Feeling out of place: Internalized age stereotypes are associated with older employees' sense of belonging and social motivation. *Work, Aging, and Retirement*, *7*(1), 61–77.

Raisborough, J., Watkins, S., Connor, R., & Pitimson, N. (2021). Reduced to curtain twitchers? Age, ageism and the careers of four women actors. *Journal of Women & Aging*, 1–12. https://doi.org/10.1080/085952841.2021.1910464

Rowson, T. S., & Gonzalez-White, M. D. C. (2019). 'I'm older but I can still do this job': The experiences of mature women in an age-sensitive occupation. *Educational Gerontology*, *45*(4), 248–258.

Sarpila, O., Koivula, A., Kukkonen, I., Åberg, E., & Pajunen, T. (2020). Double standards in the accumulation and utilisation of 'aesthetic capital. *Poetics*, *82*, 1–11. https://doi.org/10.1016/j.poetic.2020.101447

Sharit, J., Czaja, S. J., Hernandez, M. A., & Nair, S. N. (2009). The employability of older workers as teleworkers: An appraisal of issues and an empirical study. *Human Factors and Ergonomics in Manufacturing*, *19*(5), 457–477.

Shiu, E., Hassan, L. M., & Parry, S. (2015). The moderating effects of national age stereotyping on the relationships between job satisfaction and its determinants: A study of older workers across 26 countries. *British Journal of Management*, *26*(2), 255–272.

SigurÐardóttir, S. H., & Snorradóttir, Á. (2020). Older women's experiences in the Icelandic workforce – Positive or negative? *Nordic Journal of Working Life Studies*, *10*(4), 25–41.

Slevin, K. F. (2006). The embodied experiences of old lesbians. In T. M. Calasanti & K. F. Slevin (Eds.), *Age matters: Realigning feminist thinking* (pp. 247–268). Routledge.

Slevin, K. (2009). "If I had lots of money... I'd have a body makeover:" Managing the aging body. *Social Forces*, *88*(3), 1003–1020.

Sontag, S. (1997). The double standard of aging. In M. Pearsall (Ed.), *The other within us: Feminist explorations of women and aging* (pp. 19–24). Westview Press.

Spedale, S., Coupland, C., & Tempest, S. (2014). Gendered ageism and organizational routines at work: The case of day-parting in television broadcasting. *Organization Studies*, *35*(11), 1585–1604.

Steffan, B. (2021). Managing menopause at work: The contradictory nature of identity talk. *Gender, Work and Organization*, *28*(1), 195–214.

Thompson, E. H., Jr., & Langendoerfer, K. B. (2016). Older men's blueprint for 'being a man. *Men and Masculinities*, *19*(2), 119–147.

Tiggemann, M., & Zaccardo, M. (2016). 'Strong is the new skinny': A content analysis of fitspiration images on Instagram. *Journal of Health Psychology*, *23*(8), 1003–1011.

Twigg, J. (2015). Dress and age: The intersection of life and work. *International Journal of Ageing and Later Life, 10*(1), 55–67.

Van Dalen, H. P., Henkens, K., & Schippers, J. (2010). Productivity of older workers: Perceptions of employers and employees. *Population and Development Review, 36*(2), 309–330.

Walker, H., Grant, D., Meadows, M., & Cook, I. (2007). Women's experiences and perceptions of age discrimination in employment: Implications for research and policy. *Social Policy and Society, 6*(1), 37–48.

Ward, R., & Holland, C. (2011). 'If I look old, I will be treated old': Hair and later-life image dilemmas. *Ageing and Society, 31*(2), 288–307.

Warhurst, C., & Nickson, D. (2007). Employee experience of aesthetic labour in retail and hospitality. *Work, Employment & Society, 21*(1), 103–120.

Weiss, D., & Lang, F. R. (2012). 'They' are old but 'I' feel younger: Age-group dissociation as a self-protective strategy in old age. *Psychology and Aging, 27*(1), 153–163.

Chapter 6

The Price of 'Extra Layers': British Muslim Women's Work and Career

Sajia Ferdous

Abstract

In this chapter, the relations between Muslim migrant women's bodily appearances at Western workplaces, their work choices and career development are examined through the lens of embodied intersectionality. This chapter draws on exiting research reports and empirical research to also reflect on the scope of Muslim female migrants' labour market integration in the United Kingdom.

For Muslim women, wearing ethnic or religious dresses such as headscarf/ 'hijab', 'niqaab' or 'burqa' represents the quintessential identity of women belonging to their particular ethnic group or religion. These highly visible social and cultural markers are also inherently gendered. This chapter delves into understanding how Muslim migrant women wearing ethnic/religious dresses experience/encounter Western workplaces and how their embodied intersectional identities through creating barriers at the workplaces impede the process of their labour market integration, in turn, limit their work choices and further restrict their career progression/development in the long run. The discussion also shows that attention to the Muslim migrant women's workplace experiences funnelled through the process of embodied intersectionality can expose the overall racialised and gendered practices of the society, different forms of social exclusion while simultaneously indicate resistance from and agency of these Muslim women through bodily appearances in transnational contexts. This chapter also sheds lights on how these women's career and workplace experiences need to be understood outside the stereotypical Western description of gendered workplaces and how the discussion needs to be broadened in scope and encompass the spatial dynamics of migration, religion, gender and ethnicity to be able to make sense of Muslim migrant women's work choices and career in the West.

This chapter has a twofold structure – first, it looks at the relationship between self-regulating agency and voice and understanding of the

The Emerald Handbook of Appearance in the Workplace, 113–129
Copyright © 2024 by Emerald Publishing Limited
doi:10.1108/978-1-80071-174-720230007

embodiment of intersectional identities by the women themselves in the host country's society and labour market, and, second, how the changing time, space and contexts interact to play a role in terms of the host society and its labour market's acceptance and level of tolerance shown towards this group's embodied intersectional presence.

Keywords: Gender; Muslim women; intersectionality; work; identity; hijab

Introduction

For Muslim women, wearing ethnic or religious dresses such as 'hijab' (covering the head) or 'niqaab' (covering the face) or 'burqa' (covering the full body) represents the quintessential markers of belonging to particular ethnic groups or religion (Abu-Lughod, 2002; Mahmood, 2005). These highly visible socio-cultural and religious markers are inherently gendered and maybe recognised as political expressions for these women as well. In this chapter, I examine the relations between these bodily markers of Muslim women at British workplaces, their labour market choices and participation and the long-term implications of those choices and participation for their career development and prospects. In doing so, I also problematise the intersections of 'the embodiments of their gendered racial identities and ethnic belonging', 'their expressions of religious agency and sociopolitical resistance' and 'the othering process within the Western society and workplaces' in relation to their labour market integration. The discussion draws upon existing literature on Muslim women particularly in the contexts of 'veiled' appearances at Western workplaces and their impacts on those women's work trajectories. This is complemented by empirical evidence from an interview-based qualitative study conducted on South Asian British Muslim older women of Pakistani and Bangladeshi heritage living in the Greater Manchester area in the United Kingdom.

The discussion takes place at a time when contemporary debates on highly visible 'veiled'/hijabi Muslim women's presence in British society and workplaces divide the population between 'tolerant' and 'not-so-tolerant' groups. This chapter's discussion further explains how attention to Muslim women's both societal and workplace experiences in the West, funnelled through the process of 'otherness', can expose the overall racialised and gendered practices and different forms of marginalisation and social exclusion prevalent within the so-called multi-ethnic British society (Heath & Martin, 2013). This chapter emphasises the importance of understanding Muslim women's work choices and workplace experiences outside of the stereotypical Western discourses of gender appropriateness at work. It further argues that the theorisation of their experiences in the West needs to be broadened in scope and be inclusive of the aspects emerging from diverse, intersectional and spatial dynamics of migration, religion, class, gender, race, age and ethnicity, among others.

I conclude this chapter with the key argument that there is a compelling need for an alternative framework and theorisation of Muslim women's work and career in the field of work and employment research in the Western literature that (a) recognises their embodied burdens of 'otherness' (arising from wearing those extra layers of Islamic/ethno-religious clothing) as a part of their (de-)motivation for work and a barrier to their labour market integration, (b) links their religious/ethnic agency as an active constituent to their work choices and (c) shows why and how to move away from epistemic eurocentrism in order to understand Muslim women's labour market positions (i.e. their semi-absence) in Western labour markets.

Muslim Women, Islamic Attires and the West

There are still limited intellectual interests in problematising Muslim women's experiences within Western workplaces contexts. Besides, scholars also remain divided in terms of what are the best analytical lenses to study their issues, for example, whether to use secular or Islamic lenses (see Ahmad, 2003; Dhaliwal & Patel, 2012; Purkayastha, 2012). The arguments put forward by both ends of the analytical spectrum merit some careful evaluations. The 'Islamic feminism' or 'Muslim feminism' perspective is the starting point in theorisation of Muslim women in the Western societies from an Islamic viewpoint. Esack (2015) located 'Islamic feminism' as within two strands of debates – 'larger anti-colonial, anti-racist and global south' and 'Islamic historical and knowledge tradition'. However, there are cultural variations, even within the Global South countries and Islamic cultures. Therefore, the 'location' and origins of such theorisation of Muslim women's lived experiences remain critical. This is, particularly, because most of the frameworks are developed in the context of Middle-Eastern cultures that do not consider the cultural differences that South Asian, African Muslims or Muslims from other cultures may have from Middle-Eastern Arab traditions. Therefore, it must be recognised that similar to putting white women and women of colour in the same group, homogenising all Muslim women's experiences can be problematic and erroneous, especially when they only portray partial pictures of their social and labour market realities in Western labour markets.

The common concepts for understanding and representing Muslim women's narratives in the current literature can be found revolving around veil/hijabs, gendered Islamic ideologies and beliefs, religious agency, oppression and victimisation (Bullock, 2002; Dwyer, 1997, 1999). Two other themes, namely, 'essentialising their identities' and 'ignoring the intersectional nature of identities' further remain relevant for exploring Muslim women's lived experiences. Some earlier works on these topics (e.g. Skeggs, 1997) illustrated how bodies become raced and gendered differently across location and space. Mirza (2013) advanced those debates by conceptualising a post-colonial Black feminist framework of 'Embodied Intersectionality' which 'enables us to see not only how the women were constructed as recognisable visible Muslim others in discourse, but how that affective representation is signified and mediated by the body and experienced as a lived reality. The embodiment of power and disempowerment written through and within the sexed and raced body is particularly important if we are to understand how religious identity is performed, experienced and articulated through the women's subjectivity and sense of self'. (p. 13). Mirza (2013) compared 'embodied experiences' of Muslim women wearing Islamic clothing to having 'a second skin'. Drawing on in-depth interviews with Muslim women from three different heritages (Pakistani, Indian and Turkish), she investigated their issues with 'group belonging' and 'sense of self'. She argued that such an embodiment is not limited to physical appearance, but it is more profound and may manifest through the embodiment of emotions, sense of caring, among others, particularly in a transnational space (Ryan, 2008).

Islamic feminists Amina Wadud and Saba Mahmood's works also remain central and highly cited when it comes to problematising Muslim women's social positions. These scholars mainly focused on power structures and their relations to locate Muslim women's positions within the wider society. Wadud (2013) coined the term 'Gender Jihad' to problematise Muslim women's peculiar and precarious social positions and emancipation issues in the West. Within the UK context, Ahmad (2003) argued that the images, narratives and representations of Muslim women have been (unsurprisingly) fixed in the British society and in academic discourses for far too long. In her account, she showed how Muslim women were situated at the complex intersections of religion, colonialism and imperialism as well as competing discourses of race and gender (Ahmad, 2003). She argued that labelling Muslim women as the 'oppressed and victimised other' did not help them in attaining any political or social agency or power. Her viewpoint as a researcher from 'within' (as a Muslim woman researching other Muslim women) was that far from being 'passive', those Muslim women actively took part in all spheres of life, such as contributing to the household economy, upholding cultural traditions and norms and participation in political discourses as well as labour movement (also see Brah, 1996; Dale & Ahmed, 2008; Dale, Fieldhouse, et al., 2002; Dale, Shaheen, et al., 2002). She also criticised Muslim female academics for further contributing towards reproducing such discouraging narratives and victimised representation of Muslim women. Thus, despite their contributions in all spheres, they are discussed and represented negatively in popular and contemporary discourses; for example, in relation to forced marriages, arranged marriages, hijab and veil, oppression, honour killings, domestic violence, lack of voice and so on (Ahmad, 2003; Werbner, 2007). More recently, Vanzan (2016) echoed Ahmad's (2003) argument in her work on Muslim women by critiquing female Muslim scholars for reproducing the narratives of oppression and the West for using Muslim women and their bodies and beliefs to serve their political agenda. I would like to clarify my own position as an 'insider' too here – while I do fully recognise Muslim women's agency and support the criticisms of the unidirectional neoliberalist interpretations of those women's informal/hidden contributions to society and economy, we cannot ignore the additional societal/ structural burdens that they carry with them, which eventually play a pivotal role in shaping their agency.

Nevertheless, Islamic feminists must be given credits for being 'keen to claim the intersection of religion and gender in a different way' (Esack, 2015), thus advancing our understanding of Muslim women in an alternative way. That said, the Islamic feminist perspective although gives primacy to the intersections of religion and gender categories in theorising these women's lived realties, it runs the risks of undermining other mutually reinforcing factors and categories such as race, ethnicity or age in understanding Muslim women's labour market issues, especially in the Western contexts. For example, the Greater Manchester empirical study found strong evidence that older Muslim women faced more difficulties in integrating with Western labour markets because of their diverging 'sense of older-self' and 'perceptions of successful ageing' as informed by their ethnic/cultural understanding of ageing than the native white cohorts. They also held a different understanding of old-age dignity, where stepping into social roles such as grandmother discouraged them to do paid work outside the home. Nevertheless, it is widely acknowledged that specialised attention needs to be paid to 'religion', since it is no longer separate from culture and race and the nuances in its relationship with those other categories will help explore how racial profiles are created and applied within nations and states[1] (see Purkayastha, 2012).

As also mentioned above, there is counterevidence and arguments put forward by the secular feminists regarding inclusion of multi-faithism or a faith-focused lens. For instance, using evidence from their study on the United Kingdom's Southall Black Sisters (an ethnic minority feminist organisation), Dhaliwal and Patel (2012) advocated in favour of secular practices and non-inclusion of faith-focused research and policy. They argued that such an approach jeopardises the overall agenda of women's rights. The argument was based on evidence from their case studies research where women from all faiths preferred not to seek help from religious or faith-based organisations. However, one might argue that without understanding their 'Islamic' socio-community perspective, 'faith-free' secular solutions cannot be designed. Researchers, government and organisations need to work 'with' them and not 'without' or 'against' them; therefore, tailoring Islamic understanding to find solutions to their problems may be argued as the best way forward. These authors further argued that the UK government policies, laws and regulations are increasingly leaning towards associating and incorporating faith-based organisations and their views (especially, Muslim organisations). They opposed the funding of more and more of such organisations and argued that such actions are counterproductive for achieving women's freedom and rights. They stressed that a switch from multiculturalism to multi-faithism in the UK systems put other non-Muslim women's rights at risks. However, such arguments need to be further scrutinised in relation to Muslim women's embodied experiences since the bodily religious markers of Islamic attires place Muslim women in a unique highly visible position that other groups of women are not subject to making them easily identifiable as 'the other' as also argued above. There was strong evidence of this in the Greater Manchester-based study within work contexts where a 50-year-old first generation British Bangladeshi shared her embodied experiences vis-à-vis hijab at work. Her interview statements reflected the clear demarcation of race and religion within the UK society where she mentioned how many of her clients did not want her as their carer. She recalled how one of the clients used to lock the door behind her so that she could not steal anything and run away. She also faced racial abuse from that particular client when some [controversial political] news was being broadcast. The interviewee further went on to share how she complained about the issues to the office which responded to her saying that trust would have to be earned and that it would not come easy.

Non-Islamic feminist and secularist authors mostly argue in favour of using an intersectional approach to study (Muslim) women's lived experiences; for instance, Purkayastha (2012) suggested using a transnational intersectionality concept and taking transnationalism into account on a larger scale in social science research. Essers and Benschop (2009) used an intersectional lens of gender, religion and ethnicity to show the nature of agency at work in the negotiation process of identity and belonging for Muslim women who were entrepreneurs. These authors showed how 'the concept of intersectionality helps to clarify how identities in organisations are situationally, dialogically and dynamically constructed at different axes of oppression such as gender and ethnicity' (p. 418). In the field of organisation studies, too, intersectionality (Crenshaw, 1990) has been used not only to study Black women's subordinate positions but also other groups facing intersecting forms of oppression and marginalisation (Rodriguez, 2018; Rodriguez et al., 2016). However, Crenshaw's framework has been criticised for its lack of precision in explaining how to develop an analytical framework applying such a concept.

On the other hand, Islamic framings overly rely on the notions of modesty and piety and miss the point of religious patriarchy, that is, those attires which signify their belonging to a particular community, shift our focus from the substantial issues of patriarchal power culture to religion which has important and long-term implications for the Muslim women's work choices as well as their labour market participation and integration. Besides, such a lens for knowledge production also ignores the nuances of cultural variations in religious practices and traditions that affect the dualities in Muslim women's daily lived experiences in the West. Therefore, there still remains a need to place Muslim women's lives within the broader social perspectives and cultural contexts that account for structural inequalities surpassing the boundaries of gender and religion, and, of course, the borders of nation states. The intersection between gender and religion and its impact on Muslim women's work choices and decisions is debated and problematised further below to explore and understand some of the discourses and practices in the United Kingdom with regard to Muslim women's employment and career development with a specific focus on the struggle of embodiment (Mirza, 2012) and the modality of 'otherness' (Scharff, 2011).

Embodied Racial Identities and Ethnic Belongning: The Shaping of Labour Market Integration

The current literature is expansive on racial and ethnic identity politics (e.g. Anthias, 2008; Dwyer, 2000; Yuval-Davis, 2019); however, my focus will remain how religious identities play out in Muslim women's work and career through their bodily appearances (Siraj, 2011, 2012), and why their experiences remain unique

(Ahmad, 2003) to determine how to approach conceptually in understanding their positions in the wider Western societies and workplaces. Again, a substantial amount of work has been done on Muslim women's veiled identities, however, most of them have been done by migration scholars or ethnic geographers (Ahmad, 2003; Jawad & Benn, 2002; Mahmood, 2005; Mirza, 2013; Zine, 2002). In the field of work and employment, the literature still remains scant when it comes to Muslim women's work and career.

In reality, for Muslim women, both their gender and racial identities cannot be studied in isolation from 'religion' mainly because of their bodily markers of religious attires. Both in Islamic and predominantly non-Muslim cultures, the social status and public appearance of Muslim women are highly contested topics. For this discussion, I consider religion as an embedded social category that Muslim women embody and that such embodiment cuts across their other identities and agency to shape their integration with the Western society and its labour market. It also reinforces the 'othering' process and limits their social interactions and forms labour market inequalities or exclusion for them (Lewis, 1994; Modood et al., 1997; Mohammad, 1999). Some scholars argued that 'veiling' became a quintessential sign of women's oppression, essentialising their identities and that 'veil' was perceived as the symbol of gender inequality (Chakraborti & Zempi, 2012). Cooke (2008) took an intersectional approach to term Muslim women as 'Muslimwoman' to show their two identities as singular (an idea inspired by the terms 'blackwoman' and 'blackamerican' (Jackson, 2005)) and to label the saliency and visibility of such combined intersectional identities. Such visibility, of course, serves to marginalise Muslim women by making them 'easy to mark' and more vulnerable. On the contrary, Afshar (2012) argued that Muslim women lacked confidence and self-esteem despite being well-educated and articulate, overlooking the fact that Muslim women had to constantly redefine and negotiate their identities being placed within the over-lapping spheres of the Western society and the local ethnic community in Western settings (Zahedi, 2011). In the United Kingdom, a significant number of Muslim women remain out of the labour market or become irregular in wage work participation (DWP, 2021; Salway, 2007). These Muslim women are also pre-dominantly of South Asian heritage – the Pakistani and Bangladeshi groups from these diasporas also represent the majority of the Muslim population in the United Kingdom, and the women's groups have had persistent high unemploy-ment rates and economic inactivity (DWP, 2021). The race disparity audit report categorised these women as 'farthest from the labour market' and 'stay at home' groups (Cabinet Office, 2017). They are also more likely to be employed in the informal economy as well as domestic workers or care workers and caterer. More often than not, Muslim women encounter obstacles to successful integration such as discriminatory treatment in the labour market for being singled out as 'the other'. Their embodied experiences marked by their gender, racial and religious identities clearly indicate how the women's appearances can be a vantage point from which to examine their gendered career and how it is tangled differently for Muslim women.

I am also interested in exploring the power relations in employing such 'otherness' to Muslim women wearing Islamic attires, where power is clearly skewed to serve the interests of the Western employers and reinforce the patri-archal community culture. Whether it's crossing the borders of their homeland and venturing for new lives in the United Kingdom or being born in the United Kingdom in a Muslim family, not only these women grow up within the boundaries of religion and community, but they also encounter an extra layer of social boundary enforced by the 'othering process' (Ghumman & Ryan, 2013; Scharff, 2011) should they choose to or comply with religious and cultural tra-ditions of wearing a hijab or veil (Zempi, 2017). Such othering process label them socially as 'less desirable', 'an outsider' or 'the other', a process that does not cease but heightens when they enter into the world of work.

I present here some empirical evidence on this from the interviews conducted with South Asian British Muslim older women in the Greater Manchester area in the United Kingdom. The primary objectives of the study were to explore the wage work attitudes and labour market behaviour of those women in the UK labour market in the context of extended working lives for women. Data collected from 30 semi-structured interviews included life-long work trajectories/labour market experiences of those women. In their narratives, it was clear that there were variations in the levels of active efforts these women made towards labour market and social integration in the United Kingdom – some of them proactively sought and participated in wage work while some others did not make enough efforts for reasons explained below. Apart from their qualifications and language skills, one of the major barriers which deterred them from wage work was found to be 'the process of othering' in the UK labour market. The analysis showed that their efforts to integrate, participate and continue were significantly shaped by their 'othering'/embodied experiences in the UK society and labour market. All the interviewees wore ethnic and religious clothing in their everyday lives including at workplaces.

The findings of the study further showed that the cohort had firm and loyal community identities when categories of gender, religion, race and ethnicity intersected and these were expressed through the embodiment of cultural identi-ties, e.g. wearing ethnic clothing, preferring to work within the community and working jobs that were well within the boundaries of religious norms. These women felt more comfortable within the boundaries of the community since at the structural level, when their identities intersected, religious and racial identities preceded their gender identity in the UK workplaces leading to forms of labour market exclusion, including self-exclusion and self-withdrawal. These migrant Muslim women's workplace experiences reflected clear demarcation of race and religion within the UK society. More than one-third of the interviewees mentioned about their or their female family members' experiences of 'otherness' in the United Kingdom. For example, an interviewee stated in her interview how her daughter faced racial–religious abuses in the streets of Manchester where she was even pushed down on the pavement and abused by racial slurs. She further mentioned that over time, they internalised such experiences and started to believe they were 'the others'.

To further illustrate such demarcation, another interviewee account is presented here. This interviewee had been working as an elderly domiciliary carer – she shared her unique experience of 'othering' while attending to her duties of caring for an elderly person. In her account, the interviewee mentioned that she wore a 'burqa' (an Islamic dress covering the full body) to her work a couple of times when she first started working as a carer. She was wearing one too on the day of that particular event. She described that when the elderly person (a white British female) answered the door and found her standing outside, she froze in horror. The interviewee could see the fear of the 'unknown' on the face of the elderly female and the hesitation to let her inside the house. When she explained the reason why she was there, the woman insulted her by making derogatory remarks about her Islamic clothing and her religion and asked her to leave. She no longer wore a 'burqa' to work.

This particular account is helpful to understand and examine the embedded nature of exclusionary racial practices prevalent within the UK society. The social othering process and racial segregation within the society also extended to and were experienced by other female family members as stated by several other interviewees. However, such segregation and exclusion did not demoralise or discourage them in any way to stop wearing those extra layers of clothing. This simultaneously shows how these women used religious/ethnic clothing as cultural tools to show a form of resistance and agency through bodily appearances. For example, one interviewee mentioned how she always preferred to work within the community simply because she could wear ethnic clothing which made her feel more comfortable and confident. The following section further elaborates on such agency and how that shapes Muslim women's labour market participation and work choices.

Religiosity as Agency: Negotiating Work Choices and Decisions

We now turn our attention to Muslim women's agency here. As also argued above, Muslim women's agency issues need to be problematised further because of its unaccountable positioning within religion, gender and culture (Abu-Lughod, 2002; Ahmad, 2003; Vanzan, 2016). Indeed, scholars such as Mignolo (2011) continue debating decolonisation or de-Islamisation of their work choices while several others have used the Islamic feminist lens to study Muslim women's agency (e.g. Wadud, 1999). But we must recognise how Muslim women express their agency through religiosity as researchers call for changing the narratives of victimisation, giving more power to their voices, and recognising their agency (Ahmad, 2003; Vanzan, 2016).

Begum (2008) argued that agency is often lost in the process of focusing too much on the intersections of religion and culture. In her study, she used 'space' as a means to explore identity negotiation by young Bengali women in the east end of London where Islamised culture was a highly prominent theme and women living in that area used religion as a tool to negotiate, oppose and challenge the gendered space. The accounts she reported in her research showed inner conflicts relating to national and religious identity and belonging, but they also showed some agency. Mahmood (2005, 2011), on the other hand, sought to understand Muslim women's agency in living the embodied experiences through the lens of 'acts of piety' which would mean embodying religious identities by wearing Islamic/modest clothing or through practising religious (Islamic) rituals in daily lives while living in the Western societies that some may construe as symbols of resistance (Afshar, 1998) or expressions of agency. Further, Lovat et al. (2013) in their study on Muslim women in Australia found that Muslim women negotiated their agency through gendered religiosity (the gendered aspect of religiosity where women are more religious or at least display more adherence to religious norms than men) – these scholars used the term 'embedded agency' to describe such form of negotiations of agency. They also presented evidence that Muslim women believed they were highly visible in social spaces because of wearing ethnic and religious dresses, therefore, they tended to be more careful about how they represented their community and religion. The authors further argued that although in modern Australia these women felt emancipated to some extent and were aware of their equal rights to some extent, such awareness and feelings were still filtered through their Islamic beliefs and identities that toned down their voice and agency. The barriers created through the embodiment of their intersectional racial, gender and ethnic identities were heavily influenced by their sense of religiosity. They were ready to participate/integrate with the labour market only if they could reconcile with the cultural differences. The key is to understand how they use their agency and show resistance to Western workplace practices by avoiding clashes with their religious traditions and cultures. In addition, contexts play a crucial role in the articulation and expression of Muslim women's agency (McMichael, 2002).

The debates and conflicts around the issues and interplays between structure and agency are of another importance here. Away from reproducing the popular discourse and following the scholarly conventions, perhaps, we need an alternative approach to further the debates and analysis of those issues. The Greater Manchester study evidence showed that the cohort's gendered and Islamised work choices and decisions were less temporal which can be attributed to both their religious agency as well as wider social/labour market choices available to them. Their labour market integration and career trajectories did not follow linear patterns either. A host of barriers and enablers concerning the entry, integration and progression in the labour market were identified in the course of the empirical research including language barriers, outdated skills and extensive caring responsibilities throughout their life courses, among others. However, in the matter of displaying religious agency, these women consciously avoided certain types of work (e.g. bar jobs, customer-facing retail jobs) due to religious restrictions around alcohol consumption or meeting stranger men. Further, even in care work, some of the interviewees felt discouraged in caring for elderly males and preferred to care for females only, simply to conform with religious norms. The nature of jobs (e.g. take part in unpaid/charitable work more for attaining piety), environment of the workplaces (not having too many men around) and even the hours of work were matters of religious considerations for these women. Not only that, the male members of their families also played a central role in shaping those choices where every decision these women made was subject to approvals from their husbands/father-in-law/brothers.

I have already illustrated cases of the embodied religious experiences by Muslim women at both the United Kingdom's societal and structural (labour market) levels using examples of social exclusion and occupational segregation. There was further evidence in the Greater Manchester study that religion played out as a tool for legitimising the patriarchal structure at the family unit and community level which shaped the interviewees' agency and wage work attitudes, and also determined their level of overall integration with the UK labour market.

Embodied Presence at Work: Understanding the Transnational Dynamics

I have already established that we cannot ignore 'religion' as a constitutive element of embodied and lived experiences of Muslim women of colour (see Kabir, 2006). However, there are concerns regarding the role, scope and functions of religion in the appearances and experiences of Muslim women as intermediary agents. We have also seen how these concerns are amplified in the context of their work trajectories. Bhopal (1997) proposed in her work on South Asian women living in East London that there is a dichotomy of two types of South Asian women: traditional women vs highly independent women (who are successful) – she highlighted that to be successful and independent, South Asian women had to turn their back on culture and traditions and communities and become 'deviant women' (Bhopal, 1997). Such deviant women would pay less attention to 'cultural appropriateness' of 'obeying' their men and not 'overstepping' the community boundaries. Hence, we may argue that there are cultural tethering and dynamics at play in their embodiment that may or may not always work in their favour. According to Tariq and Syed (2017), the forms of sexism and racism that Muslim women face in the West are 'subtle and hard-to-prove'. In their study, they showed how Muslim women navigate the structural and societal process using their own agency, strategies (e.g. identifying a mentor to guide them or attending additional training courses) and ethnic group networks when it comes to leadership and employment. However, they also identified that intersectional inequities (arising from the intersections of gender, ethnicity, religion and family status) permeate from the societal context to the work, employment and leadership contexts, limiting Muslim women's career progression and prospects – for instance, evidence was presented of gender stereotyping by men from their own ethnicity at work. Further, there was evidence of Muslim women being discriminated at the interview stage as they were asked about their marital status and motherhood more often which may be attributed to employers' assumptions that Muslim women would leave employment soon after they get married (Dale & Ahmed, 2008; Dale, Shaheen, et al., 2002). These study findings mostly corroborated other scholarly research evidence on these groups' labour market integration and it was reiterated how particular cultural barriers for Muslim women from the Pakistani and Bangladeshi ethnic groups in the United Kingdom including patriarchal religious barriers such as lack of encouragement from families for participating in wage work both before and after marriage impede their work and career progression. However, these scholars also argued that religious agency or cultural barriers alone did not shape these women's work career, particularly for the younger age group who had higher human capital and that there might be generational differences in their behavioural patterns, although we find little evidence of this in recent labour market statistics as explained earlier (DWP, 2021). Therefore, we should be cautiously optimistic about their wage work participation despite the young groups' increased interests in education and exercising self-agency which may be thwarted by their inability to overcome the dual struggles of ethnic penalty in the labour market and patriarchal religious norms within their homes and communities.

The Greater Manchester study showed that some interviewees perceived that the quintessential identity of a Bengali or a Pakistani woman was a saree or salwar kameez and indeed made conscious choices around what to wear, expressing a sense of agency (albeit shaped by cultural norms). However, for most of them, it was part of their natural/cultural being – a carryover from their culture from which they could not separate subconsciously. The interviewees who made conscious decisions about their clothing either stated that they felt more comfortable wearing them or it stirred a sense of pride in them as being able to express their cultural identity. As for those who could not distinguish between agency and norms, they merely 'obeyed' their husbands' decisions made for them, of not wearing Western clothing. These women also chose their workplaces based on their freedom of choice around what to wear at work, for example, choosing to remain within their cultural bubble and work for community organisations or Muslim employers only.

Conclusion

This chapter has presented a relatively brief overview of how British Muslim women's embodied religious, ethnic and racial identities in the form of bodily appearances play out in their lived experiences within the Western workplace and career contexts. I particularly focused on specific lines of inquiry, for instance, how British Muslim women wearing ethnic or religious dresses navigated UK workplaces and how their embodied intersectional religious or ethnic identities not only played a central role in shaping their labour market integration process but also in limiting their work choices. In summary, there is strong support in the current literature and empirical evidence of how gendered religious embodiment might be more complex phenomena for Muslim women in a Western context. However, Islamic framings overly rely on the notions of modesty and piety and miss the point of religious patriarchy in those debates. Besides, such a lens for knowledge production also ignores the nuances of cultural variations in religious practices and traditions that affect the transnational lives of British Muslim women. Such debates not only remind us of the differences in analytical focuses studying women's issues between Western vs Islamic feminism but also urges us to re-conceptualise the labour market inequalities through a new cross-border, cross-cultural and cross-ethnic prisms.

Muslim women's embodied religious and ethnic identities are directly linked to the process of 'othering' and 'otherness' in the West, leading to create significant barriers to their overall labour market integration process, which in turn impacts their long-term career development through limiting work choices. Conversely, the religious boundaries narrowing down their work choices (e.g. bar and retail jobs) is also an indicator of expressions of their religious agency and their resistance to change. Together, these impact their long-term career prospects and trap them within the margins of a selected few professions or keep them out of the labour market.

The particular gender aspects, when positioned within and across the religious boundaries, place these women differently not only at the intersections of systems and structures but also within the hierarchies and across multiple intersecting levels of society, community and state. The empirical evidence presented on the labour market experiences of ethnic minority Muslim women from the Global South settling into the Western societies whose identities are at the intersections of age, class, race/ethnicity, gender and religion showed that a lack of sophistication in religious focus within the field of work and employment research needs to be addressed. Although the Islamic feminist lens studying Muslim women shows how religion as a cultural construct and an organising principle of society may have saliency in the wider social integration process for Muslim women, work and career research on Muslim women in the West require far more dedicated attention to their embodied burdens of otherness and their impact on these women's career and work choices. Secular framings fail to recognise the very specific issue of religious agency Muslim women consciously display in their daily lives particularly through their bodily appearances and the nuances of the relations between religiosity and gender.

One might argue, perhaps, comparing within the group differences will provide us with more clarity in understanding, e.g. how is it different for Muslim women who do not wear religious or ethnic clothing at Western workplaces? Therefore, future research needs to do more comparative studies to assess the role of religion in terms of non-hijabi vs hijabi women, which is non-existent in the current literature. Scholars also need to look beyond the ongoing debates on Muslim women's positions within society and state as victims and understand what those extra modest layers of clothing mean for Muslim women and how such representation and embodiment shape their career in the West. The goals need to be set now by scholars, of embedding 'embodiment' as a process and using it as a part of mainstream research on (Muslim) women's work and career.

Note: The Greater Manchester study from which the empirical data have been retrieved was funded by 'Just Work in Greater Manchester' project of the Work and Equalities Institute, Alliance Manchester Business School, The University of Manchester.[2]

Notes

1. In favour of her arguments, Purkayastha (2012) cited examples and evidence presented in Collins' (2010) work on how Muslims have been targeted by the US Homeland Security.
2. https://www.alliancembs.manchester.ac.uk/research/funded-projects/alliance-projects/just-work-in-greater-manchester/

References

Abu-Lughod, L. (2002). Do Muslim women really need saving? Anthropological reflections on cultural relativism and its others. *American Anthropologist, 104*(3), 783–790.

Afshar, H. (1998). Introduction: Women and empowerment—Some illustrative studies. In *Women and empowerment* (pp. 1–10). Palgrave Macmillan.

Afshar, H. (2012). *Muslim women in West Yorkshire growing up with real and imaginary values amidst conflicting views of self and society* (pp. 135–156). Taylor & Francis.

Ahmad, F. (2003). Still 'in progress?' – Methodological dilemmas, tensions and contradictions in theorizing South Asian Muslim women. In N. Puwar & P. Raghuram (Eds.), *South Asian Women in the diaspora* (pp. 43–66). Bloomsbury Academic. https://doi.org/10.5040/9781474215558.ch-003. Accessed on July 19, 2022.

Anthias, F. (2008). Thinking through the lens of translocational positionality: An intersectionality frame for understanding identity and belonging. *Translocations: Migration and social change, 4*(1), 5–20.

Begum, H. (2008). Geographies of inclusion/exclusion: British Muslim women in the East End of London. *Sociological Research Online, 13*(5), 91–101.

Bhopal, K. (1997, July). South Asian women within households: Dowries, degradation and despair. In *Women's studies international forum* (Vol. 20, No. 4, pp. 483–492). Pergamon.

Brah, A. (1996). *Cartographies of diaspora: Contesting identities* (1st ed.). Routledge. https://doi.org/10.4324/9780203974919

Bullock, K. (2002). *Rethinking Muslim women and the veil: Challenging historical & modern stereotypes.* IIIT.

Cabinet Office. (2017). Race disparity audit. https://assets.publishing.service.gov.uk/government/uploads/system/uploads/attachment_data/file/686071/Revised_RDA_report_March_2018.pdf. Accessed on July 03, 2021.

Chakraborti, N., & Zempi, I. (2012). The veil under attack: Gendered dimensions of Islamophobic victimization. *International Review of Victimology, 18*(3), 269–284.

Collins, S. (2010). The complexity of identity: Appreciating multiplicity and intersectionality. *Culture-Infused Counselling,* 247–258.

Cooke, M. (2008). Deploying the muslimwoman. *Journal of Feminist Studies in Religion, 24*(1), 91–99.

Crenshaw, K. (1990). Mapping the margins: Intersectionality, identity politics, and violence against women of color. *Stanford Law Review, 43*, 1241.

Dale, A., & Ahmed, S. (2008). Pakistani and Bangladeshi women's labour market participation. *CCSR Paper, 1*, 1–25.

Dale, A., Fieldhouse, E., Shaheen, N., & Kalra, V. (2002). The labour market prospects for Pakistani and Bangladeshi women. *Work, Employment & Society, 16*(1), 5–25.

Dale, A., Shaheen, N., Kalra, V., & Fieldhouse, E. (2002). Routes into education and employment for young Pakistani and Bangladeshi women in the UK. *Ethnic and Racial Studies, 25*(6), 942–968.

Dhaliwal, S., & Patel, P. (2012). Feminism in the shadow of multi-faithism: Implications for South Asian women in the UK. In *New south Asian feminisms: Paradoxes and possibilities* (pp. 169–188). Zed Books.

DWP. (2021). Unemployment. https://www.ethnicity-facts-figures.service.gov.uk/work-pay-and-benefits/unemployment-and-economic-inactivity/unemployment/latest. Accessed on March 16, 2021.

Dwyer, C. (1997). Contested identities: Challenging dominant representations of young British Muslim women. In T. Skelton & G. Valentine (Eds.), *Cool places: Geographies of youth cultures* (pp. 50–65). Routledge.

Dwyer, C. (1999). Veiled meanings: Young British Muslim women and the negotiation of differences [1]. *Gender, Place and Culture: A Journal of Feminist Geography, 6*(1), 5–26.

Dwyer, C. (2000, July). Negotiating diasporic identities: Young British South Asian Muslim women. In *Women's studies international forum* (Vol. 23, No. 4, pp. 475–486). Pergamon.

Esack, F. (2015). Islam, feminism and empire: A comparison between the approaches of Amina Wadud and Saba Mahmood. *Journal of Gender and Religion in Africa, 21*(1), 27–48.

Essers, C., & Benschop, Y. (2009). Muslim businesswomen doing boundary work: The negotiation of Islam, gender and ethnicity within entrepreneurial contexts. *Human Relations, 62*(3), 403–423.

Ghumman, S., & Ryan, A. M. (2013). Not welcome here: Discrimination towards women who wear the Muslim headscarf. *Human Relations, 66*(5), 671–698.

Heath, A., & Martin, J. (2013). Can religious affiliation explain 'ethnic' inequalities in the labour market? *Ethnic and Racial Studies, 36*(6), 1005–1027.

Jackson, S. A. (2005). *Islam and the Blackamerican: Looking toward the third resurrection.* Oxford University Press on Demand.

Jawad, H., & Benn, T. (2002). *Muslim women in the United Kingdom and beyond: Experiences and images.* Brill.

Kabir, N. (2006). Muslims in a 'White Australia': Colour or religion? *Immigrants & Minorities, 24*(2), 193–223.

Lewis, P. (1994). *Islamic Britain: Religion, politics, and identity among British Muslims: Bradford in the 1990s.* IB Tauris & Company.

Lovat, T., Nilan, P., Hosseini, S. H., Samarayi, I., Mansfield, M. M., & Alexander, W. (2013). Australian Muslim jobseekers: Equal employment opportunity and equity in the labor market. *Journal of Muslim Minority Affairs, 33*(4), 435–450.

Mahmood, S. (2005). Feminist theory, agency, and the liberatory subject. *On Shifting Ground: Muslim Women in the Global Era, 111,* 141.

Mahmood, S. (2011). *Politics of piety.* Princeton University Press.

McMichael, C. (2002). 'Everywhere is Allah's place': Islam and the everyday life of Somali women in Melbourne, Australia. *Journal of Refugee Studies, 15*(2), 171–188.

Mignolo, W. D. (2011). *The darker side of Western modernity*. Duke University Press.

Mirza, H. S. (2012). Multiculturalism and the gender gap: The visibility and invisibility of Muslim women in Britain. In *Muslims in Britain* (pp. 129–149). Routledge.

Mirza, H. S. (2013, January). A second skin': Embodied intersectionality, transnationalism and narratives of identity and belonging among Muslim women in Britain. In *Women's studies international forum*. (Vol. 36, pp. 5–15). Pergamon.

Modood, T., Berthoud, R., Lakey, J., Nazroo, J., Smith, P., Virdee, S., & Beishon, S. (1997). *Ethnic minorities in Britain: Diversity and disadvantage* (No. 843). Policy Studies Institute.

Mohammad, R. (1999). Marginalisation, Islamism and the production of the 'other's' 'other'. *Gender, Place & Culture: A Journal of Feminist Geography*, 6(3), 221–240.

Purkayastha, B. (2012). Intersectionality in a transnational world. *Gender & Society*, 26(1), 55–66.

Rodriguez, J. K. (2018). Intersectionality and qualitative research. In *The Sage handbook of qualitative business and management research methods* (p. 429). Sage Publications Ltd.

Rodriguez, J. K., Holvino, E., Fletcher, J. K., & Nkomo, S. M. (2016). The theory and praxis of intersectionality in work and organisations: Where do we go from here? *Gender, Work and Organization*, 23(3), 201–222.

Ryan, L. (2008). Navigating the emotional terrain of families "here" and "there": Women, migration and the management of emotions. *Journal of Intercultural Studies*, 29(3), 299–313.

Salway, S. M. (2007). Economic activity among UK Bangladeshi and Pakistani women in the 1990s: Evidence for continuity or change in the family resources survey. *Journal of Ethnic and Migration Studies*, 33(5), 825–847.

Scharff, C. (2011). Disarticulating feminism: Individualization, neoliberalism and the othering of 'Muslim women'. *European Journal of Women's Studies*, 18(2), 119–134.

Siraj, A. (2011). Meanings of modesty and the hijab amongst Muslim women in Glasgow, Scotland. *Gender, Place & Culture*, 18(6), 716–731.

Siraj, A. (2012). 'Smoothing down ruffled feathers': The construction of Muslim women's feminine identities. *Journal of Gender Studies*, 21(2), 185–199.

Skeggs, B. (1997). *Formations of class & gender: Becoming respectable* (pp. 1–200). Formations of Class & Gender.

Tariq, M., & Syed, J. (2017). Intersectionality at work: South Asian Muslim women's experiences of employment and leadership in the United Kingdom. *Sex Roles*, 77(7), 510–522.

Vanzan, A. (2016). Veiled politics: Muslim women's visibility and their use in European countries' political life. *Social Sciences*, 5(2), 21.

Wadud, A. (1999). *Qur'an and woman: Rereading the sacred text from a woman's perspective*. Oxford University Press.

Wadud, A. (2013). Inside the gender jihad: Women's reform in Islam. *Praktyka teoretyczna*, (08), 249–262.

Werbner, P. (2007). Veiled interventions in pure space: Honour, shame and embodied struggles among Muslims in Britain and France. *Theory, Culture & Society*, 24(2), 161–186.

Yuval-Davis, N. (2019). *Identity politics and women's ethnicity* (pp. 408–424). Routledge.

Zahedi, A. (2011). Muslim American women in the post-11 September era: Challenges and opportunities. *International Feminist Journal of Politics, 13*(2), 183–203.

Zempi, I. (2017). Researching victimisation using auto-ethnography: Wearing the Muslim veil in public. *Methodological Innovations, 10*(1). https://doi.org/10.1177/2059799117720617

Zine, J. (2002). Muslim women and the politics of representation. *American Journal of Islam and Society, 19*(4), 1–22.

Chapter 7

Dress Codes in a 'Singular They' World: Gender Nonbinary Identity and Expression and Employer Appearance Policies

Todd Brower

Abstract

Anyone who has recently watched television or movies can tell you that transgender, gender nonbinary or gender expansive people are becoming more visible in these media. This trend reflects the reality that younger generations are increasingly identifying with more fluid and nonbinary gender and sexual identities and are progressively expressing those identities in a more flexible and changing manner (Herman et al., 2022; Wilson & Meyer, 2021). Unsurprisingly then, those individuals are also more visible at work, including in workplaces with employer-mandated dress codes. Indeed, in 2020 the US Supreme Court decided a case involving a transgender woman, Aimee Stephens, who was fired because her employer, a funeral home, required her to conform to its gender-binary dress policy and wear clothing mandatory for people assigned male at birth, rather than appropriate for her female gender identity (*Bostock v. Clayton County*, 2020).

However, as the description of Aimee Stephens's own experience illustrates, often these employer appearance codes are based on a binary and fixed conception of gender and gender identity and expression at odds with the increasing number of workers who do not identify within those rigid parameters. Moreover, even when an employee, like Aimee Stephens herself, could have fit within her employer's dress code, the improper application of that policy to her, or employer concerns about customer or co-worker discomfort with an employee's appearance under the policy may mean that a worker's identity and expression may still conflict with a workplace appearance code. For gender nonbinary or nonconforming individuals, these complications are magnified.

The Emerald Handbook of Appearance in the Workplace, 131–154

Copyright © 2024 by Emerald Publishing Limited

All rights of reproduction in any form reserved

doi:10.1108/978-1-80071-174-720230008

This chapter explores the practical problems and barriers that employer dress codes have on employees whose gender identity and/or presentation move beyond the traditional male/female binary. Using insights from queer theory, gender expansive employees serve to interrogate fundamental assumptions behind workplace dress policies and the formal and informal ways in which these policies are policed. The chapter will explore that discordance, examine possible employer resolutions, and evaluate the strengths and weaknesses of those responses.

Keywords: Transgender; gender expansive; law; discrimination; dress code; professional; career

Introduction

Anyone who has recently watched television or movies can tell you that transgender, gender nonbinary[1] or gender expansive people are becoming more visible in these media. This trend reflects the reality that younger generations are increasingly identifying with more fluid and nonbinary gender and sexual identities and are progressively expressing those identities in a more flexible and changing manner (Herman et al., 2022; Jones, 2018; Wilson & Meyer, 2021). Unsurprisingly then, these individuals are also more visible at work, including in workplaces with employer-mandated dress codes. Indeed, in 2020, the United States Supreme Court decided a case involving a transgender woman, Aimee Stephens, who was fired because her employer, a funeral home, required her to conform to its gender-binary dress policy and wear clothing mandatory for people assigned male at birth, rather than appropriate for her female gender identity (*Bostock v. Clayton County*, 2020). The Court relied on the ordinary public meaning of the statute to hold that the prohibition on negative employment actions 'because of sex' included actions taken on the basis of an employee's sexual orientation or gender identity. In so doing, the Court sidestepped the arguments raised in the lower courts that grappled more with some underlying assumptions behind the various arguments even as it ignored others.

The intermediate appellate court recapped the issue:

> The Funeral Home nevertheless argues that it has not violated Title VII because sex stereotyping is barred only when "the employer's reliance on stereotypes ... result[s] in disparate treatment of employees because they are either male or female." According to the Funeral Home, an employer does not engage in impermissible sex stereotyping when it requires its employees to conform to a sex-specific dress code – as it purportedly did here by requiring Stephens to abide by the dress code designated for the Funeral Home's male employees – because such a policy "impose [s] equal burdens on men and women," and thus does not single

out an employee for disparate treatment based on that employee's sex.

(EEOC v. R.G. & G.R. Harris Funeral Homes, Inc., 2017, p. 572)

The intermediate court's summary raises several points relevant to this chapter. First, gender identity – how one internally conceives of their[2] gender – is different from gender presentation – how one expresses their gender to others. Second, no one, neither the employer, employee, nor court, questioned the fundamental view of gender as binary or allowing a dress code to incorporate that division. Third, the impact and workplace consequences of dress codes on transgender and gender expansive people depends on how and how much gender binaries inhere in an appearance code as well as on the gender expansiveness or conformity of the persons on whom it is imposed. Finally, it is important not to focus solely on the appearance code itself but also to interrogate the formal and informal mechanisms of jobsite implementation and enforcement.

This chapter explores the practical problems and barriers that employer dress codes have on employees whose gender identity and/or presentation move beyond the traditional male/female binary. The chapter also examines the strengths and weakness of some proposed solutions and suggests why the problem is not amenable to simple resolution.

Theory and Concepts

Disaggregating Sex, Gender Identity, Gender Expression and Sexual Orientation

Fig. 1 illustrates four different dimensions or spectra on which people may vary.

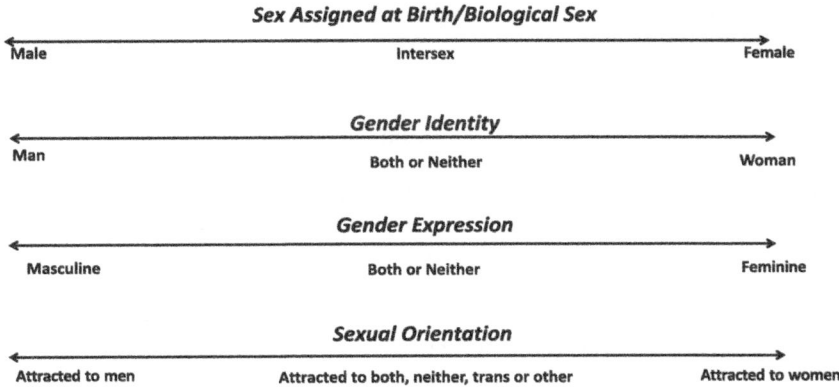

Fig. 1.   Disaggregating Sex Assigned at Birth, Gender Identity,
Gender Expression, and Sexual Orientation.
Source: © Todd Brower 2019.

The first is biological sex: the sex one is assigned at birth, usually based on genitalia and/or chromosomes. One can be assigned male, female or be born intersex with ambiguous genitalia. Biological sex is different from the second dimension, gender identity: whether one identifies as male, female, both, neither or somewhere along that second spectrum. Further, those two spectra are not only different from each other but also from the third dimension, gender expression or presentation. Gender expression is how one performs gender through clothing, make-up, hairstyles, behaviours, tone of voice (Butler, 1990) – all characteristics that may be seen as masculine, feminine, both, neither, or ambiguous from a traditionally gendered perspective. Gender expression may be linked to gender identity and/or to sex assigned at birth, but it is distinct from it. Those distinctions are not always recognised in western societies that typically aggregate sex assigned at birth, gender identity, and gender expression. However, other societies differentiate among them (Butler, 1990; Dietert & Dentice, 2009; Köllen, 2016; Pruden & Edmo, 2016).

As Butler (1990) and others have recognised, gender is neither yoked to biological sex, nor is gender identity binary. Individuals may identify at intermediate points on that dimension or entirely off of it. Terminology reflects this variation. A transgender person's gender identity is inconsistent with that assigned at birth; a cisgender person's gender identity and sex assigned at birth are congruently aligned (Köllen, 2016; Moleiro & Pinto, 2015). Some transgender persons are gender-binary; they see themselves as either a man or a woman. Within that gender binary cohort, some transgender people do not identity as transgender after their transition while others do so (Dietert & Dentice, 2009; Drescher & Pula, 2019).[3] Independent of the transgender and cisgender axis, both trans- and cisgender people can reject a binary view of gender and view themselves as having a nonbinary or more fluid gender identity (Wilson & Meyer, 2021). Thus, it is important to maintain the separation among these identities even as we recognise their overlap. These distinctions play a significant role in how dress codes affect transgender and gender nonbinary employees in the workplace and how effective proposed solutions will be.

Theoretical discussions of gender identity and expression abound (Blair & Hoskin, 2015; Goffman, 1959; Lather, 1992; Schep, 2012; Schilt & Westbrook, 2009; West & Zimmerman, 1987).[4] Drawing upon queer theory, which posits that identities, including gender, are unstable and variable (Seidman, 1996; Stein & Plummer, 1996), this chapter takes as a baseline that identities can be fluid and seeks to illuminate how fluidity in identity and its expression interact with the predominantly binary nature of employer appearance codes and the gender differentiations they incorporate.

Gender nonbinary individuals resolve gender identity and expression in complex ways (Fogarty & Zheng, 2018; Richards et al., 2016). One person with a fluid identity said:

> For me it's about having a nonbinary gender identity which essentially means my own sense of gender fluctuates. Some days I feel more masculine, some days more feminine. Some days this

varies by the hour. Some days it is so strong that my gender presentation is completely out of synch with my identity. Other days it is far less so and my gender presentation is more in line with my identity. There is no rhyme or reason to it and it is unpredictable.

(Valentine, 2016, p. 14)

Two other gender nonbinary individuals with fixed identities stated:

#1: My gender identity of genderqueer is fixed. My feelings about how that presents change on a regular basis and the presentation can be quite different, leading to external confusion.

#2: It's the same day-to-day (just slightly more to the feminine side of the centre of the gender spectrum, though I was AMAB [Assigned Male At Birth]). How I choose to express that varies. Sometimes I wish to look more masculine or feminine, but it's more like 'ooh, I haven't worn that item in my wardrobe for a while' rather than I need to wear something to better capture my identity.

(Valentine, 2016, p. 15)

These gender expansive individuals' self-descriptions explain their choices to reconcile or uncouple gender identity from gender presentation or expression. Accordingly, gender expansiveness can describe any combination of identity and/ or presentation (Factor & Rothblum, 2008; Kuper et al., 2012) as the quotes from Valentine (2016, pp. 14–15) show. One can be male-identified but express their gender with some or all female-designated clothing. Or someone may identify as gender expansive despite how they present that identity. Additionally, gender expression need not be fixed but vary over time or differ based on which aspects of gender expression the presenter chooses to emphasise (Köllen, 2016; Sawyer et al., 2016).

In contrast to the fluidity possible in individuals' own identity, social construction of gender is often created as fixed. Gender and gender identity are significant components of societal development (Dietert & Dentice, 2009). From early childhood they are composed through and for social interaction to create an oppositional binary of male/female (West & Zimmerman, 1987). Thus, gender binarism becomes rooted in social institutions like family, schools, and workplaces. That binarism is operationalised and cemented through gender performances and behaviours like clothing choice, participation in gender-segregated facilities and institutions, and sometimes through professional and leisure activities (Dietert & Dentice, 2009). Thus, gender expression is not exclusively within the control of the presenter; others may read it differently than intended by the individual (Brower, 2009).

Finally, the fourth facet or dimension, sexual orientation, is unrelated to, and not determined by, how someone identifies on the other spectra. Transgender or gender expansive individuals can be sexually and emotionally attracted to and have relationships with people of the same gender (lesbian or gay), of different genders (heterosexual or straight), of some combination of the preceding (bisexual, pansexual, queer, etc.), or neither (asexual) (Herman, 2016; Kuper et al., 2012).

Although these four dimensions are distinct and independent, employers, colleagues and others often conflate them and/or use an individual's position on one continuum to assign that individual a location on other spectra. For example, in *Doe v. City of Belleville* (1997), a male, heterosexual teen was harassed by his co-workers. They called Doe 'queer' and 'fag', referred to him as their 'bitch' and sexually molested him because they misconstrued his gender expression – his physical appearance, hair length, earring, and demeanour – to signal both femininity and gayness. The *Doe* court rejected the argument that this was nonactionable sexual orientation discrimination. It said, 'a man who is harassed because his voice is soft, his physique is slight, his hair long, or because in some other respect he exhibits masculinity in a way that does not meet his co-workers' idea of how men are to appear and behave, is harassed "because of his sex"' (*Doe v. City of Belleville.*, 1997, p. 581). LGBTQ people can also conflate these four different dimensions, sometimes deliberately. One researcher reported that some nontransgender, binarily identified lesbians use masculine gender expression as a tool to signal sexual orientation or other derivative sub-group identities (Reddy-Best, 2018).

Although the *Doe* court ruled for the plaintiff on the sex discrimination claim, its sex stereotype discussion assumed gender was fundamentally binary: men are different from women and are expected to appear that way. Indeed, the same court specifically concluded that it was not statutory sex discrimination for employers to maintain traditionally iterated gender-differentiated appearance rules (*Carroll v. Talman Savings and Loan Ass'n*, 1979). Nevertheless, in *Carroll*, the court properly differentiated sexual orientation from gender identity and expression. That distinction is also crucial in this chapter. Accordingly, although dress codes can affect lesbian, gay, bisexual and queer people (Brower, 2013) and transgender individuals (Jones, 2013), this chapter will concentrate on the interactions that those employer requirements have on gender expansive individuals, and on where they position themselves on gender identity and gender expression continua regardless of their sexual orientation.

Dress Codes

Dress codes serve many functions for employers (Brower, 2013; Middlemiss, 2018). One important reason for appearance standards is to enhance or maintain an employer's external image and/or meet customer expectations or perceived expectations (Hatzipanagos, 2021; Middlemiss, 2018). What is viewed as 'appropriate attire' in a given workplace embodies diverse meanings and expectations connected to employee status and/or organisational values (Pratt & Rafaeli, 1997). Accordingly, those decisions can affect an employee's status, career trajectory, and organisational acceptance (Dietert & Dentice, 2009; Schilt & Connell, 2007).

Further, norms are part of workplace structure and regulation. This includes the prevailing norm of collegiality and collaboration in teams and professional workspaces. Employers ordinarily expect that employees will get along with each other and work with, not against, each other (Langevoort, 2004). Dress codes integrate and reinforce these norms since they police how people perform their identity at work (Brower, 2013) – sometimes very concretely through uniforms or stringent appearance codes, at other times less formally. Accordingly, conformity/nonconformity to these policies in an employee's gender identity and gender expression performances indicate much more than illustrations of conventional gender identity or expression. They operate as stand-ins or demonstrations of agreement to workplace norms and are keys into organisational structures (Brower, 2013).

Unsurprisingly then, Pratt and Rafaeli (1997) suggest that employees frequently experience tension between wanting to conform to workplace appearance norms and thus assimilate to shared identity and desiring to assert a sense of self and individuality. This dissonance between workplace appearance demands and self-expression may be a common work experience, including for cisgender people or those who present in a traditionally gendered manner but who resist the appearance code present in their workplace (Hatzipanagos, 2021). Nevertheless, that conflict is magnified when gender dysphoria or gender nonbinarism confront employer-mandated dress codes. Accordingly, that conflict between the workplace and societal demands for binarily gendered conformity that appearance codes encapsulate, and an employee's need for expression and communication of authentic selfhood underlies the various challenges that gender expansive individuals face on the job. The resulting problem of accommodating conflicting employee needs with employers' workplace requirements is the central issue in this chapter.

For purposes of this chapter, we can divide dress codes into two basic types: gender-neutral or gender-differentiated policies. A gender-neutral appearance code applies to all persons regardless of gender: for example, black collared shirt and black trousers (*Narjes v. Absolute Health Servs.*, 2018), no jeans or sleeveless shirts (*Doud v. Yellow Cab of Reno*, 2015), conservative business attire (*McCormick v. Festiva Grp*, 2010). This group may include uniforms (Aspinall, 2017), and professional status markers like white coats for doctors (Petrilli et al., 2018) or suits for lawyers (Jones, 2013).

All male/female differentiated standards are encompassed within the second type. For example, women can wear any hairstyle, men must have short hair (*Willingham v. Macon Tel. Publ'g Co.*, 1975); women must wear prescribed 'career ensembles', men wear 'business attire' (*Carroll v. Talman Fed. Savings and Loan Ass'n*, 1979); women are expected to wear make-up, men cannot (*Jespersen v. Harrah's Operating Co.*, 2006). Gendered workplace dress codes and expectations sustain traditional binary discourses of gender and sexuality, and sometimes class (Brower, 2013) or race/ethnicity (Hatzipanagos, 2021). Skidmore (1999) examined a female only nurse's cap requirement in the United Kingdom. This visible marker distinguished female nurses from both doctors and male nursing colleagues and thus delegitimatized both their gender and status.

Gendered dress codes can also undermine women's workplace standing by highlighting attractiveness instead of competence (Brower, 2013; Dellinger & Williams, 1997; Hall, 1993). Sexualised dress for female employees has a long, often-uncontested history in retail and food service industries (Danovich, 2016; *Jespersen v. Harrah's Operating Co.*, 2006). Traditional, binary notions of gender and heteronormativity shape those policies notably when an employer uses female employees' sexuality as a marketing tool. In *Wilson v. Southwest Airlines* (1981), the airline argued that its business success with a predominantly male clientele depended on only hiring female flight attendants and outfitting them in revealing clothing. Attractive female flight attendants personified the airline's sexy image and fulfilled its advertising promise to take passengers skyward with 'love'. Although the court held the airline's refusal to hire men was sex discrimination, its dress code and underlying gendered assumptions remained unaddressed in that opinion. *Wilson* explicitly framed female employees as sexualised objects without agency who existed for male customers to react to and act upon (Rifkin, 1982; Whisner, 1982).

Female sexuality in the workplace can be exploited as in *Wilson* or restrained and sublimated. Employers sometimes assume that women need more guidance on appropriate attire and grooming than their male peers. Thus, these gendered standards implicate both female sexuality and often social class (Brower, 2013). Indeed, some have argued that makeup and grooming standards are less an attempt to impose cosmetics on women who do not wear any, and more a step towards reining in or directing women to express their gender in a preferred manner – often to not look tawdry or lower class (Avery & Crain, 2007; Paules, 1991; *Jespersen v. Harrah's Operating Co.*, 2004).

In *Carroll v. Talman Fed Savings and Loan Association* (1979), the bank required women to wear a 'career ensemble' uniform combining skirt or slacks with an employer-badged top; men wore a business suit or sport coat of their choice. The court held the policy discriminated on the basis of sex; the bank could not compel only women to wear status-denigrating uniforms or assume that only women lacked judgement to properly choose appropriate work attire. Without that disparate impact on one sex, however, *Carroll* permitted an employer to claim a business need for different dress standards for men and women if based in 'some justification in commonly accepted social norms' (*Carroll v. Talman Fed. Savings and Loan Ass'n,* 1979, p. 1032). Although the *Carroll* court struck down the dress code in that case, it retained and solidified three problematic aspects of appearance codes. The court confirmed the underlying assumption that the terms men and women are two opposing and binary categories. It required gender expression to be determined by that binary gender identity. And finally, it firmly concluded that 'commonly accepted social norms' on gender and gender expression could and should be reflected in employer dress policies.

Thus, the court's doctrinal focus on disparate employment burdens on men and women did not meaningfully interrogate the underlying binary assumptions and structure of traditional gender classifications; it reaffirmed them. Moreover, the *Carroll* plaintiff was a cisgender, binarily identified female. She challenged the bank's dress code because it demeaned her as a woman, a gender identity that neither she nor her workplace environment questioned in the slightest. Her issues were not triggered by a fluid gender expression or a mismatch between her sex assigned at birth and her gender identity. Probing those latter characteristics is essential to understanding how appearance standards affect gender expansive employees.

Gender Expansiveness and Explicitly Gender-Differentiated Dress Codes

Because binary gender is such a commonly accepted dress code norm, gender expansive and transgender people have related, but distinct, compliance issues. Gendered appearance standards present varied barriers for gender expansive individuals depending on how much and how often they diversely and/or fluidly constitute gender identity and expression. For transgender persons, additional factors are (1) whether they identify as gender binary and/or (2) how completely they harmonise their physical body post-transition with their gender identity and expression.

Some legal challenges to dress codes involved transgender plaintiffs who wished to dress consistently with their gender identity and in accord with their employers' gendered dress codes – albeit in a gender presentation different from that assigned at birth and not accepted by their employer (Jones, 2013; Middlemiss, 2018; *Bostock v. Clayton County*, 2020). Those cases remain rooted in gender binarism. Accordingly, the dress code issue is conceptually straight-forward. An employer should permit employees to dress appropriately for the gender with which they identify regardless of birth gender (Wharton, 2015); the dress code itself remains unchanged. Theoretically that solution should both meet the employer's need for business branding, marketing and uniformity (Middlemiss, 2018) while accommodating the transgender employee's authentic identity. Thus, Aimee Stephens in *Harris* should have been allowed to dress as a woman and follow the female dress code at the funeral home. In fact, that is the solution that she proposed to her employer (*EEOC v. R.G. & G.R. Harris Funeral Homes, Inc.*, 2017, pp. 568–569).[5]

Even for transgender people who see themselves as gender binary, this solution may not be cost-free, however. While it may resolve the particular appearance code issue, it may reinforce gender expectations and stereotypes and their attendant negative workplace consequences. It is a long-documented economic data point that women earn less than men even accounting for various workplace and societal dynamics (Bolotnyy & Emanuel, 2021; Schilt & Wiswall, 2008). Echoing that data, Schilt and Wiswall (2008) found that even if their actual human capital remained the same, average earnings post-transition for male-to-female transgender workers fell by approximately one-third while female-to-male transgender persons' earnings remained the same or were slightly higher. Thus, even if transgender employees are allowed to dress consistently with their gender identity, this does not remove the social and economic effects gender activates in the workplace; it may even strengthen them.

Despite possible economic and social consequences, legal doctrine has gener-ally concurred with the 'dress as the other gender with which you identify' model for transgender persons and dress codes. In 2013, Professor Jones (2013) stated that the UK Equalities Act of 2010 required employers to permit transgender persons affected by gendered dress and appearance policies to dress according to their gender identity. As previously stated, this was also Aimee Stephens's preferred resolution under Title VII, the US sex discrimination law in *Harris*. This answer, however, does not challenge gender binaries, it solidifies them. The Equalities Act/Title VII solution permits an individual to dress in a gender-conforming way, just one more suited to their gender identity. Thus, it reinforces the idea that there are two different, opposing genders; employers and employees must simply pick the right one.

Indeed, when Fernandez and colleagues studied British nonbinary persons, survey respondents specifically identified the Equalities Act's gender essentialist language and perspective as why they felt excluded from the law (Fernandez et al., 2017). Accordingly, the solution to simply present as 'the other gender' was unresponsive to gender expansive or nonbinary people's needs.

The 'dress as the other gender' solution may also be inapposite to transgender people who have not completely conformed their body to their gender identity because it ignores the realities of gender transition and elides or compresses its time frame. A transgender person's transition from gender assigned at birth to the gender with which they identify is neither simple nor quick. First, not all transition involves medical or hormonal intervention. Some transition is social, encompassing name and gender expression changes, but not necessarily physical alterations. Second, even where medical transition is undertaken, gender confirmation surgeries involve several lengthy, expensive medical procedures and entail many intermediate stages (Sangganjanavanich & Headley, 2013; Schilt & Wiswall, 2008). Transgender persons may opt for all, some, or none of those medical interventions. Accordingly, a significant number of transgender persons may have a gender presentation that is imperfectly aligned with their physical body (Schilt & Wiswall, 2008).

Thus, clothing may fit a person's gender presentation but not their body or vice versa. For example, how should a gender-differentiated policy apply to an individual who was assigned female at birth and who has partially or totally maintained their physical body post-transition, but who chooses to wear men's clothing to align with their gender identity (Wylie, 2018)? Employees may face practical difficulties reconciling partial or changing physical transition, even assuming that they wish to completely make them congruent. Moreover, co-workers and customers may notice mismatches and be uncomfortable with gender expression that incompletely conforms to or simply moves away from traditional binary expectations (Fernandez et al., 2017; Schilt & Connell, 2007). These misalignments can have important employment consequences since they may colour impressions of and attitudes towards the business itself.

The focus on customer discomfort is significant because dress codes are often part of a business's branding (Middlemiss, 2018). As in *EEOC v. R.G. & G.R. Harris Funeral Homes, Inc.* (2017), employers may worry that during or after transition, a transgender employee whose presentation cannot 'pass' as the gender with which they identify may alienate clients. 'Passing' is a problematic term since it implies that the transgender person is hiding or trying to appear as something they are not (Billard, 2019). However, in the context of these employer anxieties, it is appropriate. Passing captures the premise that customer hostility and nonacceptance stem from the belief that transgender people's gender identity and presentation are false or fake. Thus, customers' negative reactions to deception potentially can and sometimes will injure the business (*EEOC v. R.G. & G.R. Harris Funeral Homes, Inc.*, 2017).

Accordingly, even if an employer permits transgender employees to follow gendered dress codes corresponding to their gender identity, there may be a perceived misalignment between the expectations envisioned by the workplace appearance standard and an individual employee's gender presentation. That perceived misalignment may trigger concerns about corporate image management or conflict with other bases for the original or continued imposition of the appearance standard.

Gender Expansiveness and Gender-Neutral Dress Codes

A gender-neutral dress code alleviates some aspects of a gender-differentiated policy but is not a panacea. If the policy is administered in a gendered way, i.e., by having different versions of business attire for males and females, or by scrutinising more closely the choices of men or women or of differently gendered individuals, then the employer has simply replicated a gendered dress code and recreated its problems, just hidden behind facially neutral language.

The tendency to reestablish gender binarism within ostensibly gender-neutral standards is exacerbated because gender expression involves choosing among a plethora of hairstyles, jewellry, cosmetics, pitch and manner of speaking, and cut of clothing. Some choices are immediately recognisable as gender markers like facial hair, and some are more subtle like the direction buttons face on women's blouses vs men's shirts (Finney, 2016) or bust darts (Oram, 2012). Accordingly, gender can attach to dress choices even when they are labelled identically. As often occurs with workplace rules, gaps form between a policy and its implementation or between a policy and workers' use of it (Wharton, 2019).

Assume, however, that an employer's dress code is gender neutral in language and implementation. Workplaces may include people whose gender identity or presentation cannot be neatly cabined in a binary system (Clarke, 2019; Valentine, 2016). Indeed, the higher rates of youths and young adults identifying as gender expansive will mean that these individuals' presence in the workplace will substantially increase as they begin employment and thus provoke attendant jobsite conflict (Cheung et al., 2020; Trevor Project, 2021; Wilson & Meyer, 2021). The ubiquity of gendered appearance distinctions can trigger discordance between physicality and identity for gender nonbinary and transgender persons who cannot or do not wish to conform their body to their gender identity or who have fluid identities or presentations (Berks, 2019; Carroll et al., 2002; Foster, 2017; Rasmussen, 2019). Foster (2017) describes a transgender individual with an androgenous gender expression. They discuss the difficulties their presence elicits in binarily gendered spaces and the various strategies they employ to make others more comfortable with their identity and expression. Despite these strategies, their gender fluidity and nonconformity activate the predominant feeling they experience both within themselves and from others; they simply do not belong in that location.

The feeling of not belonging triggered by a discordance between one's physical body and identity and expression is not only a concern for the gender expansive individual but also for the employer and for others because work colleagues and customers share a workspace with the gender expansive person. For example:

> I know they are aware at work that I'm transitioning. But it's not official because my name hasn't changed. And I'm fortunate not only because of my specific job but just women quote unquote in general are allowed to dress fairly androgynously. And you know khakis and a polo shirt or whatever. It's not as bad as in the past when I had to wear a skirt and jacket... Even though my boss and the HR manager know I'm transitioning, the general population at work doesn't. And as I've become more androgynous on my way to being male bodied, I can tell that people are starting to wonder what's going on.
>
> (Dietert & Dentice, 2009, p. 131)

Thus, when employees' gender identity or expression do not conform to the expectations of their employers, co-workers or customers (Dietert & Dentice, 2009; Schilt & Connell, 2007), that presentation may signal to observers that gender is expressed dissonantly or imperfectly. For some gender expansive or gender fluid people who rebel against and/or play with gender markers, this consequence may be desired; for others, not (Bergner, 2019; Hornik, 2019).

Like the prior discussion of transgender employees under gender-differentiated policies, gender variability under neutral appearance codes may also affect co-workers and customers. Some employers have argued that failure to meet customer expectations around traditional gender expression and the complaints those failures generate justify termination of an otherwise satisfactory employee (*Amber Creed a/k/a/Christopher Creed v. Family Express Corp.*, 2009).

As noted earlier, dress codes often serve a branding function (Middlemiss, 2018). But exactly how that branding is concretely manifested is usually up to the employer. Although a business may be agnostic about an employee's gender identity or expression, it may insist that individuals should express gender consistently. Consistency might mean a person may be required to present uniformly in the same gender – in all of the ways in which gender can manifest during a workday. Or consistency may necessitate a gender fluid individual not vary gender expression throughout the day, work week or over the course of employment. Similarly, even if employers are unconcerned about an individual's idiosyncratic or volatile gender expression, again they may be troubled by actual or assumed customer reactions, discomfort or complaints (*e.g., Amber Creed a/k/a/Christopher Creed v. Family Express Corp.*, 2009).

Consistency demands pose a particular burden on gender fluid individuals. A 2017 study of UK gender nonbinary individuals asked respondents about their comfort in 'switch[ing] between dressing as feminine and as masculine at work' (Fernandez et al., 2017, p. 39). There were fewer positive responses on this question than on a different question about comfort with presenting as femininely or as masculinely as they liked at work, regardless of their gender. This difference suggests that gender volatility or unwillingness to present gender in a uniform or consistent way imposed greater burdens on gender nonbinary employees than would be felt by someone with a more stable and fixed gender expression, including both cis- and transgender workers with gender-binary identities.

Compliance with workplace gender expression norms is a significant source of stress and performative identity work for employees, but especially for gender expansive workers. As Bellezza et al. (2014, p. 35) noted, 'in both professional and nonprofessional settings, individuals make significant effort to learn and adhere to dress codes, etiquette and other written and unwritten standards of behavior'. As the quote recognises, it is not only employer directives that determine standards of behaviour, but colleagues may also exert a significant impact and serve a policing function in the workplace (Dellinger & Williams, 1997). Co-workers can effectively mandate workplace conformity and consistency of gender presentation through peer pressure and other jobsite regulation. Unsurprisingly then, gender expansive presentations at work draw negative attention and treatment (Dietert & Dentice, 2009; Sawyer et al., 2016; Valentine, 2016).

Some of the negative impacts should be familiar to those who study race or ethnicity and employment (Carbado & Gulati, 2000). An article on the job search website Monster.ca addressed gender expansive employees and workplace dress (Swartz, 2019). It noted that gender diverse employees may be seen as odd, or not a team player, as the expert on gender identity, as an attention seeker, or as unsuitable for promotions. These negative reactions can be seen as illustrating employer concerns about maintaining a smoothly functioning and collegial working environment – concerns ostensibly alleviated by conformity to appearance policies (Brower, 2013).

Consistent with the job seeker advice, data demonstrate that gender is salient in our interactions with others and can unconsciously colour those dealings and reactions to them (Maccoby, 1988; Sawyer et al., 2016). Thus, others may perceive an employee's gender identity or expression fluidity as aberrant or attribute erroneous significance to that lack of clarity and conflate gender nonconformity with sexual orientation (Brower, 2009; Butler, 1990; Kelly, 2019). In fact, perceptions of gender nonconformity or abnormality may even affect lesbians and gay men who are themselves gender typical but are simply sexual minorities. Some studies have found that lesbian and gay male job candidates were less likely to be invited for interviews because they were assumed to be gender nonconforming or less likely to adhere to gender appropriate job requirements (Badgett et al., 2021; Tilcsik, 2011).

Finally, although the dynamics of workplace discrimination may be similar with transgender and gender nonbinary employees, there are significant differences. Binary-identified transgender people may face disclosure of their identity across the gender binary, but nonbinary persons must disclose a gender that is outside or in the middle of a gender divide. Accordingly, the reactions of colleagues, employers and customers and the consequences of that nonbinary identity are different from those suffered by binarily gendered transgender people who conform to traditionally gendered norms (Schilt & Connell, 2007). Thus, posits Hamilton (2019), while transgender people may raise fears of gender *violation*, nonbinary individuals spark fears of gender *invalidation*. This concern that nonbinarism renders gender invalid may mean that others see their nonbinary colleagues as having a false or unreal identity. Consequently, nonbinary employees may develop identity management strategies around dress and appearance as well as pronoun usage that others find incomprehensible or strange. That unease can then affect treatment and experiences of these employees.

The consequences of these identity-management strategies may exacerbate the workplace experiences of gender expansive employees. Co-worker and employer perceptions of employee nonconformity in dress and behaviour in the workplace escalate with perceived degrees of radicalism or transgression. Accordingly, the more observers view gender 'rule breaking' as socially unacceptable, the more likely it is to be viewed negatively and result in negative employment consequences (Bellezza et al., 2014). This may result in a vicious circle. Employer, co-worker and customer discomfort with discordant or variable gender expression or identity may lead to amplified policing of appearance standards and increased demands for consistency in gender presentation (Schilt & Connell, 2007), thus subjecting gender expansive workers to increased stress and negative outcomes, and resulting in higher employer, co-worker and customer perceptions of gender rule-breaking and nonconformity.

Gender salience also extends to one's social identity and is shaped by fundamental societal and cultural beliefs (Sawyer et al., 2016). Thus, the gender of clothing may be dependent on social or group membership and attitudes (Shotter, 1993). This subjectivity can intersect with even neutral employer dress codes in unforeseen ways. For example, in *EEOC v. Patty Tipton Co.* (2012), an employer's gender-neutral standard required food service workers to wear black trousers. Megan Woodard, a fundamentalist Baptist prospective employee, requested a religious exemption from the dress code. She claimed her religion forbade her to wear male-identified clothing (trousers) and demanded the employer permit her to wear a female-identified skirt. As in other situations, the employer's dress code incorporated the masculine as neutral and nongendered (Butler, 1990; Davidson, 2016). But, for Woodard, the dress code was not gender-neutral, but gendered in a manner that contradicted her female identity and corresponding gender expression. The company eventually settled that case with the U.S. Equal Employment Opportunity Commission, providing Woodard with compensatory damages and back pay for her discriminatory termination (US Equal Employment Opportunity Commission, 2012).

Practical Impacts: A Prescription and a Proscription

What would a dress code look like that would resolve the tensions with gender expansive employees' gender identity and expression? Kelly (2019) studied queer, androgynous women's interactions with employer appearance standards; respondents proposed a dress code that would not classify uniforms or clothing based on gender. Instead, it would encompass diverse styles, tailoring, and fit to enable individual workers to decide what suited them and promoted their self-expression. Most respondents reported deliberately presenting themselves differently at different times and locations as they navigated the various spaces, relationships, and contexts of their lives and recommended a workplace dress code that would accommodate that flexibility. Finally, they stated that appearance standards that allowed workers to express their individuality at work did not compromise the professional look, or uniformity of staff (Burns, 2017). Human Resources professionals, trade unions and governmental agencies sometimes advocate for just such neutral, adaptable policies (California DFEH, 2017; SHRM.org, 2019; STUC LGBT+ Workers Committee, 2017).

Nevertheless, appearance standards meeting the above criteria would still confront engrained social norms and workplace expectations of employers, co-workers, and customers. Empirical research suggests this potential challenge will be larger than commentators and H.R. personnel may think. Dress codes comprise only part of the workplace environment but exert a significant impact on gender nonbinary or gender fluid workers. In a 2015 UK study of gender nonbinary people, Valentine (2016, p. 60) found that 51.6% of nonbinary workers reported that their employer's dress code created negative workplace experiences and forced them to adhere to gender stereotypes. Dress codes were also the negative employment experience that generated the most open-ended comments by gender nonbinary persons (Valentine, 2016, p. 61). Appearance codes provoked the third most frequent negative employment experiences in the five years preceding the study. Only being forced to pass as male/female to be accepted at work and mistakenly having wrong pronouns and names used were more significant (Valentine, 2016, p. 60).

Gender nonbinary workers reported significant additional employment consequences stemming from the disconnect between their gender fluid or gender diverse identity and expression and the demands for gender conformity on the job. 79.6% of respondents stated that they were forced to pass as traditionally and binarily gendered at work. The vast majority also experienced being misgendered either inadvertently (52.3%) or deliberately (21.0%), as well as harassment (25.1%) and name-calling (13.6%). Gender expansive individuals also reported not being given customer-facing job duties or publicly visible positions (12.5%) or being denied promotion opportunities (7.2%) based on their gender nonconformity (Valentine, 2016, p. 60).

Congruent with those negative findings, a 2017 UK study of 225 gender nonbinary workers reported potential positive consequences of gender-neutral dress policies. Fernandez and colleagues (2017) found that, along with accepting gender-neutral titles and forms, an employer having a nonbinary-inclusive dress code was the most important workplace practice that would make gender expansive people feel included there. Fully 97% of nonbinary workers thought that a gender-neutral policy would make their workplace inclusive for gender nonbinary people like themselves. Moreover, the impact of that type of appearance standard far exceeded the effectiveness of traditional employment practices like nondiscrimination policies and fairness training. However, only 50% of respondents reported that their workplaces had such a nongendered policy (Fernandez et al., 2017).

Finally, in answer to the question: 'Do you feel able to express yourself with your employer's dress codes?' only 35% said they felt comfortable; 12% said they were not at all comfortable and 54% stated sometimes/unsure (Fernandez et al., 2017). Remember that 50% of these same employees' workplaces already had what respondents classified as gender nonbinary dress codes. Thus, the percentage of negative responses to this question may reflect that even with nonbinary dress codes in place, gender expansive employees do not feel that they can express their gender in the manner they might like. This gap between policy and practice is a significant issue for employers and employees. It should serve as a caution against facile prescriptions for change in this area.

This caution should extend beyond the immediate impact of dress codes to larger employment issues. It has long been known that workplace dress affects employee self-perceptions and the perceptions of others (Kwon, 1994a, 1994b; Peluchette & Karl, 2007; Rafaeli et al., 1997; Reddy-Best, 2018). Thus, other economic effects on transgender and gender expansive people in the workplace may result from their discomfort and inability to feel they belong in the workplace.

Demographic analyses have shown that transgender and gender expansive people have fewer economic resources and are more economically vulnerable than their nontransgender or gender conforming peers (Herman et al., 2022; Wilson & Meyer, 2021). Thus, it is likely that they have fewer choices to avoid certain jobs or workplace policies (Ridge, 2009; Sheehy-Skeffington & Rea, 2017; Vollan, 2016). Nevertheless, job sorting to avoid certain workplaces or employment policies may be particularly salient here. Research on LGB employees has shown that sexual minorities work in different workplaces than do heterosexuals. Occupational sorting appears to be correlated with comfort level on the job, particularly when it is associated with more tolerant workplaces and those in which identity disclosure is less risky (Badgett et al., 2021; Plug et al., 2014). There are no available data on gender expansive people and workplace sorting. However, as the earlier quoted open-ended responses to surveys by Fernandez and colleagues (2017) and Valentine (2016) illustrate, there is reason to believe that similar dynamics may be in play with gender nonbinary employees. Thus, to the extent that dress codes reinforce traditional gender norms, they may push away gender expansive potential employees creating an even stronger appearance of unwelcomeness to those who follow.

Conclusion

These data on the opinions and experiences of gender expansive employees in workplaces with gender-neutral dress codes should serve as a reminder that employer policies and legal regimes may have limited ability to change or shape workplace culture. Informal social or workplace norms and not employer codes often limit and structure an employee's dress and gender expression (Dellinger & Williams, 1997). Nevertheless, court rulings and legal texts that validate binary employer appearance rules do affect the lives of trans and gender expansive employees, especially given law's signalling or norm-generating function (Lin, 1999; Thomas, 1993). These effects persist even as US, UK and other nations' laws have shifted significantly in favour of greater employment rights for LGBTQ workers.

Accordingly, although the US Supreme Court's *Bostock v. Clayton County* decision including sexual orientation and gender identity as prohibited bases for employment actions clarified and made uniform what was once a patchwork of varying anti-discrimination state and local laws (Lin & Cukor, 2020), it left intact the concerns of this chapter. As the facts of Aimee Stephens's own case demonstrate, finding an employer's gendered dress code to be discriminatory does not mean that it will permit transgender and gender expansive employees to express their gender honestly and appropriately. If an employer's appearance code is constructed along gender binary lines, permitting transgender employees to dress as the 'other' gender is only really appropriate for gender binary people like Aimee Stephens herself. That solution leaves behind gender nonbinary and gender expansive workers as well as transgender persons whose transition process may be at various stages short of a uniform gender presentation.

Moreover, even a gender-neutral dress code policy may still leave gender nonbinary people vulnerable. First, clothing is often itself gendered, so that appearance rules like 'white button-down shirt/black trousers' can incorporate gender sub silentio via tailoring options or style choices. Second, demands by employers, co-workers or customers for gender conformity or consistency in presentation may reinforce gender binarism even where official policies are neutral. Indeed, these unwritten policies or addenda to written dress codes may exert greater authority over employee gender expression because of the strong policing strictures of workplace norms that often contain fundamental gender binary or conformist standards (Dellinger & Williams, 1997; Reddy-Best, 2018; Valentine, 2016).

Additionally, this policing and consequent barriers to workplace equality may be invisible to employers and gender conforming work peers. As one gender nonbinary employee stated:

> Working in an environment that is not inclusive of nonbinary identities is exhausting and damaging to your mental health. You need a lot of support from outside work and strategies to keep yourself going throughout the day. It is hard because not only are you facing discrimination, no one sees it as that because they don't see nonbinary as existing.
>
> (Valentine, 2016, p. 67)

Thus, if workplaces are truly going to be inclusive of transgender and gender expansive people, the current legal requirements that dress codes permit employees to dress in accordance with their gender identity are insufficient. Attention must be paid not only to formal gender neutrality in appearance codes, but equality in gender presentations in workplace norms and interactions. That is a significantly heavier burden and one that the law is currently not addressing.

Notes

1. Although terminology relating to gender identity, gender expression and sexual orientation is fluid and sometimes contested, readers interested in a glossary of terms may review (Human Rights Campaign, n.d.; PFLAG, 2021; USC Rossier, 2020).
2. Consistent with its title, this chapter uses the pronouns 'they, them, their' to refer to an individual without assigning a specific gender. Clarke (2019), MacNamara et al. (2017) and Conlin (2011) discuss gendered pronoun usage and alternatives in detail and Trevor Project (2021) reviews the wide variety of pronouns used by youth. The chapter also prefers 'gender expansive' to 'gender nonconforming' per current usage guidelines (PFLAG, 2019).
3. Self-identification nomenclature among individuals is extremely complex and contested (Kuper et al., 2012; Factor & Rothblum, 2008). Because those distinctions are largely irrelevant to this conversation, this chapter uses more simplified and generalised classifications. For a sample of the diversity of identification labels, see Trevor Project (2021); Wilson and Meyer (2021).
4. Some theorists assert that maleness and femaleness are always hierarchical and that gender binarism reinforces patriarchy and men's superiority (Gould, 1979). This chapter does not engage that claim, nor is hierarchy part of this gender identity and binarism discussion.
5. Similarly, the July 2021 decision of the UK High Court of Justice, Queen's Bench, Administrative Division permitting the housing of transgender prisoners in single-sex facilities consistent with their gender identity and not their gender assigned at birth (The Queen (on the application of FDJ) v Secretary of State for Justice (Rev 1) [2021]), is based on a binary conception of gender.

References

Amber Creed a/k/a/Christopher Creed v. Family Express Corp., No. 3:06-CV-465, (n. d. Ind. 2009).

Aspinall, A. (2017, March 31). Cops to wear 'genderless' uniform on the beat to be more friendly to transgender people. *The Mirror*. https://www.mirror.co.uk/news/uk-news/cops-wear-genderless-uniform-beat-10137252

Avery, D., & Crain, M. (2007). Branded: Corporate image, sexual stereotyping, and the new face of capitalism. *Duke Journal of Gender Law & Policy*, *14*, 13–124.

Badgett, M. V. L., Carpenter, C. S., & Sansone, D. (2021). LGBTQ Economics. *The Journal of Economic Perspectives*, *35*(2), 141–170. https://doi.org/10.1257/jep.35.2.141

Bellezza, S., Gino, F., & Keinan, A. (2014). The red sneakers effect: Inferring status and competence from signals of nonconformity. *Journal of Consumer Research*, *41*(1), 35–54.

Bergner, D. (2019, June 4). The struggles of rejecting the gender binary. *New York Times*. https://www.nytimes.com/2019/06/04/magazine/gender-nonbinary.html

Berks, R. (2019, June 21). Otherwild owner Rachel Berks explains why we need better clothing options for nonbinary and gender nonconforming people. *TeenVogue*. https://www.teenvogue.com/story/why-we-need-better-clothing-options-for-nonbinary-and-gender-nonconforming-people

Billard, T. J. (2019). "Passing" and the politics of deception: Transgender bodies, cisgender aesthetics, and the policing of inconspicuous marginal identities". In T. Docon-Morgan (Ed.), *The Palgrave Handbook of Deceptive Communication* (pp. 463–477). Palgrave Macmillan.

Blair, K. L., & Hoskin, R. A. (2015). Experiences of femme identity: Coming out, invisibility and femmephobia. *Psychology & Sexuality*, *6*(3), 229–244.

Bolotnyy, V., & Emanuel, N. (2021). Why Do Women Earn Less Than Men? Evidence from Bus and Train Operators. *Journal of Labor Economics*. forthcoming. https://doi.org/10.1086/715835

Bostock v. Clayton County, 140 S.Ct. 1731. (2020).

Brower, T. (2009). Social cognition 'At work': Schema theory and lesbian and gay identity in Title VII. *Law and Sexuality*, *18*, 1–77.

Brower, T. (2013). What's in the closet: Dress and appearance codes and lessons from sexual orientation. *Equality, Diversity and Inclusion: An International Journal*, *32*(5), 491–502. https://doi.org/10.1108/EDI-02-2013-0006

Burns, K. (2017, November 18). What trans people really think of your dress code. *The Establishment*. Medium.com. https://medium.com/the-establishment/what-trans-people-really-think-of-your-dress-code-2111558272af

Butler, J. (1990). *Gender trouble: Feminism and the subversion of identity*. Routledge.

California Department of Fair Employment and Housing, (DFEH). (2017, November). Transgender rights in the workplace. https://www.dfeh.ca.gov/wp-content/uploads/sites/32/2017/11/DFEH_E04P-ENG-2017Nov.pdf

Carbado, D. W., & Gulati, M. (2000). Working identity. *Cornell Law Review*, *85*(5), 1259–1308.

Carroll v. Talman Fed. Savings and Loan Ass'n, 604 F. 2nd 1028 (7th Cir. 1979).

Carroll, L., Gilroy, P. J., & Ryan, J. (2002). Counseling transgendered, transsexual, and gender-variant clients. *Journal of Counseling and Development*, *80*, 131–139.

Cheung, A. S., Leemqz, S. Y., Wong, J. W. P., Chew, D., Ooi, O., Cundill, P., ... Pang, K. C. (2020). Nonbinary and binary gender identity in Australian Trans and gender diverse individuals. *Archives of Sexual Behavior*, *49*, 2673–2681. https://doi.org/10.1007/s10508-020-01689-9

Clarke, J. A. (2019). They, Them, and Theirs. (nonbinary gender identities). *Harvard Law Review*, *132*(3), 894–991.

Conlin, J. (2011, September 30). The freedom to choose your pronoun. *New York Times*. http://www.nytimes.com/2011/10/02/fashion/choosing-a-pronoun-heshe-or-other-after-curfew.html?_r=0

Danovich, T. (2016, August 24). How restaurants get away with looks-based discrimination. *Jezebel*. https://jezebel.com/how-restaurants-get-away-with-looks-based-discriminatio-1785308185

Davidson, S. (2016). Gender inequality: Nonbinary transgender people in the workplace. *Cogent Social Sciences, 2.1*, 1236511. https://doi.org/10.1080/23311886.2016.1236511

Dellinger, K., & Williams, C. L. (1997). Makeup at work negotiating appearance rules in the workplace. *Gender & Society, 11*(2), 151–177.

Dietert, M., & Dentice, D. (2009). Gender identity issues and workplace discrimination: The transgender experience. *Journal of Workplace Rights, 14*(1), 121–140.

Doe v. City of Belleville, Ill., 119 F.3d 563 (7th Cir. 1997).

Doud v. Yellow Cab of Reno, 96 F. Supp. 3d 1076, (D. Nev. 2015).

Drescher, J., & Pula, J. (2019). *Expert Q and A: Gender Dysphoria*. American Psychiatric Association. https://www.psychiatry.org/patients-families/gender-dysphoria/expert-q-and-a

EEOC v. Patty Tipton Co., 2012 U.S. Dist. LEXIS 13243.

EEOC v. R.G. & G.R. Harris Funeral Homes, Inc., 884 F3d 560 (6th Cir. 2017).

Factor, R., & Rothblum, E. (2008). Exploring gender identity and community among three groups of transgender individuals in the United States: MTFs, FTMs, and genderqueers. *Health Sociology Review, 17*(3), 235–253. https://doi.org/10.5172/hesr.451.17.3.235

Fernandez, J., Gibson, S., & Twist, J. (2017, March). Beyond the binary: Nonbinary workplace and customer experience survey. *Beyond the Binary*. http://beyondthebinary.co.uk/nonbinary-workplace-and-customer-experience-survey-2017/nonbinary-workplace-and-customer-experience-survey-1/

Finney, L. (2016, July 13). Here's why men's and women's shirts button on the opposite sides. *Today*. https://www.today.com/style/here-s-why-men-s-women-s-shirts-button-opposite-t100380

Fogarty, A. A., & Zheng, L. (2018). *Gender ambiguity in the workplace: Transgender and gender-diverse discrimination*. ABC-CLIO.

Foster, C. (2017, September 28). Dressing for the body i want, not the one i have. *Racked*. https://www.racked.com/2017/9/28/16361096/trans-body-clothing-shopping

Goffman, E. (1959). *The presentation of self in everyday life*. Doubleday.

Gould, M. (1979). Sex, gender and the need for legal clarity: The case of transsexualism,. *Valparaiso University Law Review, 13*(3), 423–450.

Hall, E. J. (1993). Waitering/waitressing: Engendering the work of table servers. *Gender & Society, 7*(3), 329–346.

Hamilton, K. M. (2019). *Does X mark the applicant? Assessing reactions to gender nonbinary job seekers*. Unpublished dissertation/thesis. Portland State University. https://doi.org/10.15760/etd.7139

Hatzipanagos, R. (2021, July 1). "A doctor was deemed 'unprofessional' for wearing hoops. Now other women of color are speaking out". *The Washington Post*. https://www.thelily.com/a-doctor-was-deemed-unprofessional-for-wearing-hoops-now-other-women-of-color-are-speaking-out/?tid=recommended_by_lily

Herman, J. (2016, March 1). LGB within the T: Sexual Orientation in the National Transgender Discrimination Survey and Implications for Public Policy. http://www.escholarship.org/uc/item/4n7727j7

Herman, J. L., Flores, A. R., & O'Neill, K. K. (2022). *How Many Adults and Youth Identify as Transgender in the United States?* The Williams Institute. UCLA School of Law. https://williamsinstitute.law.ucla.edu/wp-content/uploads/Trans-Pop-Update-Jun-2022.pdf

Hornik, S. (2019, May 2). Gender-fluid clothing is finally having its fashion moment. *LA Times.* https://www.latimes.com/fashion/la-ig-gender-neutral-fashion-20190502-story.html

Human Rights Campaign. (n.d.). *Glossary.* https://www.hrc.org/resources/glossary-of-terms

Jespersen v. Harrah's Operating Co., 392 F.3d 1076 (9th Cir. 2004).

Jespersen v. Harrah's Operating Co., 444 F.3d 1104 (9th Cir. 2006) (en banc).

Jones, J. (2013). Trans dressing in the workplace. *Equality, Diversity and Inclusion, 32*(5), 503–514.

Jones, E. M. (2018). The kids are queer: The rise of post-millennial American queer identification. In C. Stewart (Ed.), *Lesbian, Gay, Bisexual, and Transgender Americans at Risk: Problems and Solutions.* Praeger.

Kelly, K. (2019). *Wearing yourself or dressing the part: Navigating workplace dress codes as queer, androgynous women.* Unpublished dissertation/thesis. Faculty of Social Sciences, Brock University St. Catharines, Ontario, Canada. https://dr.library.brocku.ca/bitstream/handle/10464/13914/Brock_Kelly_Kailey_2018.pdf?sequence=1&isAllowed=y

Köllen, T. (2016). Intersexuality and trans-identities within the diversity management discourse. In T. Köllen (Ed.), *Sexual orientation and transgender issues in organizations.* Springer.

Kuper, L. E., Nussbaum, R., & Mustanski, B. (2012). Exploring the diversity of gender and sexual orientation identities in an online sample of transgender individuals. *The Journal of Sex Research, 49*(2–3), 244–254. https://doi.org/10.1080/00224499.2011.596954

Kwon, Y. (1994a). The influence of appropriateness of dress and gender on the self-perception of occupational attributes. *Clothing and Textiles Research Journal, 12*(3), 33–37. https://doi.org/10.1177/0887302X9401200305

Kwon, Y. (1994b). Feeling toward one's clothing and self-perception of emotion, sociability, and work competency. *Journal of Social Behavior & Personality, 9,* 129–139.

Langevoort, D. C. (2004). Overcoming resistance to diversity in the executive suite: Grease, grit, and the corporate promotion tournament. *Washington and Lee Law Review, 61,* 1615–1644.

Lather, P. (1992). Critical frames in educational research: Feminist and structural perspectives. *Theory into practice, 31*(2), 87–99.

Lin, T. E. (1999). Note: Social norms and judicial decisionmaking: Examining the role of narratives in same-sex adoption cases. *Columbia Law Review, 99*(3), 739–794.

Lin, S., & Cukor, E. (2020). *LGBTQIA+ discrimination: Employment discrimination law & litigation.* Public Law Research Paper No. 20–55, SSRN. NYU School of Law. https://ssrn.com/abstract=3679970

Maccoby, E. E. (1988). Gender as a social category. *Developmental Psychology, 24,* 755–765.

MacNamara, J., Glann, S., & Durlak, P. (2017). Experiencing misgendered pronouns: A classroom activity to encourage empathy. *Teaching Sociology, 45*(3), 269–278.

McCormick v. Festiva Dev. Grp., LLC, 269 F.R.D. 59 (D. Me. 2010).

Middlemiss, S. (2018). Not what to wear? Employers' liability for dress codes? *International Journal of Discrimination and the Law*, *18*(1), 40–51. https://doi.org/10.1177/1358229118757867

Moleiro, C., & Pinto, N. (2015). Sexual orientation and gender identity: Review of concepts, controversies and their relation to psychopathology classification systems. *Frontiers in Psychology*, *6*, 1511. https://doi.org/10.3389/fpsyg.2015.01511

Narjes v. Absolute Health Servs., 2018 U.S. Dist. LEXIS 109219.

Oram, S. (2012, June 8). It's all in the darts: Men's and women's shirt differences. *Qwear*. https://www.qwearfashion.com/home/its-all-in-the-darts-mens-and-womens-shirt

Paules, G. F. (1991). *Dishing it out: Power and resistance among waitresses in a New Jersey restaurant*. Temple University Press.

Peluchette, J. V., & Karl, K. (2007). The impact of workplace attire on employee selfperceptions. *Human Resource Development Quarterly*, *18*, 345–360. https://doi.org/10.1002/(ISSN)1532-1096

Petrilli, C. M., Saint, S., Jennings, J. J., Carusa, A., Kuhn, L., Snyder, A., & Chopra, V. (2018). Understanding patient preference for physician attire: A cross-sectional observational study of 10 academic medical centres in the USA. *BMJ Open*, *8*, e021239. https://doi.org/10.1136/bmjopen-2017-021239

PFLAG (Parents and Friends of Lesbians and Gays). (2021, January). PFLAG National Glossary of Terms. PFLAG.org. https://pflag.org/glossary

Plug, E., Webbink, D., & Martin, N. (2014). Sexual orientation, prejudice, and segregation. *Journal of Labor Economics*, *32*(1), 123–159.

Pratt, M. G., & Rafaeli, A. (1997). Organizational dress as a symbol of multilayered social identities. *Academy of Management Journal*, *40*(4), 862–898.

Project, T. (2021). Trevor Project Research Brief: Survey of Nonbinary Youth. https://www.thetrevorproject.org/wp-content/uploads/2021/07/Diversity-of-Nonbinary-Youth_-July-Research-Brief.pdf

Pruden, H., & Edmo, S. (2016). *Two-Spirit People: Sex, Gender & Sexuality in Historic and Contemporary Native America*. National Congress of American Indians Policy Research Center. https://www.ncai.org/policy-research-center/initiatives/Pruden-Edmo_TwoSpiritPeople.pdf

The Queen (on the application of FDJ) v. Secretary of State for Justice (Rev 1) [2021] EWHC 1746 (Admin). http://www.bailii.org/ew/cases/EWHC/Admin/2021/1746.html

Rafaeli, A., Dutton, J., Harquial, C., & Mackie-Lewis, S. (1997). Navigating by attire: The use of dress by administrative employees. *Academy of Management Journal*, *40*, 19–45. https://doi.org/10.2307/257019

Rasmussen, T. (2019, January 16). Eight trans and nonbinary people on personal style. *CNNStyle*. https://www.cnn.com/style/article/trans-nonbinary-style-dazed-digital/index.html

Reddy-Best, K. L. (2018). LGBTQ women, appearance, negotiations, and workplace dress codes. *Journal of Homosexuality*, *65*(5), 615–639. https://doi.org/10.1080/00918369.2017.1328225

Richards, C., Bouman, W. P., Seal, L., Barker, M. J., Nieder, T. O., & T'Sjoen, G. T. (2016). Nonbinary or genderqueer genders. *International Review of Psychiatry*, *28*, 95–102. https://doi.org/10.3109/09540261.2015.1106446

Ridge, T. (2009). *Living with poverty A review of the literature on children's and families' experiences of poverty.* Department for Work and Pensions Research Report No. 594. Department for Work and Pensions. http://webarchive. nationalarchives.gov.uk/20130314010347/http://research.dwp.gov.uk/asd/asd5/report_abstracts/rr_abstracts/rra_594.asp

Rifkin, J. (1982). Toward a theory of law and patriarchy. In P. Bierne & R. Quinney (Eds.), *Marxism and Law* (pp. 295–301). Wiley.

Sangganjanavanich, V. F., & Headley, J. A. (2013). Facilitating career development concerns of gender transitioning individuals: Professional standards and competencies. *The Career Development Quarterly, 61*, 354–366. https://doi.org/10.1002/j.2161-0045.2013.00061.x

Sawyer, K., Thoroughgood, C., & Webster, J. (2016). Queering the gender binary: Understanding transgender workplace experiences. In T. Köllen (Ed.), *Sexual orientation and transgender issues in organizations*. Springer.

Schep, D. (2012). The limits of performativity: A critique of hegemony in gender theory. *Hypatia, 27*(4), 864–880.

Schilt, K., & Connell, C. (2007). Do workplace gender transitions make gender trouble? *Gender, Work and Organization, 14*, 596–618. https://doi.org/10.1111/j.1468-0432.2007.00373.x

Schilt, K., & Westbrook, L. (2009). Doing gender, doing heteronormativity "gender normals," transgender people, and the social maintenance of heterosexuality. *Gender & Society, 23*(4), 440–464.

Schilt, K., & Wiswall, M. (2008). "Before and after: Gender transitions, human capital, and workplace experiences. *The B.E. Journal of Economic Analysis & Policy, 8*(1), 1–28.

Seidman, S. (1996). *Queer theory/sociology*. Blackwell.

Sheehy-Skeffington, J., & Rea, J. (2017). *How poverty affects people's decision-making processes*. Joseph Rowntree Foundation. https://www.jrf.org.uk/file/49906/download?token=gE5-D8_z&filetype=full-report

Shotter, J. (1993). Becoming someone: Identity and belonging. In N. Coupland & J. F. Nussbaum (Eds.), *Discourse and lifespan identity* (pp. 5–27). Sage Publications.

SHRM.org. (2019). Managing Employee dress and appearance. https://www.shrm.org/resourcesandtools/tools-and-samples/toolkits/pages/employeedressand appearance.aspx

Skidmore, P. L. (1999). Dress to impress: Employer regulation of gay and lesbian appearance. *Social & Legal Studies, 8*(4), 509–529.

Stein, A., & Plummer, K. (1996). "I can't even think straight": "Queer" theory and the missing sexual revolution in sociology. In S. Seidman (Ed.), *Queer theory/sociology* (pp. 129–144). Blackwell.

STUC LGBT+ Workers Committee. (2017, May). Gender Neutral Dress Codes A Guide for Trade Unionists. http://www.stuc.org.uk/files/LGBT/webpage/Gender%20Neutral%20Dress%20Codes%20-final.pdf

Swartz, M. (2019). Expressing your gender as nonbinary at work. https://www.monster.ca/career-advice/article/gender-expression-at-work

Thomas, K. (1993). The eclipse of reason: A rhetorical reading of Bowers v. Hardwick. *Virginia Law Review, 79*, 1805–1832.

Tilcsik, A. (2011). Pride and prejudice: Employment discrimination against openly gay men in the United States. *American Journal of Sociology, 117*(2), 586–626.

University of Southern California, Rossier School of Education. (2020, July 6). *A gender identity glossary for schools.* https://rossieronline.usc.edu/blog/gender-identity-glossary/

U.S. Equal Employment Opportunity Commission. (2012, September 4). The Patty Tipton company Agrees to Settle EEOC Religious Discrimination Lawsuit. (Press Release). https://www.eeoc.gov/newsroom/patty-tipton-company-agrees-settle-eeoc-religious-discrimination-lawsuit

Valentine, V. (2016). Nonbinary people's experiences in the UK, Scottish Trans Equality Network. https://www.scottishtrans.org/wp-content/uploads/2016/11/Nonbinary-report

Vollan, B. (2016). Does relative poverty lead to sub-optimal career decisions? *Behavioral Development Economics.* https://behavioraldevelopmentblog.wordpress.com/2016/06/17/how-much-does-relative-poverty-lead-to-sub-optimal-career-decisions/

West, C., & Zimmerman, D. H. (1987). Doing gender. *Gender & Society, 1*(2), 125–151.

Wharton. (2015, June 12). Transgender in the workplace: What firms and employers need to know. *Knowledge@Wharton.* https://knowledge.wharton.upenn.edu/article/transgender-in-the-workplace-what-firms-and-employees-need-to-know/

Wharton. (2019, February 22). Redefining gender at work: How companies are evolving. *Knowledge@Wharton.* https://knowledge.wharton.upenn.edu/article/redefining-gender-at-work/

Whisner, M. (1982). Gender-specific clothing regulation: A study in patriarchy. *Harvard Women's Law Journal, 5,* 73–119.

Willingham v. Macon Tel. Publ'g Co., 507 F2d. 1084 (5th Cir. 1975) (en banc).

Wilson v Southwest Airlines Co., 517 F.Supp 292 (ND Tex. 1981).

Wilson, B. D. M., & Meyer, I. H. (2021). *Nonbinary LGBTQ Adults in the United States.* The Williams Institute. https://williamsinstitute.law.ucla.edu/wp-content/uploads/Nonbinary-LGBTQ-Adults-Jun-2021.pdf

Wylie, J. (2018, May 13). What fashion needs to understand about being gender neutral. *Dazed.* https://www.dazeddigital.com/fashion/article/40206/1/what-fashion-needs-to-understand-about-being-gender-neutral

Chapter 8

Dressing to Be(come) a Business School Dean: Autoethnographic Accounts

Gina Grandy, Sharon Mavin and Elise Gagnon

Abstract

Women's bodies are abject and 'out of place' in organisations where (self and other) disciplining of women's bodies serve to regulate and silence women. Yet we know little about how expectations of body and appearance play out in the career decisions and everyday practices of women academic leaders. In this chapter reflexive accounts are used to explore if dress and appearance expectations have implications for women's career development and advancement, specifically in the context of business schools. The literature review and two reflexive autoethnographic accounts provided, illuminate how, through dress and appearance, the pervasiveness of hegemonic masculinity is both sustained and challenged and the potential impacts of this upon women's careers in academia.

Keywords: Abject appearance; business schools; women Deans; gender; women's leadership; bodywork; appearance; autoethnography; doing gender well; doing gender differently; respectable business femininity; women academic leaders; physicality of leadership

Introduction

Dress for the job you want, not the job you have so the saying goes. Who or what influences expectations of *appropriate* dress and appearance is tied to power relations and considerations of occupational prestige, gender, sexuality, class, race and culture. It has been argued that for women expectations of professionalism in dress and appearance are intimately tied to hegemonic masculinity (Haynes, 2012). Some research has revealed the (dark) suit as the safe call for women in business (Fotaki, 2014; Kelan, 2013), while other research has indicated that the terms of appropriate dress and appearance are more ambiguous (Mavin & Grandy, 2016a; Sinclair, 2011). Here we offer reflexive accounts to explore if

The Emerald Handbook of Appearance in the Workplace, 155–168
doi:10.1108/978-1-80071-174-720230009

dress and appearance expectations have implications for women's career development and advancement. Our particular interest is upon women Deans of university business schools. We engage in two reflexive autoethnographic accounts to illuminate how, through dress and appearance, the pervasiveness of hegemonic masculinity is both sustained and challenged. Similar to Knight et al. (2020) we use the term 'women' but we recognise the broad category of 'women' intersects with other identity markers including race, ethnicity, sexuality and class.

Women's bodies are abject and 'out of place' in organisations where (self and other) disciplining of women's bodies serve to regulate and silence women (Mavin & Grandy, 2016a, 2016b). Some contend that hegemonic masculinity, that which defines organisational life broadly, is amplified in academia. Academia is a hyper masculine and competitive environment whereby social structures of patriarchy and the masculine norm inform prevailing attitudes, practices, policies, cultures and everyday routines (Fitzgerald, 2018; Fotaki, 2014; Knights & Richards, 2003; Savigny, 2014; van den Brink & Stobbe, 2009). There is a nascent interest in the embodiment of women leaders in organisation and management studies, research which illuminates the salience of the body and appearance for women leaders and offers insights in the complexities of being a women leader (Haynes, 2012; Mavin & Grandy, 2016a, 2016b; Sinclair, 2011; Trethewey, 1999). There is, however, less on how this plays out for women and women leaders in the academy (see for exceptions, Fitzgerald, 2018; Fotaki, 2014). We take our inspiration from the work of Bell and Sinclair (2014), Fitzgerald (2018), and Fotaki (2014) who begin to surface the experiences of women academics and academic leaders in higher education and the challenges of navigating gendered expectations about clothing, grooming and performance as it relates to their body and appearance.

We believe women Deans of business are a particularly interesting site to explore expectations and implications of 'dressing the part' and career development and we aim to make a contribution in three key ways. First, women Deans and women Deans in university business schools globally are a rare breed (Henningsen et al., 2021; Lavigne, 2020). Knowing more about their experiences of becoming and being women Deans is important in addressing some of the barriers women confront. This may also pave new ways for career advancement for women in academia. Second, the lived experiences of two of the authors as women Deans of business schools inform this exploration. We draw from these experiences as we engage in this reflexive autoethnographical approach to the topic. In doing so, we contribute to studies of reflexivity and learning (e.g. Corlett & Mavin, 2018; Hibbert et al., 2021). Third, we seek to extend the extant literature on the complexity of women's gendered experiences of dress and appearance in the workplace (e.g. Mavin & Grandy, 2016a, 2016b; Trethewey, 1999), and more specifically in the academic setting and for women leaders in academia (e.g. Abbasi, 2013; Bell & Sinclair, 2014; Fitzgerald, 2018; Fotaki, 2014).

In what follows we look to literature related to women's embodiment in organisations. Specifically, we discuss how women are abjected in organisations and how that manifests through expectations of body and appearance. We also discuss how expectations of embodiment surface for women and women leaders in academia, serving to impede career development and silence women. We then offer two reflexive autoethnographical accounts of our own career development as it links to gender and appearance as women Deans of business schools. We conclude with thoughts for future research and continued reflexive practice as researchers of gender and women leading in business schools.

Literature Review

We understand gender as socially reconstructed through social activities; historical, cultural and embodied praxis within a web of complex power dynamics through which perceived biological sex is tied to particular scripts or associations of masculinity and femininity (Grandy & Mavin, 2020; Helms Mills & Mills, 1999; Mumby & Ashcraft, 2006). Organisations are gendered contexts where a masculine order shapes gender relations.

Women's Abjected Bodies in Organisations

Labour is an embodied practice (Brunner & Dever, 2014) and bodies map out relations of power and identity (Haraway, 1990) in organisations (Gimlin, 2007). The physical body is an important facet of professionalism and thus an important embodied representation of a perceived identity (Haynes, 2012). Yet, Brunner and Dever (2014) in their research on sexual harassment at work conclude that 'troubling bodies' (p. 463) are women's bodies, not men's. Women are rendered visible and invisible by their bodies in organisations.

'Women leaders have been definable by bodies, reproductive capacities and shaped by expectations of what is perceived to be respectable for women's bodies, i.e. "what should be worn, what mannerisms, demeanour, voice, size and shape are appropriate [read respectable femininity]" (Sinclair, 2011, p. 119)' (Mavin & Grandy, 2016a, p. 382). In the neoliberal context, Mavin et al. (2019) refer to the economies of visibility, where women's bodies are subject to commercial exchange and commodification, yet are silenced and restricted through policing of bodies. Economies of visibility explain how neoliberal logic not only commodifies women bodies as a brand but also offers them up for attention, scrutiny and criticism. Not only are women's bodies commodified, their credibility is realised when they conform to the subjective expectations of what a proper idealised feminine woman leader *should* be (Mavin & Grandy, 2016a). A credibility which affords them a fragile privilege at best (Mavin & Grandy, 2016a). Women leaders therefore continually work on their identities, aware of their bodies and appearance (Mavin & Grandy, 2016a, 2016b).

We have argued elsewhere how women leaders' bodies are abjected in organisations (Mavin & Grandy, 2016b), whereby the feminine/maternal body is subject to simultaneous intrigue and disgust (Kristeva, 1982). Even the threat of pregnancy can mark a women leader as suspect to abjection (Gatrell et al., 2017). We theorised that women leaders must manage the ambiguity of being both one (holding power through a leadership role) and other (through their out of place maternal bodies). We developed 'abject appearance' to explain a dynamic, dialectical and relational process through which women elite leaders manage felt ambiguities of their 'in-between' (Tyler, 2011, p. 1490) or 'abject' (Kristeva, 1982) status. This abjection of women's bodies is evident in how women leaders' privilege, accumulated through their position, is destabilised and always incomplete due to their embodied femininity. In their struggles to maintain their privilege, and therefore credibility, women leaders engage in a relational and discursive process of 'respectable business femininity' through disciplining self, in relation to others, body and appearance regimes (Mavin & Grandy, 2016a). We recognise that the body is more than appearance and that it is both social and material (Meriläinen et al., 2015) but similar to our work on respectable business femininity, here we focus on the visual gaze.

Bodies of Women (Leaders) in Academia as Barriers to Advancement

Academia has been said to be marked by three forms of gender segregation: vertical, horizontal and contractual (Knights & Richards, 2003). Women are especially under-represented in higher level positions (vertical), are scattered disproportionately across disciplines (horizontal), and are found in higher proportions in part-time and term positions (contractual) (Knights & Richards, 2003). The gendered environment in academia has been referred to as a 'chilly climate' (Sandler, 1986), where women are not recognised for their achievements, or valued in the same way as their men colleagues (Acker & Feuerverger, 1996; Hall & Sandler, 1982). Moreover, women are less likely to seek promotional opportunities when they identify an environment where sexist attitudes are encountered on a day-to-day basis, which in turn, normalises the expectations that women do not wish to progress (Savigny, 2014). The extant literature has identified many barriers to career advancement for women academics. Some of these obstacles relate to the job itself, such as a lack of a flexible work environment, work–life balance difficulties and required geographical mobility (Fritsch, 2015; Kalaitzi et al., 2017). Other barriers are specific to the culture in academia, citing male-dominated networks, stereotypes and a lack of mentoring (Acker & Feuerverger, 1996; Fritsch, 2015; Kalaitzi et al., 2017; van den Brink & Benschop, 2011). Our interest here is upon physical appearance and embodiment as one such barrier or challenge that women in academia must navigate.

Studies have shown that academics (men and women) who dress more formally (e.g. suit or suit-like) are viewed as more credible and more expert-like (see, for example, Lightstone et al., 2011; Sebastian & Bristow, 2008) but are also less likeable.[1] Both Bell and Sinclair (2014) and Fotaki (2014) bring attention to the feminine body in academia and how this plays out for women. Bell and Sinclair (2014) were interested broadly in the gendered bodily performance and sexualities of academic life, and specifically in arguing for a more nuanced understanding of eros and eroticism. In illuminating the role of bodies in academia and the gendered experience of academic life as part of their work, they adopt an autoethnographic storytelling approach and present selected personal experiences and those of other women academics (Bell & Sinclair, 2014). As it relates specifically to women's bodies in academia, some of those accounts reveal how: women academics can be sexualised by students; men colleagues police, inadvertently or otherwise, women academics' bodies and appearance; women academics respond to, resist, comply with such gendered expectations about their body and appearance; and women's size and their breasts mark them out as different, or less credible (Bell & Sinclair, 2014). Other studies provide further support for their conclusions. Women academics have reported being objectified by both colleagues and students (Cole & Hassel, 2017), having the male gaze directed to their chests (Savigny, 2017), having been viewed as less credible due to their petite and feminine appearance (van den Brink & Benschop, 2011), as well as having observed sexist behaviour and comments directed towards women – but not men (Savigny, 2014).

Abbasi (2013) engaged with eight women academics in a small, private liberal arts university in the United States to explore the dress choices of these women. There were no faculty requirements regarding dress at the institution. Drawing from Roach-Higgins and Eicher (1992, p. 1), Abbasi (2013, p. 6) defined dress as '"an assemblage of modifications of the body and/or supplements to the body" including styling one's hair, wearing make-up and perfumes, garments, and accessories'. Abbasi (2013) notes that there were varied conceptualisations of 'professional dress' and that expectations of appropriate professional dress as expressed by the women academics was rather ambiguous. For example, some said wearing make-up was part of being put together, while others felt make-up was not part of appropriate dress for women academics. Another expressed that only suits denoted professional dress, while another expressed that suits were too formal and appropriate only for special occasions. Nearly all of them, however, expressed that dress and appearance should help to distinguish faculty members from students. Despite the differences in expectations of appropriate dress and appearance, Abbasi (2013, p. 1) concluded, 'dress, for them, is a means of controlling and shaping who they view themselves to be into an appropriate external image of how they must be.'

Fotaki's (2014) work further extends our understandings of dress and appearance of women academics. Fotaki (2014) drew from the work of Irigaray (1985) and Kristeva (1982) to explain how, through the female body, women are excluded and out of place in academic institutions because of the pervasiveness of the male symbolic order. She interviewed 23 women academics in nine UK management and business schools (full professors, senior lecturers, lecturers and research associates). The study reveals how the denial of the feminine/female body enacted within the dominant discourses and comments about the material aspects of a woman's identity and their ways of being an academic in this context (e.g. 'too emotional'), serve to silence women literally and figuratively. The work also highlights how this manifests itself through self-regulation by women, for example, in wearing suits, wearing clothing in 'gender neutral' colours such as black, as well as disciplining the body through hair styles and weight maintenance. While this empirical work did not account for women in senior leadership roles in academia, it does illuminate critical insights into how women's bodies can be both abjected and disembodied in this context, the pressures and complexities that women in academia confront and how they attempt to navigate through that for career success.

Fitzgerald's (2018) work brings us closer to understanding what this means for women leaders in academia. Fitzgerald (2018) looked at the experiences of 30 senior women leaders in academia (in Australia and New Zealand), with an interest in how they navigate expectations about their clothing, grooming and image. She concluded that women had to meet expectations for both dress ('looking good') and behaviour ('being good'). Her work resonates with our own work on 'doing gender well and differently' (Mavin & Grandy, 2012, 2013) where through body, appearance and other performative aspects, women leaders in academia 'are simultaneously required to negotiate an inherently masculine culture, yet at the same time are expected to exercise a level of femininity' (Fitzgerald, 2018, p. 1). We argue that the former requires doing gender differently and the latter doing gender well. In 'looking good' the women academic leaders in Fitzgerald's study attempt to 'mask and monitor their feminine and 'out of place' bodies through their dress and physical appearance in order to be seamlessly woven into the organizational fabric and not be marked by their bodily difference to their male colleagues' (p. 2). These women both conform (e.g. through wearing suits) and also resist (e.g. through the use of colours or wearing scarves) to the masculine norm. Fitzgerald (2018) describes 'being good' as a 'bodily performance in which women discipline their own bodies, appearance and behaviours to display their outward conformity to a learned femininity' (p. 2). For example, some of the women in Fitzgerald's (2018) research enacted a results driven, target focused and direct approach, yet were often simultaneously criticised when they didn't engage with particular norms of femininity (e.g. caring; consultative). Fitzgerald's (2018) work extends the women in leadership literature by illustrating that within the context of academia, women leaders are at risk of receiving criticism or losing credibility if they do not *appropriately* discipline their bodies. Fitzgerald (2018) further demonstrates the complexities women leaders face – leadership is expected to be performed through physical embodiment, yet for women expectations of appropriate embodiment are ambiguous and contradictory.

In the reflexive accounts by the first two authors that follows we seek to further unravel how dress and appearance expectations have implications for women's career development, both sustaining and challenging hegemonic masculinity.

Reflexive Accounts by Two Women Business School Deans

As gender and leadership researchers, we (the first two authors) are intrigued by the *required* bodywork of women at work. Over 20 years, we have engaged in reflexive discussions about our own bodies and appearance at work, questioning our practices, our self-other judgements and our assumptions. We have also published on gendered expectations of body and appearance for women, including how our own lived experiences influence our interest in this area of research (e.g. Mavin et al., 2014; Mavin & Grandy, 2016a, 2016b). We have lived experiences as women leaders in academia. One author as a two times Dean in a business school in Canadian universities and one previously holding Dean and Director appointments at three different universities in the United Kingdom. Our lived experiences as women business Deans have been marked by self and other disciplining of body and appearance to do gender well and differently. Our lived experience also tells us that business school Deans need to be seen as both credible academics (to internal constituents) and credible business professionals (to external constituents). Here we offer our reflexive accounts to illuminate how through dress and appearance the pervasiveness of hegemonic masculinity can be both sustained and challenged for women leaders in academia.

We adopt a moderate autoethnographic approach (Wall, 2016) where we link personal experiences to social, cultural and political issues while attempting to critique 'within a cultural context with a vision and hope for change' (p. 5). Similar to Beck et al. (2018) who offer an autoethnograpic account as researchers of women's experiences of menopause and work, we offer a type of 'memory work' (Haug, 1999) – a feminist methodology whereby we remember and relive our experiences together as authors, rewriting and reinterpreting through shared meaning making of our retrospective retellings.

Story One

As a woman Dean of a university business school, I work hard to retain an impression of professionalism through my armour. My armour often includes a suit jacket (with a dress or trousers), especially if I am going to meetings with other business school Deans, students or external constituents to the university, or participating in video recordings or photo shoots. This felt need to look a certain type of professional through my attire started as early career bodywork. As a young woman academic my vulnerability around being viewed as insufficiently competent, experienced knowledgeable and credible in the classroom was made visible by students and others. Students would regularly approach me outside the classroom in conversations about topics that were personal and private (e.g. asking me how old I was; was I in a relationship) and older men students in particular would openly challenge my knowledge on topics in ways that were very different than I had ever witnessed experienced by my men colleagues. I loved teaching but I felt both exposed and silenced, my 'gender and age as intersecting forms of difference' (Beck et al., 2018, p. 259). I adopted the suit as a shield of credibility. It wasn't always a neutral colour but it was a suit nevertheless. I felt it distinguished me as different from the students in the classroom so close to my own age and aligned me more with how well-experienced business professionals presented themselves. I carried this through my pre leadership roles in academia with some variation (e.g. wearing dresses) but always wearing something I felt was more formal and more professional than the students in my classroom.

I never knew a woman business Dean until my co-author became a Dean and she reinforced my notion of the professionalism (and credibility) of the suit in positions of leadership for women (and men). Other salient cues have reinforced for me the apparent importance of certain notions of appropriate appearance and dress for women academic leaders. A story recounted to me by a woman university president stays with me. She felt rendered silent early in her academic leadership career when search consultants presenting at a women in academic leadership conference depicted the ideal presentable (woman) president as one with straight (read controllable) hair, pearls and a suit. None of which she felt aligned with her appearance, marking her out of place.

I am acutely aware that my neoliberal tendencies to look the part and do gender well are often at odds with my strong desire to do gender differently through exaggerated femininity (e.g. bright pink lipstick; big curly hair; bright coloured suits). I had one wall of my work office painted bright pink to insert, what I have described as, 'some femininity' in the Dean's Office. I want to be and see myself as a tempered radical (Meyerson & Scully, 1995) shaking the hegemonic masculine system from within with blasts of vibrant femininity. As I progress in my tenure as a woman academic leader, as an Associate Dean first and now Dean of business, I struggle more and more with a nagging feeling that at most all I am doing is hanging onto and reinforcing hegemonic femininity. A femininity that is tied to attracting the male gaze and sexual availability (Nussbaum, 1995); a seductive femininity that makes me feel special and beautiful and one I often wear proudly. I am left contemplating how my age and gender (now as I creep to 50) again mark my difference, a difference that is now even more fragile because I will soon no longer be able to perform hegemonic femininity. I also begin to wonder more and more how I am a failed feminist, kidding myself that I am tempered radical. Am I failing myself and other women because I am not brave enough to shake free of my desire to enact hegemonic femininity? Have I done anything to unsettle those embodied expectations which also leave those who do not identify with the gender binary feel unwelcomed because their bodies too are out of place?

On the days when I make mental space to challenge those body expectations, I look for contrary examples of my bodywork to see if those women Deans are viewed as less credible or competent. Mostly they aren't. I notice other women Deans (including in business) who dress and look differently (e.g. no suit, no make-up, vibrant coloured hair) and who appear to have their credibility intact – who aren't excluded or silenced because of their difference. And yet on other days I still catch myself internally abjecting women who are in academic leadership roles (in and outside business schools) and who do not align with my embedded markers of appropriate professional appearance. If others can enact their deanship as credible leaders outside those narrow body and appearance boundaries as I (and others) have defined, then what part do I play in sustaining hegemonic masculinity rather than embracing their courage in being tempered radicals?

Story Two

It started when I was promoted to Associate Dean as the only woman on the senior team, amidst the perfume of suits, when I became ultra-aware of how my body should be presented as part of a credible team. Not just a suit but a dark black or navy suit, with a top not so low as to show cleavage. The promotion meant attendance at 'black tie' events representing my organisation. This was trickier still. So visible against the sameness of men in black and white, like a rare white peacock regardless of the colour I wore. Knee-to-floor-length gown, evening dress or palazzo-cut pants – a black dress as a classic option were recommended to 'blend in' or fuchsia pink or red to make a 'splash' amongst the penguins, when I was more confident in resisting. Always aware of being the other. As part of resistance, I used these experiences in my teaching of gender and diversity and research into women leaders and Managers. Yet while I conformed to the dress and appearance expectations, my otherness was accentuated regardless of what I wore or how I looked. My body disrupted the 'flow' of 'business as usual' and at times, even international rituals, when, for example (there are hundreds of examples), at a dinner with corporate partners a business school colleague toasted to the 'women in the room' – there was only me (again) – all eyes on me – humiliating. When I travelled in the limousine with the VIP – as I had short legs so wouldn't take up much room – I hate being short. Or when along with university colleagues we would 'relax' at the hotel pool after an international graduation – horrendous. These were situations where I did have a choice, to speak or not, yet hegemonic masculinity reflected in professional etiquette or respectable business femininity, gagged and silenced me.

As Associate Dean and then Dean, on the way to work, via dropping off my daughter at nursery and then school, I'd put my makeup on in the car and always wore lipstick. I was conscious at all times – on high alert of the judging of my body that I knew was always happening – particularly when making 'whole school' presentations, where what I said was less important than how I looked... My resistance was my hair – never short enough and always curly. And I was never thin enough – not like those women CEOs and politicians who keep to the same pant suit and short, blond bob – they know how they are judged.

My second Dean position was in a less corporate, more social sciences university where the suit was rejected in preference for individuality and in most circumstances as a woman I was in the majority. This was so liberating and came at the same time as I was researching postfeminism, corporate and moderate feminism and women leaders in the Financial Times Stock Exchange (FTSE). I learned to let go of the body armour, camouflage and to 'relax' what I wore. I was able to be 'me' in ways I hadn't been before. We researched women leaders' misrepresentations in the media and studied how gendered expectations of women's bodies come about and are perpetuated (e.g. resisting and making sense of my experiences).

The next Dean move was to a culture I experienced as toxic masculinity, reflected in 'hidden' rules to be complied with and submitted to, certain ways of asserting power and dominance and systemic issues related to a gender order (SHRM, 2021) reflected in 97% men Professors. While there was lack of corporate expectation, the gender balance meant I was completely aware – on high alert – of how my body was abjected – symbolic of my outsider status and lack of credibility.

No longer a Dean or Director, my hair is long, curly, I wear little makeup, mostly flat shoes and no suits – I am old enough for my body to no longer be subject to a certain gaze – but I inhabit a body that remains abjected, not yet credible enough.

Reflexivity engages me in questioning my ways of being; it has a 'self-referential characteristic of "bending-back" some thought upon the self (Archer, 2009, p. 2) and is always a self-monitoring of, and a self-responding to, our thoughts, feelings and actions as we engage' (Corlett & Mavin, 2018, p. 379). In relation to this story, my reflexivity has focused on how my body and bodywork changed to reflect each of the organisational cultures where I was a 'leader'. There are signs that I should have been more attuned to. I am baffled by the ambiguities of seduction and resistance in my claims for credibility. Why didn't I interrogate these cultures for what they were – scrutinise their inclusivity and readiness for a woman leader, the signals of the diversity of the university and openness (or not) of the cultures (regardless of public statements) rather than internalising a focus on my bodywork and resisting through my research?

Concluding Thoughts

As we continue to reflect on our lived experiences as women business school Deans we ponder what this means for other women Deans in business schools or those aspiring to become Associate Deans and Deans in business schools. First, we have become acutely aware of the physicality of leadership as women deans in business schools. Women Deans are hyper-visible. Our focus in this chapter has been on the visual gaze but we recognise that the physicality of leadership extends far beyond that (e.g. how our bodies tense and breathing changes in stressful situations). As the number of women holding these positions slowly increase (at least white women), we may begin to stand out less because of our recognised sex category or gender. Regardless, these positions affect our bodies – how we present ourselves and how we are able to maintain healthy (re: stress free) bodies. Our position is less about advocating for women to do gender well or differently through their bodies, and more about being aware of one's body needs and raising consciousness about how others' may interpret your bodywork and the institutional expectations and pressures to conform. Second, we hope we have come to place in our careers where we have learned to pay closer attention to what isn't said in interviews (about the cultural expectations) and to look more closely at material and symbolic clues that often go unnoticed during interviews (e.g. what appears to be the 'dress code' for faculty members in the school, Vice Chancellor, advisory board members) to better understand what subtle hints and explicit signals are being offered. Understanding those cultural and climate clues might help to better assess what it will 'really be like' to work there for the woman considering the position. Third, we encourage women to become more aware of their own bodywork and expectations (of themselves and others) in a business school context. In doing so, it serves to bring to the surface underlying assumptions about perceived professionalism and credibility. Such assumptions have implications for women, men (is the suit a measure of professionalism for men?) and non-binary academics in the context of business schools.

In their work on gender bias and self-selection and the link to deanship ambition of women and men professors, Henningsen et al. (2021) suggest 'policies to increase the number of women in university deanships should make salient the presence of other women in these roles and also the potential of these roles to fulfil communal career goals' (p. 1). We believe that such an approach serves to reinforce gender stereotypes (e.g. women will be interested in leadership roles to fulfil communal career goals). Yet, we recognise there is much to uncover in understanding the career path of women academic leaders. In this chapter, we offer a previously unspoken version of what we, as women leaders in academia, experience as Associate Deans and Deans. In surfacing our stories and rendering ourselves vulnerable as leaders and as women, we recognise how invisible 'appearance in the academic work place' is in mainstream research and in organisational academic practice – but the powerful impact this has for women academic leaders. It is important to continue this conversation and to challenge and resist by making public the impact of gendered body and appearance via academic leadership programmes, career coaching and mentoring and in future research.

Note

1. In the Lightstone et al. (2011) study formal dress and reduced likeability was amplified for men.

References

Abbasi, L. (2013). "Their image of me": A phenomenological study of professional dress choices of female professors. In *Proceedings of the New York State Communication Association.* Vol. 2021, Article 4. https://docs.rwu.edu/cgi/viewcontent.cgi?article=1055&context=nyscaproceedings. Accessed on September 1, 2021.

Acker, S., & Feuerverger, G. (1996). Doing good and feeling bad: The work of women university teachers. *Cambridge Journal of Education, 26*(3), 401–422.

Archer, M. S. (Ed.). (2009). *Conversations about reflexivity.* Routledge.

Beck, V., Brewis, J., & Davies, A. (2018). The post-re/productive researching the menopause. *Journal of Organizational Ethnography, 7*(3), 247–262.

Bell, E., & Sinclair, A. (2014). Reclaiming eroticism in the academy. *Organization, 21*(2), 268–280.

Brunner, L. K., & Dever, M. (2014). Work, bodies and boundaries: Talking sexual harassment in the new economy. *Gender, Work and Organization, 21*(5), 459–471.

Cole, K., & Hassel, H. (2017). *Surviving sexism in academia: Strategies for feminist leadership.* Routledge, Taylor & Francis.

Corlett, S., & Mavin, S. (2018). Reflexivity and researcher positionality. In C. Cassell, A. Cunliffe, & G. Grandy (Eds.), *The SAGE handbook of qualitative business and management research methods* (pp. 377–399). Sage. Chapter 23.

Fitzgerald, T. (2018). Looking good and being good: Women leaders in Australian universities. *Education Sciences, 8*(54), 1–12. https://doi.org/10.3390/educsci 8020054

Fotaki, M. (2014). No woman is like a man (in academia): The masculine symbolic order and the unwanted female body. *Organization Studies, 34*(9), 1251–1275.

Fritsch, N. (2015). At the leading edge – Does gender still matter? A qualitative study of prevailing obstacles and successful coping strategies in academia. *Current Sociology, 63*(4), 547–565. https://doi.org/10.1177/0011392115576527

Gatrell, C., Cooper, C. L., & Kossek, E. E. (2017). Maternal bodies as taboo at work: New perspectives on the marginalizing of senior-level women in organizations. *Academy of Management Perspectives, 31*(3), 239–252.

Gimlin, D. (2007). What is 'body work'? A review of the literature. *Sociology Compass, 1*(1), 353–370.

Grandy, G., & Mavin, S. (2020). Informal and socially situated learning: Gendered practices and becoming women church leaders. *Gender in Management: International Journal, 35*(1), 61–75.

Hall, R., & Sandler, B. (1982). The classroom climate: A chilly one for women. In *Project on the Status and Education of Women.* Association of American Colleges.

Haraway, D. (1990). A manifesto for cyborgs: Science, technology, and socialist feminism in the 1980s. In L. Nicholson (Ed.), *Feminism/Postmodernism* (pp. 190–233). Routledge.

Haug, F. (1999). Memory work as a method of social science research: A detailed rendering of memory work method. http://www.friggahaug.inkrit.de/documents/ memorywork-researchguidei7.pdf. Accessed on September 1, 2021.

Haynes, K. (2012). Body beautiful? Gender, identity and the body in professional services firms. *Gender, Work and Organization, 19*(1), 489–507.

Helms Mills, J., & Mills, A. J. (1999). Rules, sensemaking, formative contexts and discourses in the gendering of organizational culture. In N. Askernasy, C. Wilderom, & M. Peterson (Eds.), *Handbook of Organizational Culture and Climate* (pp. 55–70). Sage.

Henningsen, L., Eagly, A. H., & Jonas, K. (2021). Where are the women deans? The importance of gender bias and self-selection processes for the deanship ambition of female and male professors. *Journal of Applied Social Psychology*, 1–21. Early View. https://doi.org/10.1111/jasp.12780

Hibbert, P., Beech, N., Callagher, L., & Siedlok, F. (2021). *After the pain: Reflexive Practice, emotion work and learning.* Organization Studies. OnlineFirst. https://doi. org/10.1177/01708406211011014

Irigaray, L. (1985). *This sex that is not one.* Cornell University Press.

Kalaitzi, S., Czabanowska, K., Fowler-Davis, S., & Brand, H. (2017). Women leadership barriers in healthcare, academia and business. *Equality, Diversity and Inclusion: An International Journal, 36*(5), 457–474. https://doi.org/10.1108/edi-03-2017-0058

Kelan, E. (2013). The becoming of business bodies: Gender, appearance and leadership development. *Management Learning, 44*(1), 45–61.

Knight, L., Gray, E., & Blaise, M. (2020). Powerful dressing. Artfully challenging sexism in the academy. In C. A. Taylor, J. Ulmer, & C. Hughes (Eds.), *Transdisciplinary feminist research: Innovations in theory, method and practice.* Taylor & Francis.

Knights, D., & Richards, W. (2003). Sex discrimination in UK academia. *Gender, Work and Organization, 10*(2), 213–238. https://doi.org/10.1111/1468-0432.t01-1-00012

Kristeva, J. (1982). *Powers of horror: An essay on abjection.* Columbia University Press.

Lavigne, E. (2020). The demographics and career paths of Canadian deans: Gender, race, experience, and provenance. *Studies in Higher Education, 45*(9), 1949–1960.

Lightstone, K., Francis, R., & Kocum, L. (2011). University faculty style of dress and students' perception of instructor credibility. *International Journal of Business and Social Science, 2*(15), 15–22.

Mavin, S., Elliott, C., Stead, V., & Williams, J. (2019). Economies of visibility as a moderator of feminism: 'Never mind Brexit. Who won Legs-it!' *Gender, Work and Organization, 26*(8), 1156–1175.

Mavin, S., & Grandy, G. (2012). Doing gender well and differently in management. *Gender in Management: International Journal, 27*(4), 218–231.

Mavin, S., & Grandy, G. (2013). Doing gender well and differently in dirty work. *Gender, Work and Organization, 20*(3), 232–251. (Note: Online 4 August 2011). https://doi.org/10.1111/j.1468-0432.2011.00567.x

Mavin, S., & Grandy, G. (2016a). Women elite leaders doing respectable business femininity: How privilege is conferred, contested and defended through the body. *Gender, Work and Organization, 23*(4), 379–396.

Mavin, S., & Grandy, G. (2016b). A theory of abject appearance: Women elite leaders' intra-gender 'management' of bodies and appearance. *Human Relations, 69*(5), 1095–1120. (Note: Online First 2015). https://doi.org/10.1177/0018726715609107

Mavin, S., Grandy, G., & Williams, J. (2014). Experiences of women elite leaders doing gender: Intra-gender micro-violence between women in management. *British Journal of Management, 25*(3), 439–455.

Meriläinen, S., Tienari, J., & Valtonen, A. (2015). Headhunters and the 'ideal' executive body. *Organization, 22*(1), 3–22.

Meyerson, D., & Scully, M. (1995). Tempered radicalism and the politics of ambivalence and change. *Organization Science, 6*(5), 585–600.

Mumby, D. K., & Ashcraft, K. L. (2006). Organizational communication studies and gendered organization: A response to Martin and Collinson. *Gender, Work and Organization, 13*(1), 68–90.

Nussbaum, M. (1995). Objectification. *Philosophy & Public Affairs, 24*(4), 249–291.

Roach-Higgins, M. E., & Eicher, J. B. (1992). Dress and identity. *Clothing and Textiles Research Journal, 10*, 1–8.

Sandler, B. (1986). *The chilly climate revisited: Chilly for women faculty, administrators and graduate students.* Association of American Colleges.

Savigny, H. (2014). Women, know your limits: Cultural sexism in academia. *Gender and Education, 26*(7), 794–809.

Savigny, H. (2017). Cultural sexism is ordinary: Writing and re-writing women in academia. *Gender, Work and Organization, 24*(6), 643–655. https://doi.org/10.1111/gwao.12190

Sebastian, R., & Bristow, D. (2008, March/April). Formal or informal? The impact of style of dress and forms of address on business students' perceptions of professors. *Journal of Education for Business, 83*(4), 196–201.

SHRM. (2021). *How toxic masculinity is ruining your workplace.* https://www.shrm.
org/hr-today/news/all-things-work/pages/how-toxic-masculinity-is-ruining-your-
workplace-culture.aspx. Accessed on September 14.

Sinclair, A. (2011). Leading with body. In E. Jeanes, D. Knights, & P. Martin (Eds.),
Handbook of Gender, Work and Organization (pp. 117–130). John Wiley & Sons.

Trethewey, C. (1999). Disciplined bodies: Women's embodied identities at work.
Organization Studies, 20(3), 423–450.

Tyler, M. (2011). Tainted love: From dirty work to abject labour in Soho's sex shops.
Human Relations, 64(11), 1477–1500.

van den Brink, M., & Benschop, Y. (2011). Slaying the seven-headed dragon: The
quest for gender change in academia. *Gender, Work and Organization, 19*(1),
71–92.

van den Brink, M., & Stobbe, L. (2009). Doing gender in academic education: The
paradox of visibility. *Gender, Work and Organization, 16*(4), 451–470.

Wall, S. S. (2016). Toward a moderate autoethnography. *International Journal of
Qualitative Methods, 15*(1), 1–9.

Chapter 9

Appearance Matters: Appearance Management in Political Careers

Minita Sanghvi and Nancy Hodges

Abstract

Today, appearance is an integral aspect of a politician's image and personality and therefore his or her brand (Budesheim & DePaola, 1994; Sanghvi &
Hodges, 2015; Smith & French, 2009). While appearance is critical to political marketing, most of the research focusing on appearance in politics is
experimental in nature (Lenz & Lawson, 2011; Olivola & Todorov, 2010;
Todorov et al., 2005). This study investigates the importance of appearance
for marketing politicians through a qualitative interpretivist framework that
offers implications for theory. Moreover, this chapter offers a specific focus
on the importance of appearance for female politicians.

Research shows women face greater scrutiny on their appearance (Carlin
& Winfrey, 2009; Sanghvi, 2018). This chapter examines myriad of issues
women in politics face based on their appearance. It also examines how
women have successfully managed the issue of appearance at local, state and
national levels. Thus, this study delivers a multifaceted view of the topic and
facilitates the understanding of how appearance management enters into the
political marketing process.

Keywords: Women; appearance management; image; careers; political
brands; gender

As more women run for office in the United States, politics becomes an important
career choice for many women. In 2022, approximately 31.5% of the city council
seats in the top 100 towns, 26% of Mayors in towns over 30,000 people, 32.7% of
the state legislature seats and 27.9% in US Congress were held by women
(CAWP, 2023). The unexpected loss of Secretary of State Hillary Clinton to
Donald Trump in the US presidential elections in 2016 led to an unprecedented
boom in women's interest in political participation. For example, in 2018 we saw

The Emerald Handbook of Appearance in the Workplace, 169–184
Copyright © 2024 by Emerald Publishing Limited
All rights of reproduction in any form reserved
doi:10.1108/978-1-80071-174-720230010

476 women ran for the United States House of Representatives (CAWP, 2023) compared to 273 in 2016. These numbers continued to grow with 585 women candidates running for the 435 seats in the US House of Representatives in 2020 (CAWP, 2023).

Politics may not necessarily be categorised as 'display work' as described by Mears and Connell (2016) with regards to careers that have a dominant visual component, such as modelling and acting; nevertheless, however we know that having 'the right look' is a critical component to women's success in careers, including politics (Nickson, 2018; Peluchette & Karl, 2018; Sanghvi & Hodges, 2015). Appearance management has become a critical aspect in political campaigns and can significantly affect election outcomes (Hoegg & Lewis, 2011; Rosenberg et al., 1991). In today's fast paced visual culture, voters gauge a politician's competence, intelligence, integrity and trustworthiness from his or her appearance (De Landtsheer et al., 2008; Franklin & Zebrowitz, 2016; Garzia, 2013; Lenz & Lawson, 2011; Rockey et al., 2022; Sanghvi, 2018).

Several studies indicate that a large section of voters respond almost exclusively to emotional appeals (De Landtsheer et al., 2008; Guzmán & Sierra, 2009; O'Shaughnessy, 1990). Campaigns are creating strategies, positioning the political candidate as a brand and winning votes by communicating messages to people that are grounded in emotional appeals. Millions of dollars are spent communicating the right look and image to the people. In some ways, looking the part has become more critical to winning voters than a candidate's policies, voting record or endorsements (Guzmán & Sierra, 2009; Hoegg & Lewis, 2011; Jackson, 2003; Lawson et al., 2010; Lenz & Lawson, 2011). Today, appearance is an integral aspect of a politician's image and personality and therefore his or her brand (Budesheim & DePaola, 1994; Sanghvi & Hodges, 2015).

This study investigates the importance of appearance for marketing politicians through a qualitative framework that offers implications for theory. This study also offers consideration of how the role of appearance differs for female politicians compared to male politicians, and how it impacts their success in the political landscape. This study provides a multifaceted view of the topic and facilitates the understanding of how appearance management enters into political careers and the political marketing process.

Literature Review

Gregory Stone's (1962) pivotal article in the field of appearance management defines appearance as a social transaction that helps to establish identity. That is, according to Stone (1962), identities are 'established and mobilised' via appearance (p. 28). When an individual dress themselves, they are concurrently addressing an audience whose response to that dress is crucial in order to validate one's identity (Stone, 1962). Kaiser (1997) defines appearance as a composite image made by the human body, including any 'modifications, embellishments or coverings of the body that are visually perceived; a visual context that includes clothing as well as the body' (p. 4). For Kaiser (1997), appearance management is defined as a process that starts with planning, thinking about or evaluating the social consequences of one's appearance. Aune and Aune (1994) posit that initial impressions are based on one's appearance and therefore define appearance management as the 'grooming or preening behaviour in humans' (p. 259). Thus, appearance encapsulates not only a person's clothing but also their hair colour and styles, body modifications such as tattoos and piercings, jewellery, accessories, body language, voice and posture. Consequently, the management of an appearance involves the following:

(1) everything one does to dress oneself using modifications and supplements;
(2) the process of planning, organising and making decisions to dress oneself; and
(3) assessing the personal and social implications of such decisions (Kaiser, 1997).

There are often multiple meanings communicated by appearance; however, such meanings can also be vague and undercoded (Miller-Spillman et al., 2012). Each appearance includes several systems of communication within it, such as colour, texture and silhouette (Damhorst, 1990). According to Damhorst (1990), the 'nonlinguistic, gestalt, structural, undercoded' properties of appearance create a multifaceted method of communication (p. 2). Appearance is also used as a conduit for communicating an individual's identity and can communicate such identity dimensions as social class, religious beliefs, group membership, rebellion, style and power (Nelson, 2000; O'Neal, 1999; Roach-Higgins & Eicher, 1992).

Although appearance impacts perceptions of self and others as a mode of non-verbal communication, it can also impact behaviour (Johnson et al., 2008). Uniforms, such as those worn by police, the military and airline pilots impact people's perceptions of power and authority and affect behavioural responses (Johnson et al., 2008; Johnson & Lennon, 1999). O'Neal (1999) suggests that dress is a political instrument used to influence formal and informal relationships. Humans are highly visual by nature and often rely on appearance to judge the goals of others (Johnson & Lennon, 1999). Relatedly, appearance orientation is the level of emphasis one puts on personal appearance and includes how critical an individual's looks are to him/her and the extent of grooming behaviour he/she engages in to manage his/her appearance (Davis et al., 2001; Johnson et al., 2008).

Brannon (1993) suggests two perspectives to use in the study of appearance management: (1) a self-system theoretical orientation and (2) a behavioural-system theoretical orientation. According to Brannon (1993), the self-system theoretical orientation comprises thoughts and feelings about oneself, how those thoughts and feelings become strategies to conceal and reveal and the expression of those strategies in dress and self-presentation. The behavioural system encompasses thoughts and feelings about social implications of dress, how those thoughts and feelings manifest into selection strategies for a specific instance and for the desired effect on social interactions via impression management (Brannon, 1993).

Similarly, Kaiser (1997) defines appearance management as thinking, planning, organising, paying attention to, experimenting with, self-expression of and the act of creating one's appearance. In the next section, we examine how appearance works in the political arena.

Appearance and Political Marketing

There is scant research that specifically examines the role of appearance management in politics. Over the years as the political marketing literature has evolved, politicians have increasingly been treated as brands (Jackson, 2003; Smith & French, 2009) and appearances are a part of the packaging that sells the brand (Jackson, 2003). The appearance of a candidate is a critical piece of the candidate's brand image, and one that could affect voter perceptions about the candidate's moral fibre, competence and leadership qualities, which, in turn, could affect election results (Goudge & Littrell, 1989; Kwon, 1994; Lawson et al., 2010). Politicians use props and non-verbal cues such as ties, hats, hairstyles and jewellery to accentuate certain aspects of themselves based on the situation, and do so to demonstrate behaviours that are attuned with social values and expectations that they think look good to the public (Mohamed & Gardner, 2004).

Appearance management is an integral aspect of several studies in the political branding literature, though not acknowledged as such. For example, according to Guzmán and Sierra (2009), a political candidate's brand image is built on three factors: (1) the physical attributes of the politician, (2) the politician's personality and (3) the politician's pledges to the populace. Appearance management strategies help with the first two factors by highlighting certain facets of a candidate's physical attributes as well as aid in manipulating the impressions of certain aspects of the candidate's personality to win the election and maintain the image of an effective leader. Similarly, appearance management is also a factor in building a politician's image and personality which is a crucial aspect of the politician's brand (Cwalina & Falkowski, 2015; Falkowski & Michalak, 2014) as well as creating what is now considered a celebrity based political age (Seawright, 2013). The fact that appearance is utilised but unacknowledged may be intentional as we see from Scammell's (2015) study wherein she agrees that appearance is a part of a politician's brand image, but calls it 'frippery' (p. 9) and something that is insignificant to political scientists and not worth paying a lot of attention to. However, the next section examines the significant impact that appearance has on the success of a female politician.

Appearance Management and Female Politicians

Appearances are important for women in as much as the culture places a strong emphasis on how women look, including their clothing and grooming practices (Rudd & Lennon, 2000). A woman's appearance can affect perceptions of her professionalism and intelligence, and is a critical part of her success in the workplace (Kwon, 1994). For instance, Goudge and Littrell (1989) found that in the workplace, dress is often added to the equation of job skills and luck equalling a job applicant's success. Likewise, Kwon (1994) found that clothing enhances a person's perceptions of his/her occupational attributes such as responsibility, professionalism, efficiency and so on. Women use appearance as a tool to increase perceptions of competence and boost their value in the social and work arenas (Johnson et al., 1994; Kwon, 1994).

The research on appearance for female politicians focuses on the greater propensity among the media, other politicians and the general public to focus on the female political candidate's physical appearance, clothing, hair and shoes instead of more substantive issues (Falk, 2010; Sanghvi, 2014; Uscinski & Goren, 2011). Lizotte and Meggers-Wright (2019) found that focus on women's appearance, specifically her attractiveness, impacted her negatively on issues such as intelligence and competence. Several other studies showcase the damaging effects of sexism and gender stereotyping on women's participation in politics (Lammers et al., 2009; Sanghvi, 2018). Several studies point to the negative bias in media coverage for female politicians and media's propensity to focus on appearance with respect to female candidates (Falk, 2010; Mandziuk, 2008; Sanghvi & Hodges, 2015). Falk (2010) studied female presidential candidates in the United States to uncover that the media reports on a female candidate's clothes more often than that of males. Focus on Governor Palin's appearance led to lower estimation of her competence and a lower intention to vote for McCain and Palin's 2008 Republican ticket.

Clearly, appearance management is a critical aspect of current political branding strategies and therefore deserves further attention in the literature. That is even more so the case for female politicians who face a greater scrutiny on their appearance.

Method

To address the purpose of this study, data were collected through in-depth interviews and focus groups with a total of 42 participants involved in various aspects of politics and political marketing. Overall, participant selection reflected a purposive sampling method, in that we chose 'informants from populations that manifest that phenomenon of interest and are ideally suited to illuminate the phenomenon' (Wooten, 2006, p. 189). Participants were recruited through referrals such as personal contacts at Political Action Committees (PAC) political parties and affiliations, as well as through a network of political consultants. These connections helped us gain access to other participants, from politicians to staff members, aides, political consultants, media, volunteers and PAC members (See Table 1).

The participants included eight politicians at various levels of office, from local to national and from legislative to executive office, including a Governor, a Senator, a State Senator, two State Representatives, two Mayors and a city council member. Several staffers, aides and political consultants, as well as PAC

Table 1. Participant Information.

No.	Name	Job Description
1	Victoria Burns	Governor
2	Sue Ellen Rowland	Senator
3	Joy Lancaster	State Senator
4	Elizabeth Stanton	State Representative
5	DeShawn King	State Representative
6	Patricia Mitchell	Mayor
7	William Kane	Mayor
8	Rashida Davis	City Council Member
9	Anna Belle Crawford	Former Senior White House official
10	James Pippen	Congressional Staffer for a Senator
11	Nicole Christensen	Director on presidential campaign
12	Andrea Fearrington	Political consultant
13	John Duckworth	Political consultant
14	Oliver Andrews	Political consultant
15	Jacob Ratner	Political consultant
16	Adriana Kablitz	Political consultant
17	Samantha Wilkes	PAC member, and political consultant
18	Alexandra Margozzini	Political Director at PAC
19	Kevin Dixon	Political Director at Super PAC
20	Lucy Little	Field Director at Super PAC
21	Kate Renou	Political Director at PAC and Senior Party Official
22	Harold Smith	Congressional District Chair, Political candidate
23	Polly Michaels	Political Consultant
24	Jeffrey DeMaio	State PAC Political Director
25	Michael Armstrong	Author, Opinion-Editor, Journalist
26	David Spurlock	Editor, Journalist
27	Miranda Rudlin	Campaign Fundraiser, Volunteer
28	Alice Keens	Precinct Chair, County office holder, Volunteer
29	Kathleen Edwards	County office manager, Volunteer
30	Joseph Puccio	Senior district official, Volunteer
31	Anne Mancini	Registered Voter/Retired
32	Elizabeth Bennett	Registered Voter/Retired
33	Elina Funar	Registered Voter/Retired
34	Virginia Nilsen	Registered Voter/Working

Table 1. *(Continued)*

No.	Name	Job Description
35	Jessica Vera	Registered Voter/Working Part Time
36	Deborah Larssen	Registered Voter/Working
37	Kurt Hubbard	Registered Voter/Working
38	Linda Mooney	Registered Voter/Working
39	Brittany Page	Registered Voter/Working
40	Vivienne Marsh	Registered Voter/Working
41	Mary Elizabeth Ray	Registered Voter/Working
42	Jason O'Connor	Registered Voter/Working

political directors, were also interviewed. Pseudonyms are used in place of real names to protect each participant's confidentiality.

For the purposes of this study, semi-structured questions were used, which helped give direction to the interviews, and focus groups, yet allowed for openness to new directions that unfolded during the process (Rubin & Rubin, 1995). Once the data were collected, we followed the analysis procedures as outlined by Spiggle (1994) to organise the data, deduce meaning and draw conclusions that helped the thematic framework that describe the data.

By selecting politicians from local, legislative and executive levels, the role of appearance management in political marketing could be examined in depth and detailed descriptions of experiences achieved at a range of levels (Hesse-Biber & Leavy, 2004).

Interpretation

Appearance is a critical piece for most politicians. Participants in this study described how various aspects of their appearance would be discussed and focused upon, not just by the media, but by volunteers and voters as well. The most common issues brought up by participants with respect to appearance include the fact that men have it easier because they have a uniform in the suit. Likewise, men's hairstyles offer little variation and therefore less room for error. The same holds true for hemlines, which calls forth questions related to pantyhose (to wear it or not to wear it).

Workwear: The Male Politician's Uniform

Most participants talked about men's dress as a uniform. That is, as State Senator Lancaster says, 'Men have a simple uniform and when they wear it, no one particularly notices'. State Senator Lancaster thinks that men face judgement about their appearance only when they break out of this uniform. She provided the example of Mitt Romney wearing jeans in 2012 Presidential election at various campaign rallies and received widespread media coverage on it. Some of the attention was positive, while some poked fun at the candidate with funny memes and pictures. Similarly, Obama wearing a tan suit at a news conference caused a national news cycle with politicians, media, fashion critics and image consultants weighing in (Farzan, 2019).

According to State Senator Lancaster, it is very rare that a male politician's clothing or appearance is discussed. As she explained, 'You rarely get someone saying to the guy, "You should wear brown shoes, you should not wear black shoes, you shouldn't wear khakis." [Laughs] I mean, you don't get that as much with guys'. It is interesting to note that the mere suggestion was humourous to State Senator Lancaster, indicating the extent to which even participants thought that the idea was ridiculous.

Although male politicians may have standardised wardrobe choices with few options, in contrast, female politicians have an extensive range of dress and appearance decisions that they must be mindful of. This means there is much greater room for error regarding women's appearance, making it doubly difficult for them to avoid criticism, as their appearance is usually a focal point to begin with. Participants pointed in particular to decisions about how to wear their hair, whether to be formal or casual, and what hem length is most appropriate.

The Long Job Interview

Today political campaigns can last for months or even years. For example, Senator Elizabeth Warren announced her intentions to run in the 2020 presidential election on 31 December 2018, almost two years (23 months) before the actual election. And former President Donald J. Trump announced his candidacy for the 2024 election on 16 November 2022 (24 months) earlier. This is earlier than planning for the 2016 presidential elections which started officially in May 2015 (18 months before the actual election). Political consultants see campaigns as a long interview process that puts the political candidate on display for an extended period of time. As Andrea Fearrington, a political consultant, explained, 'Campaigning is nothing but a long job interview…and you have to present a certain way. You have to look as if you are credible. And certainly, appearance plays a role in that'.

When asked what goes into making a politician 'look credible' she responded that a politician, regardless of gender, needs to look clean, well-kept and look professional. She believes that if politicians appear well-kept and professional then voters think they are responsible and will take care of the details.

> If someone is well-kept and well-presented then they will present well on your behalf, represent you well. And they are probably responsible if they take the time to care of themselves and present themselves in a positive way physically. If people take care of the details then they will take better care of you.

Nicole Christensen, a political consultant specialising in women's votes, also uses the long interview analogy when she talks about campaigning. She explained, 'As voters we are interviewing a candidate for a job'. Similar to job interviews, candidates must present themselves seriously to be taken as serious contenders for the position. She adds, 'When you campaign for a job it *does* matter how you dress or how you present yourself'.

David Spurlock (media editor) explained that politicians dress up because they want people to believe they are committed to their jobs, stating, 'They want people to think they are serious about their jobs, they take it seriously and they are trying to do a good job'. Mayor Patricia Mitchell concurs, 'You have to dress for job. . .and I think it is very important because this is a serious job'. In addition, Kate Renou (political director) suggests that a well-groomed, attractive, fit candidate shows discipline and commitment to the job and the people that person represents. She states 'If you don't care about your appearance what is to say you care about going to work every day and being a good representative and taking care of the people. People in America just expect to see that kind of presentation and stature from their elected officials'.

Additionally, in the age of social media and smart phones, politicians must be prepared to be photographed or videotaped anywhere at any point and these photos and videos can go viral within minutes. Hence appearance is something that a politician needs to consider on a regular basis. Likewise, the appearance of the politician is something voters also take into consideration. For example, Virginia Nilsen (voter) thinks that President Obama got elected because he has the 'winner look'. Similarly, Mary Elizabeth Ray (voter) believed Kennedy's 'vibrancy' helped win him the election. According to Jessica Vera (voter), some voters may use appearance cues to make the decision about whom to vote for if they are undecided. She explained that 'some people might really be motivated to vote if there is something that is exciting about that person. Like when people got excited about voting for Obama. And back with Reagan, he probably traded on being a movie star'.

Gendered Expectations in the Political Workplace

When discussing appearance with Senator Rowland, the issue of pantyhose arose. She talked about how while she was running for office she attended a seminar conducted by the National Women's Political Caucus on how to win an election. In the seminar, female candidates were advised to carry an extra pair of pantyhose at all times. Senator Rowland explains in greater detail as to why the Caucus made the suggestion:

> Because if you are in a debate or you are out, if people notice a run in your hose, it is a whole different ball game. In terms of your appearance, it was a whole different challenge, because people won't pay attention to what you are saying, because they can't think beyond the fact that you have a run in your hose.

Clearly, the pantyhose issue is a problem unique to women, in as much as men do not wear them. Female politicians also need to consider regional differences in appearance expectations. That is, apparel choices that may be acceptable for a female politician in one state may not work in another. If some states expect her to wear pantyhose and some do not, how does she please all audiences in a nationwide televised debate? Pantyhose may seem like a rather minor issue, but one that a female politician running in a presidential race might have to consider, while her male counterpart would not. Because they more or less wear a uniform, men are exempt from considerations of such details that can take time and energy away from the issues at hand.

Another appearance-related issue, albeit one that has changed in recent years, is hats. Hats may not be as popular anymore or much of an issue in the lives of most female politicians today, but when Hattie Carraway, the first female politician elected to serve a full term as a senator came to the Senate in 1932, she was not allowed to wear hats on the floor. According to Senator Rowland, this was a big problem for her:

> The first woman to be elected to the Senate in her own right was Hattie Caraway in 1932. Talk about scrutiny. She had lost her husband, so she had completed the final two years of his term and then chose to run for election, which shocked everybody. But she was still in mourning so she wore black. Back in the day it was considered inappropriate for a woman to be out in public without a hat, but it is against Senate rules to wear a hat on the floor of the Senate because it was rude if a man wore a hat indoors. But for a woman it as really more of an issue of whether she was being appropriate or not. There has always been this kind of scrutiny, as woman became a greater part of the political atmosphere. [Another congresswoman Bella Abzug] from New York. . .was very flamboyant and she wore hats and she was definitely incensed that she was not allowed to wear hats on the floor. But that was the rule. You don't change the rules of the House or the Senate easily. [Laughs]

This excerpt, rich in history, is a clear reminder of how appearance rules have changed over the years. A mixed blessing, participants' responses highlight the extent to which having choices is not always a good thing, especially when female politicians are being scrutinised for either following or not following social norms.

The themes discussed in this section highlight how different facets of appearance can impact a politician running for office in America. In this long job interview process, also known as the campaign, the candidate must find ways to communicate the message to make connections between myriad different voters with different perspectives.

From National to Local: Appearance Matters

While the previous section examined the varied ways politicians are expected to 'look the part', in this section the role of appearance at various levels in politics such as the national, state and local level is examined. The literature is limited to the study of politicians on the national stage, yet appearance also plays a key role in local campaigns. The importance of appearance at all levels in politics is examined here.

Appearance expectations may be different depending on the scale of the election. For example, local elections are often small affairs wherein the candidate's appearance plays a key role, as they embody the message in meet and greets at coffee houses or go door-to-door asking for support. Smaller campaigns for town, city, board and county level often have small budgets and limited financial resources. Participants explained that communicating the messaging in local campaigns with limited dollars is a challenge, in that, what a candidate does not have in airtime he or she has to make up for in personal contacts with voters. Hence the candidate becomes the living embodiment of the message. As Council member Rashida Davis put it, 'the deliverer of that message is who is showing up at your door...that is all a part of the message'. Miranda (fundraiser) further explained that, 'appearance expectations are different for every level of politician'. Local elections may have different expectations for Mayor and for city council or county legislators.

According to Governor Burns, voters often know their local politicians, such as a member of a local planning board or a local village alderman, because they meet them in church, or at school, at clubs or around town. Often times, at the city level, voters know the political candidate and have seen them live and work in the community, therefore the emphasis is not particularly on appearance. Moreover, compared to national political candidates, the media scrutiny is comparatively lower for local political candidates, especially as it relates to their appearance.

While appearance expectations may be lower for local candidates, all participants think that politicians should be dressed neatly, be tidy and look professional. As Harold explains, voters even 'have an image in their heads about what a city council member should look like. You have to look professional in their minds'. Local politicians also have an advantage of being able to customise their appearance to their audience in a way that politicians at the national level cannot do. As DeShawn points out, 'People are looking for representation and leadership based off of the issues that concern them. But before you have that conversation, they have to be comfortable with you and your dress'. DeShawn tailors his clothes based on his audience '...just like you tailor a speech'. Several other local political candidates said they do that too, in that Rashida believes 'you need to know your demographic'. William agrees and he explains how he tailors his clothes based on who he is going to meet with. To meet farmers, William says he would wear 'a pair of Wrangler jeans, a plaid shirt and a hat' but to meet high profile donors he would 'wear a grey suit with a muted red tie'. Similarly, to meet soccer moms, James would 'wear a short sleeve shirt and khaki pants [with] some tennis shoes'. Although customising one's appearance is easier at a local or state level, DeShawn thinks it would be more difficult to tailor appearances for a Senate seat or a Presidential race.

> When you are going across state or you are going across the country there are so many elements, so many constituencies, so many neighbourhoods and communities. It is the difference between trying to get 6000 votes and trying to get hundreds of thousands of votes...you would have to play it safer.

As the target office gets higher, the focus on appearance seems to get stronger, as Governor Burns points out, 'Once you get beyond a certain mass amount of people the relationships are more superficial because you don't know the people and you judge the politician on what they look like, what they say and what they promise'.

Due to the paucity of media coverage and limited dollars, politicians at the local level also use appearance management as a tool to create their own styles, which, over time, can become embedded in the psyche of the voter, building strong brand images. Doing so can work as a device to help the voter recognise the political candidate or differentiate them in a crowd. Miranda (fundraiser) and Alice (precinct chair) mention Edna Mae (name changed) a veteran, Black state representative who is well-known for wearing hats. Miranda believes that Edna Mae may have started wearing hats to characterise herself as a part of an appearance management strategy. She proposes that 'white folks, especially in the south, think all Black women look the same. So (Edna Mae) sets herself apart because she's always the one with the hat'. As Alice (precinct chair) pointed out, 'Edna gets a lot of mileage out of those hats'. Wearing hats not only helps her get noticed among other African–American candidates but it also creates connections through her religious background. As Elizabeth (state legislator) describes, 'It is something she believes in and it goes back to her culture'. DeShawn (state legislator) thinks that Edna Mae 'does it for branding purposes. She has totally branded herself as "the hat lady". People expect to see a hat when they see Edna Mae.' Time in office is also important. As a newcomer to the general assembly, DeShawn explained that, 'Once a district gets to know you...it becomes less likely that your appearance matters. For me, I am building that brand so it is more critical for me to think about the way I dress'.

Elizabeth (state legislator) sees her political brand as 'the little old lady in tennis shoes'. DeShawn (state legislator) is in agreement, 'Elizabeth, she dresses like a grandmother...like you just want to hug her'. Managing her appearance in a way that creates a persona of a grandmother helps voters to feel comfortable and see Elizabeth as warm and approachable. In political marketing theory, the political candidate is often considered as a brand (De Landtsheer et al., 2008). Appearance management is often utilised to project perceived personality traits, thereby creating market-oriented political brands that live up to the aspiration of the voter audience (De Landtsheer et al., 2008). Edna Mae and Elizabeth, both politicians working at the state level, have built their specific brands through appearance.

Discussion

Consumers often buy brands that are coherent and congruent with their self-image in an attempt to reaffirm perceptions of perceived self (Aaker, 1996). Similarly, voters will choose a political candidate that they identify with. As participant responses reveal, politicians that pay attention to appearance and want to 'look the part' of serious, committed candidates who represent the fabric of America seek to appear more likeable and form connections with their constituents.

In the case of Edna Mae, DeShawn and Elizabeth, appearance management allows local politicians to create a specific brand image in the minds of their voters. When these politicians create a brand identity accompanied by strong visual or symbolic imagery, it can simplify the recall and recognition process for voters. A candidate can package the message in a simple format in a way voters can quickly decipher and commit to memory. In a fast-paced visual culture where images and sound bites need to quickly convey the political candidate's brand identity to the voters, appearance management goes a long way in helping get the message across in an effective manner.

To understand how 'looking the part' helps politicians in their campaigns and builds their brand in political marketing, various important aspects of appearance emerge. Based on the data, a candidate's appearance communicates aspects important to being an elected official: credibility, honesty, competence, responsibility to themselves and their constituents, seriousness as well as their ability to identify with and relate to their constituents; all of these aspects help the candidate 'look the part' for the job of a particular office. There are many aspects to a candidate's image and political brand, including political ideology, their platform, positions on certain issues and political background (Cosgrove, 2012; Newman, 1999). Findings of this study indicate the important and multifaceted ways that a candidate's appearance also impacts image, political brand and political careers.

Conclusion

As campaigns cost billions of dollars in the United States, politics becomes lucrative business and an important career path for many aspiring politicians. Although some studies have focused on the appearance of the politician (De Landtsheer et al., 2008), no study has examined the issue comprehensively. By doing so, this study contributes to the growing body of literature on appearance management and its role in seeking office by politicians. Future studies could focus on the impact of appearance on careers with a greater emphasis on intersectionality and issues such as race, religion, sexual orientation and the role of these factors in the careers of politicians. Furthermore, future studies can explore other positions where appearance plays a critical role in the success of careers.

References

Aaker, D. A. (1996). *Building strong brands*. The Free Press.

Aune, R. K., & Aune, K. S. (1994). The influence of culture, gender and relational status on appearance management. *Journal of Cross-Cultural Psychology, 25*(2), 258–272.

Brannon, E. L. (1993). Affect and cognition in appearance management: A review. In S. J. Lennon & L. D. Burns (Eds.), *Social science aspects of dress: New directions* (pp. 82–92). Monument: International Textiles and Apparel Association.

Budesheim, T. L., & DePaola, S. J. (1994). Beauty or the beast? The effects of appearance, personality, and issue information on evaluations of political candidates. *Personality and Social Psychology Bulletin, 20*(4), 339–348.

Carlin, D. B., & Winfrey, K. L. (2009). Have you come a long way, baby? Hillary Clinton, Sarah Palin, and sexism in the 2008 campaign coverage. *Communication Studies, 60*(4), 326–343.

CAWP. (2023). *Current numbers.* Center for American Women and Politics. https:// cawp.rutgers.edu/facts/current-numbers

Cosgrove, K. M. (2012). *Political branding in the modern age: Effective strategies, tools and techniques* (pp. 107–123). Routledge Handbook of Political Marketing.

Cwalina, W., & Falkowski, A. (2015). Political branding: Political candidates positioning based on inter-object associative affinity index. *Journal of Political Marketing, 14*(1–2), 152–174.

Damhorst, M. L. (1990). In search of a common thread: Classification of information communicated through dress. *Clothing and Textiles Research Journal, 8*(2), 1–12.

Davis, C., Dionne, M., & Shuster, B. (2001). Physical and psychological correlates of appearance orientation. *Personality and Individual Differences, 30*(1), 21–30. https://doi.org/10.1016/S0191-8869(00)00006-4

De Landtsheer, C., De Vries, P., & Vertessen, D. (2008). Political impression management: How metaphors, sound bites, appearance effectiveness and personality traits can win elections. *Journal of Political Marketing, 70*(3/4), 217–238.

Falk, E. (2010). *Women for president: Media bias in nine campaigns.* University of Illinois Press.

Falkowski, A., & Michalak, M. (2014). Backward framing and memory evaluation in political elections. *Journal of Political Marketing, 13*(1–2), 85–107.

Farzan, A. N. (2019). *Five years ago, Obama was blasted for wearing a tan suit. Now, it's used to contrast him with Trump. The Washington Post.* https://www. washingtonpost.com/nation/2019/08/28/tan-suit-scandal-obama-trump/

Franklin, R. G., Jr., & Zebrowitz, L. A. (2016). The influence of political candidates' facial appearance on older and younger adults' voting choices and actual electoral success. *Cogent Psychology, 3*(1), 1151602.

Garzia, D. (2013). Can candidates' image win elections? A counterfactual assessment of leader effects in the second Italian republic. *Journal of Political Marketing, 12*(4), 348–361.

Goudge, B. S., & Littrell, M. A. (1989). Attributions for job acquisition: Job skills, dress and luck of female job applicants. *Clothing and Textiles Research Journal, 7*(4), 19–26.

Guzmán, F., & Sierra, V. (2009). A political candidate's brand image scale: Are political candidates brands? *Brand Management, 17*(2), 207–217.

Hesse-Biber, S. N., & Leavy, P. (2004). *Approaches to qualitative research: A reader on theory and practice.* Oxford University Press.

Hoegg, J., & Lewis, M. V. (2011). The impact of candidate appearance and advertising strategies on election results. *Journal of Marketing Research, 48*(5), 895–909.

Jackson, T. E., Jr. (2003). Brand marketing in today's cluttered political marketplace. *Campaigns and Elections,* 30–31.

Johnson, K. K. P., Crutsinger, C., & Workman, J. E. (1994). Can professional women appear too masculine? The case of the necktie. *Clothing and Textiles Research Journal, 12*(2), 27–31.

Johnson, K. K. P., & Lennon, S. J. (1999). *Appearance and power.* Berg.

Johnson, K. K., Yoo, J. J., Kim, M., & Lennon, S. J. (2008). Dress and human behavior: A review and critique. *Clothing and Textiles Research Journal, 26*(1), 3–22.

Kaiser, S. B. (1997). *The social psychology of clothing: Symbolic appearances in context.* Fairchild.

Kwon, Y.-H. (1994). The influence of appropriateness of dress and gender on the self-perception of occupational attributes. *Clothing and Textiles Research Journal, 12*(3), 33–39.

Lammers, J., Gordijn, E. H., & Otten, S. (2009). Iron ladies, men of steel: The effects of gender stereotyping on the perception of male and female candidates are moderated by prototypicality. *European Journal of Social Psychology, 39*(2), 186–195.

Lawson, C., Lenz, G. S., Baker, A., & Myers, M. (2010). Looking like a winner: Candidate appearance and electoral success in new democracies. *World Politics, 62*(4), 561–593.

Lenz, G., & Lawson, C. (2011). Looking the part: Television leads less informed citizens to vote based on candidate's appearance. *American Journal of Political Science, 55*(3), 574–589.

Lizotte, M., & Meggers-Wright, H. J. (2019). Negative effects of calling attention to female political candidates' attractiveness. *Journal of Political Marketing, 18*(3), 240–266. https://doi.org/10.1080/15377857.2017.1411859

Mandziuk, R. M. (2008). Dressing down Hillary. *Communication and Critical, 5*(3), 312–316.

Mears, A., & Connell, C. (2016). The paradoxical value of deviant cases: Toward a gendered theory of display work. *Signs: Journal of Women in Culture and Society, 41*(2), 333–359.

Miller-Spillman, K. A., Reilly, A., & Hunt-Hurst, P. (2012). *The meanings of dress.* Fairchild.

Mohamed, A. A., & Gardner, W. L. (2004). An exploratory study of interorganizational defamation: An organizational impression management perspective. *Organizational Analysis, 12*(2), 129–145.

Nelson, N. J. (2000). Listening to Jane Cunningham Croly's 'Talks with Women': Issues of gender, dress, and reform in Demorest's Monthly Magazine. *Clothing and Textiles Research Journal, 18*(3), 128–139. https://doi.org/10.1177/088730 2X0001800302

Newman, B. I. (1999). *Handbook of political marketing.* Sage Publications.

Nickson, D. (2018). The importance of how you look for getting in and getting on in the workplace. In A. Broadbridge & S. Fielden (Eds.), *Research handbook of diversity and careers.* Edward Elgar Publishing.

O'Neal, G. S. (1999). The Power of Style: On Rejection of the Accepted. In K. K. P. Johnson & S. J. Lennon (Eds.), *Appearance and power* (pp. 127–140). Bloomsbury Academic.

Olivola, C. Y., & Todorov, A. (2010). Elected in 100 milliseconds: Appearance-based trait inferences and voting. *Journal of Nonverbal Behavior, 34,* 83–110.

O'Shaughnessy, N. (1990). *The phenomena of political marketing.* St. Martin's Press.

Peluchette, J. V. E., & Karl, K. (2018). 'She's got the look': Examining feminine and provocative dress in the workplace. In A. Broadbridge & S. Fielden (Eds.), *Research handbook of diversity and careers.* Edward Elgar Publishing.

Roach-Higgins, M. E., & Eicher, J. B. (1992). Dress and identity. *Clothing and Textiles Research Journal, 10*(4), 1–8. https://doi.org/10.1177/0887302X920 1000401

Rockey, J. C., Smith, H. M., & Flowe, H. D. (2022). Dirty looks: Politicians' appearance and unethical behaviour. *The Leadership Quarterly, 33*(2), 101561.

Rosenberg, S. W., Kahn, S., & Tran, T. (1991). Creating a political image: Shaping appearance and manipulating the vote. *Political Behavior, 13*(4), 345–367. https://doi.org/10.1007/BF00992868

Rubin, H. J., & Rubin, I. S. (1995). *Qualitative interviewing: The Art of hearing data.* Sage.

Rudd, N. A., & Lennon, S. J. (2000). Body image and appearance management behaviors in college women. *Clothing and Textiles Research Journal, 18*(4), 163–177.

Sanghvi, M. (2014). *Marketing the female politician: An exploration of gender, appearance, and power.* The University of North Carolina at Greensboro.

Sanghvi, M. (2018). *Gender and political marketing in the United States and the 2016 presidential election: An analysis of why she lost.* Palgrave Macmillan.

Sanghvi, M., & Hodges, N. (2015). Marketing the female politician: An exploration of gender and appearance. *Journal of Marketing Management, 31*(15–16), 1676–1694.

Scammell, M. (2015). Politics and image: The conceptual value of branding. *Journal of Political Marketing, 14*(1–2), 7–18. https://doi.org/10.1080/15377857.2014.990829

Seawright, D. (2013). "Cameron 2010": An exemplification of personality-based campaigning. *Journal of Political Marketing, 12*(2–3), 166–181. https://doi.org/10.1080/15377857.2013.781477

Smith, G., & French, A. (2009). The political brand: A consumer perspective. *Marketing Theory, 9*(2), 209–226.

Spiggle, S. (1994). Analysis and interpretation of qualitative data in consumer research. *Journal of Consumer Research, 21,* 491–503.

Stone, G. (1995/1962). Appearance and the self. In M. Roach-Higgins & J. Eicher (Eds.), *Dress and identity* (pp. 19–39). Fairchild.

Todorov, A., Mandisodza, A. N., Goren, A., & Hall, C. C. (2005). Inferences of competence from faces predict election outcomes. *Science 308*(5728), 1623–1626.

Uscinski, J. E., & Goren, L. J. (2011). What's in a name? Coverage of Senator Hillary Clinton during the 2008 Democratic Party. *Political Research Quarterly, 64*(4), 884–896.

Wooten, D. B. (2006). From labeling possessions to possessing labels: Ridicule and socialization among adolescents. *Journal of Consumer Research, 33,* 188–198.

Chapter 10

Status Effects of Attractiveness at Work

Tonya K. Frevert, Tarya Bardwell and Lisa Slattery Walker

Abstract

In this chapter, we outline the evidence regarding the status effects of physical attractiveness in the workplace. We frame the effects of attractiveness as power and status dynamics shaped by the context of the workplace. Attractiveness serves as a social status that mostly provides benefits in the workplace, although the results are not uniformly positive. We first explain attractiveness as a status characteristic and how it operates in general social interactions. We then examine these effects across three typical yet significant career development milestones in a worker's life: (1) the selection and hiring process of employment, (2) day-to-day interactions with colleagues and co-workers and (3) in leadership roles and positions.

Keywords: Attractiveness; status; power; selection; leadership; workplace and career

Introduction

Physical attractiveness, often described as 'attractiveness' or 'beauty' in research, has been studied extensively in many domains, including biology, sociology, psychology and organisational behaviour. Numerous studies on job-related outcomes of physical attractiveness were described in a meta-analysis conducted by Hosoda et al. (2003). In general, attractiveness in research studies is determined by perceiver evaluations.

Examples of the aspects of attractiveness common in the research include: facial symmetry (Thornhill & Gangestad, 1999); body weight and obesity (Burmeister et al., 2017; Gordon et al., 2018); and facial attractiveness (Little et al., 2011; Thornhill & Gangestad, 1999). Confounds of attractiveness (race/ethnicity, sex and/or gender, age, changing beauty standards, etc.) are sometimes considered. Various perspectives are taken as well – most recently evolutionary arguments are common (e.g. Lee et al., 2015; Rhodes, 2006; Sugiyama, 2015).

The Emerald Handbook of Appearance in the Workplace, 185–196

Copyright © 2024 by Emerald Publishing Limited

All rights of reproduction in any form reserved

doi:10.1108/978-1-80071-174-720230011

The evolutionary psychology perspective on attractiveness posits that attractiveness is used by others as an indicator of health and genetic compatibility.

In this chapter, however, we frame the effects of attractiveness as power and status dynamics shaped by the context of the workplace. Attractiveness serves as a social status that mostly provides benefits in the workplace, although the results are not uniformly positive. We first explain attractiveness as a status characteristic and how it operates in general social interactions. We then examine these effects across three typical yet significant career development milestones in a worker's life: (1) the selection and hiring process of employment, (2) day-to-day interactions with colleagues and co-workers and (3) in leadership roles and positions.

Attractiveness as a Status Characteristic

Attractiveness plays an important role in day-to-day social interaction. We think that a useful way to envision this social dynamic is by thinking of physical attractiveness as a status characteristic. As such, attractiveness can be seen as carrying expectation states, as originally defined by Berger et al. in 1977 (Webster & Driskell, 1983). In their definition, a status characteristic is 'any characteristic of actors around which evaluations of and beliefs about them come to be organised', such as gender, race, age, attractiveness and education (Berger et al., 1980, p. 479).

Ridgeway (1997) subsequently identified the concept of status beliefs, a set of ideas about competence that become associated with certain states of various characteristics, in this case, attractiveness. These beliefs exist below the level of consciousness, but drive our decisions and judgements about who is competent and to whom influence should be granted. In many ways, these beliefs act as self-fulfilling prophecies, as attractive people are given more opportunities to display their competence and are evaluated more favourably regardless of actual competence. Status beliefs serve to bias evaluations and reward and persistently re-create status differences between attractive people and those who are deemed less attractive.

All status characteristics have at least two states, e.g. attractive/beautiful and not attractive/ugly. These states 'are differentially evaluated in terms of honour, esteem, or desirability' and thus become 'stabilised beliefs about how an individual possessing a given state of the characteristic will perform or behave' (Berger et al., 1980, p. 482). The states (beautiful versus ugly) will be differentially evaluated in the culture (Webster & Hysom, 1998), such that one state (e.g. attractive) will be viewed higher/more desirable than the other state (e.g. unattractive).

The theoretical definition of a diffuse status characteristic of which attractiveness is an instance (Berger et al., 1977, pp. 93–94) has three parts:

(1) There are at least two states, differentially evaluated. Individuals acknowledge it is 'preferable, fortunate, better' to have one state than another.

(2) The characteristic carries specific performance expectations consistent with the society's evaluation of the states. Individuals believe that certain tasks can be performed more skillfully by those possessing the socially favoured state.

(3) The characteristic also carries general performance expectations consistent with the evaluation of its states. Individuals believe that those possessing the favoured state can perform 'most tasks' more skillfully than those possessing other states.

Thus, if (1) individuals know that this society grants advantages to attractive people rather than unattractive people, (2) they see attractive people as more competent or as better able to perform any specific task than those who are less attractive, and (3) they see attractive people as outperforming unattractiveness people at 'most tasks', then attractiveness meets the definition of a diffuse status characteristic in this society.

In situations where the scope conditions of the theory of status characteristics (task interaction that requires collective orientation of group members) apply, attractiveness serves to privilege the beautiful. We will review, however, evidence from many types of workplace situations – those that fit the scope of expectation states theory and those that do not. The evidence suggests that the effects of attractiveness, while especially profound in task-focused and collectively oriented groups, are also present in many other types of social interaction – and even when no true interaction takes place. Furthermore, the effects of attractiveness may accumulate over the life course or the course of a career, such that attractive individuals gain influence that compounds over time into general social advantage while unattractive individuals lose influence that compounds over time into general social disadvantage. For example, individuals deemed attractive as they journey through the workplace acquire higher status and influence that subsequently becomes higher status and more influential in the workplace as a leader. However, as unattractive individuals do not benefit over the life course in this manner, they are thus penalised by the spread of adverse effects of status disadvantage. We next discuss how the status characteristic of attractiveness plays out in the first milestone of career development, beginning with the selection and hiring process of employment.

Attractiveness at Work: Employment Selection

Although many workplaces take great pains to scientifically evaluate job applicants according to merit and skill (e.g. Schmidt & Hunter, 1998), evaluation and judgement of an applicant's appearance – and therefore associated assumptions of ability and job fit – inevitably influence selection (e.g. Paustian-Underdahl & Walker, 2016). Attractiveness biases may be borne out of mate selection in evolutionary psychology. This heuristic arises in the workplace and produces selection biases (Luxen & Van De Vijver, 2006). The 'what is beautiful is good' heuristic (Dion et al., 1972) – has long demonstrated that assumptions of goodness increase perceptions of other positive traits (Guerrero, 2017). In a work context, this might mean that an attractive candidate is perceived to be more competent or a better fit for a job (Lowman et al., 2019). Below, we examine the role of attractiveness in the selection and hiring process of employment, the first milestone of career development.

Studies that examine the relationship between attractiveness and employment selection demonstrate that it is frequently influenced by a number of other characteristics, such as sex of both applicant and evaluator (e.g. Agthe et al., 2010; Hosada et al., 2003), job type (e.g. Paustian-Underdahl & Walker, 2016), and impression management strategies (i.e. acknowledgement of one's beauty; e.g. Hebl & Kleck, 2002). Research methods in studying attractiveness typically use the same general quasi-experimental design strategy whereby photographs of people who are separately evaluated for varying levels of attractiveness are presented to research participants playing the role of hiring managers. These 'hiring managers' are then presented with these piloted images and asked to make a hypothetical hiring decision. Overall, when controlling for interaction effects such as evaluator traits or additional information about applicant qualifications, those applicants rated attractive are selected over those who are not, demonstrating the influence attractiveness has on hiring decisions.

To explain this phenomenon, research demonstrates that the assumption 'what is beautiful is good' is often at play in employment selection practices (Dion et al., 1972; Dipboye et al., 1977). For example, Cristofaro (2017) examined facial and body attractiveness on perceptions of personality. He suggested that beauty is used by proxy to make inferences about an applicant's personality and perceived job fit. However, the nature of this relationship seems to change when also accounting for gender in perceptions of job fit. Paustian-Underdahl and Walker (2016) found that attractiveness will improve perceived job suitability for men, and reduce it for women, in typically male-type jobs. This bias is in effect when attractiveness is considered irrelevant. However, if attractiveness is considered relevant – for example, in sales jobs – this effect is no longer found because, despite being female, attractive women have a key qualification for the job. Additionally, women are often stereotyped as more communal (e.g. concerned about others) while men are often stereotyped as agentic (e.g. taking charge). Generally, those who are perceived as more attractive are also more towards the extremes of their gender. In other words, attractive men are perceived as 'masculine' and attractive women as 'feminine'. For this reason, perceptions of agency are positively associated with perceived suitability for male-typed jobs; attractiveness moderates the relationship between sex and perceived agency, such that attractive men and unattractive women are perceived as the most agentic.

A technique that has been tested to reduce discrimination in hiring is *acknowledging*. By acknowledging a stigmatised identity, an applicant signals that they have some control over the identity (Hebl & Kleck, 2002). Although past research on acknowledging was conducted on physical traits that are almost universally perceived as negative in hiring (e.g. obesity and physical disability), Johnson et al. (2014) tested acknowledging for attractive women applying to male-typed jobs (specifically, a job in construction). Undergraduate student participants were provided with a bogus applicant packet which included a photo and an interview transcript. Pictures were either of an attractive or unattractive woman paired with one of three versions of the interview transcript in which the applicant acknowledged either their beauty, their sex or nothing. The acknowledgements were conveyed via the hypothetical job applicants' answers to a question about their qualifications: (1) acknowledgement of beauty – *I know that I don't look like your typical construction worker, but...*, (2) acknowledgement of sex – *I know that there are not a lot of women in this industry but...*, or (3) no acknowledgement at all. The physically attractive applicant was rated significantly higher on job suitability when she acknowledged her appearance or when she acknowledged her sex, but not when she did not acknowledge. For the unattractive applicant, her ratings were actually significantly lower when she acknowledged her appearance, but there was no significant difference when she acknowledged her sex. This finding suggests that the interviewer responds better when the interviewee calls attention to an aspect of herself that is more universally positive. Gender may be more relevant to the types of traits that the interviewer is seeking. Traits of communality, or supporting others in one's social circle, are often considered feminine traits, while more independent or even aggressive tendencies are often more masculine (Abele, 2003; Lowman et al., 2019). These signals of gender typicality based on one's sex and attractiveness (e.g. agentic or communal) were also integrated into Johnson et al.'s (2014) acknowledgement study. They found that participants' perceptions of an applicant's counter-communality and masculinity mediated the relationship between acknowledgement and ratings of employment suitability, such that acknowledgement made them seem more counter-communal, more masculine, and more suited to the male-typed job. These findings suggest that individuals have some control over how they are perceived based on attractiveness, and that strategies such as acknowledgement, can be used to mitigate attractiveness bias.

As we have demonstrated, the roles of applicant gender and job type have been fairly thoroughly researched in the relationships between attractiveness and selection. However, the role of the person making hiring decisions is also relevant. Research in social psychology (e.g. Maner et al., 2007) suggests that people are attentive to attractive *opposite-sex people for mate-seeking behaviours* while appraising attractive *same-sex people for threatening behaviours*. Agthe et al. (2010) applied these findings in a selection context by proposing that pro-attractiveness tendencies would only be found in opposite-sex selection. They tested their hypotheses by having college students evaluate same-sex or opposite-sex scholarship applicants as either highly, moderately, or unattractive applicants. Agthe et al. found that the effect of attractiveness is contingent on the sex pairings of the applicant-evaluator dyads (same sex versus different sex). Specifically, high applicant attractiveness increases the likelihood of selection for opposite-sex pairings, as opposed to same-sex pairings. For example, a male evaluator is more likely to select an attractive female applicant than an attractive male applicant, and a female evaluator is more likely to select an attractive male applicant than a female applicant. Interestingly, Agthe et al. (2010) actually found a bias *against* attractive female applicants when the evaluator was female, but this bias was only present with female–female pairings. In a second study, Agthe et al. (2010) evaluated the role of evaluator attractiveness. For highly attractive evaluators, evaluations were generally unaffected by the biases described in their first study. For moderately attractive evaluators, however, these biases were present.

Attractiveness has long been an important research issue in job selection, and its relevance may be increasing with the use of social media (Roth et al., 2016). Although the merits and legality of using social media is an ongoing debate (see Slovensky & Ross, 2012), research demonstrates that this practice is becoming more common (Winter, 2013). Viewing applicants' social media activity allows hiring managers to access information they might not see otherwise; and, although screening for 'red flags' is often the cited reason for this practice, it also allows hiring managers to view photographs and get information on applicant attractiveness earlier in the hiring process (before learning more about applicants during interviews, for example). Research has found that other forms of discrimination, such as sex- and race-based discrimination, are enabled through this screening process. Van Iddekinge et al. (2016) found that using Facebook did not uniquely predict variables such as turnover and performance, but did predict adverse impact based on sex and race. There may be some variation across social media sites, as some are more focused on job-related networking (e.g. LinkedIn; see Roulin & Levashina, 2019). It is possible, for example, that people are more likely to attend to attractiveness on a platform where employment qualifications are not the focus. Researchers such as Paustian-Underdahl and Walker (2016) point out the potential relevance of social media-based job screening in attractiveness and Roth et al. (2016) highlight the need for future research on this front.

Attractiveness at Work: Interactional Power

Even beyond the hiring and selection processes, attractiveness plays an important role at work. Interactions among co-workers continue to show the effects of individual attractiveness. We next examine the role of attractiveness in day-to-day interactions with colleagues and co-workers, the second milestone of career development.

According to status characteristics theory, those in the high state of a characteristic like attractiveness are expected to have high states of other valued characteristics, such as intellectual competence. Webster and Hysom (1998) demonstrated that such expectations will persist, even when attractiveness is unrelated to task performance. In turn, each state is associated with performance expectations (perceived competence of skills); ergo an attractive person will be perceived to be more competent with better abilities than an unattractive person (Webster & Hysom, 1998). This perceived competence and ability translates into higher performance expectations without limit as to where those expectations apply, thus making attractiveness a diffuse status characteristic. Attractiveness will confer social advantages in many domains of life (e.g., the workplace and interactions with colleagues) for those individuals possessing the desired state (Webster & Driskell, 1983).

As summarised in Frevert and Walker (2014), many studies have demonstrated the status effects of attractiveness in workplace settings at the level of co-workers. In general, a person who possesses the state of being attractive rather than unattractive is seen as more desirable, worthy, and competent. Jackson et al. (1995) found that when people interact with one another, individuals who are ascribed by others to be high in attractiveness are evaluated differently than individuals who are ascribed to be low in attractiveness.

Thus, the benefits that attractiveness typically confers to the physically attractive in social interactions may also yield status inequalities that again advantage the physically attractive. In addition, this inequality is separate from sexual attraction but clearly is conveyed through status association. For example, Haas and Gregory (2005) examined power differences that emerge in female-only dyads differentiated by attractiveness. They found that the more attractive partners showed higher influence than the less attractive partners by making the second accommodate their behaviour to them by verbally expressing their compliance. Status competition was also found among dyads with low and average attractive partners, as all participants used status characteristics to negotiate their relative positions. Those in the lower position (less attractive) were deferential while those in the higher position (more attractive) were dominant (more power), suggesting that attractiveness is power of display or referent power.

A study by Mulford et al. (1998) examined the link between attractiveness and cooperation in an exchange relationship, such as one would find with co-workers. In general, participants were more likely to cooperate with those they found attractive, while also expecting those they saw as attractive to cooperate more often. Clearly, these tendencies will be beneficial to those who are more attractive as they will get the cooperation and support of their co-workers at a higher level than those who are less attractive. Subjects' ratings of their own attractiveness were positively correlated with the likelihood to cooperate with those they rated as highly attractive. In terms of gender, men who see themselves as more attractive will cooperate more often with men, although women who see themselves as more attractive will cooperate less often with women. This finding suggests that women who perceive themselves as attractive are inclined to be in competition with each other. Mulford et al. (1998) concluded that being seen by others as attractive encourages productive exchange because the perception of attractiveness is associated with expectations of cooperative behaviour.

Other studies have also examined the relationship between attractiveness and social interactions, including those among co-workers. Using a sample of college students, Dollinger (2002) found that when presenting self-descriptive photo essays, physically attractive participants depicted more social connectedness in their pictorial narratives than their less attractive peers, which suggests that more attractive people may have more successful social interactions resulting in more social relationships – which again may be very beneficial in the workplace. In an experimental lab study that simulated a workplace, Mobius and Rosenblat (2006) found that physically attractive workers demonstrated both communication and social skills that positively correlated with wage raises after interacting with their employers, even after controlling for worker confidence. These studies show that more attractive individuals tend to be more successful in everyday exchange than less attractive peers. The benefits of such success may lead to attractive people being advantaged in their ability to get tasks completed at work. This advantage will likely yield more favourable job performance reviews and evaluations, which, in turn, culminates over time into promotion and career advancement for the attractive employee (Frevert & Walker, 2014).

Attractiveness at Work: Leadership

Lastly, we examine the role of attractiveness in leadership roles and positions, the third milestone of career development. Humanity has long sought to identify the qualities that comprise a 'perfect' leader (Van Vugt & Grabo, 2015). This quest is perhaps most collectively visible in politics, whereby presidents, prime ministers, governors, and other civic representatives are routinely evaluated and assessed via public elections. Numerous studies have demonstrated that politicians perceived to be more physically attractive than their opponents tend to be more politically successful and win elections (Frevert & Walker, 2014; Efrain & Patterson, 1974; Praino et al., 2014; Rosar & Klein, 2014). The tendency for people to associate physical characteristics with leadership can be traced throughout history to our earliest origins. For example, during times of war, leaders with more masculine features are preferred as a sign of dominance that can respond to acts of physical aggression and conflict (Van Vugt & Grabo, 2015). In contrast, during times of peace, leaders with more feminine features are preferred as a sign of trustworthiness that can promote cooperation and diplomacy. In times where stability and tradition are desired by followers, leaders with older faces are preferred; in times where innovation and growth are desired by followers, leaders with younger faces are preferred. These preferences demonstrate that certain facial characteristics are ascribed status values that act as proxy indicators of leaders' perceived competence in their ability to meet followers' needs, particularly in the context of the demands of the larger environment.

These leader preferences and resulting leadership selection patterns also show up in the context of the workplace. Leadership can be generally defined as the disproportionate influence an individual has on a group to achieve a common goal (Northouse, 2010; Van Vugt & Grabo, 2015). Following the advent of mass production and industrialisation in the nineteenth century, humanity's ongoing quest for 'perfect' leaders shifted focus to individual traits and innate characteristics (e.g. the 'Great Man' theory of leadership; see Harrison, 2018). Trait approaches to leadership are problematic, however, for they are biased towards men and privilege masculine behaviours in perceptions of good leadership, thus precluding women and devaluing feminine behaviours. Additionally, trait theories do not take the *interaction* between leaders and followers into consideration. More recently, leadership studies focused more on trying to understand leadership behaviours that successfully facilitate group members achieving their goals, such as leaders who define group members' roles and let followers know what is expected of them (i.e. structure) as well as leaders who demonstrate that followers' well-being, comfort, and contributions matter (i.e. nurture; Guerrero, 2017).

It appears that we cannot escape humanity's earliest inclinations, however, for attractiveness still looms large in leadership selection and evaluation. Numerous studies generally indicate positive ratings and outcomes for attractive leaders, whose looks are attributed to greater perceptions of competence, intelligence, popularity and success (Van Vugt & Grabo, 2015), even when controlling for gender, ethnicity and age (Guerrero, 2017). These outcomes may be somewhat disheartening to those who desire a workplace where merit and effort yield successful career development, but research studies examining if attractiveness *predicts* who becomes a leader demonstrate mixed results, as such decisions are made from too little information (Van Vugt & Grabo, 2015). If attractiveness was a true predictor of leadership, it would suggest that 'if the most competent individual were always selected, then all leaders would be highly effective, which is not the case' (Antonakis & Eubanks, 2017, p. 272). Though there is correlational evidence that leaders' attractiveness is linked to companies financial performance (Antonakis & Eubanks, 2017; Van Vugt & Grabo, 2015), such a true predictor of leadership would again suggest that all businesses with attractive leaders are successful. As numerous companies 'fail' every year (Kücher et al., 2020), successfully navigating the complexity of the global economic marketplace requires more than leaders' good looks.

Conclusion

In this chapter, we discussed attractiveness as a status characteristic in the workplace. As we have demonstrated, numerous studies over the last several decades across the social sciences and business management demonstrate that attractiveness serves as a social status at work that yields many benefits over the course of a career, as attractive people are evaluated more favourably in terms of perceived competence and ability. These benefits accumulate over time into general social advantage that can be especially beneficial during significant career development milestones in a worker's life – when being considered and hired for a job, when interacting with colleagues and co-workers and when being promoted into leadership roles and positions. During employment hiring and selection processes, attractiveness is influenced by both applicants' and evaluators' sex, job type and impression management strategies. During interactions with co-workers, individuals who are deemed to be attractive are rated as more desirable, worthy and competent than their less attractive peers. Lastly, attractive leaders are ascribed to be more competent, intelligent, popular and successful, though attractiveness is not a perfect predictor of leadership. While attractiveness generally accumulates over the life course as a benefit, it is not a *guarantee* of success. As the old adage goes, 'looks can be deceiving'.

References

Abele, A. E. (2003). The dynamics of masculine-agentic and feminine-communal traits: Findings from a prospective study. *Journal of Personality and Social Psychology, 85*(4), 768–776. https://doi.org/10.1037/0022-3514.85.4.768

Agthe, M., Spörrle, M., & Maner, J. K. (2010). Don't hate me because I'm beautiful: Anti-attractiveness bias in organizational evaluation and decision making. *Journal of Experimental Social Psychology, 46*(6), 1151–1154.

Antonakis, J., & Eubanks, D. L. (2017). Looking leadership in the face. *Current Directions in Psychological Science, 26*(3), 270–275.

Berger, J. H., Fisek, F., Norman, R. Z., & Zelditch, M., Jr. (1977). *Status characteristics and social interaction: An expectation-states approach.* Greenwood Pub Group.

Berger, J., Rosenholtz, S. J., & Zelditch, M., Jr. (1980). Status organizing processes. *Annual Review of Sociology, 6*(1), 479–508.

Burmeister, J. M., Taylor, M. B., Rossi, J., Kiefner-Burmeister, A., Borushok, J., & Carels, R. A. (2017). Reducing obesity stigma via a brief documentary film: A randomized trial. *Stigma and Health, 2*(1), 43.

Cristofaro, M. (2017). Candidates' attractiveness in selection decisions: A laboratory experiment. *Baltic Journal of Management, 12*(4), 390–407.

Dion, K., Berscheid, E., & Walster, E. (1972). What is beautiful is good. *Journal of Personality and Social Psychology, 24*(3), 285–290.

Dipboye, R. L., Arvey, R. D., & Terpstra, D. E. (1977). Sex and physical attractiveness of raters and applicants as determinants of resume evaluations. *Journal of Applied Psychology, 62,* 288–294.

Dollinger, S. J. (2002). Physical attractiveness, social connectedness, and individuality: An autophotographic study. *The Journal of Social Psychology, 142*(1), 25–32.

Efrain, M. G., & Patterson, E. W. J. (1974). Voters vote beautiful: The effect of physical appearance on a national election. *Canadian Journal of Behavioural Science/Revue canadienne des sciences du comportement, 6*(4), 352–356.

Frevert, T. K., & Walker, L. S. (2014). Physical attractiveness and social status. *Sociology Compass, 8*(3), 313–323.

Gordon, H. L., Walker, L. S., Gur, S., & Olien, J. L. (2018). Obesity and gender as status beliefs. *Social Science Research, 71,* 11–18.

Guerrero, L. (2017). *In the eye of the beholder: Exploring the role of the perception of physical attractiveness in leadership* Doctoral dissertation. Our Lady of the Lake University.

Haas, A., & Gregory, S. W. (2005). The impact of physical attractiveness on women's social status and interactional power. *Sociological Forum, 20*(3), 449–471.

Harrison, C. (2018). Leadership research and theory. In *Leadership theory and research: A critical approach to new and existing paradigms* (pp. 15–32). Palgrave Macmillan.

Hebl, M. R., & Kleck, R. E. (2002). Acknowledging one's stigma in the interview setting: Effective strategy or liability? *Journal of Applied Social Psychology, 32*(2), 223–249.

Hosoda, M., Stone-Romero, E. F., & Coats, G. (2003). The effects of physical attractiveness on job-related outcomes: A meta-analysis of experimental studies. *Personnel Psychology, 56*(2), 431–462.

Jackson, L. A., Hunter, J. E., & Hodge, C. N. (1995). Physical attractiveness and intellectual competence: A meta-analytic review. *Social Psychology Quarterly, 58*(2), 108–122.

Johnson, S. K., Sitzmann, T., & Nguyen, A. T. (2014). Don't hate me because I'm beautiful: Acknowledging appearance mitigates the "beauty is beastly" effect. *Organizational Behavior and Human Decision Processes, 125*(2), 184–192.

Kücher, A., Mayr, S., Mitter, C., Duller, C., & Feldbauer-Durstmüller, B. (2020). Firm age dynamics and causes of corporate bankruptcy: Age dependent explanations for business failure. *Review of Managerial Science, 14*, 633–661.

Lee, S., Pitesa, M., Pillutla, M., & Thau, S. (2015). When beauty helps and when it hurts: An organizational context model of attractiveness discrimination in selection decisions. *Organizational Behavior and Human Decision Processes, 128*, 15–28.

Little, A. C., Jones, B., & DeBruine, L. M. (2011). Facial attractiveness: Evolutionary based research. *Philosophical Transactions of the Royal Society, 366*, 1638–1659.

Lowman, G. H., Harms, P. D., & Mills, M. J. (2019). The influence of job candidates' physical appearance on interview evaluations: A prototype matching model. *Journal of Personnel Psychology, 18*(2), 55.

Luxen, M. F., & Van De Vijver, F. J. (2006). Facial attractiveness, sexual selection, and personnel selection: When evolved preferences matter. *Journal of Organizational Behavior, 27*(2), 241–255.

Maner, J. K., Gailliot, M. T., Rouby, D. A., & Miller, S. L. (2007). Can't take my eyes off you: Attentional adhesion to mates and rivals. *Journal of Personality and Social Psychology, 93*(3), 389–401.

Mobius, M. M., & Rosenblat, T. S. (2006). Why beauty matters. *The American Economic Review, 96*(1), 222–235.

Mulford, M., Orbell, J., Shatto, C., & Stockard, J. (1998). Physical attractiveness, opportunity, and success in everyday exchange. *American Journal of Sociology, 103*(6), 1565–1592.

Northouse, P. G. (2010). *Leadership theory and practice* (5th ed.). Sage Publications.

Paustian-Underdahl, S. C., & Walker, L. S. (2016). Revisiting the beauty is beastly effect: Examining when and why sex and attractiveness impact hiring judgments. *International Journal of Human Resource Management, 27*(10), 1034–1058.

Praino, R., Stockemer, D., & Ratis, J. (2014). Looking good or looking competent? Physical appearance and electoral success in the 2008 congressional elections. *American Politics Research, 42*(6), 1096–1117.

Rhodes, G. (2006). The evolutionary psychology of facial beauty. *Annual Review of Psychology, 57*, 199–226.

Ridgeway, C. L. (1997). Interaction and the conservation of gender inequality: Considering employment. *American Sociological Review, 62*(2), 218–235.

Rosar, U., & Klein, M. (2014). The physical attractiveness of front-runners and electoral success. In M. Steinbrecher, E. Bytzek, U. Rosar, & S. Roßteutscher (Eds.), *Europa, europäische Integration und Eurokrise* (pp. 197–2009). Springer VS.

Roth, P. L., Bobko, P., Van Iddekinge, C. H., & Thatcher, J. B. (2016). Social media in employee-selection-related decisions: A research agenda for uncharted territory. *Journal of Management, 42*(1), 269–298.

Roulin, N., & Levashina, J. (2019). LinkedIn as a new selection method: Psychometric properties and assessment approach. *Personnel Psychology, 72*(2), 187–211.

Schmidt, F. L., & Hunter, J. E. (1998). The validity and utility of selection methods in personnel psychology: Practical and theoretical implications of 85 years of research findings. *Psychological Bulletin, 124*(2), 262.

Slovensky, R., & Ross, W. H. (2012). Should human resource managers use social media to screen job applicants? Managerial and legal issues in the USA. *info*, *14*(1), 55–69.

Sugiyama, L. S. (2015). Physical attractiveness in adaptationist perspective. In D. M. Buss (Eds), *The handbook of evolutionary psychology* (pp. 292–343). Wiley & Sons.

Thornhill, R., & Gangestad, S. W. (1999). Facial attractiveness. *Trends in Cognitive Sciences*, *3*(12), 452–460.

Van Iddekinge, C. H., Lanivich, S. E., Roth, P. L., & Junco, E. (2016). Social media for selection? Validity and adverse impact potential of a Facebook-based assessment. *Journal of Management*, *42*(7), 1811–1835.

Van Vugt, M., & Grabo, A. E. (2015). The many faces of leadership: An evolutionary-psychology approach. *Current Directions in Psychological Science*, *24*(6), 484–489.

Webster, M., Jr., & Driskell, J. E., Jr. (1983). Beauty as status. *American Journal of Sociology*, *89*(1), 140–165.

Webster, M., Jr., & Hysom, S. J. (1998). Creating status characteristics. *American Sociological Review*, *63*(3), 351–378.

Winter, J. L. (2013). Social media and talent acquisition: Emerging trends and implications. In R. F. Miguel (Eds), *The promise and perils of social media data for selection*. Symposium presented at the 28th Annual Conference of the Society for Industrial and Organizational Psychology, Houston, TX.

Chapter 11

Lookism Knows No Age: Aesthetic Labour in Women's Careers

Marjut Jyrkinen, Mira Karjalainen and Linda McKie

Abstract

This chapter draws from research on aesthetic labour, gender, management and organisation studies and research on women's careers. We base our analysis on two empirical data sets, namely interviews with women mid-managers in Finland and Scotland, and interviews with highly positioned expert women in Finland in knowledge work. Women in different phases of their careers and life experience manifold pressures on appearances, and are increasingly aware of the demands to 'look good and sound right'. We address how these pressures impact on women managers' and experts' well-being and career plans.

Keywords: Women in managerial and expert positions; knowledge work; age; career; appearance; aesthetic work

Introduction

Women in different phases of their working life experience many pressures to 'look good, behave appropriately and sound right'. In this chapter, we consider how these pressures impact on women managers' and experts' well-being and career plans in the context of knowledge work jobs. Our analysis draws upon two empirical data sets, namely, interviews with women mid-managers in Finland and Scotland, and interviews with highly positioned expert women in Finland. The first group consists of more experienced senior women working in what might be considered as traditional workplace structures and the second group of younger women in earlier stages of their professional career, working in low hierarchy organisational contexts.

The Emerald Handbook of Appearance in the Workplace, 197–211
Copyright © 2024 by Emerald Publishing Limited
All rights of reproduction in any form reserved
doi:10.1108/978-1-80071-174-720230012

Knowledge work refers to labour that is of an intellectual nature and which requires higher education qualifications (Alvesson, 2001). In knowledge work, tasks vary in complex ways and require problem-solving and creativity, inter-linking with relative autonomy and independence on decision-making (Costas & Kärreman, 2016). The majority of the workforce in knowledge contexts consists of highly educated and highly specialised professionals (Alvesson, 2004). In many cases, a significant, albeit unspoken, requirement for knowledge work is to be able to convey/to convince the clients, colleagues or stakeholders that you are expert in your field. The control of the body and its presentation, as physically fit, healthy and of an appropriate weight, can be said to be seen as symptomatic of being in control of one's rationality and corporeal presence (Haynes, 2012), as well as one's appearance regarding 'looks', hair-do, make-up and dress do. In knowledge work, managers are often considered as role models for appropriate work behaviour and dress code. In expert positions, work often includes contacts with clients, other business representatives and decision-makers. We argue that look-ism sets many pressures for women managers and experts, although aesthetic work is done also for other women colleagues.

Theoretical Framework

Lookism refers to workplace discrimination based on physical appearance (Tietje & Cresap, 2005). It can occur at all stages in working life from recruitment to retirement, as well as in different phases of career development. Lookism is difficult to track and discuss in organisations, and hard to evidence and seek redress, through organisational and court proceedings. Legal forms of discrimi-nation in Europe generally cite gender, age, disability and race, among others, as basis of discrimination. Lookism can include elements of all these as part of (other) physical signifiers that are not per se named in legislation, and this multifaceted nature of lookism makes it (even) more complicated to evidence.

We approach lookism through the lens of aesthetic labour, namely managing and self-control over appearance in working life (for instance, Witz et al., 2003), which includes demands and implicit or more explicit dress, appearance and behaviour codes in an organisation. Aesthetic labour has been studied in partic-ular in service and hospitality sector organisations, such as hotels, airlines and retail companies (Hochschild, 1983; Helms Mills, 2002; Mears, 2014; Williams & Connell, 2010). However, there is less research on lookism and aesthetic labour in managerial and expert positions as well as in the context of knowledge work organisations (see Karjalainen et al., 2016; Meriläinen et al., 2015; McKie & Jyrkinen, 2017).

Mears (2014, p. 1332) emphasises that aesthetic labour 'encompasses work in which individuals are compensated, indirectly or directly, for their own body's looks and affect'. Thus, aesthetic labour is understood as an embodied form of work demands, which can be beneficial for the person's working life success. The related terms include Gimlin's (2007) concept of body work, which refers to the unpaid work individuals do to modify their own bodies. The 'techniques of the self' (Mauss, 1992), Foucault's (1988) 'self-technologies', Bourdieu's (1984) 'embodied body capital' and Hochschild's (1983) 'emotional labour' have been significant for the development of the '"body work" that comes with feeling' (cf. Mears, 2014, p. 1331; Witz et al., 2003). According to Mears (2014), body work can be understood as unpaid work on one's own body, such as weight management practices, which differs from bodily labour that refers to paid work on others' bodies (for instance, by hair-dressers, cosmetologists or personal trainers). In aesthetic labour, Mears argues, two elements are crucial, namely how it 'reproduces intersectional hierarchies by making social positions–gender, race, and class–clearly marked in space and unequally valued', and 'assessments of good looks are grounded in power relations, which the service economy reproduces in assigning differential value to workers according to interlocking social positions' (Mears, 2014, p. 1337).

We echo Mears (2014) that aesthetic labour is strongly gendered, racialised and classed, but highlight that it is also 'aged', i.e. related in particular to demands of 'agelessness' or 'youthfulness' of senior women as well as 'matureness' and 'professional looks' of younger women (McKie & Jyrkinen, 2017). It reproduces and reinforces the idea that 'looking good and sounding right' is in particular part of women's work – attractiveness, suitable mannerism, style and the ability to relate well with people are feminine soft skills in many work contexts. In addition to appearance, there are often embedded gendered expectations that affect the performance of embodied actions and impressions, especially of emotional intelligence and empathy work (Hochschild, 1983; Ridgeway, 2011). At the same time, particular appearances seem to be expected increasingly also from men, for instance, in managerial work (Meriläinen et al., 2015).

Women's career paths often differ from those of men's (see discussion below). There are many embedded expectations in relation to different genders' suitable physical appearance and behaviour, which come to play in everyday work practices and through overt and covert gender stereotypes. We understand gender as socially constructed, built but also as re-reinforced in everyday life and through discourses, and thereby to be in constant flux. Organisations, societies and working lives are socially constructed, but at the same time women have different levels of agency, albeit, constrained by a range of forces and factors (Alvesson & Willmott, 2002), such as aesthetic work and lookism.

Management may intentionally mobilise aesthetic labour of certain groups of people (Caven et al., 2013; Witz et al., 2003), often women, such as recruiting 'suitably looking' young women to positions which demand public presentations or communication with business clients. At the same time, women managers may themselves practice self-vigilance, and feel pressured, at least covertly, to be presentable to other women, and thereby to do aesthetic labour. In our earlier work, we evidenced and analysed women managers' self-control and survival in gendered and sexualised working place through the concept of 'MyManagement' (McKie & Jyrkinen, 2017). As part of the wage-labour exchange and as partners in a psychological contract (Rousseau, 2001), employees are expected to follow explicit but also more implicit rules of the workplace, also as regards dress, appearance and behaviour codes. These relate to physical appearance, style of dress, physical demure and communication with male, female and colleagues of other genders, subordinates, (other) managers and clients. Shilling (2011, p. 339) argues that routine behaviours are 'modes of connection' that shape 'appearance, pleasures, pains and capacities in particular directions'. He contends that through 'body work the minutiae of individual action with the "structural" issues of society, culture and economy' connect. Women's careers are often not linear, but instead often 'kaleidoscopic' (Mainiero & Sullivan, 2006) and relate to multidimensional and cyclic sceneries in personal life and care obligations. Gender-based discrimination, career breaks because of multifarious care responsibilities and work–life (un)balance impact on many women's working life in different positions. Preciousness of one's own time is common in managerial and expert work, and thereby intensive aesthetic work for suitable looks is an additional challenge.

In addition to formal qualifications and flexibility as regards time to be used for actual work tasks, managers and experts may be expected to attend after-work events, semi-official occasions and over-the-weekend seminars or conferences. Formal receptions can be a crucial part of the work which might imply representability, suitable manners and dressing up. Meriläinen et al. (2015) emphasise the relevance of the embodied co-presence (energy, intensity), voice (toughness for men, charisma and warmth for women) and capability (fitness, physical condition) to construct an 'ideal' executive body and presence. Regardless of many progressive legislation and policies on gender-based discrimination, the 'ideal' continues to be a white, male able-bodied manager in many organisational contexts to fit in the embedded demands (Johnson et al., 2018; also see Acker, 1990). In this chapter, we demonstrate that embodiments and aesthetic labour are more central in managerial and expert level positions than perhaps previously recognised.

The Data

In the following sections, we address aesthetic labour through two data sets that highlight different dimensions among women of different ages. As noted above, the first consists of interviews with senior women managers in what might be considered traditional organisations, such as finance and engineering firms. The second data set comprises younger women in low or no hierarchies forms of organisations. In both projects, data were analysed through thematic content analysis (Guest et al., 2012).

Senior Women Managers

In the first data set, women ranged in age from early 40s to 60s. The focus of this project was on gender, age and careers in Finland and Scotland. It was interesting to note that talking about looks ran alongside discussions of notable points in career development such as recruitment and promotion. There were notable similarities across the two countries. Women managers encountered unwanted, often sexist comments on their looks, and this was especially intense in early stages of their career. Looks were also discussed with reference to pressures to be convincing and professional, but at the same time to be able to express style and 'femininity'; to negotiate and empathise.

Gendered Presentability

Pressures to look 'young' or ageless were discussed in many interviews, such as by Lisa:

> Why is it that older colleagues [women] try to look so young? It seems that people condition themselves to this... When I look at the managers in our organisation, the women are quite well groomed and slim even in older age unlike some men .... Image is very important. Sometimes I wonder if I should also be more elegant. (Lisa, late 50s)

Lisa emphasised that the pressures to look presentable arose from all genders. In addition to a male gaze and re-sexualisation of women's bodies (Evans et al., 2010), other women's evaluations had an influence on women's efforts to look young, 'well groomed and slim'. Lisa stated that 'appearance is interesting, as women tend to dress up for other women'. The female gaze was not necessarily always gentle and supportive. Some relatively harsh comments on other women's appearance were expressed:

> When I look at my younger colleagues, sometimes I think good grief, as some can have so much make-up and hair out of control [wild] .... Perhaps they look at me like an old matron. (Elisabeth, late 50s)

Elisabeth paid a lot of attention to her appearance and made an effort to look good but she also felt under the gaze of other women and speculated about the views of younger colleagues. For self-esteem and career progress, even well-meant patronising by senior colleagues may be hurtful. Somewhat paradoxically, Elisabeth said that she likes to dress up in a 'youngish' way, and wears 'shortish skirts' and 'nice dresses'. Elisabeth also proudly asserted that she often gets positive comments from other women of a similar age; 'you're looking so good at your age!' Thus, lookism can form 'a damned if you do, damned if you don't' dilemma in different career phases, demands to carefully balance with a 'proper' dressing up which signals professionalism, but being 'feminine' enough and to represent one's own personality. This echoes with Trethewey's (1999, p. 443) study where women talked about the fine line of dressing up to be successful in their working life. To reveal too much of their bodies resulted in dire consequences, such as the loss of credibility, flirtation or sexualised comments and looks.

Ironically some women noted that you could also be 'too good looking' and this was a particular concern for younger women, and at earlier stages of their careers, as they might not be taken seriously enough in managerial roles. Shellie (in her 60s, Finland) was a bit hesitant but shared how her (appealing) looks had been problematic and caused her feelings of being 'looked at' and uncomfortable in official contexts: 'I remember how concerning it was to hear so called compliments such as "this beautiful lady" during a meeting or so'. Her experience was not unique and presented the gendered nature of how women managers were evaluated often firstly as women, not as competent colleagues or clients; thus, for instance, keeping slim can be part of a range of embedded duties in professional life. Impacts of rigorous weight control for suitable appearance and beauty ideals might be serious for physical and mental health, including eating disorders in their different forms (Bordo, 2003).

Looks proved to be a balancing act; how to fit in to the workplace and yet be yourself:

> When I was younger, I made myself up more... and I still do [dress and make up carefully]. When I got comments that 'Layla is always so dressed up', I then wondered if I were overdoing it. (Layla, 60s)

> Gender is a topical issue and one of the longest revolutions [impacting on] women... I can say that I dye my hair blond, I have blue eyes, I wear pink lipstick... In terms of gender, I have to live in a certain way to be [acceptable] or to fit in, you know it is going to be your money and you spend on your looks. (Leticia, 40s)

In Leticia's interview, the cost and worth of looks was brought up – to fit in to working life demanded a certain amount of aesthetic labour. Looks were a presupposed extra cost and commitment on the part of women. Some women felt obliged to explain why they do aesthetic work and argued that they pay attention to their looks for their organisation, their career and for themselves. Earlier studies indicate that in recruitment, people who are considered physically attractive are in stronger positions and more likely to be hired. Similar kind of bias is seen in compensation, as 'attractive' workers tend to receive higher salaries (Mahajan, 2007). Thus personal investments in looks, including careful balancing with dressing up with personal style but not too 'feminine' or provocative way, may seem rational for many women (see Trethewey, 1999).

The responsibility to 'fit in' becomes an individualised and complex task for women in organisations. As Huppatz (2009, p. 50) comments, 'femininity is generalised as a female condition', and therefore managerial women often need to engage in the field and the social relations and networks, and carefully consider how to find out and follow the embedded rules and regularities which are not openly spoken nor explicit. For instance, Claudia spoke about the pressures to 'keep yourself fresh' to survive in her area of business, advertising, where the looks and beauty are elements of sales of products:

This is a very young industry and people reach the top of their career potential in their early thirties. ...So you have to keep yourself fresh and motivated. (Claudia, late 40s)

Rebelling Against Aesthetic Labour and Lookism Pressures

There were also disruptions to the pressures to look or behave in certain ways. Some interviewees reflected how they cherish one's appearance and femininity, but embedded, gendered expectations also bothered them. Celeste spoke of feeling irritated in cases where women flirt around men 'like bees to honey' and wanted to distance herself from that kind of behaviour. She continued:

> I think gender has impacted on my career; I mean sadly in a men's world being attractive you can play this card a little bit... In a beautiful summer [day] I wore a nice dress, white jacket and high heels and I was tanned and did my hair nicely and wore nice make-up. He [male superior] said that 'you look like a girl' and then I [played this card], sat next to him rather than opposite, crossed my legs and so on... I am not that attractive but have passion and brains... When you see beautiful women flirting around them [men] like bees to honey, I think I don't want to be in that club. Talk to my brain or piss off. I mean I'm not everyone's cup of tea. (Celeste, 40s)

Celeste expressed concern on flirting and yet used her looks and bodily proximity to play 'a card'. These are complex responses, and certain looks and behaviours some women were aware of as tactical moves. At times this can result in sexualisation and infantilisation, but may also be tactics for career progression.

Efforts to manage and control one's appearance in working life impacts many women (for instance Witz et al., 2003), but in our data there were also women managers who explicitly said that they are not affected by pressures of lookism:

> I have never felt that I should be more feminine or something more particular, as I have never been like that, never felt that I would have a mannequin body or to be brilliantly beautiful. (Samantha, 50s)

> We learn how to present ourselves in the world... So there are certain kind of clothes I wear and certain ways in which I present myself that will fit in so that I don't stand out... because I have learnt the behaviour whether it is what I look like, whether it is how I speak, behaviour that is acceptable with anyone and in any settings. Men have probably learnt that probably more – how many men do you see in unusual clothes? They are all in suits. ...When I started studying [as an adult] I started wearing flat shoes and I was more free to wear the kind of clothes I wanted to ...

there were comments that 'she is wearing student clothes' and they [friends] were making a judgement about what I look like in terms of what I have become... it was never said in a nasty way, it was all sort of friendly joking, but it was still a recognition of difference. (Stephanie, 60s)

These examples contest the taken-for-granted roles of aesthetic labour and looks, and thereby manifest agency in relation to their bodies and behaviours albeit of pressures from outside (see Alvesson & Willmott, 2002). However, both Samantha and Stephanie were in stable positions and had impressive careers, which moved across a number of organisations. It could well be that economic certainty and self-reliance are protective mechanisms for aspects of lookism. Further, older age may influence this too. We now turn to younger women's experiences of lookism and pressures both from inside and outside work organisations to reflect further on the impact of age.

Professional Women in Low/No-Hierarchy Organisations

We now turn to data from two companies in the knowledge work sector that provide business-to-business services to both private and public organisations. These organisations celebrate friendship and low/no hierarchy management philosophy, and rely on highly professionalised workforce (Alvesson, 2004). In both organisations, the workforce is rather young – mostly millennials, extending to some born in late 1970s. The first organisation, which is given the pseudonym 'CommUnity', is a male-dominated firm with approximately one-third of female employees operating in several European countries. The second, 'ComPany,' is a female-dominated organisation operating in Finland. The research participants were knowledge professionals, women in their 20s, 30s and early 40s. The data consists of total 26 interviews, accompanied by diaries: 19 face-to-face interviews at first round, eight work boundaries diaries written by participants and seven second-phase interviews conducted face-to-face and by email, and additional discussions with company owners and leaders. The interviews and boundary-diaries focused on blurring boundaries of work, including aesthetic, emotional and spiritual labour (Hochschild, 1983; Karjalainen, 2022; Witz et al., 2003), and boundaries between work and non-work (Desrochers & Sargent, 2003; Fleming & Spicer, 2004). All research participants were white able-bodied highly educated professionals, who identified as cis-women. This homogenous group represents well both the organisations and the industry, although in the industry there is variation in the gender ratio across the field.

Looking Competent – Professional Women in Low/No Hierarchy Talk About Aesthetic Labour

The women in two low/no hierarchy organisations were highly skilled, educated and successful in a very competitive business sector. Yet they worried about their appearance in several ways: as a company that projects certain images and brings added-value to their product through a certain look, as individuals in a competitive business sector that deals intensely with clients and as individuals within organisations experiencing peer pressure.

ComPany had a reputation of bringing with its professionals a 'certain extra' to the deal by looking good and being presentable. The professionals brought up in the interviews and diaries the experienced unspoken demands on appearance. As Beata, a mid-manager in her early 30s, reflects: 'It is an unwritten rule in our organisation that if we go somewhere to present, we bring added value. [—] For example, we wear colourful or distinguishable clothes by Finnish designers'. This added value, 'the look', was brought up in several interviews and the employees are well aware of it. Monica, a professional in a leadership position in mid 30s, identified strongly with the company having a major role in it:

> If I'm presenting something, knowing that all eyes are on me, and also all client situations – then I think it over, for I have to project a certain image of myself. Am I considered a professional, or... There is an expected value in it. Sometimes I enjoy it, though. (Monica, mid 30s)

The strategy of doing extensive aesthetic labour as a firm, albeit bringing attention and attracting clients, causes an unfortunate backlash as Patricia (early 30s) explained: 'People come to tell me "Oh, you are working at ComPany!" That "Women of ComPany" are here and there. And that we supposedly look all the same and are alike'. Thus, the company strategy may turn into a form of structural sexism, as the women working in the organisation are put under a label based on 'organisational looks' (Witz et al., 2003).

There were evident pressures for a certain appearance promoted in the knowledge work business-to-business sector, as the majority of work is conducted for clients, and thus looks that communicate competence, are considered a prerequisite. In this setting, the question of the right appearance is strongly related to age, looks and dress (Haynes, 2012).

The issue of credibility and looking competent interplays with age. As the workers in these companies are generally young – mostly millennials – the question of age is also raised as a problem of looking too young. This was discussed also in the other firm, CommUnity, in which most professionals were also under 40. Abigail from CommUnity, a professional in her early 30s and relatively early stages of her professional career states: 'I have noticed that people consider me younger than I am. Because of that – at least if there is an important client – I try to look older with certain clothes and such'. It has been noted (Duncan & Loretto, 2004; see also McKie & Jyrkinen, 2017) that a woman is never a right age – for younger professional women it means trying to look older; to look credible and therefore someone to be taken seriously. Sarah, who in her 30s is already relatively far in her career, spoke about feedback she has received on her colleague, based on her looking too young for the client's liking:

> We have had such cases in which the client has demanded [replacement] – clearly because the other person looks a bit childish... I remember being furious for her sake, for it was clear that something in her appearance or personality irritated the client. (Sarah, early 30s, ComPany)

Youth fades, grey hairs and wrinkles appear. Then the worry of looking too young quickly moves to concerns about retaining youthful looks:

> There are many unspoken pressures on weight and also ageing and such. I have never been looks-oriented, I have even now chapped lips, but I have more important things to worry about than chapped lips. But, in the same breath I have to say that I have lately thought about the looks – I turn soon 35. (Nina, mid 30s, ComPany)

Nina who was in a management position expressed her frustration in the expectations of being well groomed and interested in looks. Yet she started to ponder her own view on the business of appearance as she is getting older – and perhaps jumping straight from looking too young to the category of trying to look younger.

The third dimension is the request to follow the appropriate dress code for each situation. Kate in 20s, a manager at CommUnity, spoke about the dress code in her company hiring young professionals:

> We have guides, but people have had quarrels about them too. We had an actual code before; one should dress 10% better than the client does. That was for the consultants [not the back office]. But, it was abandoned for it was distressing for so many. That is where the contradiction lies, we expect professional looks, especially in Sweden – there are differences between countries – you have to be immaculate. But at the same time it is... a bit... forbidden to talk about appearance. (Kate, mid 20s)

Kate reported several double standards in CommUnity on appearance, such as the unwritten rule that one should not focus too much on one's looks as it could be interpreted as vanity, or the renouncement of dress code. Wishing the dress code back, she sometimes found the debate around appearance frustrating.

Yet, for many millennials, dressing according to the code – spoken or unspoken – was a problem. Anne told about the struggles of trying to fit in to the corporate dress code while remaining herself:

> I have had to buy smart shirts and stuff, things that did not belong to my style before. At one point, I had a major inner struggle of how to find smart clothes that I could wear also outside work. At

some point I went shopping, trying to find something to wear, something I could wear and feel being myself. I have had to put some thought in it. (Anne, mid 20s, ComPany).

These implicit or more explicit organisational appearance and dress codes (Witz et al., 2003) form a maze of expectations the millennials try to fulfil while staying true to their own understanding of themselves. This kind of aesthetic labour may cause stress to millennials, whose careers in competitive sector has just started, and they might also have less financial resources required for 'proper' dressing up.

Peer Pressure, Looking Right Inside the Organisation

Taken that both organisations celebrate friendship and low/no hierarchy management philosophy, it is surprising how pressures of looking right play such a role in these organisations, specifically in the female-dominated ComPany. Especially wearing the 'right clothes' seems to cause stress, as many workers' report feeling pressure on dressing in the right style. Sarah, in her early 30s reflects on the dressing style in ComPany: 'I find it really stereotypical, so many of us wear exactly the same black winter coat by COS [an international brand specialising in clothing young professional women], for example... it is a certain kind of ...a mould'. This 'mould' consists of certain brands and style that some felt is outside their reach, due to the lack of money, time, self-esteem or interest.

Madeleine, a professional also in her 30s, spoke about her low self-esteem regarding her appearance, when working in the organisation where everyone seemed to reach higher standards in looks and clothes than she does:

> I do feel pressure. In our office, as noted [smiles wryly], are really young folks and really good-looking folks [gives a laugh], and many invest in dress. It is a bit, the norm for dress is Finnish design and Marimekko [an iconic design brand from Finland] and alike [gives a laugh]. Not skirt suit style, but people put a lot of effort in dressing nicely. Some people use dress rentals, they have more public performances as part of their job, more than I do. But, when you think of the general atmosphere..., it creates a certain standard, which I will never reach. (Madeleine, mid 30s)

The pressure was felt not only in way of dressing but in general appearance. Madeleine continued, reflecting on her memory of a photo shoot that the company organised to have a representable employee group photo for the marketing purposes:

> Well, I wouldn't like to say this – but I say it anyways [gives a laugh]. There was a group photo taken of us, we were standing in a row on a shore [gives a laugh], well, then it was published. So I was

a bit. . . well [laughs]. . . that It is not nice to be in that row. [—] I was the fattest and the shortest [laughs], next to me there were standing these fashion model size 28-year-olds. (Madeleine, mid 30s)

Madeleine felt she does not fit into the appearance standards of the company, comparing herself to '28-year olds'. This may cause a negative outlook on one's career prospects in a company that is noted for its employees looking presentable and dressing according to a certain code. Yet the pressure of looking fresh affects all ages, as a professional in mid-20s confessed:

Everybody looks so good here, and it is really taxing for me [gives a laugh], because I often look very tired and I do not have the energy to do my make-up every morning when I come to work and for me its ok, but then I notice sometimes that 'O my God, how tired one can look! Why does no one else look tired'. (Jessica, mid 20s)

In these organisations, there are several interweaving standards, many unspoken and unwritten. These promote a 'right' appearance, including dress, style and make-up (see Williams & Connell, 2010). Women workers are left alone in the labyrinth of expectations, dress codes, hints and examples set too high for them to achieve. Many of these expectations are not management driven, but set by co-workers in a supposed atmosphere of friendship.

Summary and Recommendations

Through comparing and contrasting the two data sets, we have evidenced the complex ways in which lookism impacts on the lives of women. In one data set, a woman commented that you need to 'keep yourself fresh', while a younger woman from the second study notes that she has 'to look competent.' Younger women evidently felt pressured not to appear too young lest they be considered inexperienced and potentially less reliable than their skills and work experience demonstrate. Older women talked of pressures to appear young, energetic and active and thus capable, in contrast to the commonly held images of the elder male statesman manager as silvered haired, sedentary, paternalistic and a trustworthy leader. Women are constantly reflecting upon their looks and expressing concerns about how seriously or competent they might be perceived by colleagues and clients.

Some companies have dress codes and these codes place disproportionate financial as well as psychological and physical pressures on women. Further, the gaze is experienced from women towards women as well as from men to women. Compliments from colleagues and clients are, at times, perceived as scrutiny. Few women seem immune to the pressures of lookism and those few who dismissed it in our data spoke of their self-confidence, secure situation and wider support for their careers; they recognise lookism but can dismiss the pressures.

Given the societal prevalence of lookism, what recommendations could we offer? Companies can and do express dress codes in ways, which are less prescriptive and offer ease of comfort to perform your job. This includes encouraging comfortable shoes and not dictating dresses or suits. However, as recent social movements have found, there remain both written and unspoken codes. For example, the movement in Japan which challenged the policy of wearing high heels for reception staff and the movement to reduce the pressures on women in the City of London to wear tailored suits and high heels. Both of these grew through social media and drew upon wider social movements, which are challenging the presumptions made about looks and femininity.

Nevertheless, aesthetic labour remains a powerful demand in many roles, which at times, such as in nursing, emerges from health and safety concerns, but is all too often driven by embodied notions of company or organisation images and brandings. The policy and everyday changes required necessitates working bottom up and top down, to continue pressures through social movements and media, while working with business and professional associations to remove or relax policies on appearance.

Our analysis should be set in the wider context of notable growth in anti-ageing treatments, cosmetic surgery and grooming services, such as nail and blow dry bars. The beauty, fitness and well-being industries are omnipresent with men now drawn further into the orbit of lookism. For women, however, the contradictions and pressures of lookism add to the multiple challenges of forging a career including indirect discrimination in recruitment, promotions and the gender pay gap. This chapter evidences the aged defined nature of lookism and how for women the sense of being different and not quite correct is evident across their careers.

References

Acker, J. (1990). Hierarchies, jobs, bodies: A theory of gendered organisations. *Gender & Society*, *4*(2), 139–158.

Alvesson, M. (2001). Knowledge work: Ambiguity, image and identity. *Human Relations*, *54*(7), 863–886.

Alvesson, M. (2004). *Knowledge work and knowledge-intensive firms*. Oxford University Press.

Alvesson, M., & Willmott, H. (2002). Identity regulation and organisational control: Producing the appropriate individual. *Journal of Management Studies*, *39*(5), 619–644.

Bordo, S. (2003). *Unbearable weight. Feminism, Western culture and the body* (Tenth Anniversary Edition). University of California Press.

Bourdieu, P. (1984). *Distinction: A social critique of the judgment of taste*. Harvard University Press.

Caven, V., Lawley, S., & Baker, J. (2013). Performance, gender and sexualised work. Beyond management control, beyond legislation? A case study of work in a recruitment company. *Equality, Diversity and Inclusion: An International Journal*, *32*(5), 475–490.

Costas, J., & Kärreman, D. (2016). The bored self in knowledge work. *Human Relations*, *69*(1), 61–83.

Desrochers, S., & Sargent, L. D. (2003). *Boundary/border theory and work-family integration. A Sloan work and family encyclopaedia entry*. Chestnut Hill.

Duncan, C., & Loretto, W. (2004). Never the right age? Gender and age-based discrimination in employment. *Gender, Work and Organization*, *11*(1), 95–115.

Evans, A., Riley, S., & Shankar, A. (2010). Technologies of sexiness: Theorizing women's engagement in the sexualization of culture. *Feminism & Psychology*, *20*(1), 114–131.

Fleming, P., & Spicer, A. (2004). 'You can check out anytime, but you can never leave': Spatial boundaries in a high commitment organization. *Human Relations*, *57*(1), 75–94.

Foucault, M. (1988). In L. Martin, H. Gutman, & P. Hutton (Eds.), *Technologies of the self. A seminar with Michel Foucault* (pp. 16–49). University of Massachusetts Press.

Gimlin, D. (2007). 'What is 'body work'? A review of the literature. *Sociology Compass*, *1*, 353–370.

Guest, G., MacQueen, K. M., & Namey, E. E. (2012). *Applied thematic analysis*. Sage Publication. Sage Research Methods online.

Haynes, K. (2012). Body beautiful? Gender, identity and the body in professional services firms. Gender. *Work and Organization*, *19*(5), 489–507.

Helms Mills, J. (2002). Employment practices and the gendering of Air Canada's culture during its Trans Canada Airlines days. *Culture and Organisation*, *8*(2), 117–128.

Hochschild, A. R. (1983). *The managed heart. Commercialization of human feeling*. University of California Press.

Huppatz, K. (2009). Reworking Bourdieu's 'capital': Feminine and female capitals in the field of paid caring work. *Sociology*, *43*(1), 45–66.

Johnson, S. K., Keplinger, K., Kirk, J. F., & Chan, E. T. (2018). The perils of pretty: Effects of personal appearance on women's careers. In A. Broadbridge & S. Fielden (Eds.), *Research handbook of diversity and careers* (pp. 129–144). Edward Elgar.

Karjalainen, M. (2022). Workplace mindfulness as practice of well-being and productivity. In G. Mossiere (Ed.), *New spiritualties and the culture of well-being* (pp. 99–116). Springer.

Karjalainen, M., Niemistö, C., & Hearn, J. (2016). Tietotyöalan voittajan tyyli [The Winning Style of Knowledge-workers]. In T. Kinnunen, I. Korte-lainen ja, & J. Parviainen (Eds.), *Ruumiillisuus ja työelämä* (pp. 165–181). Vastapaino.

Mahajan, R. (2007). *The naked truth: Appearance discrimination, employment, and the law. Asian American Law Journal*, Vol. 14, 165–203.

Mainiero, L., & Sullivan, S. (2006). *The opt-out revolt: Why people are leaving companies to create kaleidoscope careers*. Davies-Black Publishing.

Mauss, M. (1992). Techniques of the body. In J. Crary & S. Kwinte (Eds.), *Incorporations* (pp. 455–476). MIT Press.

McKie, L., & Jyrkinen, M. (2017). MyManagement: Female managers meet the sexualised and gendered working life. *Gender in Management: International Journal*, *32*(2), 98–110.

Mears, A. (2014). Aesthetic labor for the sociologies of work, gender, and beauty. *Sociology Compass, 8*(12), 1330–1343.

Meriläinen, S., Tienari, J., & Valtonen, A. (2015). Headhunters and the 'ideal' executive body. *Organization, 22*(1), 3–22.

Ridgeway, C. L. (2011). *Framed by gender: How gender inequality persists in the modern world*. Oxford University Press.

Rousseau, D. M. (2001). Schema, promise and mutuality: The building blocks of the psychological contract. *Journal of Occupational and Organizational Psychology, 74*, 511–541.

Shilling, C. (2011). Afterword: Body work and the sociological tradition. *Sociology of Health & Illness, 33*(2), 336–340.

Tietje, L., & Cresap, S. (2005). Is lookism unjust? The ethics of aesthetics and public policy implications. *Journal of Libertarian Studies, 19*, 31–50.

Trethewey, A. (1999). Disciplined bodies: Women's embodied identities at work. *Organization Studies, 20*(3), 423–450.

Williams, C. L., & Connell, C. (2010). 'Looking good and sounding right': Aesthetic labour and social inequality in the retail industry. *Work and Occupation, 37*(3), 349–377.

Witz, A., Warhurst, C., & Nickson, D. (2003). The labour of aesthetic and the aesthetics of organization. *Organization, 10*(1), 33–54.

Chapter 12

Appearance Discrimination in Hiring: Challenges and Dilemmas for Managers in the United States

Bahaudin G. Mujtaba, Frank J. Cavico and Tipakorn Senathip

Abstract

Appearance is part of a person's non-verbal communication, and looks are often associated with the perceived 'attractiveness' of individuals for hiring practices in the workplace. As such, physical attractiveness can be a 'prized possession' when it comes to leaving a positive impression on managers who are interviewing candidates. In the twenty-first century environment, our society seems to be more obsessed with physical appearance than ever before because society has conditioned us to associate beauty with other favourable characteristics. Of course, such appearance norms, regarding attractiveness, 'good looks' and beauty are linked to years of socialisation in culture, cultural norms and materialistic personality standards.

In a business context, managers and employers often make hiring decisions based on the appearance and attractiveness of the job applicants since outward appearance seems to play a significant role in which candidates eventually might get the job. Physically attractive job applicants and candidates tend to benefit from the unearned privilege, which often comes at a cost to others who are equally qualified. Preferring employees who are deemed to be attractive, and consequently discriminating against those who are perceived as unattractive, can present legal and ethical challenges for employers and managers. In this chapter, we provide a discussion and reflection of appearance-based hiring practices in the United States with relevant legal, ethical and practical implications for employers, human resources professionals and managers. We focus on 'lookism' or appearance discrimination, which is discrimination in favour of people who are physically attractive. As such, we examine federal, state and local laws regarding appearance discrimination in the American workplace. We also offer sustainable policy recommendations for employers, HR professionals and

The Emerald Handbook of Appearance in the Workplace, 213–232
Copyright © 2024 by Emerald Publishing Limited
doi:10.1108/978-1-80071-174-720230013

managers on how they can be fair to all candidates in order to hire, promote and retain the most qualified professionals in their departments and organisations.

Keywords: Lookism; beauty; brand; appearance; professional; discrimination; laws

Introduction

Appearance is an important part of our society as it affects hiring decisions in almost all industries (Cavico et al., 2012). For example, once the basic requirements for the job qualification are met, Hollywood directors are likely to hire the best-looking actors for movie parts, though as per the infamous Harvey Weinstein sexual harassment and abuse case, some of these attractive female actors had to submit to sexual advances as a *quid pro quo* for being hired. Moreover, like the movie industry, television stations want the most 'attractiveness' in their journalists and news anchors, and universities make the first offer to the most professional looking faculty members to represent their organisations (Dworkin & Squire, 2019; Gomez, 2012; Schwantes, 2019; Zakizenski, 2005). James (2008, p. 229) indicates that '. . .outward appearance plays a significant role in everyday life. Magazines and television programs that illustrate America's obsession with appearance overrun society. Consequently, employers realize that looks do matter, and their hiring decisions reflect this simple fact'. Corbett (2011, p. 625) has mentioned, 'society's affinity for beauty seems to have real economic consequences for people'. Physically attractive workers, on average over a lifetime, tend to make around $230,000 more money than their ordinary-looking colleagues do in the United States, according to economist Daniel Hamermesh (2011, p. 47; Cavico et al., 2013). To further illustrate, Hamermesh indicates that the best-looking women made 8% more than the average-looking women and that the best-looking men earned 4% more (Bogner, 2011). Most people would agree that appearances do effect first impressions, and all human beings tend to be at least partially or initially be influenced by how a person looks. While there is nothing wrong with getting the best person for the job, managers must be very careful to make sure they are not discriminating against others who are not perceived as the most 'attractive' candidates simply because of their religious wardrobe, skin colour, age, ethnic backgrounds, disability, gender and/or other such legally protected categories (Mujtaba & Cavico, 2016).

Corbett (2007, p. 153) underscores that 'at the beginning of the twenty-first century, American society was obsessed with physical appearance'. James (2008, pp. 629–30) mentions that when two equally qualified applicants apply for a position, managers are more likely to hire the applicant that they perceive as more attractive since they 'associate beauty with other favorable characteristics'. These appearance perceptions of what is considered attractiveness, 'good looks' and beautiful, are based on years of socialisation, cultural norms and societal standards (Mahajan, 2007; Steinle, 2006). Mahajan (2007, p. 182) warns, 'Relying on culture-bound judgments for appearance may reinforce existing prejudices and stereotypes. Such judgments have...more to do with society's...appearance expectations'.

Appearance also affects a customer's perception of the company and its overall brand value. Consequently, some employers might formally use appearance-based hiring as a marketing technique. For example, firms such as Abercrombie & Fitch, the Gap, L'Oreal and some hotel chains have tried to develop an attractive sales force by hiring workers who are seen as pretty, handsome, good-looking and sexy (Cavico et al., 2013). Greenhouse (2003, p. 21A) quoted the Abercrombie communications director, who said that his company preferred to hire sales assistants, who are known as 'brand representatives', who 'looked great' and who will serve as 'ambassadors' for the brand. Abercrombie has had the brand of the 'classic American' and 'preppy' look and style, which, has been somewhat problematic for them, as they were sued for mainly preferring young, white, blond-haired, blue-eyed applicants while supposedly discriminating against Muslims who wear hijab as well as Black applicants. (Mujtaba & Cavico, 2016). As a result of the lawsuits and the concomitant adverse publicity Abercrombie & Fitch changed its policy and the retailer has stopped hiring workers based on body type and physical attractiveness, and it also will give employees more leeway in what they wear to work. The company said too that it would no longer feature 'sexualised marketing' (McGregor, 2015).

A civil rights lawsuit also would ensure for similar discrimination against job applicants with disabilities, who of course could do the job with a reasonable accommodation (Cavico & Mujtaba, 2014). As such, managers must be aware of Civil Rights laws and thus should make ethical and fair choices in their hiring and promotional decisions. Yet, there is still latitude in the law to discriminate based on appearance, that is, hiring based on 'good looks', so long as there is no connection between an appearance standard and a protected category under Title VII of the Civil Rights as well as other federal and state/local civil rights laws. So, the authors would advise managers to take heed of the old maxim: 'be good, but if you can't be good, be careful'!

Civil Rights Laws

Employers, managers and human resources professionals should know that civil rights laws in the United States make it illegal to discriminate against an employee or job applicant because of his or her race, colour, religion, sex, national origin, age (40 or older) and disability as these characteristics are all 'protected' categories (Cavico et al., 2013). Moreover, as a result of the seminal Supreme Court decision in 2020 in *Bostock v. Clayton County, Ga.* (2020), the prohibition against discrimination based on sex now encompasses protections for gays and lesbians, transgenders and sexually transitioning people. One would hope that this includes non-binary individuals (those who are not solely male or female), but the court cases will eventually provide clarity and confirmation. The aforementioned civil rights laws are federal in nature and apply throughout the land in the United

States, and these laws are enforced by the Equal Employment Opportunity Commission (EEOC). However, it is certainly permissible for a state, county or municipal government entity in its own 'local' law to afford more protections to employees and job applicants, for example, prohibiting discrimination based on political affiliation or beliefs (Cavico & Mujtaba, 2014).

The EEOC actually can proceed to court on behalf of the complaining employee who reports any illegal discrimination towards him or her based on protected categories. Generally, in the context of discrimination pursuant to Title VII of the Civil Rights Act, the plaintiff employee must show that: (1) he or she is in a class protected by the statute; (2) the plaintiff applied for and was qualified for a position or promotion for which the employer was seeking applicants; (3) the plaintiff suffered an adverse employment action, for example, the plaintiff was rejected or demoted despite being qualified, or despite the fact that the plaintiff was performing his or her job at a level that met the employer's legitimate expectations; (4) after the plaintiff's rejection or discharge or demotion, the position remained open and the employer continued to seek applicants from people with the plaintiff's qualifications (Cavico et al., 2012). The presence of these elements gives rise to an inference of discrimination. The burden of proof and persuasion is on the plaintiff employee to establish the prima facie or initial case of discrimination by a preponderance of the evidence (*Gul-E-Rana Mirza v. The Neiman Marcus Group, Inc.*, 2009). Accordingly, in an appearance discrimination case the employee or job applicant would have to demonstrate that his or her appearance is integrally tied to a protected category under civil rights laws, for example, religious beliefs mandating beards and/or long hair, and thus the employee would be converting a legal 'mere' appearance discrimination situation into an illegal discrimination lawsuit, for example, a religious discrimination one, including the failure to make a reasonable accommodation to the employee's religious beliefs.

Title VII of the Civil Rights Act of 1964 prohibits discrimination by employers, labour organisations and employment agencies on the basis of race, colour, sex, religion and national origin. The Act applies to both the private and public sectors, including state and local governments and their subdivisions, agencies and departments. An employer subject to this act is one who has 15 or more employees for each working day in each of 20 or more calendar weeks in the current or preceding calendar year. One of the principal purposes of the Act is to eliminate job discrimination in employment (Mujtaba, 2014). However, while Title VII of the Civil Rights Act protects employees and job applicants from discrimination based on the protected categories of race, colour, sex, national origin and religion, appearance or 'attractiveness' is not included as a protected category. Therefore, it is not always illegal to discriminate based on appearance, for example, by hiring only attractive people (Cavico et al., 2012; Mujtaba & Cavico, 2016). Yet if 'mere' appearance can be linked to a protected category under civil rights laws, for example, religious-based dress, then the case would be a 'simple' religious discrimination one (Cavico et al., 2012; Mujtaba & Cavico, 2016).

Appearance as Race or Colour Discrimination

Accordingly, if an appearance-based case can be connected to race or colour or religious discrimination, then one can have a viable civil rights lawsuit. James (2008, pp. 648–49) states that appearance policies can be tied to race discrimination 'when the policies involve race-linked or race-specific physical traits'. In one case, an agency instituted a race discrimination lawsuit against a restaurant and pub in Georgia because the employer wanted employees who were 'attractive cast members' (EEOC, Press Release, 9/26/2011). According to the EEOC, the restaurant violated Title VII for firing an African-American employee due to her race and colour because she was 'too dark'. In another race- and colour-based lawsuit, it is alleged that the Bass Pro Shops managers repeatedly refused to hire non-white workers as clerks, cashiers and managers as they may not have fit in with the 'company profile' (Zimmerman, 2011).

Similarly, Greenhouse (2003) reported the case of the Mandarin Hotel in California, which was settled for over $1 million. The hotel was accused of race discrimination for discharging nine employees, majority non-white because they were 'too ethnic'. Corbett (2011, p. 634) mentions the case Abercrombie & Fitch, which wanted its sales personnel to have an 'A&F Look'. Consequently, Abercrombie & Fitch was sued for race discrimination because the 'A&F Look' mainly meant hiring those who were young, 'preppie' and 'white' looking. James (2008, p. 655) points out that the plaintiffs in the A&F case successfully connected appearance-based discrimination to race, resulting in negative publicity regarding the company's hiring policies and practices (Cavico et al., 2013).

Appearance as Religious Discrimination

If an employee's appearance can be tied into the employee's religious beliefs or practices, the employee may have a viable Title VII religious discrimination claim. For example, the EEOC instituted a lawsuit against UPS on behalf of an employee, a Rastafarian, who was refused accommodation to the company's appearance policy. The employee's manager said that he did not want any employees 'looking like women on (his) management team' (EEOC, Press Release, 2015). In addition, the EEOC brought another failure to accommodate lawsuit against UPS in the case of a Muslim employee who had a beard due to his religious beliefs and who asked for accommodation to the company's appearance policy that employees in customer-contact positions could not have beards. The employee was told to shave his beard and that 'God would understand', or accept a lower paying job (EEOC, Press Release, 2015). In 2018, however, UPS paid $4.9 million to settle the lawsuit, which was the largest class action religious discrimination settlement in history. As part of the settlement the company now will allow employees to seek an accommodation for their beards as well as long hair if such appearance is motivated by religious beliefs and practices (Bloomberglaw, 2018).

Appearance as Sex Discrimination

Appearance in the form of an attractiveness standard can result in illegal sex discrimination pursuant to civil rights laws when the appearance standard is applied to women but not men; that is, the female employee or job applicant must demonstrate that she was treated differently than a similarly situated male employee or applicant (Corbett, 2011). In such a situation the case is not one of mere appearance discrimination but rather a straightforward case of disparate treatment sex discrimination because the company standard (of being 'pretty' or 'sexy') is only applied to women and not men. However, for a disparate treatment civil rights discrimination case evidence of a purposeful intent or animus to discriminate based on a protected category is required, and of course such evidence may be difficult to obtain, though circumstantial or indirect evidence, such as the use of 'code words' creating an inference of bad discriminatory intent, is permissible in addition to direct evidence (Cavico and Mujtaba, 2014). The use of a code word or words simply gives rise, according to the courts, to an inference of discrimination, that is, the code word is indirect or circumstantial evidence of discrimination, which establishes an initial legal case, which of course can be rebutted, but now the burden of proof and persuasion is on the employer and if it cannot come forth with a legitimate job-related reason for the job action, the plaintiff employee prevails on his or her discrimination case. Furthermore, appearance requirements that are based on sexual stereotypes are impermissible. For example, in the California appeals court case of *Yanowitz v. L'Oreal* (2003), a male executive's order to a manager to fire a female employee because the employee was not sufficiently 'good looking enough' and not 'hot enough' to sell perfume was deemed to be illegal sex discrimination when no similar attractiveness standards were applied to male employees. Women, therefore, cannot be subject to different and more severe and burdensome appearance requirements than men (Cavico & Mujtaba, 2020).

Height and weight requirements must be applied to both male as well as female employees; otherwise, the employer could be liable for disparate treatment based on sex pursuant to Title VII. For example, in one federal appeals court case, the court ruled that the employer acted illegally when the employer's maximum weight standards were applied to the exclusively female position of 'flight hostess' but not to a similar though exclusively male position of 'director of passenger service' (*Gerdon v. Continental Airlines*, 1982). Similarly, there is a federal appeals case where the court found that the weight policy of United Airlines was discriminatory. Although both men and women were subject to the weight requirements, the court found that the airline was imposing a more burdensome weight policy on women by requiring that female flight attendants adhere to maximums for a medium-framed person, but male flight attendants were allowed to reach maximums for a larger-framed person. However, Fowler-Hermes (2001) relates a federal district court case where the employer's appearance requirement of a 'thin and cute' sales force prevented a 270-pound woman from obtaining a promotion to an outside sales position. The employer admitted that the woman was denied a promotion because of her weight, but there was no gender discrimination pursuant to Title VII because the plaintiff woman could not identify one overweight male in the outside sales force. Weight, therefore, is not a protected class under Title VII, and, consequently, discrimination based on weight alone is not per se illegal. Nevertheless, height and weight requirements may disproportionately limit the employment opportunities of certain protected groups; consequently, unless the employer can show that these requirements are necessary for performance of the job, they may be viewed as illegal pursuant to federal civil rights laws. The EEOC advises employers to avoid inquiries about height and weight unless job-related (EEOC, Pre-Employment Inquiries, and Height and Weight, 2011).

In examining the employment-appearance-gender case law, the conclusion is that subjecting women but not men to appearance and attractiveness requirements is illegal sex discrimination. Accordingly, so long as the appearance discrimination is not connected to sex discrimination and that any appearance standards are applied equally to men and women, then the appearance discrimination is legal.

Appearance as National Origin Discrimination

If appearance discrimination can be connected to national origin discrimination, then the aggrieved employee can have a viable civil rights lawsuit. Corbett (2011, pp. 637–638) notes that the 'seeds of a national origin claim' can be planted when 'a particular fashion was so closely associated with a particular race or national-origin group that to discriminate on the basis of fashion was the equivalent of discrimination based on race or national origin'. Discrimination based on a person's ethnic appearance violates the law. For example, the EEOC instituted a lawsuit on behalf of a Muslim pilot who was fired because his appearance was too Arab-looking (EEOC, Press Release, 2003; Mujtaba & Cavico, 2016).

One should remember that a person's dress and fashion are changeable; but one's national origin is not; and neither is one's height. Accordingly, the EEOC warns that an employer's minimum height requirements might have a disproportionate impact, and consequently screen out applicants of a particular national origin, such as Hispanics and Asians; thus, such a policy would be against the law unless it is related to the job and necessary for the employer to operate its business in a safe or efficient manner (Cavico et al., 2012). Therefore, so long as the appearance discrimination is not connected to national origin, the appearance discrimination is legal.

Business Necessity Defence

Civil rights laws under Title VII also provide a 'business necessity' defence in disparate or adverse impact cases for all protected characteristics. In a disparate or adverse impact case there is no intentional discrimination; rather, a policy of the practice of the employer, for example, a weight or height requirement, has a disparate, that is, disproportionate, or adverse impact on a protected category of employees or job applicants. Nonetheless, the policy can be upheld if justified by the employer on grounds of 'business necessity', for example, weight and height requirements for flight attendants (Cavico & Mujtaba, 2014). Regarding age discrimination cases under the Age Discrimination in Employment Act (ADEA), there is an additional defence, called the 'reasonable factors other than age' (RFOA) test. Pursuant to the RFOA, if an employment action, for example, 'downsizing' as a result of a merger, has a disparate or adverse impact on older workers protected by the ADEA, the employer has a defence if it can point to factors other than age, for example, eliminating duplication in positions or reducing healthcare costs the employer has a viable defence (Corbett, 2007, p. 176; James, 2008, pp. 665–66).The practical result of the RFOA test is to vitiate a great deal of the protections of the ADEA. In Title VII cases, assuming that an employer's neutral employment practices or policies have a disparate or adverse impact, and that appearance was a protected characteristic because appearance is directly or indirectly connected to a protected characteristic, the employer would have available the business necessity defence. In addition to the business necessity defence, civil rights law provides another defence – the 'bona fide occupational qualification' defence.

Bona Fide Occupational Qualification (BFOQ) Defence

Title VII of the Civil Rights Act does not prohibit all discrimination in employment. There is a notable exception, in essence, legal discrimination – the 'bona fide occupational qualification' exception. Pursuant to the BFOQ doctrine, employers are allowed to discriminate based on sex, national origin and religion (but not race or colour) if a particular characteristic is reasonably necessary to the normal operations of a business or enterprise (Corbett, 2007, 2011; Mahajan, 2007; Steinle, 2006).

One BFOQ sex appearance case was the federal district court case of *Wilson v. Southwest Airlines Company* (1981). Southwest Airlines embarked on its 'Love' marketing campaign, wherein the company hired exclusively female flight attendants and ticket agents, preferring attractive ones and making them wear sexy 'hot-pants' and 'go-go boots', and aimed the marketing campaign at male business fliers. The company admitted it discriminated against male applicants for customer contact positions; and offered the BFOQ doctrine as a defence, contending that hiring the women was reasonably necessary for the continued operation of the airline. The court, however, disagreed; and explained that the primary business of the airline was to provide air transportation and not to provide a vicarious sexual service; and thus, the airline was denied the protection of a BFOQ exception (*Wilson v. Southwest Airlines*, 1981). Corbett (2007, p. 177) concludes that 'if the BFOQ defence were incorporated into appearance-based discrimination law, as it almost surely would, courts would have to decide whether to interpret it as narrowly as they have for sex or age'. That is, since the BFOQ doctrine is in essence legal discrimination based on certain characteristics, such as sex or age (but never colour or race), the courts have been hostile to the doctrine and consequently have construed it narrowly to afford more fulsome job opportunities for women and older workers who can do the job successfully regardless of their gender or age.

The most famous (or perhaps infamous) BFOQ case dealt with the Hooters restaurant chain. As related by Corbett (2011, p. 646; 2007, pp. 167–68), the EEOC commenced a lawsuit against Hooters because the restaurant refused to hire males for the position of 'Hooters girls'. Hooters defended the lawsuit by contending that being a woman was a BFOQ for being a Hooters girl. The restaurant chain then commenced a public relations campaign to make the federal agency look ridiculous. Ultimately, a settlement was reached that permitted Hooters to continue its hiring practice of selecting only women for 'Hooters girls', that is, servers, but which also expanded other employment opportunities for males in the form of gender-neutral positions. Hooters 'victory' notwithstanding, the BFOQ defence would be a difficult defence to sustain, *assuming* that appearance was deemed to be a protected category under civil rights laws.

An employer generally is permitted to discriminate in employment by making hiring and other business and employment determinations based on appearance in the sense of attractiveness and 'good looks'. However, if the employer's appearance standards can be connected to Title VII's protected categories, then the employer could confront 'conventional' discrimination lawsuits. Discrimination based on appearance is not per se illegal under Title VII. Nonetheless, two other major civil rights laws must be considered in the context of appearance discrimination – the Age Discrimination in Employment Act (ADEA) and the Americans with Disabilities Act.

Americans With Disabilities Act (ADA)

Similar to redress on Title VII and the ADEA, if one's appearance can be linked to a disability, then an applicant or employee may be able to utilise the ADA to secure redress from discrimination. Appearance policies can be challenged pursuant to the ADA, but only if the employer's appearance policy was based on, implicates, or functions to discriminate based on disability. That is, the employee or applicant will need evidence – direct or circumstantial/inferential – that the determination not to hire or promote him or her was based on and motivated by a legally recognised disability and not by the applicant's or employee's appearance. Therefore, like Title VII law, pursuant to the ADA mere discrimination based on appearance is not legally actionable; and consequently the applicant's or employee's appearance must be linked by evidence to his or her legally recognised disability.

An employer's height and weight appearance requirements could trigger the ADA. The EEOC, however, advises that 'normal deviations' in height or weight, which are not the result of any physiological defect or disorder or physical abnormality, are not disabling impairments covered by the Americans with Disabilities Act. For example, in the federal district court case of *Underwood v.*

Trans World Airlines (1989), the court ruled that a mildly overweight flight attendant, who had not been clinically diagnosed as having any medical disorder, did not have an impairment under the ADA. Being overweight, therefore, generally is not construed or regarded as a legal disability; however, severe obesity, defined as body weight more than 100% over the norm, is an impairment (EEOC, Notice Concerning the Americans with Disabilities Act Amendments Act of 2008, 2011). Fowler-Hermes (2001) relates that for weight to be considered a disability, one must be 'morbidly' obese; and emphasises that the purpose of the ADA is to protect the truly disabled, and thus the statute should not be used as a 'catch-all' for appearance discrimination. Appearance also may raise to the level of a disability protected by the ADA when a person is deemed to have an impairment due to a 'stigmatic' condition, for example, severe burns. Such impairment does not by itself substantially limit a major life activity as required by the ADA; however, such a condition is deemed by the EEOC to be an impairment because the negative attitudes and reactions of others to the condition render it a substantially limiting to the person afflicted. Consequently, such a person may be continuously denied employment due to the employers' fears about negative reactions from customers, clients or co-workers. Such a person would thus have a 'disability' and would be protected by the ADA (Equal Employment Opportunity Commission, Notice Concerning the Americans with Disabilities Act Amendments Act of 2008, 2011). James (2008, pp. 651–52) indicates that, 'a few disfigurement claims under the ADA...have largely been settled out of court. In consequence, the ADA currently offers limited redress for victims of discrimination based on some aspect of their physical appearance'. Accordingly, as with Title VII and the ADEA, unless the appearance discrimination can be connected to a disability or an impairment pursuant to the ADA, the appearance discrimination is legal. In addition to lawsuits based on employers violating the aforementioned civil rights statutes, federal civil rights laws also allow a lawsuit by an employee against his or her employer for retaliating against the employee for seeking to vindicate rights protected by the civil rights statutes (Cavico et al., 2013).

Since the United States is a federal system of government with a federal, that is, national government as well as constituent government entities, states, employers and managers must be aware of the potential applicability of state and local civil rights law affecting the employment relationship.

State and Municipal Civil Rights Laws

Although federal civil rights laws do not protect against appearance discrimination unless the discrimination can be linked to a protected category, there are a few states and localities that do protect against appearance discrimination (Rhode, 2010). Initially, the EEOC points out that regarding specifically height and weight inquiries and requirements that a number of states and localities have laws that explicitly prohibit discrimination on the basis of height and weight, unless the height and weight requirements are predicated on the actual requirements of the job (Equal Employment Opportunity Commission, Pre-Employment Inquiries and Height and Weight, 2011). Recognising the underlying unfairness of 'lookism' practiced by employers under the guise of the employment at-will principle, state and local governments have tried to fill the void in this area due to the federal government's inability to act. Often this situation is typical in the area of employment law, where local jurisdictions act as experimental 'laboratories' for pressing, progressive social change to address their local populace's concerns. For example, in the void of federal level protections, many state and local jurisdictions have taken the lead in outlawing discrimination in employment based on sexual orientation or preference (Cavico et al., 2012, pp. 9–13, 2012). Regarding appearance, Michigan, Santa Cruz, San Francisco, California and Washington, D.C., have passed laws prohibiting discrimination because of weight (Capell, 2007; Corbett, 2007; James, 2008; Rhode, 2010). Furthermore, the District of Columbia, Urbana, Illinois, Madison, Wisconsin and Santa Cruz, California, have passed laws prohibiting discrimination based on some aspect of personal appearance (Corbett, 2007; James, 2008).

State Level Civil Rights Laws

Michigan passed the Elliott-Larsen Civil Rights Act of 1976, which banned employment discrimination specifically based upon height and weight, along with other traditional protected classes (Mich. Comp. Laws Ann. Section 37.2102 (2004)). Although the statute does not explicitly include attractiveness as a protected appearance characteristic, it specifically mentions that height and weight are appearance factors that are protected. The previously discussed evidentiary 'burden-shifting', used when addressing federal discrimination complaints in the workplace, also applies to allegations under this code provision (*Harrison v. Olde Financial Corp.*, 1998).

Although not a 'state jurisdiction', Washington, D.C.'s anti-discrimination laws are considered some of the broadest in the nation preventing employers from discriminating based on 'looks' and actually identifying 'personal appearance' as a protected class (D.C. Code Ann. § 2–1402.11(a) (2001)). The provision proffers an 'external' definition of 'personal appearance' as follows: 'Personal appearance' means the outward appearance of any person, irrespective of sex, with regard to bodily condition or characteristics, manner or style of dress and manner or style of personal grooming, including, but not limited to, hairstyle and beards (D.C. Code Ann. § 2–1401.02 (22) (2010)). One would assume that tattoos and piercings would also be covered by the broad language of the act. However, although the District of Columbia provision states that discrimination is prohibited based on personal appearance, it allows exceptions that are available for business necessity and reasonable business purposes, such as clothes, hair styles and beards not interfering with uniforms or safety gear of 'first-responders'.

Municipal Level Civil Rights Laws

Howard County, Maryland, is a county level governmental entity in the United States that makes it unlawful for employers, employment agencies and unions to discriminate based on 'personal appearance' (Howard County Code, Title 12, Subtitle 2, Sec. 12.208 Human Rights (2012)). This code defines personal appearance as an 'outward appearance of a person with regard to hairstyle, facial hair, physical characteristics or manner of dress. It does not relate to a requirement of cleanliness, uniforms or prescribed attire, when uniformly applied, for admittance to a public accommodation or to a class of employees' (Howard County Code Title 12, Subtitle 2, Section 12.201(XV) Human Rights (2012)). It is interesting to note that the law does not explicitly include piercings and tattoos, though one could make a reasonable argument that they are covered by the 'physical appearance or manner of dress' language in the law.

Relying on city codes to protect employees and applicants from this type of workplace appearance discrimination will offer very little additional protection, as only a few of these exist. The cities of Santa Cruz, California, San Francisco, Urbana, Illinois, Binghamton, New York and Madison, Wisconsin extend some protections in avoiding 'lookism' in the workplaces within their geographic city limits. Santa Cruz's code provision begins with explaining its very liberal public purpose of eliminating 'arbitrary discrimination', including that based upon weight, height and physical characteristics, but not necessarily outward 'appearance' since this specific term was removed and replaced with 'physical characteristics' in the final version of the ordinance passed in 1992 (Santa Cruz, Cal. Mun. Code §9.83.010). 'Physical characteristics' is 'A bodily condition or bodily characteristic of any person which is from birth, accident, or disease, or from any natural physical development, or any other event outside the control of that person including individual physical mannerisms. Physical characteristics shall not relate to those situations where a bodily condition or characteristic will present a danger to the health, welfare or safety of any individual' (Santa Cruz, Cal., Mun. Code §9.83.020(13)).

The substitution of 'physical characteristics' for 'appearance' was due to the considerable objections from local business owners who felt that 'self-expression' that offends others should not be protected under the ordinance. These objections ultimately resulted in the ordinance being passed in a weaker version; and thus, employers were able to legally evaluate workers based upon the messages conveyed by their outward appearances attributed to tattoos, artificial hair colour and clothing (Post, 2000). The law arguably would apply to physical characteristics altered by cosmetic surgery; yet presumably since the cosmetic surgery should enhance one's appearance there should be no legal or practical issues.

Urbana, Illinois and Madison, Wisconsin join Santa Cruz in attempts to outlaw discrimination based on 'personal appearance'. Urbana's municipal code defines 'personal appearance' as 'the outward appearance of any person, irrespective of sex, with regard to bodily condition or characteristics, such as weight, height, facial features, or other aspects of appearance. It shall not relate, however, to the requirement of cleanliness, uniforms, or prescribed attire, if and when such requirement is uniformly applied for admittance to a public accommodation or to employees in a business establishment for a reasonable business purpose' (Urbana Mun. Code 12–37 & 12–39). Madison's Equal Opportunities Ordinance is very similar; and defines 'personal appearance' as 'the outward appearance of any person, irrespective of sex, with regard to hairstyle, beards, manner of dress, weight, height, facial features, or other aspects of appearance. It shall not relate, however, to the requirement of cleanliness, uniforms, or prescribed attire, if and when such requirement is uniformly applied for admittance to a public accommodation or to employees in a business establishment for a reasonable business purpose' (Madison Code, Chap. 23, Sec. 39.03(2) (bb) (2010)).

Other municipalities are not as aggressive in their efforts to address 'lookism'. The remaining municipalities limit their code provisions to the physical attributes of 'height and weight' rather than the more encompassing 'physical appearance' definition. Article 33 of the San Francisco Municipal/Police Code bars discrimination based on one's weight and height in both employment, housing and in contracting; and states that 'It shall be unlawful for any person to do any of the following acts wholly or partially based on actual or perceived race, religion ….weight, height, association with members of classes protected under this chapter or in retaliation for opposition to any practices forbidden under this chapter for an employee or applicant for employment'. The city of Birmingham, New York also limits its appearance discrimination code provision to 'height and weight'; and defines those terms as 'Weight is a numerical measurement of total body weight, the ratio of a person's weight in relation to height or an individual's unique physical composition of weight through body size, shape and proportions'. Furthermore, they mention, 'Height is a numerical measurement of total body height, an expression of a person's height in relation to weight, or an individual's unique physical composition of height[1] through body size, shape, and proportions' (City of Birmingham, Chapter 45, Human Rights Law (2010)).

There is, overall, minimal state and local law dealing explicitly and even indirectly with appearance discrimination. Nonetheless, people, perhaps many people, believe that appearance-based discrimination is morally wrong and unfair; and thus they may believe that 'surely employers cannot legally fire someone based on physical appearance alone. ...(T)his is not the case, however, because most state legislatures have not enacted laws prohibiting appearance-based discrimination, and most never will' (Corbett, 2011, pp. 625–26). In general, there is legislative concern that it is an overly broad, vague and amorphous legal standard, very difficult to precisely define, consequently resulting in a substantial increase in workplace discrimination lawsuits and a further 'clogging up' of the courts. Furthermore, James (2008) worries that if too many state and local jurisdictions did enact appearance discrimination laws, then these laws will be vague and overbroad as well as not uniform and consistent, and as a result would engender inconsistent results and apprehension on the part of the business community. Nonetheless, in the vast majority of jurisdictions, appearance discrimination, particularly in the form of attractiveness, is not a protected characteristic pursuant to federal, state or local civil rights law; thus, as a general rule, it is legal to discriminate based on appearance. However, due to the absence of federal protections and the paucity of law on the state and local level, presently, there are proposals to amend civil rights laws to encompass appearance discrimination as a protected category.

Employer and Employee Analysis

Notions of appearance in the sense of attractiveness, 'good-looks', beauty and sexiness certainly can affect employment opportunities. 'Undoubtedly, people make decisions based on exterior stereotypes and frequently form opinions supported solely by prejudice' (James, 2008, p. 629). The effect can be deleterious. Corbett (2007, p. 157) fears that '...the relatively unattractive (aesthetically challenged, if you please) lose out on opportunities and benefits that are generously bestowed on the attractive'. Consequently, if an employee is not deemed to be sufficiently attractive, this appearance factor can supersede more pertinent criteria, such as the employee's knowledge, skills and qualifications (Cavico et al., 2013). Mahajan (2007, p. 170) deems appearance policies to be 'troubling because they facilitate the judging of employees based on qualities unrelated to job performance'. Moreover, 'appearance policies can reflect certain prejudices, and adversely affect the individuals against whom they are enforced' (Mahajan, 2007, p. 170).

However, if the employee has a 'good' appearance, his or her attractiveness may unduly influence the perception of the employer as to the capabilities and qualifications of the employee. Corbett (2011, pp. 632–33) opines that 'attractive people often evoke sympathy, admiration, forgiveness, or other milk of human kindness in situations in which unattractive people do not'. Similarly, Mahajan (2007, pp. 167–68) deems this psychological phenomenon to be the 'halo effect', whereby an employee is rated positively on one criterion, appearance in the context herein, and this factor unduly influences the employer's evaluation of the employee on other criteria, such as abilities and qualifications. Furthermore, Mahajan (2007, p. 168) relates: 'In fact, the empirical evidence suggests that in the context of employment decision-making, the more attractive a person, the more likely she (or he) is to be hired and the more highly she will be paid'. As such, Mahajan (2007, pp. 166–167) points to a study which 'found that more socially desirable traits, such as likeability, honesty, and competence, were attributed to the attractive individuals, whereas less attractive individuals were deemed lazy and counterproductive'. Furthermore, James (2008, p. 637) relates an economic study on beauty and employment, which 'found that "plain" people earned between five and ten percent less than "average-looking" people, who earned five percent less than "good-looking" people'. So, while there certainly may be negative consequences for the 'appearance challenged', at least for securing some employment opportunities, that 'pain' is counterbalanced to some degree by the 'pretty' who are preferred and hired.

In addition, it should be underscored that employers are granted certain discretion pursuant to civil rights laws on how they run their businesses. Not all discrimination is illegal. Managing a workforce in an efficient, effective and profitable manner is surely a legitimate interest. As Corbett (2007, p. 166) explains, in US society, in addition to preventing employment discrimination, 'a very strong goal at the other extreme is respecting employers' prerogatives to operate their businesses in ways they deem appropriate to create jobs, generate profits, and contribute to a robust economy'. Moreover, as emphasised in the legal analysis, an appearance policy is not automatically illegal pursuant to Title VII and other civil rights laws unless the employer's appearance policies and standards can be connected to one of the protected categories in Title VII or other laws. Employers could have very practical, and quite rational, business reasons for preferring the 'pretty' in employment. Image can be a very important factor for an employer, and attractiveness can be an essential component of that image. Employers, for example, could be seeking to satisfy perceived customer preferences or to maintain a certain image or brand with the public. James (2008, p. 638) states that 'employers often support using appearance as a factor in hiring when beauty has a direct effect on profitability'. Furthermore, James (2008, p. 638) relates that 'market analysts agree that employees' outward appearances reflect on the product and the brand image'. Similarly, as emphasised by Corbett (2007, p. 154), 'businesses were convinced that customers would buy what they had to sell if their employees were attractive'. Furthermore, attractiveness may be directly related to the functions of a particular job. Modelling, of course, emerges as an obvious example. As further explained by James (2008, p. 670), these functions can '. . .include playing a certain role, appealing to a particular market, displaying the company's image, and looking the part'. Moreover, 'some employers may simply prefer to hire attractive women as a matter of personal taste, but many believe that their businesses will enjoy higher profits as a result of such hires' (Corbett, 2011, p. 646). Similarly, Steinle (2006, pp. 262–263) points out that 'to survive in a competitive marketplace, employers increasingly seek to tap into today's "lookist" culture by ensuring that their employees create a salable image. Often, this is achieved through hiring on the basis of personal attractiveness'. Similarly, Mahajan (2007, p. 173) relates that employers can 'capitalize on women's sexuality in order to attract customers'. As such, broadening civil rights laws to encompass appearance protections, particularly as to attractiveness, would certainly undermine employers' discretion to establish appearance standards. Employers are also concerned about being mired in frivolous appearance lawsuits, especially by 'eccentric' employees (Steinle, 2006). Corbett (2007, p. 166) agrees, noting: 'When the goal of reducing discrimination would encroach too much on other important goals, such as employer's autonomy of decision-making, some in society will speak up about the potential excesses of employment discrimination law'. Employers, therefore, in the form of image, customer satisfaction, profitability and success, surely can benefit from having the discretion to hire and to keep attractive (as well as presumably qualified) employees.

Implications and Recommendations

Legally, an employer as a general rule can discriminate based on appearance in the form of attractiveness, but an employer must exercise caution since an appearance standard might be connected to a Title VII, ADEA or ADA protected category, thereby triggering a civil rights discrimination lawsuit. As such, Mahajan (2007, p. 203) emphasises that 'the first step to protecting individuals adversely affected by employer-imposed appearance policies is to recognize the discriminatory potential of those policies, particularly those that serve as proxies for discrimination based on suspect categories, such as gender and race'. For example, an employer may be able to discriminate in hiring by preferring 'good-looking' job applicants; but if that appearance standard results in the hiring of only young, white employees, then the employer could be sued pursuant to Title VII and the ADEA. Similarly, as explained by Corbett (2007, p. 164): 'It is not illegal for employers to discriminate on the basis of certain physical characteristics – those covered by existing discrimination laws. Thus, if an employer discriminates on the basis of wanting a certain "look," and that look is "young" or "white" or "American", then the discrimination is illegal under the existing employment discrimination laws'. The employer must be cognizant that the employee will need sufficient evidence to sustain a case of impermissible discrimination. Perhaps there will be direct evidence, such as a memo or email, stating that an applicant was not hired or promoted because he or she was 'Black' or 'too old', that will reveal evidently the employer's intent to discriminate, not on appearance per se, but on illegal race or age grounds. Such a direct evidence approach naturally would be a more effective legal tactic; yet obtaining direct evidence of a wrongful intent to discriminate is difficult. However, the employer also must be cognizant that indirect or inferential evidence can also be used to demonstrate a wrongful intent to discriminate. For example, the use of such 'code words' in making negative employment determinations, such as 'too ethnic', 'too foreign-looking', 'too dark', 'young bloods', 'young guns', 'go-getters', 'youthful appearance', 'appeal to youth demographics', 'appeal to youth market', 'all American look', 'trendy', 'preppie', 'hip' and 'with it', may take the case out of the non-actionable appearance category, and place it squarely by means of inferential evidence in a viable civil rights violation category, such as race, colour or age discrimination (Cavico et al., 2013).

Employers, therefore, can and must take precautions to preclude attractiveness or appearance lawsuits. As such, if an employer deems it necessary or even beneficial to have an attractiveness standard, or perhaps a concomitant height or weight standard, the employer must make sure that discriminatory elements are not built into the standard or that the standard is applied in a discriminatory manner. Most importantly, men and women, Blacks and whites and people of different races, religions and nationalities must be treated in a comparable and fair manner. Appearance and attractiveness cannot legally or morally be used as a pretext for impermissible discrimination. Managers should be particularly sensitive to insidious prejudice exhibited against transgender and transsexual individuals in the workplace based purely on their outward appearance and mannerisms. There should be 'zero tolerance' for the use of insulting code words like 'cross-dressers' or 'drag queens' in the workplace to describe these individuals. Employers and managers now must be keenly aware that the US Supreme Court ruled in 2020 in a 6-3 decision in the case of *Bostock v. Clayton County, Ga.* (2020) that Title VII protects employees from discrimination because they are gay or transgender. Business managers consequently have a legal as well as moral obligation to take the lead in preventing this type of real discrimination against such vulnerable groups of individuals as well as preventing other forms of discrimination. Confronting such prejudice 'head-on', by appropriate diversity and sensitivity education and training and articulating and enforcing a corporate code of conduct to protect against physical appearance as well as other forms of discrimination, is a characteristic of a legal, ethical, forward-thinking, socially responsible and smart employer.

Conclusion

Appearance discrimination can be connected to a protected category, and thus converted into a discrimination claim based on race, colour, sex or any other protected characteristic under civil rights laws. However, if a person, perhaps regarded as 'unattractive', cannot tie his or her appearance-based lawsuit to a protected category under federal, state or local civil rights laws, that person will not have legal redress. Managers should lead by example with forward-thinking and protective written policies that are sustainable over time, where the legal system has so far fallen short in offering sufficient protections to all workers regardless of outward appearance.

The objective is to create an organisation that is founded on the core values of legality and morality. Morality means treating people – job applicants, employees and all others – as valuable and worthwhile human beings deserving of dignity and respect. Consequently, any action or policy that treats people as a thing, tool, instrument or a simple 'means to an end' is immoral. Likewise, any action that is demeaning, disrespectful, offencive, abusive or bullying is an immoral action that must be adjured. Morality supersedes legality; and thus, an action even if arguably legal is not permissible from an ethical standpoint if it is immoral. The core value of respect also encompasses the important corollary values of sensitivity, diversity and cultural awareness and competence in the organisation's treatment of its employees and all its stakeholders. Awareness of and adherence to these fundamental values will go a long way to ensuring that the firm is, and is truly perceived as, a moral as well as a legal one. Job applicants will want to work for such an organisation, employees will want to continue working there, customers and clients will want to do business with such a firm, good relations will be achieved in the local community and government regulators will have no problem with a company that acts legally and morally. Accordingly, acting in an ethical and legal manner is the 'right' thing to do as well as the 'smart' thing to do!

Note

1. For further information on state and municipal law as well as national law and
   foreign legal perspectives, see the following: Managing Employee Dress and
   Appearance (SHRM, 2021) and Regulating Appearance in the Workplace: An
   Employer's Guide to Avoiding Employment Discrimination (The National Law
   Review, 2021).

References/Cases

Bloombergnews.com. (2018). UPS Settles U.S. Suit Alleging Bias Over Long Hair,
   Beard. https://news.bloomberglaw.com/daily-labor-report/ups-settles-u-s-suit-
   alleging-bias-over-long-hair-beards-1. Accessed on May 24, 2021.

Bogner, E. (2011). Beauty pays. *Business Insider*. businessinsider.com/beauty-pays-
   daniel-hamermesh- 2011. Accessed on May 24, 2021.

Bostock v. Clayton County, Ga., 140 S.Ct. 1731 (2020).

Capell, P. (2007, October 2). Why weight-discrimination cases pose thorny legal tests
   (p. B4). The Wall Street Journal.

Cavico, F. C., & Mujtaba, B. G. (2014). *Legal challenges for the Global Manager and
   entrepreneur* (2nd ed.). Kendall-Hunt Publishing Company.

Cavico, F. J., & Mujtaba, B. G. (2020). *Business law for the Entrepreneur and Manager*
   (4th ed.). ILEAD Academy.

Cavico, F. J., Muffler, S. C., & Mujtaba, B. G. (2013). Appearance discrimination in
   employment: Legal and Ethical implications of "Lookism" and "Lookphobia".
   Equality, Diversity and Inclusion: An International Journal, 32(1), 89–119.

Cavico, F. J., Muffler, S. C., & Mujtaba, B. G. (2012). Appearance discrimination,
   "Lookism" and "Lookphobia" in the workplace. *Journal of Applied Business
   Research*, 28(5), 791–802.

City of Binghamton, Chapter 45 Human Rights Law, Sections 45-2, 45-3, and 45-4
   (2010).

Corbett, W. R. (2011). Hotness discrimination: Appearance discrimination as a mirror
   for reflecting on the body of employment discrimination law. *Catholic University
   Law Review*, 60, 615–652.

Corbett, W. R. (2007). The ugly truth about appearance discrimination and the beauty
   of our employment discrimination law. *Duke Journal of Gender Law & Policy*, 14,
   153–183.

Dworkin, L. B., & Squire, M. B. (2019, June 28). "You look marvelous!" avoiding
   appearance-based discrimination at work. *Insight*. newsbloomberglaw.com/us-law-
   week.insight/dworkin. Accessed on July 5, 2022.

Equal Employment Opportunity Commission - EEOC. (2011). *Fact sheet. What you
   should know about appearance discrimination*. http://www.eeoc.gov/eeoc/
   publications/upload/immigrants-facts.pdf. Accessed on October 10, 2019.

EEOC. (2011). *Notice Concerning The Americans with Disabilities Act Amendments
   Act of 2008", Section 902 Definition of the Term Disability*. http://www.eeoc.gov.
   policy/docs/902cm.html. Accessed on November 7, 2011.

EEOC. (2011). *Pre-Employment Inquiries and Height and Weight*. http://www.eeoc.
   gov;aws/practices/inquiries_height_weight.cfm. Accessed on November 7, 2011.

EEOC. (2011, September 26). Press Release – K&J Roswell/the Tilted Kilt Sued by EEOC for Race Discrimination. http://www.eeoc.gov/eeoc.newsroom/release/9-26-11.cfm. Accessed on November 7, 2011.

EEOC. (2003, July 17). *Press Release – Muslim Pilot Fired Due to Religion and Appearance.* http://www.eeoc.gov/eeoc.newsroom/release/7-17-03.cfm

EEOC. (2015, July 15). Press Release – EEOC Sues UPS for religious discrimination. http://www.eeoc.gov/eeoc.newsroom/release/7-15-15.cfm. Accessed on October 10, 2019.

EEOC. (2011). *Prohibited Employment Policies/Practices.* http://www.eeoc.gov/laws/practices/index.cfm November 7, 2011

Fowler-Hermes, J. (2001, April). *Appearance-based Discrimination Claims Under EEO Laws* (p. 32f). The Florida Bar Journal.

Gerdon v. Continental Airlines, 692 F.2d 602 (9th Circuit 1982).

Gomez, E. (2012, January 31). Should Business Worry About Appearance-Based Discrimination in the Workplace. *Forbes.* forbes.com/sites/evangelinegomez/2012/01/31. Accessed on July 5, 2022.

Greenhouse, S. (2003, July 13). *Looks aren't everything – unless you want a job* (p. 21A). The Miami Herald.

Gul-E-Rana Mirza v. The Neiman Marcus Group, Inc., 649 F. Supp.2d 837 (2009); 2009 U.S. Dist. LEXIS 38102.

Hamermesh, D. (2011). *Beauty Pays: Why Attractive People are More Successful* (p. 47). Princeton University Press.

Harrison v. Olde Financial Corp., 225 Mich. App. 601, 572 N.W.2d 679, 681 (Mich Ct. App. 1998).

Howard County Code, Title 12, Subtitle 2, Sec. 12.208 Human Rights. (2012). County Council of Howard County, Maryland. https://howardcounty.granicus.com/MetaViewer.php?view_id=2&clip_id=2410&meta_id=77126/https://law.justia.com/codes/maryland/2015/article-gsg/title-20/subtitle-12/section-20-1202

James, H. R. (2008, Winter). If you are attractive and you know it, please apply: Appearance based discrimination and employer discretion. *Valparaiso University Law Review, 42,* 629–677.

Madison, Wis. Gen. Ordinance, Chapter 39, Equal Opportunities Ordinance, Sections 39.03(1) and Section (2)(bb) (2010).

Mahajan, R. (2007). The Naked Truth: Appearance Discrimination, Employment, and the Law. *Asian-American Law Journal, 14,* 165–213.

McGregor, J. (2015). *Washington Post.* Abercrombie & Fitch says it will no longer hire store workers based on their 'body type or physical attractiveness'. washingtonpost.com/news/on-leadership/wp/2015/04/24/Abercrombie-fitch. Accessed on May 25, 2021.

Michigan Comp. Laws, Section 37.2102 (2004).

Mujtaba, B. G. (2014). *Managerial skills and practices for global leadership.* ILEAD Academy.

Mujtaba, B. G., & Cavico, F. J. (2016). Weight and Appearance at Work: Legal Concerns Related to Race, Ethnicity, and Gender. In M. Foegen Karsten (Eds.), *Part I – Chapter 2 in "Gender, race and ethnicity in the workplace: Emerging issues and enduring challenges* (pp. 27–42). Praeger. ISBN-13:978-1-4408-3369-4

Post, R. C. (2000). Prejudicial Appearances: The Logic of American Antidiscrimination Law. *Faculty Scholarship Series, Paper 192*, 5–6; also found at 88 California. Law. Review. 6 (2000).

Rhode, D. L. (2010). The injustice of appearance. *Stanford Law Review, 61*(5), 1033–1099. https://www.stanfordlawreview.org/print/article/the-injustice-of-appearance/

Santa Cruz California Municipal Code, Santa Cruz, Ca. Mun. Code Section 9:83.010-9.83.120 (1992).

Schwantes, M. (2019, October 12). New research reveals why appearance discrimination is making workplaces even more toxic. *Inc.* Inc.com.marcel-schwantes. Accessed on July 5, 2022.

Steinle, A. T. (2006,Fall). Appearance and Grooming Standards as Sex Discrimination in the Workplace. *Catholic University Law Review, 56*, 261–306.

The National Law Review (Vol. 11, Number 145, 2021). *Regulating Appearance in the Workplace: The Employer's Guide to Avoiding Employment Discrimination.* https://www.natlawreview.com/article/regulating-appearance-workplace-employer-s-guide-to-avoid-employment-discrimination-#:~:text=Employers%20institute%20dress%20codes%2C%20appearance,do%20not%20violate%20Title%20VII. Accessed on May 25, 2021.

Underwood v. Trans World Airlines, 710 F. Supp. 78 (S.D.N.Y. 1989).

Urbana, Il., Code of Ordinances Sections, Chapter 12, Human Rights Article III, Sections12-37, 12-39, and 12-62 (a).

Yanowitz v. L'Oreal USA, Inc., 131 Cal. Rptr. 2d 575 (Ca. App. 2003).

caWilson v. Southwest Airline Company, 517 F. Supp. 292 (N.D. Texas 1981).

Zakizenski, K. (2005). The prevalence of lookism at hiring decisions: How federal law should be amended to prevent appearance discrimination in the workplace. *University of Pennsylvania Journal of Labor and Employment Law, 7*(2), 431–461.

Zimmerman, A. (2011, September 22). U.S. Accuses Bass Pro Shops of Bias. *The Wall Street Journal*, B4.

Chapter 13

Legislating Against Lookism in Australia

Chris Warhurst, Richard Hall and Diane Van Den Broek

Abstract

Aesthetic labour explains how employees are required to look and sound the part in many contemporary workplaces. That such corporeality affects workers' employment prospects, including career progression, is now well documented in research. As such, it can result in employment discrimination based on physical features, more commonly known as 'lookism'. However, very few jurisdictions proscribe lookism, and little is known about the efficacy of those that do. Based on archival research, this chapter examines the procedures and operation of physical features inclusion in an Equal Opportunity Act in one jurisdiction that does proscribe 'lookism – the state of Victoria in Australia. As the first analysis of such laws, the chapter provides an important opportunity to assess the efficacy of legal attempts to address employment discrimination based on employee appearance. In so doing, it draws out lessons about the legal challenge to lookism.

Keywords: Aesthetic labour; Australia; career progression; discrimination; equal opportunity law; lookism

Introduction

In 2009, amid huge international media attention, Riam Dean, an employee of fashion retailer Abercrombie & Fitch in London, took the company to an employment tribunal claiming that she had been discriminated against because her appearance – more particularly her prosthetic arm fell foul of the company's 'looks policy'. The tribunal heard that the company had a 45-page handbook outlining this policy, which went as far as listing acceptable hairstyles and fingernail length. After describing how she felt 'personally diminished [and] humiliated', the tribunal found in the complainant's favour and awarded her more than £9000 for injury to her feelings, loss of earnings and wrongful dismissal (Malvern, 2009; Pidd, 2009, n.p.)

The Emerald Handbook of Appearance in the Workplace, 233–248

Copyright © 2024 by Emerald Publishing Limited

All rights of reproduction in any form reserved

doi:10.1108/978-1-80071-174-720230014

The propensity of employers to hire, train, reward and promote employees based on their appearance is now mainstreamed and termed 'aesthetic labour' (Warhurst & Nickson, 2020). This labour has the potential to create a new form of employment discrimination based on workers' appearance, popularly called 'lookism' (Warhurst et al., 2009). This lookism is not considered to be an illegal form of discrimination in the United Kingdom where Dean's case was heard. Successful challenges to lookism in the United Kingdom by trade unions or organisations concerned with equality have used legislation centred on race, sex and, as the Dean case exemplifies, disability discrimination, which entails a claim being based on a protected category.

Indeed very few jurisdictions proscribe lookism. In Australia, Victoria (*Equal Opportunity Act* 1995) and the Australian Capital Territory (ACT) (*Discrimination Act* 1991) have anti-discrimination legislation which include 'physical features' as protected attributes. Victoria is a state and the ACT a territory with within the Australian federal system of government that have legislative authority. The Victorian and ACT Acts mean that a worker should not be discriminated against on the basis of height, weight or other bodily characteristics (which have been broadly defined to include tattoos, piercings and other forms of self-expression such as hairstyle/facial hair/make-up). Although why physical features was included is not clear – even among the politicians speaking to its inclusive – the legislation sought to regulate forms of discrimination not captured in existing attributes such as sex, age, religion, race etc.

This chapter examines the procedures and operation of 'physical features' inclusion in the Victorian Act. As the first analysis of such laws, the chapter provides an important opportunity to assess the efficacy of legal attempts to address employment discrimination based on employee appearance. In so doing it draws out lessons about the legal challenge to lookism. The files available to us included historical cases relating to the first 10 years of the Act. We were also able to interview some of the senior officers of the Victorian Equal Opportunity Commission (EOC) (since renamed the Victorian Equal Opportunity and Human Rights Commission) responsible for dealing with complaints related to the Act.

The next section provides a short overview of aesthetic labour, employee appearance and lookism. The following sections then outline and evaluate the efficacy of the Act as law. The concluding remarks suggest how workers might be better protected from lookism in the future.

Aesthetic Labour, Employee Appearance and Lookism

There is now a significant body of research highlighting how employees looking and sounding 'the part' is an important feature of many contemporary workplaces. Employers mobilise, develop, deploy and commodify these embodied employee dispositions through processes of recruitment, selection, training, management and reward, transforming them into a 'style' of service encounter intended to appeal to the senses of customers and/or clients. This aesthetic labour is typically manifest in employees' dress, speech and body language and supports organisations' image and/or brand (Warhurst & Nickson, 2020). Employer expectations of dress and presentation might include the absence of facial piercings and jewellery, tattoos, or short/long hair as well specific preferences around body height/weight and size. These preferences are evident in many high-profile service industries' companies, such as Virgin Airlines in Australia, French Connection in the United Kingdom and Abercrombie and Fitch in the United States (e.g. Devine, 2004; Pettinger, 2004; Spiess & Waring, 2005).

While mainstreamed in the service industries, the importance of workers' appearance extends into other industries, even manufacturing (Warhurst et al., 2012). A number of studies have demonstrated that labour market pay and career premiums and penalties exist for workers as an outcome of their perceived physical attractiveness (e.g. Hamermesh, 2011; Rhode, 2010; Sierminska, 2015). Hamermesh and Biddle (1994, p. 1174) state that workers of above average beauty earn around 10 to 15% more than workers of below average beauty for example. Employers also benefit from this perceived attractiveness, Hamermesh (2011, p. 7) notes: having workers with good looks 'affect[s] the bottom line of companies'.

Despite appearance being increasingly accepted as legitimate in employment decisions, its functional need is questionable says Adamitis (2000, p. 195): 'for most jobs appearance has no bearing on an individual's ability to perform'. Those employees deemed to be relatively unattractive or 'aesthetically challenged', in Corbett's (2007, p. 157) words, may nevertheless find themselves facing looks-based discrimination or 'lookism'. Ayto (1999, p. 485) defines lookism as 'prejudice or discrimination on the grounds of appearance (i.e., uglies are done down and beautiful people get all the breaks)', noting the term was first used in print by the *Washington Post* in the late 1970s. Tietje and Cresap (2005, p. 32) observe that 'In our society aesthetic capital, like other kinds of capital, is unequally distributed'. With employers using this unequally distributed 'capital' to, in the phraseology of economists, 'sort' the workforce, lookism has entered the lexicon of employment discrimination.

Providing protection from employment discrimination based on their appearance can be difficult. As Tietje and Cresap (2005) note, discrimination based on looks can be mediated by social markers such as race, class and sex, with these markers often difficult to disentangle. Furthermore, Tietje and Cresap note, lookism 'may be difficult to see as a prejudice because judging people on the basis of how they look is in many areas of life an indisputable good', citing the example of sexual attraction (p. 37). However, when lookism becomes discriminatory or exclusionary in an economic sector or social context it is much more likely to be considered abnormal, pernicious and unfair (Adamitis, 2000; Fleener, 2005).

Nonetheless, the exploitation of employee appearance is regarded as legitimate by many employers. In their review of appearance standards and dress codes in the United Kingdom and United States, Hay and Middlemiss (2003) note that a managerial prerogative is generally accepted that gives employers 'the right to lay down rules imposing appearance standards for their employees' and which allows employers to 'control the way their employees are dressed (e.g. clothing) or groomed (hair, jewellery, etc.)' (2003, p. 69). This managerial prerogative, these authors note, has been repeatedly reinforced by the courts in a range of case law in the United Kingdom and United States.

This managerial prerogative is, however, tempered by the need to not discriminate against employees on account of their sex, race, religious belief or other 'protected' status or characteristic, which might include physical disability or impairment. The exception occurs when an employer can argue that a certain characteristic or attribute is a Bona Fide Occupational Qualification (BFOQ). In assessing what physical characteristic constitutes a BFOQ, the courts have generally rejected arguments that the characteristic reflects the preference of customers or co-workers or is part of the 'company image' (Fleener, 2005, p. 1305). Generally, the attribute must be a requirement for performing the core duties of the job to be considered a BFOQ, such as the situation where particular physical characteristics are needed to ensure the authenticity or credibility of a dramatic or artistic performance, entertainment, photographic or modelling work (Equal Opportunity Commission Victoria, 2003).

Thus, employers may prescribe the appearance of employees as part of a business strategy so long as that prescription does not transgress existing discrimination legislation. In this respect, while there are no national laws in the United Kingdom, the United States or Australia prohibiting discrimination based on appearance, plaintiffs are potentially able to seek relief from lookism where appearance discrimination is related to an established ground of unlawful discrimination such as sex, race, religion or disability. It was this approach that was taken in the Riam Dean case against Abercrombie and Fitch. The case was successful because the tribunal ruled that, in relation to the company's looks policy, Dean was wrongfully dismissed after being the victim of disability discrimination. In most Anglophone jurisdictions, therefore, employees subjected to lookism might, in some circumstances, be able to seek relief where the discrimination can be related to sex, race or disability discrimination. As a result, however, discrimination on the basis of appearance per se, provided it is unrelated to race, sex or disability, is not unlawful. Lookism's omission from discrimination law can create practical challenges for potential claimants and can also mask a discriminatory practice on the part of employers.

However, there are a few jurisdictions in which physical appearance has been legislated as unlawful discrimination. At least five local jurisdictions in the United States identify physical appearance or aspects of appearance as prohibited grounds for discrimination: Michigan prohibits 'height and weight' discrimination, the District of Columbia (DC) and Urbana in Illinois both prohibit 'personal appearance' discrimination, Santa Cruz in California prohibits discrimination on the basis of 'physical characteristics' and Madison in Wisconsin proscribes 'physical appearance' discrimination (Baron, 2005; Corbett, 2007). These prohibitions can be broadly or narrowly defined. DC adopts a broad approach, defining 'personal appearance' as 'the outward appearance of any person, irrespective of sex, with regard to bodily condition or characteristics, manner or style of personal grooming, including, but not limited to, hair style and beards' (quoted in Adamitis, 2000, p. 210). By contrast, Santa Cruz adopts a narrow approach, restricting 'physical characteristics' to immutable characteristics: 'a bodily condition or bodily characteristic of any person which is from birth, accident or disease, or from any natural physical development, or any event outside the control of that person' (quoted in Adamitis, 2000, p. 210).

Understanding the efficacy of such laws is important and analysis of the Victorian law in Australia provides that opportunity. It is a state in which the definition also seems to have evolved. Analysis enables assessment of the efficacy of legal instruments intended to address discrimination based on employee appearance and also helps identify more general lessons about such legal instruments.

Physical Features Discrimination and the Equal Opportunity Act 1995 (Victoria)

To date, Victoria and the ACT are the only state jurisdictions in Australia to recognise physical appearance as an unlawful ground of discrimination under its Equal Opportunity legislation. The 1995 legislation in Victoria added to existing grounds of discrimination including: sex, sexuality, marital status, pregnancy, race, impairment and age. As part of a substantial enlargement of the grounds of discrimination, the reforms added 'physical features' including direct and indirect discrimination pertaining to employment as well as education, the provision of goods and services, accommodation, by clubs, in sport and in local government. Although the parliamentary debates of the time shed relatively little light on the rationale for including physical features, officers from the Victorian Commission indicated that they had long received a range of complaints pertaining to matters concerning body shape and size and length, colour and style of hair that did not, at the time, fit clearly into any of the existing categories of discrimination.

While introducing discrimination on the basis of physical features in employment as part of the new Act, the Victorian Government was at pains to emphasise the need to weigh this new prohibition against the rights of employers to insist on appropriate standards of dress and presentation. Speaking during the Second Reading debate, one government member emphasised the 'balance' that the new legislation was attempting to strike, with specific reference to the physical features ground:

> The act enshrines particularly well a balance in dealing with discrimination on the basis of physical features. Employers should be able to say that their employees should dress and appear reasonably in all forms appropriate to the workplace. Employees should not be excluded from the workplace because of their height, weight, size or birthmarks. We are not talking about a person's general appearance. That strikes a balance between the needs of one and the rights of the other without government unduly impinging on a private sphere of activity.
>
> (Doyle, 1995, n.p)

The Act defines 'physical features' as 'height, weight, size or other bodily characteristics' (s.4). While presumably narrower in scope than 'physical appearance', 'physical features' might be taken to include both immutable attributes inherent to the person's 'natural appearance', as well as mutable attributes – characteristics over which the person has, in some sense, or at some time, had some control or chosen. The phrase 'bodily characteristics' seems to more directly refer to primary rather than secondary characteristics. The Attorney General proposing the bill was in little doubt that the definition was restricted to primary attributes 'over which the person may not have much control'. In defending the definition of 'physical features' in the Bill, she stated:

> Society places too much emphasis on a person's bodily characteristics, over which the person may not have much control. For instance, a person may not have any control over a birthmark across his or her face. A person's physical features should not be used to judge the suitability of the person for a job. . . . The attribute of physical features is not intended to include such things as tattoos or body piercing which a person may choose to acquire.
>
> (Wade, 1995, n.p.)

In this passage, the Attorney General appears to suggest that immutability is the key quality of a 'physical feature' for the purposes of the Act. The implication is that discrimination on the basis of attributes which are chosen by the person, or are within their control, should not be regarded as unlawful. While the Attorney General purported to have a clear view on the matter, not all government members debating the Bill were so clear. For example, one member argued that the Bill 'says community discrimination will not be tolerated on the basis of physical features. Why should I have to change the way I look?' (Phillips, 1995, n.p.). This viewpoint would seem to suggest that social identity as expressed bodily should be included within the scope of the Act.

At the same time, the legislation clearly established the limited right of employers to set dress and appearance standards. The 'standards of dress and behaviour' exception in s.24 is relatively broad: 'An employer may set and enforce standards of dress, appearance and behaviour for employees that are reasonable having regard to the nature and circumstances of the employment.'

The Commission provided guidance to employers and employees on the balance between an employee's right to freedom from discrimination on the grounds of their physical appearance and the employer's right to set dress and appearance standards. The guidelines state that 'it is against the law to discriminate against an employee . . . because of their dress or appearance'. The guidelines also state that 'an employer can create and maintain an image for their organisation that best suits their industry and their clients' needs by setting reasonable standards of dress, appearance and behaviour' (EOC, n.d). Despite the publicity and educative work of the Commission subsequent to the introduction of the Act, the matter of where the balance is struck between an employee's right to freedom from discrimination on the grounds of their physical appearance and the employer's right to set dress and appearance standards remains uncertain. Instead, when providing examples of 'common concerns' the Commission's publicity seemed more concerned to warn employers against introducing rules which contravene other grounds of discrimination. For example, it advises that:

- asking men to wear a collar and tie or women to wear skirts and dresses may discriminate on the basis of sex;
- insisting on a clean shaven look or a particular hairstyle may discriminate on the basis of physical features or religious beliefs;
- some workers may have tattoos for religious or cultural reasons (EOC, n.d.).

In addition to its publicity and educative work, the Act also provides for the operation of the Commission, which, under s.161 is to receive and investigate complaints. The Commission operates a complaints-based, investigation and referral process for all cases of alleged discrimination falling within the Equal Opportunity Act. However, the Commission has investigative and conciliation powers only; it is able neither to make binding judicial determinations nor enforce the law. Where conciliation fails or where the complainant so elects, matters can be referred by the complainant to the Victorian Civil and Administrative Tribunal (VCAT), which exercises judicial powers. It is this operation of the law and, through that operation, its efficacy that is now examined.

Procedural and Jurisdictional Issues With the Physical Features Law

The prohibition on discrimination based on physical features became law in 1995. Review of cases in the Act's first 10 years of operation suggests that a number of procedural and jurisdictional issues have arisen.

The Relative Obscurity of the Physical Features Discrimination Jurisdiction

Physical features is only one of 20 grounds of unlawful discrimination under Victorian law. Analysis of the records of enquiries received by the Commission indicates that physical features discrimination is a relatively uncommon source of complaint. In the period 1995–2005, 1876 enquiries were made about discrimination related to physical features, of which 1421 became cases. Of this latter number, 639 related to employment.

As we have noted elsewhere, over the 10 years of the Act, on average, physical features was ranked 10th out of the 20 possible attributes initiating enquiries from employees to the Commission. In the early years of the Act, physical features ranked around 13th. However it had risen to 7th by 2005. The top-ranked attribute by enquiry for 2005 was disability at 16.7% of total enquiries; sex and age both represented less than 5%; physical features 2%. Enquires about physical features are, therefore, significant relative to other possible discriminatory attributes covered by the Act and its relative salience is increasing (Warhurst et al., 2012).

More recently, the Commission's 2017–2018 Annual Report stated that physical features complaints were more common in employment (133 complaints) compared to goods and services (73) or education (14). These crude measures cannot be taken to suggest that physical features discrimination is uncommon in Victoria; only that it is a relatively infrequent type of enquiry or complaint compared to disability and sex for example.

One likely reason for the relatively small number of enquiries and complaints is the lack of recognition among the public that discrimination on the basis of physical features is unlawful, possibly due to poor understanding of the scope of discrimination law. As one Commission officer noted, 'most people do associate discrimination laws with race, sex and disability, that's part and parcel of this area of the law. But I don't think it [physical features] has a very high profile in the community'. Another officer explained: 'It's canvassed probably when someone comes to us on the enquiry line and actually raises an issue, and then we inform them that there is this category of physical features that it may fall under, and you may wish to pursue a complaint under that attribute.'

Moreover, the vast majority of enquiries and complaints that involve aspects of physical features also concern other forms of discrimination. In virtually all cases of registered complaints mentioning 'physical features' and employment in the period 1999–2005, the complaints concerned grounds of discrimination in addition to physical features – commonly sex, disability and/or race discrimination.

The Commission's Lack of Enforcement Powers

Under the legislation, the Commission lacks any capacity to enforce any decisions or determinations. The primary function of the Commission is to receive and investigate complaints and to offer conciliation as a means of encouraging the parties to resolve their differences without resort to the courts. While this function is laudable, it is apparent that conciliation is successful in only a minority of cases. While the data held by the Commission do not allow firm conclusions, they were estimated by one officer that about half of the complaints were declined (because the matter lacked substance or because the respondent's behaviour fell into an exempt category) and that most of the matters that were unable to be conciliated were referred by the complainant to the VCAT. When asked about problems with the current jurisdiction, one officer cited the Commission's lack of enforcement powers: '. . . some people call us "toothless tigers" – that we don't have any power to actually enforce what we do'.

The Commission does have a limited power to initiate its own investigation where: (a) the VCAT refers a matter to it for investigation which appears to contravene the Act or (b) it becomes aware of a possible contravention while exercising its educative functions. Under that educative function the Commission is required to disseminate information relating to unlawful discrimination and has the power to report to the Minister on matters arising as a result of its educative function. However, the power to initiate has been used rarely and the educative function of the Commission, while clearly valuable, is of less significance than its function of receiving and investigating complaints. As a result, the Commission is compelled to take a relatively piecemeal approach to the issue of lookism (and other forms of discrimination).

Discrimination in Recruitment Is Rarely the Subject of a Complaint

Despite the law covering job applicants, one key area where the Commission's complaints-based approach appears ineffective in combating lookism concerns discrimination at the point of job hire. None of the archival cases involved a complaint concerning discrimination on the basis of physical features at recruitment or selection. All the archived employment cases related to complainants who were already in employment – a point confirmed by the officers.

Given that research of aesthetic labour has revealed that, in services at least, hiring on the basis of worker appearance is frequent (e.g. Nickson et al., 2005; Spiess & Waring, 2005), it seems highly unlikely that lookism is not occurring at the point of recruitment and selection in Victoria. It is more likely that the lack of complaints reflects the practical difficulty in demonstrating that a given applicant is rejected for reasons of physical appearance when employers (and recruitment consultants) are required to give few reasons for their decisions and can always provide alternative, lawful reasons. Similarly, for existing employees, under-performance was often given as a reason for employment termination rather than any physical features of the complainant. In both cases – recruitment and termination – discrimination (physical or otherwise) can be very difficult for employees to prove.

However, Commission officers suspected that the concealment of discrimination on the grounds of physical features was not uncommon. One officer identified recruitment agencies as a particular source of concern: 'I think they [recruitment agents] are wise in what they do, but I think their practices at times are quite discriminatory. They have these pre-employment forms they get candidates to fill out that are quite intrusive in relation to personal attributes that are covered under the Act, and I think that they're culling.'

Lack of Clarity Regarding the Legal Definition of 'Physical Features'

As we noted above, the issue of defining 'physical features' attracted attention among parliamentarians at the time of the passage of the Act. While the Attorney General claimed to have a clear view of the limits of the provision, case law since that time has created ambiguities. The Commission's subsequent 'frequently asked questions' website is equivocal on the matter of whether mutable physical attributes (such as piercings) are 'physical features' or not. In response to a question of whether a school pupil can be sent home for wearing a facial piercing, the website advises that 'Unfortunately, this is not a black and white case', noting that while the VCAT has found tattoos to constitute a 'physical feature' no ruling had been made on the question of piercings (EOC, 2003).

It is apparent, therefore, that the meaning of 'physical features' has evolved since the legislation came into force. Despite the original intention of the Attorney General, subsequent decisions of the VCAT have confirmed that tattoos can be considered physical features. While the Commission website suggests that piercings are yet to be classified as 'physical features' one officer stated that they were now considered by the VCAT to be 'bodily characteristics'. The lack of clarity around the definition of physical features was a concern another officer commented:

> I think clarity in the Act is an absolute starting point and no matter how clearly parliament states an intention in an Act one day, ten years down the track it's going to lose that clarity. And we usually say to VCAT to add that clarity and it just hasn't happened to the extent that we would have liked, particularly in relation to physical features ...

This officer went on to suggest that if the VCAT was to offer declaratory opinion about the appropriate definition of physical features, it would greatly assist the work of the Commission and allow it to provide better assistance to complainants and respondents.

Evidentiary Issues Associated with Establishing Discrimination

In order to establish a case of unlawful discrimination under the Victorian law, the complainant must establish that the relevant attribute (i.e. a physical feature) was 'a substantial reason' for their adverse treatment. 'Direct discrimination' is further defined as occurring where 'a person treats ... someone with an attribute less favourably than the person treats ... someone without that attribute, or with a different attribute, in the same or similar circumstance' (s.8(1)). This formulation effectively means that a complainant needs to demonstrate that, firstly, they were treated less favourably than someone else without their attribute, and, secondly, that their attribute was 'a substantial reason' for that adverse treatment.

These requirements create a major evidentiary burden for a complainant. Firstly, the comments of the officers interviewed, and some of the file notes and investigation reports analysed, appear to confirm that it is a valid defence to the allegation of discrimination for an employer to argue that there are other employees who share the same physical feature(s) and who have not been treated adversely. This existence appears to be taken as evidence that the attribute was not likely to be the grounds for the discrimination. Secondly, in order to make their case, the complainant might also need to be able to refer to another employee, one without the attribute and in a similar circumstance, who has received more favourable treatment. It is likely that in many cases it might be difficult, if not impossible, to find another employee in 'a similar circumstance' to make this comparison, for example among agency workers. This dependency on an ability to make comparisons appears to be a consequence of the wording of the relevant section of the Act.

Practical Disincentives for Pursuing a Physical Features Discrimination Claim

It is evident from the archival and interview data that many enquirers and complainants complaining about discrimination on the grounds of physical features are genuinely distressed at the treatment that they have received. Enquiry line staff and senior officers confirmed that it was virtually unheard of for a complainant to be disingenuous, frivolous or vexatious. Despite an acute feeling of hurt, and a strong perception that the adverse treatment is associated with their physical attribute, many enquirers decline to pursue their complaints to formal status or to the VCAT. It needs to be recognised that a legal process, even one as informal and conciliatory as the Commission process, which involves an employee taking legal action against their employer, has potentially severe consequences for an employee. According to one of the officers:

> ... in the employment context people are making highly fraught decisions pressing a complaint through us and just preserving their employment. ... A lot of people across the board are completely intimidated by the process and I think it just becomes worse when a person is in current employment and they know for a fact that we will contact their employer to discuss the complaint.

Ultimately, this disinclination to proceed with a complaint suggests that while anti-discrimination legislation might have the advantage of establishing more clearly the right of employees to be free from lookism, it suffers from the disadvantage of being too costly, in personal and professional terms, for the aggrieved to assert that right. The fear of job loss or curtailed career prospects are also huge motivators to remain silent in the face of discrimination as is the potential to waste both time and money on what may end up being a difficult claim to prove.

Concluding Remarks: Towards More Effective Regulation of Lookism?

In 2015, a new CEO jettisoned Abercrombie & Fitch's formal looks policy.[1] Nevertheless, sorting employees on the basis of appearance continues to be widespread in particular segments of the labour market in which aesthetic labour is salient, for example in retail and hospitality (Warhurst & Nickson, 2020). While these routine interactive services account for only part of the service sector, they comprise a significant proportion of all services employment. Employee appearance also plays a more subtle but potentially no less decisive role in other services industries and beyond (Warhurst et al., 2012). The lookism that can occur is problematic because it perpetuates prejudice based on harmful stereotypes and facilitates the making of employment decisions on irrational, unfair and arbitrary grounds. For workers, it jeopardises their job and career prospects; in short, hampering their capacity to get in and get on in work.

Anti-lookism legislation can be one solution. However, analysis of Victoria's physical features discrimination law shows that it has made only a modest and limited contribution to reducing appearance-based employment discrimination. There are emergent procedural and jurisdictional reasons for the law's limited efficacy. First, that physical features discrimination is illegal in Victoria is not well known among employers, employees and the public. This obscurity suggests a need for a stronger educative function for the Commission. Second, the effectiveness of the Commission's role in enforcing the law is compromised by its lack of enforcement powers. Greater public recognition of lookism as a prohibited form of discrimination and more ready enforcement would assist in addressing the third problem – the failure of the law to provide an avenue for redress to job applicants. Demonstrating unlawful discrimination during recruitment and selection is always difficult for plaintiffs given the characteristic lack of evidence concerning the (real) reasons for the selection of successful applicants (and, more importantly, the non-selection of unsuccessful applicants). If the provisions had greater visibility, employers, recruiters, human resource officers and consultants might have more cause to question the role that appearance plays in informing and shaping their selection preferences and processes. Fourth, the lack of clarity concerning the definition of physical features warrants the attention of policymakers. While the meaning of statutory provisions is invariably shaped by judicial decisions, the definition of 'physical features' in Victoria creates confusion and needs clarification from policymakers. Fifth, the current evidentiary burden is significant for complainants but may be aided to an extent by the provision of greater definitional clarity. Finally, although it was noted that these points might better establish employee rights with respect to discrimination, the costs for workers of asserting these rights can be high, both in terms of their employment with their current employer and any potential future career prospects.

In reviewing US laws related to appearance discrimination, commentators have reached different conclusions about the best way forward. Some strongly support legislation explicitly prohibiting appearance discrimination (Adamitis, 2000; Baron, 2005; Fleener, 2005), others are opposed to these laws (Barro, 2003) or advocate only their very limited application (Corbett, 2007). By contrast, some have argued that as financial benefits accrue disproportionately to good-looking people, employers should be entitled to hire good-looking employees particularly in customer service roles on the grounds that they are more productive or successful, and hence, profitable (Barro, 2003).

In response to these arguments, we contend that employment discrimination law has both an industrial justice purpose and a social transformation purpose. In relation to the industrial justice purpose, job applicants and employees should be protected from irrational, unfair and arbitrary discrimination. To the extent that physical appearance is unrelated to the capacity of an individual to undertake the core duties of a position, then its consideration in employment decisions is irrational. To the extent that physical appearance is immutable and largely beyond the control of the individual, then its consideration in employment decisions is unfair. The socially transformative purpose is also important. Such laws can make a vital contribution to changing people's attitudes towards the role and status of physical attractiveness in society and in employment in particular. The contemporary obsession with body image and the idealised constructions of beauty are associated with health problems associated with body image, and with psychological problems associated with low self-esteem, anxiety and depression (APPG on Body Image, 2012). Employment discrimination law has a role here. Virtually all employers, employees and job applicants in the advanced economies know, for example, that it is illegal to discriminate on the basis of sex and race. While legislation has not eradicated sexism and racism at work, it has made a significant contribution to reducing its acceptance and overt practice, and victims do have reasonable recourse of redress – surely welcome developments and demonstration of the potential socially beneficial contribution of the law.

If these arguments are accepted, the issue then becomes enactment. Advocates of appearance discrimination laws have proposed a variety of models. Adamitis (2000, p. 220) advocates restricting the meaning of 'appearance' to '(1) physical characteristics, (2) grooming and attire that is associated with some already-protected category, and (3) grooming and attire that has some other cultural or historical significance'. She also proposes that employers should be able to make a defence based on the grounds of BFOQ or 'business necessity'. Fleener (2005) suggests restricting 'appearance' to just 'immutable or semi-immutable' characteristics, with exceptions where BFOQ can be established. Both of these commentators therefore advocate a definition of 'appearance' largely restricted to immutable physical features over which the individual has little or no control, while also retaining the prohibition on appearance regulations which have a discriminatory impact on women (or men) in particular, or on members of racial, ethnic, religious and other 'protected' groups. While this approach has some merit, it does invite the problem of distinguishing between immutable and mutable physical characteristics. In an era of increasingly sophisticated cosmetic surgery such distinctions may prove increasingly difficult. Another problem with this approach is that it tends to regard physical appearance as akin to a disability. While the law should certainly cover appearance characteristics such as disfigurement, it might also usefully extend to aspects of appearance such as tattoos and piercings which might more often be thought of as mutable. Lastly, restricting the discriminatory ground to largely immutable physical features will do little to strike at the most objectionable lookism at work, which is typically associated with favouring job applicants or employees who the employer regards as 'good-looking' at the expense of others deemed less physically attractive but who might be equally or even more capable of doing the job. If laws are to be developed that might constructively address this kind of lookism, then a broader definition of 'appearance' is surely required.

The alternative approach therefore is to adopt a broad definition of 'appearance' aligned, for example, with the definition of 'personal appearance' used in the DC regulations, and then identify defences or permissible exceptions to that rule. Under this proposal it would be unlawful to adversely treat an individual on account of their physical appearance, subject to the following exceptions: first, an employer can insist that an employee abides by a dress and grooming policy provided that policy is consistently, fairly and reasonably applied to all employees and provided that policy is reasonable given the nature of the job, workplace, business and industry; second, where the physical appearance requirement is a BFOQ for the job (such as modelling or firms that demand corporate uniforms); third, where the physical appearance characteristics of the employee might endanger the health and safety of any person. Reforming the law in this way would have the effect of more clearly and unambiguously identifying physical appearance and the basis of inappropriate lookism in the labour market as the target of this type of employment discrimination law. It would also signal that the basic presumption of the law is that an employee's physical appearance and attractiveness is irrelevant to their rights and opportunities at work and in the labour market, and that this presumption is subject only to the reasonable exceptions that an employer may be able to establish in the cases of a reasonable dress and grooming policy, and where certain physical characteristics might be required to do the core duties of the job, or ensure health and safety. While some jurisdictions, such as Victoria, have taken steps to legislate against lookism, the journey to prohibition is not yet complete.

In the meantime, future research might compare our findings with the second decade of the Act in Victoria – though again negotiating access in a way that assures the analysis of cases will be required. It would also be useful to compare our findings about the procedural and jurisdictional issues with the Act in Victoria with the similar Act in the ACT in Australia as well as with legal initiatives that seek to proscribe discrimination based on physical features in other jurisdictions, for example within the United States in Michigan and Santa Cruz. The findings from this evidence would help create a body of evidence about what works that could then be used to assess the desirability and feasibility of changing the Equality Act (2010) in the United Kingdom to include physical features. As the Riam Dean illustrates, there is currently ambiguity or what might be termed a legal 'grey area' (Warhurst & Nickson, 2020), in the United Kingdom over the legitimacy of workplace policies that can result in lookism and which can negatively affect the careers of employees and lead to adverse publicity and financial penalties for employers. Providing legal clarity would, therefore, be beneficial to both employees and employers.

Note

1. The reason may be the fall in sales arising from the company's marketing approach based on the employment of young, attractive workers that made some potential customers feel excluded (Berfield & Rupp, 2015).

References

Adamitis, E. (2000). Appearance matters: A proposal to prohibit appearance discrimination in employment. *Washington Law Review*, 75, 195–223.

All Party Parliamentary Committee on Body Image (APPG on Body Image). (2012). *Reflections on body image.* All Party Parliamentary Group on Body Image and Central YMCA. http://ymca-central-assets.s3-eu-west-1.amazonaws.com/s3fs-public/APPG-Reflections-on-body-image.pdf

Ayto, J. (1999). *20th century words.* Oxford University Press.

Baron, S. (2005). (Un)lawfully Beautiful: The Legal (De)construction of Female Beauty. *Boston College Law Review, 46,* 359–389.

Barro, R. (2003). The economics of beauty. *Across the Board, 40*(3), 7–8.

Berfield, S., & Rupp, L. (2015). *The aging of Abercrombie & Fitch.* Bloomberg. https://www.bloomberg.com/news/articles/2015-01-22/how-abercrombie-and-fitch-and-ceo-michael-jeffries-lost-u-dot-s-dot-teens

Corbett, W. (2007). The ugly truth about appearance discrimination and the beauty of our employment discrimination law. *Duke Journal of Gender Law & Policy, 14*(1), 153–178.

Devine, M. (2004). Stop pretending: Dressing sexy comes with a price. *Sun-Herald.* 4 April, 15.

Doyle, R. (1995, May 25). Equal opportunity bill – Second Reading, Parliament of Victoria Hansard. http://tex.parliament.vic.gov.au/bin/texhtmlt?form=VicHansard.adv

Equal Opportunity Commission Victoria. (n.d.). *Building quality in the workplace: Dress and appearance in the workplace.* http://www.eoc.vic.gov.au

Equal Opportunity Commission Victoria. (2003). *Physical features.* http://www.eoc.vic.gov.au/materials/brochures/physical.html

Fleener, H. (2005). Looks sell, but are they worth the cost? How tolerating looks-based discrimination leads to intolerable discrimination. *Washington University Law Quarterly, 83,* 1295–1330.

Hamermesh, D. (2011). *Beauty pays.* Princeton University Press.

Hamermesh, D., & Biddle, J. (1994). Beauty and the Labor Market. *The American Economic Review, 84*(5), 1174–1194.

Hay, O., & Middlemiss, S. (2003). Fashion victims, dress to conform to the norm, or else? Comparative analysis of legal protection against employers' appearance codes in the United Kingdom and United States. *International Journal of Discrimination and the Law, 6,* 69–102.

Malvern, J. (2009, August 14). Abercrombie & Fitch told to pay disabled worker Riam Dean £9,000. *The Times.* www.timesonline.co.uk/tol/news/uk/article6795327

Nickson, D., Warhurst, C., & Dutton, E. (2005). The importance of attitude and appearance in the service encounter in retail and hospitality. *Managing Service Quality, 15*(2), 195–208.

Pettinger, L. (2004). Brand Culture and Branded Workers: Service Work and Aesthetic Labour in Fashion Retail. *Consumption, Markets and Culture, 7*(2), 165–184.

Phillips, W. (1995, May 25). Equal opportunity bill – Second reading. Parliament of Victoria Hansard. http://tex.parliament.vic.gov.au/bin/texhtmlt?form=VicHansard.adv

Pidd, H. (2009, June 24). Disabled student sues Abercrombie & Fitch for discrimination. *Guardian.* www.guardian.co.uk/monay/2009/jun/24/abercrombie-fitch-tribunal-riam-dean

Rhode, D. (2010). *The beauty bias.* Oxford University Press.

Sierminska, E. (2015). Does it pay to be beautiful? *IZA World of Labour, 161*(June), 1–10.

Spiess, L., & Waring, P. (2005). Aesthetic labour, cost minimization and the labour process in the Asia Pacific airline industry. *Employee Relations, 27*(2), 193–207.

Tietje, L., & Cresap, S. (2005). Is lookism unjust? The ethics of aesthetics and public policy implications. *Journal of Libertarian Studies, 19*(2), 31–50.

Wade, J. (1995, May 4). Equal opportunity bill – Second Reading, Parliament of Victoria Hansard. http://tex.parliament.vic.gov.au/bin/texhtmlt?form=VicHansard.adv

Warhurst, C., & Nickson, D. (2020). *Aesthetic labour.* Sage.

Warhurst, C., van den Broek, D., Hall, R., & Nickson, D. (2009). Lookism: The new frontier of employment discrimination? *Journal of Industrial Relations, 51*(1), 131–136.

Warhurst, C., van den Broek, D., Nickson, D., & Hall, R. (2012). Great expectations: Gender, looks and lookism at work. *International Journal of Work, Organization and Emotion, 5*(1), 72–90.

Chapter 14

Appearance, Aesthetic Labour and Corporate Social Responsibility

Peter Waring

Abstract

International evidence of corporate demand for 'aesthetic labour' has stim-ulated a growing and important literature on the strategic, commercial, legal, gendered and ethical aspects of this labour process (see Spiess & Waring, 2005; Warhurst & Nickson, 2009; Warhurst et al., 2000; Waring, 2011; Witz et al., 2003). There is some evidence to suggest that the growth in 'Diversity and Inclusion' strategies and practices by larger firms provides a level of recognition of the need to avoid discriminatory practices based on the physical characteristics of employees whether these be overt, structural or as a result of unconscious bias. It is argued that the emergence of 'Diversity and Inclusion' strategies are not just in response to regulatory demands or an enlightened 'character over characteristics' approach to hiring, but stems from a desire to meet contemporary Corporate Social Responsibility (CSR) expectations. In turn this corporate motivation is frequently driven by commercial concerns such as the need to attract and retain capital and talent.

In this chapter, the intersection of aesthetic labour, appearance-based discrimination, corporate Diversity and Inclusion strategies and CSR is explored. Through the examination of Fortune 500 'Diversity and Inclusion' strategies and approaches to CSR, the intent behind the resourcing of 'Diversity and Inclusion' and its relationship to CSR is critically assessed. This critical assessment discloses both genuine efforts to reject unethical forms of 'lookism' or 'appearance-based discrimination' but also several contradictions. These include contradictions between the rhetoric of diversity and CSR and the continuation of aesthetic labour strategies for commercial advantage. Further, the research finds that the physical representation of 'Diversity and Inclusion' efforts are sometimes themselves exploited for commercial gain.

The Emerald Handbook of Appearance in the Workplace, 249–272
Copyright © 2024 by Emerald Publishing Limited
All rights of reproduction in any form reserved
doi:10.1108/978-1-80071-174-720230015

Keywords: Aesthetic labour; appearance; corporate social responsibility; discrimination; diversity; inclusion; practices; policies

Introduction

Twenty years ago, pioneering research by Warhurst et al. (2000) and Nickson et al. (2003) in the United Kingdom found credible evidence that some employers sought to commodify the aesthetic qualities of their employees. Their argument, primarily based on empirical examples from services organisations, was that some employers either actively discriminated in favour of employees who 'looked and sounded' right for their firm, or that employers (re)organised the physical appearance of their employees in a way that supported a particular organisational aesthetic. This seminal research proved to be an insightful and welcome addition to the labour process literature, and complemented a burgeoning literature on emotional labour (see Hochschild, 1983). Witz et al. (2003, p. 37) described these efforts as 'aesthetic labour', in which the physical characteristics of employees are 'mobilised, developed and commodified' for strategic and commercial gain. Warhurst et al. (2000, p. 7), for instance, refer to the example of an upmarket clothing store in Britain in which employers selected young people from middle-class backgrounds because they could be assured that they would sound 'right' and look right for their mainly middle-class customers.

Selection criteria that discriminates in favour of certain candidates because of their looks is perhaps the most obvious way in which firms are said to extract aesthetic labour but not the only means. Spiess and Waring (2005), for instance, discussed training and development methods along with 'grooming guides' in the airline industry as further means by which the appearances of employees are managed for commercial purposes. They also identified examples from among low cost airlines in Asia that not only controlled the 'look' of airline flight attendants, but represented that appearance as a sexualised appeal to consumers.

The aesthetic labour literature rightly draws attention to the moral and ethical dimensions of this particular corporate strategy, and this is mirrored in the literature on the law of discrimination based on lookism (see Waring, 2011 for a review). For example, Adamitis (2000, p. 1) has argued that consideration of appearance is 'not justified, rational or beneficial to society' given that in most positions, 'appearance has no bearing on an individual's ability to perform'. Fleener (2005) has also argued that appearance-based discrimination is objectionable and, if tolerated, would cause harm to those without these qualities and potentially exacerbate undesirable social and psychological pressure on women in particular. On the other hand, there are those legal contributors to the literature such as Corbett (2007, p. 166) who assert that efforts to regulate 'lookism' would be too much of an infringement of managerial prerogative and would be difficult to enforce in any case.

Corbett's (2007) second point resonates with Waring (2011), acknowledging the difficulties of those alleging appearance-based discrimination to bring successful actions against errant employers. Nonetheless, it is contended in this chapter that appearance-based discrimination lies in stark contrast with the widespread adoption of Diversity and Inclusion policies and practices in large corporations. The nomenclature of 'Diversity and Inclusion' has largely replaced that of equal opportunity in which the justification for hiring on merit alone and building inclusive workplace cultures centres on both the moral and business imperative. The latter suggesting that productivity improves, turnover decreases and talent is better utilised if a firm executes strong Diversity and Inclusion practices.

The balance of this chapter is organised into four sections. In the next section, the relationship between Diversity and Inclusion and Corporate Social Responsibility (CSR) is explored. In particular, the next section demonstrates how the growth in CSR has tended to promote Diversity and Inclusion as part of labour-related criteria that it prioritises. The section that follows outlines the methodology used while the third section discusses the results of the empirical study. Finally, the concluding section draws together the strands of the key arguments while also highlighting likely future trends.

Diversity and Inclusion and CSR

From its inception, CSR or the notion that business firms owe social responsibilities beyond maximising profit and complying with the law has tended to focus on the employment relationship as a focus of concern. This stems from its lengthy heritage which can be traced to the moral principles evident in the management philosophy of Robert Owen and the Quakers. For the Quakers, treating labour with dignity flowed naturally from their Christian view of the unique worth of every human being. Similar religious views of the need to respect the dignity of human labour can be found in other monotheist faiths. For instance, the Islamic faith is said to promote the fair treatment of labour, while in Catholicism, the Papal Encyclical of 1891, *Rerum Novarum* supported the rights of labour including to form unions. For the Welsh textile entrepreneur, Robert Owen, the vicissitudes of working conditions in the industrial revolution led him down the path of experimenting with factory reforms and utopian socialist communities (Carrasco, 2007).

These early impulses unquestionably contributed to the development of CSR and the idea that a firm needs to protect the interests of labour, community and environment. CSR is, however, not without its critics. It has proved to be a concept and practice that is contentious because of the strong challenges it has attracted from both ends of the political spectrum. For instance, those on the right and adherents to economic rationalism frequently mount their objections based on the premise articulated by Milton Friedman (1970) that the singular responsibility of the corporation is to maximise its profits. Any move beyond this motivation, they argue, would be akin to socialism by stealth. From the left, CSR has also been criticised as essentially being a mere public relations activity designed to gloss over structural inequalities and corporate malfeasance. Hanlon (2008), for example, has argued that CSR, far from challenging business, further embeds capitalist social relations.

Additionally, CSR has been criticised for its lack of conceptual clarity, which Van Oosterhout and Heugens (2008) claim stems from a proliferation of definitions and its normative origins, describing what corporations or any business entity ought to do as opposed to how they actually behave. Crane et al. (2008, p. 6) have also identified that CSR is weakened by the different types of organisations which hold a wide variety of views on and towards CSR.

Notwithstanding these critiques, CSR as both concept and practice has continued to grow in influence. Academic interest in the subject and growing acknowledgement throughout the private sector has reached a level where it cannot be thought of as empty rhetoric (Waring & Lewer, 2004). The number of firms that produce CSR or sustainability reports has expanded significantly (see Gray, 2001) while bibliometrics reveal strong academic interest in the subject (Van Oosterhout & Heugens, 2008).

Furthermore, commercial pressures have driven the widespread adoption of CSR norms. For instance, consumer boycotts of goods that have been 'unethically' produced, increasing popular concern over climate change, environmental degradation and concern over the exploitation of labour (Dahlman et al., 2008; Smith, 2003). Financial pressure for companies to consider their social responsibilities has also stemmed from the rise of socially responsible investment (SRI) (or ethical investment), shareholder activism and the development of the United Nation's Global Compact and related Global Reporting Initiative (GRI). It is worth noting that four of the 10 principles of the Global Compact focus on labour rights. Of most importance to this chapter is Principle 6 which refers to 'the elimination of discrimination in respect of employment and occupation' (UN Global Compact, 2021).

Finally, the business imperative for CSR has become difficult for the private sector to ignore. The mainstreaming of SRI principles has deeply impacted both equity and debt markets. It is now standard practice for banks to consider Environmental, Social and Governance (ESG) risks before extending business loans. 'Green Bonds' are also commonplace and most mutual funds also incorporate sustainability principles in their investment decisions as do most pension funds (Schoenmaker & Schramade, 2019). Further, an increasing body of research has found positive correlations between CSR and firm success. Turban and Greening (1996), for instance, discovered that a firm's corporate social performance is related positively to its reputation and to its attractiveness as an employer. Furthermore, in a meta-analysis of studies of the relationship between corporate social performance and corporate financial performance, Orlitzky et al. (2003) conclude that there is a positive association indicating that CSR does generate financial rewards.

Diversity and Inclusion strategies and CSR are often intertwined and mutually reinforcing. To demonstrate a commitment to CSR, firms frequently cite their commitment to equal employment opportunity (EEO) and thus are eager to present their Diversity and Inclusion credentials. The policy and practices of Diversity and Inclusion are, in turn, strengthened by an acknowledgement that firms owe this social responsibility to the workforce. Hence, in studying aesthetic labour and appearance-based discrimination, it is critical to examine the intersection between

and community categories. The level and type of detail presented also varied between the corporations which were reviewed. Some disclosed highly detailed reporting with substantial data (the majority), while a minority revealed far less detail and only general policy commitments and goals. Some firms made use of established reporting frameworks such as the GRI while others reported against CSR strategic goals.

Diversity and Inclusion

Aside from Berkshire Hathaway and Fannie Mae, all companies with a clear CSR policy or the like were also found to have a stated commitment to 'Diversity and Inclusion' or EEO. The research taxonomy (please see appendix) has attempted to capture the key message, statement or aphorism that each company used to sum up their commitment and approach to Diversity and Inclusion. Some companies presented very high stated aspirations such as Ford and Boeing, for example, to become the most diverse and inclusive companies 'on Earth'.

Other firms tried to explain the meaning that they attached to Diversity and Inclusion. For instance, Johnson & Johnson declared that Diversity and Inclusion means that 'everyone belongs', while for Intel it means valuing individual perspectives. For United Technologies, the term simply means 'All in'. For most firms, Diversity and Inclusion was usually defined in terms of ensuring that their workforce was broadly reflective of the communities that they serve. A few companies also built upon this standard definition of diversity to suggest that they also sought diversity of cognitive styles. For instance, IBM referred to seeking 'diversity of thought and experience' and Alphabet (parent of Google) referred to the need for diversity of thinking so that more 'inclusive algorithms' can be developed.

A number of firms sought to frame their commitment to Diversity and Inclusion (D and I) not only in moral or legal terms, but also in commercial terms. For example, ExxonMobil insisted that a strong Diversity and Inclusion approach was a competitive advantage. Cardinal Health claimed that an inclusive culture 'inspires more innovations and helps to retain key talent'. Verizon Communications stated that Diversity and Inclusion was a business imperative and competitive advantage, while mortgage provider Freddie Mac simply state that it is 'smart business'.

Most firms discussed the hiring and training strategies they had implemented to ensure that women, people of colour and other minorities were employed in percentages that were consistent with the diversity of the US population. Almost all firms provided statistical detail to evidence this or to demonstrate that the composition of their workforce was well on the way to reflecting the broader US population. A few companies claimed (using their data sets) to have achieved more diverse workforces than the US population. Some firms provided very detailed data sets to demonstrate diversity not just in the workforce, but at all hierarchical levels within the workforce. One company, Chevron, also indicated that they tied executive compensation to the achievement of Diversity and

Inclusion performance indicators. Others provided more information on their policies and practices but did not provide very detailed data on workforce composition.

One important observation is that no firms explicitly referenced appearance-based discrimination or any terms that could be construed as referring to appearance-based discrimination. Some firms detailed their anti-discrimination or non-discrimination policies (sometimes also referred to as EEO). A good example is CostCo Wholesale who state 'All decisions regarding recruiting, hiring, promotion, assignment, training, termination, and other terms and conditions of employment will be made without unlawful discrimination on the basis of race, color, national origin, ancestry, sex, sexual orientation, gender identity or expression, religion, age, pregnancy, disability, work-related injury, covered military or veteran status, political ideology or expression, genetic information, marital status, or any other protected status'. Rather than listing all the legally protected categories (that still exclude appearance), some firms simply indicated that they did not tolerate discrimination in any form. This suggests a level of vagueness when it comes to appearance-based discrimination in the firms reviewed, and a reticence to unequivocally state the firm's opposition to appearance-based discrimination.

While all firms did not specifically identify appearance-based discrimination, a number discussed the positive ways in which they were addressing the explicit and implicit bias that might lead to appearance-based discrimination. For example, it was interesting to note the large number of top Fortune companies have engaged in unconscious bias training (UBT) which is designed to bring to the surface, individual's implicit biases or learned stereotypes which are said to be deeply ingrained but nonetheless can influence managerial decisions and behaviour (see Lee, 2005). Proponents of UBT argue that such awareness is crucial to reducing negative associations that are appearance-based. The evidence of the effectiveness of this training though is still keenly debated. While some studies (see Bezrukova et al., 2016; Jackson et al., 2014) suggest that UBT can raise awareness and reduce negative appearance-based associations, others do not find any enduring positive behavioural change after the interventions (see Forsher et al., 2019).

Another frequently cited tool designed to support Diversity and Inclusion efforts are employee resource groups (ERGs) – sometimes described as business resource groups or affinity groups. These groups, facilitated by employers, bring together employees who share characteristics or common life experiences. ERGs' purpose is to provide employees (typically regarded as being in the minority) with support, coaching career development and also a representative voice with management. Frequently, ERGs have been formed to support women, people of colour and employees who identify as being in the LGBTQI community, veterans among many others. The review of the top 50 Fortune companies indicated that a significant majority had formed such groups and considered them to be extremely useful for promoting Diversity and Inclusion. What is less clear is whether ERGs play a positive role in addressing appearance-based discrimination. While not explicitly referenced, it would seem likely that ERGs formed to support minority groups within the workplace would also assist in addressing appearance-based discrimination or at the very least, be oppositional to any instances of such discrimination. Nonetheless the internal operations and outcomes of ERGs is unquestionably a topic for future research.

Concluding Thoughts

The analysis of the CSR reporting of the top US corporations has demonstrated an acute concern for Diversity and Inclusion and the avoidance of discriminatory employment practices but less direct evidence of the avoidance of appearance-based discrimination. Indeed it was evident from the review that companies tended to attach greater weight to Diversity andInclusion than perhaps other employment matters such as fair wages or freedom of association. The attention and resources devoted to Diversity and Inclusion, at least in the context of CSR reports, appeared to rival environmental concerns. While it is easy to dismiss such reports as embodying mere rhetoric, the evidence contained within many reports of the considerable efforts regarding education & training, establishment of ERGs, senior management commitment and the presentation of workforce data and associated goals suggested that this was a concrete and central concern for many of the largest corporations in the United States. It is possible to infer that such efforts have implications for appearance issues in the workplace. The considerable 'weight' of resources invested is clearly designed both to raise awareness and to eliminate negative behaviours and decisions based on the inherent characteristics of individual staff.

Three important caveats though ought to be kept in kind. First, the companies represented the largest corporations in the United States – a country with a strong history of litigation around civil rights and equal opportunity matters. So it could be assumed that these companies would have the resources and the motivation to make these investments in Diversity and Inclusion. Second, while these commitments may reflect genuine intent, it was interesting to note that the images that accompanied Diversity and Inclusion reports could themselves be considered an effort to represent a particular workforce aesthetic. Frequently it was observed that images of multiracial groups of employees or minority employees accompanied a firm's Diversity and Inclusion credentials, which could be construed as an effort to commercialise employee appearance or to leverage appearance to influence corporate reputation. To be clear, this is not the moral equivalent of an airline purposefully advertising the aesthetic characteristics of its flight attendants, in a crass sexualised appeal to consumers. Nonetheless it does illustrate the pervasiveness of aesthetic labour as a resource even in corporate efforts to broadcast a firm's commitment to diversity. Finally, it should also be observed that although most firms made strong stated commitments to Diversity and Inclusion, there was far less concrete reference to 'appearance' or 'appearance-based discrimination'. Where 'appearance' was referred to, it was only in fairly vague terms suggesting that 'appearance-based discrimination' may not be a primary consideration or that some firms might actively be avoiding clear statements on this topic for perhaps commercial or legal reasons.

The fact that Diversity and Inclusion commitments and the underpinning evidence is accessible through CSR reports demonstrates the very real influence of SRI or ESG Investing on the decisions managements make in this space. Accessing these growing pools of investible capital while also demonstrating that firms are well managed is clearly a strong part of the motivation for these efforts. This kind of investing criteria was once the preserve of specialist SRI funds but increasingly there is evidence of the mainstreaming of these principles to influential pension and sovereign wealth funds. Of course as many of the companies reviewed were keen to point out good Diversity and Inclusion practices are likely to be good for business. They should reduce the risk of employment discrimination litigation, and as a number of firms testified, they help to attract and retain talented employees and possibly help certain firms to reach a broader and larger consumer base. This enlightened approach, whether driven by commercial or moral imperatives, is likely to normalise the fundamental objection to the corporate manipulation of aesthetic labour.

References

Adamitis, E. (2000). Appearance matters: A proposal to prohibit appearance discrimination in employment. *Washington Law Review*, *75*, 195–223.

Bezrukova, K., Spell, C., Perry, J., & Jehn, K. (2016). A meta-analytical integration of over 40 years of research on diversity training evaluation. *Psychological Bulletin*, *142*(11), 1227–1274.

Carrasco, I. (2007). Corporate social responsibility, values, and cooperation. *International Advances in Economic Research*, *13*, 454–460.

Corbett, W. (2007). The ugly truth about appearance discrimination and the beauty of our employment discrimination law. *Duke Journal of Gender Law & Policy*, *14*(1), 153–178.

Crane, A., McWilliams, A., Matten, D., Moon, J., & Siegel, D. S. (Eds.). (2008). *The Oxford handbook of corporate social responsibility* (pp. 156–172). Oxford University Press.

Dahlman, F., Brammer, S., & Millington, A. (2008). Barriers to proactive environmental management in the United Kingdom: Implications for business and public policy. *Journal of General Management*, *33*(3), 1–20.

Fleener, H. (2005). Looks sell, but are they worth the cost: How tolerating looks-based discrimination leads to intolerable discrimination. *Washington University Law Quarterly*, *83*, 1295–1330.

Forsher, P., Lai, C., Axr, J., Ebersole, C., Herman, M., Devine, P., & Nosek, B. (2019). A meta-analysis of procedures to change implicit measures. *Journal of Personality and Social Psychology*, *117*(3), 522–559.

Friedman, M. (1970, September 13). The social responsibility of business is to increase its profits. *New York Times Magazine*.

Gray, R. (2001). Thirty years of social accounting, reporting and auditing: What (if anything) have we learnt? *Business Ethics: A European Review*, *10*(1), 9–15.

Hanlon, G. (2008). Rethinking corporate social responsibility and the role of the firm – On the denial of politics. In A. Crane, A. McWilliams, D. Matten, J. Moon, & D. S. Siegel (Eds.), *The Oxford handbook of corporate social responsibility* (pp. 156–172). Oxford University Press.

Hochschild, A. (1983). *The Managed Heart: Commercialisation of human feeling.* University of California.

Jackson, S. M., Hillard, A. L., & Schneider, T. R. (2014). Using implicit bias training to improve attitudes toward women in STEM. *Social Psychology of Education: An International Journal, 17*(3), 419–438.

Lee, A. (2005). Unconscious bias theory in employment discrimination litigation. *Harvard Civil Rights – Civil Liberties Law Review, 40*, 481.

Nickson, D., Warhurst, C., Cullen, A., & Watt, A. (2003). Bringing in the excluded? Aesthetic labour, skills and training in the 'new' economy. *Journal of Education and Work, 16*(2), 185–203.

Orlitzky, M., Schmidt, F. L., & Rynes, S. L. (2003). Corporate social and financial performance: A meta-analysis. *Organization Studies, 24*(3), 403–442.

Schoenmaker, D., & Schramade, W. (2019). *Principles of sustainable finance.* Oxford University Press.

Smith, N. C. (2003). Corporate social responsibility: Whether or how? *California Management Review, 45*(4), 52–76.

Spiess, L., & Waring, P. (2005). Emotional and aesthetic labour, cost minimisation and the labour process in the Asia Pacific airline industry. *Employee Relations, 27*(2), 193–207.

Turban, D. B., & Greening, D. W. (1996). Corporate social performance and organizational attractiveness to prospective employees. *Academy of Management Journal, 40*(3), 658–672.

United Nations (UN) Global Compact. (2021). *The ten principles of the Global Compact.* www.unglobalcompact.org. Accessed on November 19, 2021.

Van Oosterhout, J., & Heugens, P. P. (2008). Much ado about nothing: A conceptual critique of corporate social responsibility. In A. Crane, A. McWilliams, D. Matten, J. Moon, & D. S. Siegel (Eds.), *The Oxford handbook of corporate social responsibility* (pp. 156–172). Oxford University Press.

Warhurst, C., & Nickson, D. (2009). 'Who's got the look? Emotional, aesthetic and sexualised labour in interactive service's. *Gender, Work and Organization, 16*(3), 385–404.

Warhurst, C., Nickson, D., Witz, A., & Cullen, A. (2000). Aesthetic labour in interactive service work: Some case study evidence from the 'new' Glasgow. *The Services Industries Journal, 20*(3), 1–18.

Waring, P. (2011). Keeping up appearances: Aesthetic labour and discrimination law. *Journal of Industrial Relations, 53*(2), 193–207.

Waring, P., & Edwards, T. (2008). Socially responsible investment: Explaining its uneven development and human resource management consequences. *Corporate Governance: An International Review, 16*(3), 135–145.

Waring, P., & Lewer, J. (2004). The impact of socially responsible investment on human resource management: A conceptual framework. *Journal of Business Ethics, 52*(1), 99–108.

Witz, A., Warhurst, C., & Nickson, D. (2003). The labour of aesthetics and the aesthetics of organization. *Organisation, 10*(1), 33–54.

Appendix: Review of the Top 50 Fortune 500 Companies

Rank	Company	Revenue (2018 in USD$M)	CSR	Diversity and Inclusion Policy	Reference to Appearance Discrimination
1	Walmart	514,405	ESG Report + Culture, Diversity and Inclusion Report	Everyone included. By fostering a workplace culture where everyone is – and feels – included, everyone wins. Becoming a stronger business is about having an awareness and appreciation not only for our cultural similarities and differences but also for our unique and diverse backgrounds.	Vague reference to diversity of 'experiences, styles, identities and abilities...' focus on training (e.g. inclusive leadership expectations), associate resource groups and Diversity and Inclusion metrics.
2	ExxonMobil	$290,212	Yes – Global Diversity Framework	Diversity and Inclusion of thought, skill, knowledge and culture make ExxonMobil more competitive, more resilient and better able to navigate the complex and constantly changing global energy business.	Vaguely – Our Global Diversity Framework and Standards of Business Conduct govern ExxonMobil employment practices, including policies for recruitment, hiring, promotions and salary administration. The

					Standards support our commitment to provide EEOs, prohibit discrimination in the workplace and align with applicable laws in the countries where we operate.
3	Apple	$265,595	Yes – Apple Values	At Apple, Diversity and Inclusion means bringing everybody in. We welcome all voices and all beliefs. Differences not just celebrated but essential.	No – but focus on diverse hiring practices and diversity metrics.
4	Berkshire Hathaway	$247,837	No	Sustainability link to companies within Berkshire's portfolio	Not Available
5	Amazon.com	$232,887	Yes – sustainability reporting – Amazon is strongly committed to conducting our business in a lawful and ethical manner, including engaging with suppliers who respect human rights, provide safe and inclusive workplaces and promote a sustainable future.	Yes – building an inclusive culture	No – at Amazon, Amazonians examine the intersection of gender with race, sexual orientation, disability status, veteran status and other dimensions of diversity.

(Continued)

(Continued)

Rank	Company	Revenue (2018 in USD$M)	CSR	Diversity and Inclusion Policy	Reference to Appearance Discrimination
6	UnitedHealth Group	$226,247	Yes – Social Responsibility Reporting	Workforce diversity metrics reported	No
7	McKesson	$208,357	Corporate Responsibility	Yes – we work to create and maintain an inclusive environment where everyone brings their authentic self to work and enjoys great employee experiences at every touchpoint.	No
8	CVS Health	$194,579	Yes – CSR Report	We believe diversity and innovation go hand in hand, which is why we're committed to continuously promoting diversity in the workplace and supply chain.	No
9	AT&T	$170,756	Corporate Responsibility Reporting	Yes – separate Diversity and Inclusion report – CEO – 'For a company to be its best it needs strong, engaged talent at every level. And that requires a workforce, leadership team	No – but strong focus on reporting hiring outcomes

10	AmerisourceBergen	$167939.6	Corporate Citizenship Report	and board of directors as diverse and inclusive as the customers and communities it serves'. Yes – 'to engage our workforce, we create an inclusive culture that prizes diversity'.	No – but references 'unconscious bias' training
11	Chevron	$166,339	Corporate Responsibility Reporting	Yes – 'we're a proud proponent of diversity in the workforce, and we support an inclusive workplace that values the diversity of ideas'.	No – but references unconscious bias and diversity training. Diversity and Inclusion metrics also tied to executive compensation.
12	Ford Motor	$160,338	Yes – Sustainability Report	Yes – 'we aspire to become the most inclusive and diverse global company'. Ford member of CEO action for Diversity and Inclusion pledge.	No – but clear statement on no tolerance of discrimination.
13	General Motors	$147,049	Sustainability Report	An integral part of GM's mission to build a workplace of choice is creating an inclusive culture that welcomes and celebrates a diverse workforce.	No – but stated zero tolerance for discrimination

(Continued)

(Continued)

Rank	Company	Revenue (2018 in USD$M)	CSR	Diversity and Inclusion Policy	Reference to Appearance Discrimination
14	Costco Wholesale	$141,576	Sustainability Commitment	We aim to have a diverse workforce that is representative of the communities where we do business, and to foster an inclusive environment.	No – all decisions regarding recruiting, hiring, promotion, assignment, training, termination and other terms and conditions of employment will be made without unlawful discrimination on the basis of race, colour, national origin, ancestry, sex, sexual orientation, gender identity or expression, religion, age, pregnancy, disability, work-related injury, covered military or veteran status, political ideology or expression, genetic information, marital status or any other protected status.

15	Alphabet	$136,819	Sustainability Report	Yes (separate diversity report) – 'Building a world where progress, equitable outcomes, Diversity and Inclusion can be realities both inside and outside our workplace.	No – but comprehensive reporting of 'representation data'. Creating more 'inclusive' algorithms. ERGs.
16	Cardinal Health	$136,809	Yes – Corporate Citizenship Report	Yes – 'We know that an inclusive culture helps us to attract and retain the very best talent. An inclusive culture inspires more innovations and produces better more far-reaching products and services'.	No – but priority to promote gender and racial diversity. Tracks hiring outcomes and performance ratings to check for bias.
17	Walgreens Boots Alliance	$131,537	Yes – CSR Report	To deliver our commitment to equal opportunities for everyone across our employment practices, policies and procedures.	No – but states ' we work hard to attract diverse people to care for our customers and patients everywhere we do business'.
18	JP Morgan Chase	$131,412	Yes – ESG Report	Yes – 'cultivating a diverse and inclusive work environment'.	No – but 'we hire based on merit using objective criteria and standard processes for assessing and selecting candidates'.

(Continued)

(Continued)

Rank	Company	Revenue (2018 in USD$M)	CSR	Diversity and Inclusion Policy	Reference to Appearance Discrimination
19	Verizon Communications	$130,863	Yes – CSR Report	Yes – 'Business imperative and a competitive advantage'.	No – Verizon's policy is to provide EEO to all persons without regard to race, colour religion, age, gender, pregnancy, sexual orientation, gender identity and expression, national origin, disability, marital status, citizenship status, veteran status, relationship or association with a protected veteran, military status or any other legally protected classifications.
20	Kroger	$121,162	ESG Report	Yes – 'Diversity and Inclusion have been among Kroger's values for decades'.	No – but states 'we invest in associates of different ethnicities and cultures because we value them and want our teams to reflect the communities they serve'.
21	General Electric	$120,268	ESG Report	Not published in ESG Report.	No – reference to Fair Employment Practices only.

22	Fannie Mae	$120,101	No	Not referenced – mention of 'sustainable communities'.	No
23	Philips 66	$114,217	Yes – Sustainability Report	No – but reference to EEEO.	No – but 'Philips 66 is an EEO employer and all employees and qualified applicants will receive consideration for employment without regard to race, colour, religion and other protected categories.
24	Valero Energy	$111,407	Yes – ESG Report	Yes – 'We foster a culture that supports Diversity and Inclusion...'	No
25	Bank of America	$110,584	Yes – Human Capital Report	Yes – Discussion around 'diverse representation' at all levels. 'We strive to mirror the communities we serve'.	No – but monitor Diversity and Inclusion metrics every month.
26	Microsoft	$110,360	Yes – ESG Report	Yes – 'Diversity and Inclusion grounded in a growth mindset.	No – but focus on an 'Inclusion Index' (a measure of workforce inclusivity) and presentation of workforce demographics. UBT.

(Continued)

(Continued)

Rank	Company	Revenue (2018 in USD$M)	CSR	Diversity and Inclusion Policy	Reference to Appearance Discrimination
27	Home Depot	$108,203	Yes – CSR Report	Yes – 'our workforce is more ethnically diverse than the US working population'.	No – but 'we are intentional in our efforts to build a workforce that reflects the communities in which we do business'. UBT for hiring managers.
28	Boeing	$101,127	Yes- 'Our Principles'	Yes – 'strive to be most equitable, diverse and inclusive company on Earth'.	No – but discussion of business resource groups.
29	Wells Fargo	$101,060	Yes – Corporate Responsibility Report	'We value and promote Diversity and Inclusion in every aspect of our business and at every level of our organisation'.	No – but focus on '44% of our US workforce was ethnically diverse'.
30	Citigroup	$97,120	Yes – Environment and Social Information	Yes – 'Commitment to diversity is core to Citi's values'.	No – but 'more than 80% of our colleagues participated in virtual UBT'.
31	Marathon Petroleum	$97,102	Yes – Sustainability Responsibility Report	Yes – 'We foster a collaborative inclusive team environment'.	No – but focus on diversity training including UBT.

32	Comcast	$94,507	Yes – Values Report	Yes – 'Our values are shaped by working to promote diversity, equity and inclusion among our employees, customers and audiences'.	No – but focus on diversity metrics and business resource groups.
33	Anthem	$92,105	Yes – Corporate Responsibility	Yes – 'Diversity and Inclusion makes us a stronger organisation'.	No – but unconscious bias education, cultural competency training and transgender inclusion.
34	Dell Technologies	$90,621	Yes – Social Impact Plan	Yes – 'Cultivating a culture of inclusion is a business imperative'.	No – focus on diversity metrics and ERGs.
35	Du Pont de nemours	$85,977	Yes – Sustainability Reporting	Yes – 'Become one of the world's most inclusive companies with diversity well ahead of industry benchmarks'.	No – some limited reference to equal opportunity and elimination of discrimination.
36	State Farm Insurance	$81,732.2	Yes – ESG	Yes – 'Diversity and Inclusion is central to everything we do'.	No – but reference to ERGs.
37	Johnson & Johnson	$81,581	Yes – Citizenship and Sustainability Reporting	Yes – 'Diversity at J&J means you belong'.	No – but discussion of ERGs.

(Continued)

(Continued)

Rank	Company	Revenue (2018 in USD$M)	CSR	Diversity and Inclusion Policy	Reference to Appearance Discrimination
38	IBM	$79,591	Yes – Corporate Responsibility Report	Yes – 'Diversity of thought, experience and personal identity among IBMers improves our company's innovation, agility, performance and engagement'.	No – but discussion of support for Equality legislation.
39	Target	$75,356	Yes – CSR Report	Yes – 'We champion a more inclusive society by having an inclusive work environment'.	No – 'but goal to ensure team equitably reflects the qualified applicant pools within communities we serve'.
40	Freddie Mac	$73,598	Yes – Our People Report	Yes – 'We value diversity because it's smart business'.	No – but discussion of ERGs
41	United Parcel Service	$71,861	Yes – ESG	Yes – 'We're continuing to build a business that supports and celebrates diversity'.	No – but focus on business resource groups.
42	Lowes	$71,309	Yes – Corporate Responsibility Report	Yes – 'Foster an inclusive culture that enables everyone who touches our business to thrive and contribute to our success'.	No – but discussion on anti-discrimination training and unconscious bias classes.

43	Intel	$70,848	Yes – Corporate Responsibility Report	Yes – 'We value the unique perspectives of every individual'.	No – but focus on diversity metrics and ERGs and diverse hiring panels.
44	Metlife	$67,941	Yes – Corporate Responsibility	Yes – 'A diverse workforce and culture of inclusion are integral to how we do business and how we serve our customers'.	No – but discussion of 'employee networks' and train recruiters to be mindful of potential bias in hiring.
45	Proctor & Gamble	$66,832	Yes – Our Impact	Yes – 'Everyone valued, everyone included. Everyone performing at their peak'.	No – but discussion of 'affinity groups' and diversity recruiting. Employee rights policy stresses non-discrimination of any legally protected factor.
46	United Technologies	$66,501	Yes – Social Impact	Yes – 'All in'.	No – but discussion of 115 ERGs and diversity/ equality awards.
47	FedEx	$65,450	Yes – Citizenship Report	Yes – 'We value our people and promote diversity in our workplace and in our thinking'.	No – but reference to diversity metrics.
48	PepsiCo	$64,661	Yes – Sustainability Reporting	Yes – 'Diversity is a moral and business imperative'.	No – but discussion of visible and invisible diversity.

(Continued)

(*Continued*)

Rank	Company	Revenue (2018 in USD$M)	CSR	Diversity and Inclusion Policy	Reference to Appearance Discrimination
49	Archer Daniels Midland	$64,341	Yes – Sustainability Reporting	Yes – 'ADM's culture promotes inclusion in all roles, at all levels'.	No – but referencing to addressing unconscious bias in the workplace and diversity metrics.
50	Prudential Financial	$62,992	Yes – Corporate Responsibility Reporting	Yes – 'Racial equity and inclusion are core business imperatives'.	No – but focus on building a diverse talent pipeline.

Chapter 15

Advising Clients on Appearance: Ethical Tensions and Positive Conversations

Julia Yates

Abstract

The impact of appearance on career development is well-documented. We know with some certainty that those blessed with good looks, a sense of style and a winning smile have an advantage at all stages of the job application process, and throughout their careers, with the most aesthetically pleasing being more likely to be given jobs, higher salaries and promotions (Baert & Decuypere, 2014; Toledano, 2013). What then should those who offer career advice make of this? Should career advisers, coaches, HR professionals and line managers be advising their clients and employees on how to improve their looks? At one level, the answer to this question seems obvious: if the advisers know it can make a difference, of course they should try to help their clients to look more professional or better appropriate for the role, to give them every chance of success in their chosen field. But on closer inspection, this assumption is fraught with challenges. How far should the practitioners go? How can one give advice without causing offence? And most crucially, how could this tacit support of an arguably unfair and superficial value system be justified? In this chapter, I will explore some of these issues, drawing on research conducted with career advisers, counsellors and coaches and will offer some practical guidelines for all those who might find themselves tempted to offer advice.

Keywords: Appearance; attractiveness; career development; career practitioners; career advice; professional

Introduction

In 2016, I conducted some research into career practitioners' experiences and views of the role of appearance in their career conversations. My co-authors and I wanted to find out how central the topic was to their work, how well equipped

The Emerald Handbook of Appearance in the Workplace, 273–285
Copyright © 2024 by Emerald Publishing Limited
All rights of reproduction in any form reserved
doi:10.1108/978-1-80071-174-720230016

they felt they were to handle the conversations and how they approached the topic. The findings (reported in more detail in Yates et al., 2017; Yates & Hooley, 2018) suggested that questions about appearance were playing on the minds of the practitioners' clients, and that the practitioners too felt that the topic, for the most part, was an appropriate one for a professional career conversation. With 96% of the practitioners in our survey reporting that they had discussed or would discuss some aspect of appearance with their clients, it seemed clear that the topic was relevant for both clients and practitioners. But it was not quite that straightforward. The practitioners felt some ethical tensions around the subject and were not always sure how best to manage the conversations effectively. We will explore these two issues in turn.

Ethical Tensions

The career professions have a long standing and strongly held commitment to social justice (Sultana, 2014). Underpinning much of practitioners' motivation is a desire to make the world a better and a fairer place, and a strong strand of career practitioners' work is aimed at changing the system. Practitioners spend time in their day-to-day work making sure that girls believe they can succeed as engineers, that working class boys feel that law firms will be interested in them and supporting people with disabilities as they negotiate adjustments in the workplace. Career practitioners also work directly with employers to help them create environments that are welcoming and hospitable to all, and with political organisations influencing and shaping policy (Career Development Institute, CDI, 2014).

The idea that attractive people get better breaks is yet another example of the way the world of work discriminates, and it is clearly unfair that just by accident of birth, and regardless of their ability to do the job, some people's paths to career success are easier than others'. Given the career practitioners' commitment to social justice, one might assume that these professionals would try to ensure that their clients don't change their appearance to conform to social norms, aiming to disrupt the social systems and create a fairer society. But while career practitioners might despise this unjust discrimination in society and rail against it, they work with individuals, and are contracted to help expedite their client's passage towards their career goal; and this will often involve encouraging them to comply with employers' expectations.

This tension was clear to see in the participants in our study: advising a client to change how they look to accommodate employers' prejudices did not sit easily with them, yet they also feared that they would be letting their clients down if they failed to mention something that might help them get the job they wanted. If a brief chat about the importance of making sure that an outfit is clean and ironed could give their client the edge in a job interview, then surely it would be wrong to avoid the subject.

Of course, a salient point, and one that sets 'lookism' apart from other kinds of discrimination, is that people *can* change their appearance, at least to some degree

(Hooley & Yates, 2015). They can choose different clothes, they can wear make-up and they can cover up tattoos. These are things that are fairly easily changed and people do often, quite voluntarily, alter their image and play around with how they look. It is also widely accepted that different work settings have their own codes of appearance, explicit or implicit (Hazen & Syrdhal, 2010), and it is common for people to adopt quite a different image at work from that which they display at home. Employers might well argue that the appearance of their employees is a key part of their brand, and that their reputation depends, to some degree, on the appropriate appearance of their staff. But just because you can change your appearance doesn't mean that you should have to, and accepting that it is individuals who should change their appearance, rather than employers who should change their expectations, perpetuates the unjust status quo.

Career practitioners are then left with a dilemma: should they encourage clients to present themselves just the way they want to, and focus their professional efforts on working with employers to reduce bias and change assumptions in society, or should they work with the individual clients to help them achieve their career goals by encouraging them to change themselves in order to fit into the existing, unfair system? The former approach aligns better with practitioners' overall worldview, but the second offers a much more expedient way to help improve the lives of the clients sitting in front of them, and this is important to career practitioners too.

A useful framework for understanding these ethical tensions comes from Watts (2015) who proposes a sociopolitical analysis of career guidance. Watts notes that there are two driving forces in the academic field of career guidance: sociological and psychological. The sociological approaches, primarily focused on the structures within society, would hold that practitioners should not encourage individuals to change their appearance to meet employers' expectations, as this perpetuates an unjust system; psychological theories, more concerned with the individual, would suggest that practitioners should encourage clients to conform to employer expectations, to give them the best possible chance to achieve their career goals.

The psychological theories, Watts suggests, have tended to dominate in this field, within both practice and research, because career guidance is, in essence, a service delivered to individuals. At the point of delivery, the theories and values which are most relevant to the client will prevail and practitioners, therefore, will inevitably find that these psychological approaches have more relevance to their everyday practice. Yet they are widely criticised (Bimrose, 2019; Richardson, 2012; Sultana, 2014). Even the humanist approach to career guidance (Ali & Graham, 2006; Rogers, 1961), in which the practitioner facilitates the individual to be their authentic self and avoids influencing the client's direction of thought or behaviour, has been criticised for its tacit acceptance of the neoliberal agenda. Its critics argue that a non-directive focus simply encourages individuals to conform to the prevailing social mores within the labour market and fails to apply a critical lens to the existing systems, or disrupt the status quo (Roberts, 1977, 2009).

Arguably these critics are doing the practitioners a disservice. There are times when the two sets of values are simply at odds with each other, and the practitioner has to make a choice. They cannot act to support the client with their personal short-term goal, while acting to change the social structures: facilitating one impedes the other, and, ultimately, the career professional is employed to work with individuals, and to support their individual progression into or within the workplace. The practitioners' hands are tied by the context in which they work and the expectations of both their employers and their clients.

Watts (2015) concludes that practitioners should be aware of both psychological and sociological approaches, and while they will, most often, adopt psychological approaches to meet the specific needs of the individual client, they should, where it is judged appropriate, raise alternative ideas with clients and negotiate the approach that feels most suitable. This advice was reflected in the position that the practitioners in our study took. While they wrestled with the tension, they generally concluded that it was, at least sometimes, appropriate to talk to their clients about appearance; more tricky was knowing quite how to go about this.

Managing Conversations

The practitioners in our study were aware of how personal and potentially wounding conversations about appearance could be, how important their working relationships with their clients were, yet how fragile, and how subjective the whole topic is. They knew the conversations needed to be handled with great care. To this end, the practitioners had developed and made use of a range of strategies, which allowed them to raise or discuss appearance in a positive way. Their strategies made sure that they did not avoid these difficult conversations, but also that they did not damage the clients' self-esteem or their working relationships, and instead led to clients having a greater understanding of changes they could make, and a clear assessment of the pros and cons of making those changes.

Appearance has not traditionally played a big part of the standard professional training of career practitioners. It is not covered in initial training courses, such as the Qualification in Career Development accredited by the Career Development Institute in the United Kingdom (UK Commission on Employment and Skills – UKCES, 2014), and is rarely mentioned in professional training or practitioner text books. The practitioners in our study had devised their own strategies individually, through trial and sometimes quite painful error. But views about the strategies that seemed to be most effective were widely shared, and while the practitioners seemed a little cautious about the whole area, it seems that they had, between them, devised a thoughtful and wide-ranging set of tools. The framework below sets out a summary of the practitioners' strategies for dealing sensitively and ethically with issues of appearance in career conversations. The remainder of this chapter will examine this in more detail, looking at whether it is appropriate to address the topic at all, and, if so, how is it best to talk about it.

Should the Topic Be Raised at All?

The first decision that practitioners must make is whether to raise the topic at all. Some aspects of appearance can be highly sensitive, so practitioners need to be aware that raising the issue carries a risk.

What, Specifically, Is the Issue?

Not all aspects of appearance are equal and the more personal the issue is, the more risk it carries. Issues to do with clothing, body language and style can be less sensitive than those to do with weight and personal grooming, so raising the topic of what to wear at a job interview, or how to nail the perfect handshake might be less likely to cause offence or damage a client's self-esteem. Questions of weight or cleanliness have the potential to be hurtful, so should be considered carefully and raised cautiously.

A judgement needs to be made about the significance of the issue. Some aspects of appearance might make a minimal difference in a job interview – a firm handshake has been shown to have a small positive impact (Stewart et al., 2008), but will rarely make or break a job interview. Other issues will carry more weight: an interview candidate who looks as though they haven't washed in a week would have to be an outstanding contender in every other way to stand a chance of a job offer. If the issue could make all the difference to a client, then it might be right to raise it. If a change might only lead to a possible or marginal improvement, it might not be worth the risk.

It is also important to consider whether the aspect of appearance is something that the client is actually able to change. Aspects of body language such as eye contact are generally automatic and not usually under people's conscious control – encouraging a client to try to make more eye contact may be very difficult for them to do and the intervention could risk making an unconfident client yet more anxious. Some changes in appearance can be costly, and recommending that an already heavily indebted student invest in a new suit might just not be realistic. Other changes can take time. Clients may be able to lose weight, but there is a limit on how sylphlike one can get over the course of a weekend, and sending a client in to their job interview faint with hunger will probably not see them performing at their best.

Is This a Real Knowledge Gap for the Client?

Given the risks that can accompany a discussion about appearance with a client, it is useful to ascertain whether it is a genuine gap in information for the client. Is there a good reason to think that they do not realise that they should present neatly at an interview or that their facial tattoos will not endear them to every employer? Appearance is a dominant construct in our society and most people do generally have an awareness of how they fit into the social hierarchy of good looks. Raising the topic when a client is already painfully aware that they are overweight or badly dressed may add nothing.

There are groups of clients whose knowledge about the norms and expectations of the contemporary UK workforce may not be very up-to-date and a practitioner might then feel more inclined to raise these topics with particular clients. Younger clients, who may not have spent much time at work at all, might find it useful to talk through what level of formality might be expected for them at a job interview or at work. Those who have been living or working overseas might feel a bit out of touch about conventions within the UK labour market, and those who have had a period of unemployment or who have been away from the workforce altogether for sometime might gain in confidence if they are able to talk through the current conventions of workplace attire. Clients looking to change sector could find a discussion about appearance valuable: a move from a law firm to an NGO, or from advertising to the civil service, might entail a change in workplace expectations and clients might feel more confident about how they present themselves if they have thought through the culture of their new industry. If a client does not fit into any of these categories, it may well be that they are quite aware that they do not look the part.

How Could the Conversation Help?

Clearly, there is no point in raising a difficult and potentially damaging topic with a client if it is not going to help. I have talked a bit so far about the importance of appearance in job selection – we know that looking the part and being well-groomed and attractive make a difference to people's chances of succeeding at the interview stage, but there are other possible benefits to a discussion about appearance.

Image and appearance can also be a marker of identity, and as such can hold clues to the kinds of environments in which people might feel most comfortable (Barnard, 2002; Cutts et al., 2015). Different occupations, industries or organisations have their own social identities, and the style typically adopted by the members of a particular group reflects the group identity (Hazen & Syrdhal, 2010). As such, people's reactions to the outfits and images typically seen in different workgroups can offer a valuable insight to their own values and goals. A discussion about whether a client would feel comfortable in the formal attire expected in the professional services industry, the uniform of a retail environment, or the highly fashionable casual wear expected in some media companies could help a client think about how they would fit in within a particular work-culture, and this could lead to insights about their values, expectations and identity.

Discussions about appearance can risk damaging clients' self-esteem, but addressing these issues can also sometimes lead to a boost in clients' confidence. If an individual is feeling unconfident about their fashion choices, perhaps unsure about what kind of formality is appropriate for a job interview, whether they should cover up their tattoos and what their future employer might feel about their beard or dyed hair, a conversation with a career practitioner could help them to clarify their own views. This could lead them to feel more confident about their choices and perhaps allow them to present themselves with more poise at interview, or on their first day at work.

Who Is the Right Person to Deliver This Message?

The last thing to consider, when choosing whether to raise the topic at all, is whether the practitioner is the right person to deliver the message. First, any information given must be accurate and up-to-date. The whole field of how to dress and present oneself at work is complex and subjective (Parmentier et al.,

2013), and it may well be that the practitioner is not, in all honesty, fully up to speed with the nuances of what is appropriate in all contexts. They may feel sure of their ground when it comes to personal hygiene and grooming, but perhaps less confident in the level of formality expected at an interview, or the reactions of an employer to piercings. Perhaps they are familiar with the conventions in some industries, but not others, or maybe their knowledge is a little out of date. In these circumstances, it might be more fruitful to invite the client to take advice from someone with more relevant or recent experience, or suggest they check the prospective company's website for images that might give some clues as to the expectations.

Some of the practitioners in our survey felt that they would not be a credible conduit for some messages about appearance. One or two felt that they themselves perhaps were not particularly elegant, fashionable or slim, and were concerned that their own appearance might diminish the impact of their advice to others on how to look good. Other practitioners wondered if demographic differences between themselves and their clients might make the conversation less comfortable. One older male career adviser felt it would be entirely inappropriate to discuss clothing with a young, female client and others commented that these conversations might have more impact between practitioners and clients who were the same sex and the same sort of age. These kinds of challenges can be overcome, and I would not want to suggest that only fashion-conscious practitioners, the same age and gender as their clients are qualified to have these discussions, but it may be worth considering whether a client might gain more from a conversation with their friends, their colleagues or from some online research. Practitioners could also consider producing some written material to handout, or including a page on the service website which addresses issues or appearance in an impersonal context.

If the practitioner decides at this stage that the topic is indeed a suitable one to raise with their client, the next step is to consider some strategies that can ensure that the message is delivered in a positive and constructive way, increasing the client's self-esteem and strengthening the working relationship with the two.

How Best to Raise the Topic?

In this second part of the framework, I offer some practical suggestions for the conversations themselves, for maximising impact and minimising risks. The two key dangers associated with these conversations that the practitioners in our survey identified were (i) the potential damage to their clients' self-esteem and (ii) a risk to the working relationship between the practitioner and client. These both are important to preserve. We know that high levels of confidence make a significant difference to people's chances of success in job interviews and in their career development more generally (Betz, 2004; Judge & Bono, 2001; Songqi et al., 2014). A well-meaning comment from a professional might ensure that their client has neat and tidy hair at a job interview, but if it makes the client feel more anxious and less sure of themselves, then on balance, their chances of interview success are probably reduced. The second issue is the relationship between the client and practitioner which has long been shown to be at the heart of any therapeutic intervention (de Haan et al., 2013; Masdonati et al., 2009), and a solid foundation to the relationship allows the conversations to delve deeper. An ill-timed piece of feedback and advice, delivered before the client feels safe, can cause a damaging rift between practitioner and client.

Protect the Working Relationship

Central to a good professional relationship is unconditional positive regard. This term was used by Rogers in 1961, in his exploration of approaches to counselling and underpins effective career conversations. Unconditional positive regard is the non-judgemental stance adopted by the practitioner which communicates to their client their belief that the client is basically an ok person (*positive regard*) and that this belief is unshakable, and is not dependent (or *conditional*) on anything they say or anything they do. Unconditional positive regard is achieved through authentic and deep empathy. A sincere effort to understand the client, how they are feeling and why they have made the choices they have made can lead to a real understanding between the practitioner and the client which helps the two to work together, as a team, to move forwards. If the client can feel this unconditional positive regard from the practitioner, they are then much more likely to take any comments and advice in the spirit in which they are intended and are less likely to find words offencive or to be embarrassed by their own perceived lack of sophistication.

Once the professional relationship is on solid ground, the practitioner must be thoughtful about their language, expressing their views tentatively and sensitively and making sure that they are acutely aware of their client's reaction to their comments. This can allow the conversation to delve deeper but ensures that the practitioner can pull back the moment they see that they have gone far enough. Asking permission can be another useful approach. The practitioner could suggest to their client that they have had an idea and ask whether they could raise a slightly personal topic. This acknowledges, up front, that the message might be a difficult one to hear, and as well as allowing the client just to say 'no, I'm not feeling robust enough to hear this now', it gives both client and practitioner permission to keep a close eye on the client's feelings, and to back away from the discussion if needed.

Finally, and very much in keeping with the tone of any career conversation, it is important to remember to deliver any message using positive suggestions rather than critical comments. Suggesting that a client might want to treat themselves to a haircut or a new pair of shoes before their interview, and pointing out how this might make them feel more confident on the day, clearly feels like a much more positive message than drawing their attention to their scruffy appearance.

Depersonalise

One of the most widely used strategies from the practitioners in our survey was depersonalisation. Practitioners addressed the issue of appearance but approached it in such a way that it did not feel personal to the client themselves.

This allowed them to discuss the topic at some depth without risking hurting them or causing offence.

Practitioners made the topic less personal by focusing on the role rather than the person. If discussions can be angled around the requirements of the job, the organisation or the context, then the client can see any choices around appearance as being part of a role they are playing, rather than anything to do with their personal identity. A discussion that focuses on how people generally dress for interviews, or the value that accountancy firms place on making sure their client-facing employees reflect the brand of the organisation, can help a client to make positive choices about their appearance, without feeling that they are compromising their own identity.

Many of the practitioners from our survey work with groups and found that this was an excellent forum for raising issues of appearance. This group context ensures that the individual clients do not think that the topic is being raised because of something that they are doing wrong, and because the discussions are inevitably general, the messages that can be communicated can be stronger than those that are suitable within a one-to-one. A follow-up one-to-one meeting can then build on the more general issues raised in the group session and address the specific needs of the client.

Citing external sources can be an effective way to deliver a meaningful message. A relevant piece of research, or a quote from a conversation with an employer, can feel like a message from a third party, and the risk to the working relationship between the client and the practitioner client is, therefore, minimised. Having summarised a third party's view, the practitioner and client can then discuss the issue together, collaboratively, perhaps leading to a valuable conversation that explores the client's reaction to the idea that looking a certain way may enhance their chances of success. The client might then make the choice to stick to their own image, or they might choose to embrace the look that is most likely to get them the job. Either way their choice will be an informed one and they may well feel additionally confident about their appearance having talked it over.

Adopt a Non-directive Approach

Alongside these strategies to depersonalise the topic, a non-directive approach can ensure that a discussion about appearance is conducted in a way that works for the client. With this approach, it is the client who identifies the questions or problems, and who finds the answers or solutions which best suit them. The thorny ethical tensions discussed earlier in this chapter are not as salient, as the practitioner is not making any decisions about whether the client should or should not change themselves in order to conform to society's unfair biases.

Non-directivity is a core aspect of a humanistic approach to counselling (Rogers, 1967). The key assumption underpinning this philosophy is that individuals are their own best experts: however empathic or knowledgeable a practitioner might be, they are never going to understand their client's context the way the client themselves can, and so their advice is not going to be as relevant or valuable as the client's own opinion. The practitioner's role, therefore, should be to help the client to think the dilemma through themselves and to facilitate the client listening to their own inner voice and reaching their own conclusions. With a topic such as appearance, which could engender quite diverse ethical opinions, a non-directive approach could be a useful way to manage the conversation to make sure that the ethical position adopted reflects the client's position, and not the practitioner's.

A non-directive practitioner will discuss appearance only if the topic is first raised by the client. Even if the practitioner feels that their client would benefit from a discussion about how they look, a non-directive approach holds that it is not the practitioner's role to decide what the client would find useful. The practitioner might ask the client what they want to discuss, invite them to consider whether there is anything else they want to raise, encourage them to explore any possible reasons they can think of which might help in hindering them in their pursuit of their goals, but ultimately, if the client does not raise the topic of appearance, then the practitioner should assume that they do not want to talk about it. If the client does indicate that they would find it useful to talk about their image, then it would also be down to the client to choose which particular aspects of appearance to focus on – they can then make their own choices about which elements they feel they would benefit from discussing and which they feel are too personal.

The non-directive approach holds that the practitioner is not an expert in the topic, and, indeed, it would be difficult for a career practitioner to build up a comprehensive expertise in this field. Dress codes vary from one industry to another and from one organisation to another, and they change year by year. It would be more than a full time research job just to keep up-to-date with the current norms and expectations. On top of that, it is a very subjective topic, and the practitioner and the client might not share the same opinions, leading perhaps to confusion rather than clarity for the client.

Accepting then the principle that people are their own best experts, the practitioner's role in a conversation about work-related appearance should be to help the client to think through the topic for themselves. The practitioner could ask a series of open questions 'What do you think you might wear to the interview?', reflect their answers back to them 'So, what you are saying is. . .' and invite them to explore their own opinions 'How would you feel about having to cover up your tattoos every day at work?'. If a client were to ask the practitioner for an opinion, they would deflect the question back to them 'That's a really important question. I wonder how you could find out the answer?'.

Conclusion

Appearance is clearly relevant to careers, and people at work make choices about their appearance which will have an impact on their career paths (Baert & Decuypere, 2014; Toledano, 2013). In this chapter, I approach the topic from the perspective of professionals who support people with their career development. While we might understand that appearance impacts career, it is not necessarily a position that we need to approve of or accept as inevitable. In acknowledging this, career practitioners are faced with an ethical dilemma: do they rail against the unjust social norms and refuse to do everything they can to facilitate their client's career success, or do they support their client but in doing so co-operate with an unfair system? Advice here comes from both Watts (2015) and the experienced practitioners in our study, who suggest that practitioners should support clients to achieve their own goals, which may involve advising them to conform to social conventions, but should be alert to the broader impact that this might have, and be open to treating the topic in a different way if it seems appropriate. For practitioners who decide that they should address these issues, I have proposed an empirically derived framework (Fig. 1), drawing on the expertise of career advisers, counsellors and coaches. The framework offers practitioners some guidance, helping them make the choice about whether to

---

1. Should the topic be raised at all?
  1. **What, specifically, is the issue?**
     i.   How personal is it?
     ii. Does it really need to be raised?
     iii. Could the client change it?
  2. **Is this a real knowledge gap for the client?**
     i.   Are they young, with limited experience in the workplace at all?
     ii. Have they been living overseas?
     iii. Have they been out of the workplace for some time?
  3. **How could the conversation help?**
     i.   Could it help the client to get a job?
     ii. Could it help them to clarify their own career goals?
     iii. Could it lead to a boost in self-esteem?
  4. **Who is the best person to deliver this message?**
     i.   Does the practitioner know the answer?
     ii. Will the practitioner have credibility delivering the message?
     iii. Is the client going to feel comfortable having that discussion?

2. How best to raise the topic?
  1. **Protect the working relationship using:**
     i.   Unconditional positive regard
     ii. Sensitive language
     iii. Positive suggestions
  2. **Depersonalise the issue**
     i.   Focus the discussion on the role not the person
     ii. If practical, raise the topic first in a group setting
     iii. Rely on external sources, for example, quoting employers, or the findings of research
  3. **Adopt a non-directive approach**
     i.   Allow the client to raise the topic
     ii. Allow the client to decide which features to focus on
     iii. Don't present as an expert on the topic
     iv. Encourage the client to work out their right answers for themselves

Fig. 1.   A Framework for Addressing Appearance in Career Conversations.

address the topic with their clients, and offers some pragmatic suggestions for their conversations – helping to make sure that the topics are discussed effectively but sensitively. More conversations about this topic are needed, and I hope this framework stimulates debate, allowing practitioners and clients to develop the ideas and refine the suggestions, and leads the profession to adopt a clearer position and an effective set of techniques.

References

Ali, L., & Graham, B. (2006). *The counselling approach to careers guidance.* Routledge.

Baert, S., & Decuypere, L. (2014). Better sexy than flexy? A lab experiment assessing the impact of perceived attractiveness and personality traits on hiring decisions. *Applied Economics Letters, 21,* 597–601. https://doi.org/10.1080/13504851.2013.877564

Barnard, M. (2002). *Fashion as communication.* Routledge.

Betz, N. E. (2004). Contributions of self-efficacy theory to career counseling: A personal perspective. *The Career Development Quarterly, 52*(4), 340–354.

Bimrose, J. (2019). Guidance for girls and women. In J. Athanasou & H. Perera (Eds.) *International handbook of career guidance* (pp. 385–412). Springer.

CDI. (2014). *Code of ethics.* http://www.thecdi.net/Code-of-Ethics

Cutts, B., Hooley, T., & Yates, J. (2015). Fitting in or being yourself? How undergraduates plan to use hair, clothes and make-up to smooth their transition to the workplace. *Industry and Higher Education, 29*(4), 271–282.

de Haan, E., Duckworth, A., Birch, D., & Jones, C. (2013). Executive coaching outcome research: The contribution of common factors such as relationship, personality match, and self-efficacy. *Consulting Psychology Journal: Practice and Research, 65*(1), 40.

Hazen, L., & Syrdhal, J. (2010). Dress codes and appearance policies: What not to wear at work. *Colorado Lawyer, 39,* 55–63.

Hooley, T., & Yates, J. (2015). If you look the part you'll get the job. Should career professionals help people to enhance their career image? *British Journal of Guidance and Counselling, 43*(4), 438–451.

Judge, T. A., & Bono, J. E. (2001). Relationship of core self-evaluations traits—Self-esteem, generalized self-efficacy, locus of control, and emotional stability—With job satisfaction and job performance: A meta-analysis. *Journal of Applied Psychology, 86*(1), 80–92.

Masdonati, J., Massoudi, K., & Rossier, J. (2009). Effectiveness of career counselling and the impact of the working alliance. *Journal of Career Development, 36*(2), 183–203.

Parmentier, M.-A., Fischer, E., & Reuber, A. R. (2013). Positioning person brands in established organizational fields. *Journal of the Academy of Marketing Science, 41,* 373–387. https://doi.org/10.1007/s11747-012-0309-2

Richardson, M. S. (2012). A critique of career discourse practices. In *Social constructionism in vocational psychology and career development* (pp. 87–104). Sense Publishers.

Roberts, K. (1977). The social conditions, consequences and limitations of careers guidance. *British Journal of Guidance and Counselling, 5*(1), 1–9.

Roberts, K. (2009). Opportunity structures then and now. *Journal of Education and Work, 22*(5), 355–368.

Rogers, C. R. (1961). *On becoming a person.* Houghton Mifflin.

Rogers, C. R. (1967). *Person to person: The problem of being human: A new trend in psychology.* Real People Press.

Songqi, L., Huang, J. L., & Mo, W. (2014). Effectiveness of job search interventions: A meta-analyticreview. *Psychological Bulletin, 140*(4), 1009–1041. https://doi.org/10.1037/a0035923

Stewart, G. L., Dustin, S. L., Barrick, M. R., & Darnold, T. C. (2008). Exploring the handshake in employment interviews. *Journal of Applied Psychology, 93*(5), 1139–1146.

Sultana, R. G. (2014). Pessimism of the intellect, optimism of the will? Troubling the relationship between career guidance and social justice. *International Journal for Educational and Vocational Guidance, 14*(1), 5–19. https://doi.org/10.1007/s10775-013-9262-y

Toledano, E. (2013). May the best (looking) man win: The unconscious role of attractiveness in employment decisions. *Cornell HR Review.*

UKCES. (2014). National Occupational Standards. *UKCES.* http://nos.ukces.org.uk/Pages/index.aspx

Watts, A. G. (2015). Socio-political ideologies of guidance. In T. Hooley & L. Barham (Eds.), *Career development policy and practice: The Tony Watts Reader* (pp. 171–186). Highflyers.

Yates, J., & Hooley, T. (2018). Advising on career image: Perspectives, practice and politics. *British Journal of Guidance and Counselling, 46*(1), 27–38. https://doi.org/10.1080/03069885.2017.1286635

Yates, J., Hooley, T., & Bagri, K. K. (2017). Good looks and good practice: The attitudes of career practitioners to attractiveness and appearance. *British Journal of Guidance and Counselling, 45*(5), 547–561.

Chapter 16

The Visibility of Invisibility: Exploring Criminal History Appearance and Implications to Careers

Nicole C. Jones Young and Kemi S. Anazodo

Abstract

Criminal history has been conceptualised as a socially stigmatised identity. From this perspective, we can understand criminal history as invisible, concealable and 'not readily apparent to others' (Chaudoir & Fisher, 2010, p. 236). Although previous periods of incarceration cannot be detected per se, during this chapter, we present several elements, such as embodiment, appearance-based inferences (i.e. assumptions of what a criminal history looks like), and information as proxy (e.g. résumé gaps, credit history), which may contribute to individual assessments and interpretations of the appearance of a criminal history. Once perceived, these elements may contribute an array of unique career experiences as individuals with a criminal history seek to navigate their employment experience. Therefore, this chapter offers insight into how the appearance of criminal history information, particularly when presented without a thorough explanation, may be left to interpretation and bias throughout the employment experience.

Keywords: Criminal history; stigma; employment; visibility; appearance; inclusion

Appearance suggests a process or emergence of visibility. From an employment perspective, appearance is relevant to individual interpretations of self and the interpretations of relevant organisational stakeholders. Criminal history has been conceptualised as a socially stigmatised identity (Anazodo et al., 2019), which is generally considered to be invisible and concealable in that it 'is not readily apparent to others' (Chaudoir & Fisher, 2010, p. 236). Although prior convictions

The Emerald Handbook of Appearance in the Workplace, 287–300
doi:10.1108/978-1-80071-174-720230017

and periods of incarceration may not necessarily be outwardly detected, criminal history can appear visible through direct questions, self-disclosure and receipt of information from credible sources, which all may occur during various stages of the employment process. Thus, as the appearance of criminal history shifts from invisible to visible, it will undoubtedly affect individuals as they navigate the hiring process and subsequent employment.

According to the most recent report from the World Population Prison Brief (Walmsley, 2018), the United States had the highest prison population rate in the world, with over 5.5 million individuals included in the correctional population (i.e. prison, jail, parole or probation; Kluckow & Zeng, 2022). Despite the high level of incarceration in the United States, approximately 95% of those incarcerated will be released and return to the community (Hughes & Wilson, 2020). However, upon returning to the community, the labour market experiences of those with a criminal history are generally bleak, frequently characterised by low employment, low wages, weak social networks and job connections, as well as an erosion of employment skills (Visher et al., 2011). Unsurprisingly, the unemployment rate for those with a criminal history is typically high, ranging between 18.4% and 43.6% (Couloute & Kopf, 2018). Although maintaining stable employment is consistently recognised as one of the primary means to ensure individuals' success after obtaining a criminal history (Visher et al., 2011), when criminal history is revealed or detected, it is often one of the most detrimental stigmas during the employment process (e.g. Holzer et al., 2006; Pager, 2003).

Why does this matter to organisations? It matters because organisations do not exist apart from society, but within it. Employing individuals with a criminal history correlates with several community and social justice benefits such as less crime, greater public safety, reduced costs for the government and taxpayers, improved community attitudes towards individuals with a criminal history (Graffam et al., 2008) and reduced recidivism (Griffiths et al., 2007; Ruddell & Winfree, 2006). Despite these advantages, criminal history continues to appear and interfere with hiring because employers are allowed to ask about this personal, yet stigmatised characteristic. By contrast, other characteristics such as race, religion, sex, age, disability, national origin and genetic information have been deemed 'protected' (U.S. Equal Employment Opportunity Commission, 2020a), meaning they are generally not to be considered in employment-related decisions. In fact, consideration of one or more of these characteristics while making an employment-related decision may be subject to a claim of employment discrimination. Apart from policies such as Ban the Box, which prohibit employers from requesting criminal history information until later in the employment process (Avery, 2019), or Open Hiring, which does not explicitly consider any aspect of an individual's background (Conscious Company, 2018), employers *can* consider an individual's criminal history when making an employment decision.

This chapter offers insight into the relevance of the appearance of criminal history during employment. We explore the role of criminal history as it relates to employment, how it may be experienced by individuals who possess a criminal history, including those who have been incarcerated, and how the imagery associated with criminal history may affect subsequent career progression.

Embodiment

Embodiment suggests that a series of 'cognitive processes are deeply rooted in the body's interactions with the world' (Wilson, 2002, p. 625). As it pertains to the lived experience of incarceration and employment pursuits that follow, embodiment represents the central function of the body, having been situated in incarceration for a time, as a formative influence on the mind (Wilson, 2002). From this perspective, cognition is situated in historical, social and physical interactions with the prison environment (see Ziemke, 2003). For example, in exploring the perspectives of incarcerated and formerly incarcerated women, many of the women describe themselves as 'marked' or 'tattooed' by incarceration (Moran, 2012; Zaitzow, 2011). From this perspective, the embodied individual is described by the spaces or circumstances that one has been exposed to (Moran, 2012).

Individuals are distinctly aware of their outward appearance, which can serve as a personal indicator or projection of their social role in employment spaces (see Green, 2003; Kaiser et al., 2003; Rafaeli et al., 1997), affecting individual appraisals of self, their work trajectory and experience (Kimle & Damhorst, 1997). While navigating their careers, individuals may assess a job based on whether there is congruence between the visible aspects of an organisation's identity and their own social or desired identity. For instance, in a study by Kimle and Damhorst (1997) female executives held 'personal image priorities' (p. 62) and articulated a preference working for business firms that possessed organisational identities that were similar to their own social identities.

The effects of embodiment are further understood by considering stigma internalisations, which describes an individual's acceptance of devaluing social experiences as a reflection of who they are (Moore et al., 2013). Internalisation has been linked to low self-esteem, depression and social isolation (Corrigan & Shapiro, 2010; Corrigan et al., 2006). Even if individuals are not exposed to overt discrimination, internalised stigma can affect whether they challenge or address their devalued status (Campbell & Deacon, 2006), further hindering one's ability to successfully integrate into employment.

The relationship between embodiment and stigma internalisation as related to employment may be that individuals view employment as a means to attain a positive self-image. For instance, in a study we conducted with women who were incarcerated in the Mid-Atlantic, US (Young & Anazodo, 2020), several women responded to the question, 'how do you want to show up and be seen?', with strong affirmations noting a desire to be perceived by others as 'self-confident', 'reliable', 'happy', 'positive', 'good person' and 'strong' (p. 516). However, embodiment of a criminal history can also result in less positive feelings such as lowered esteem and sadness. As articulated by a male participant who had been incarcerated for 20 years, and was now housed in a work release facility (Young et al., 2019), he described how incarceration affected his self-worth '...It saddened

me to the point where I think I've laid in a bed for like two days straight...'
(p. 86). He went on to explain how steady employment would be an opportunity
to attain the relevance during the time he missed, 'I just want to work hard for the
next ten, 15-plus years... I just want to be relevant'.

Regardless of how strongly an individual embodies their experience of criminal
history or incarceration, employment contexts often require revealing this information or have it uncovered. This reality may interfere with individuals' felt need
to manage the reputation, image and impressions that others have of them
(Tedeschi, 2013).

Appearance-Based Inferences of Criminality

How would you describe an individual with a criminal history? Does a particular
appearance come to mind? Rapid, unconscious and mental representations tend
to be based on minimal interactions, but may inform individual – and employer –
interpretations of criminality. In a study conducted by Valla et al. (2011), participants were asked to distinguish between headshots of individuals the
researchers denoted as 'criminals' and 'non-criminals'. The participants were able
to do so reliably, highlighting a potential consensus regarding the appearance of
'criminals' and 'non-criminals'. These categorisations may be particularly problematic within the realm of employers, as substantial bias exists in perceptions of
appearance, and assessment based on these judgements may not be accurate
(MacLin & Herrera, 2006).

As Valla et al. (2011) found, participants' judgements were not accurate for
assessing the specifics of the offence, such as the crime committed and nature of
the crime (i.e. violent/non-violent), both of which have been found to be important predictors of employer willingness to hire (see Griffith & Young, 2017;
Society for Human Resource Management and Charles Koch Institute, 2018).
Yet, assumptions of criminality have employment consequences, such as low
wages and low wage growth (Western, 2002), with employment opportunities
often concentrated into particular industries (Lichtenberger, 2006). While
numerous examples exist, we highlight four visible factors that may affect interpretation of criminal history during the employment process.

Race. Particularly in the United States, race plays an integral role in the
appearance and assumption of a criminal history. Societal images of criminals
continue to reinforce the image of a Black male criminal (Welch, 2007). Assumptions
about Black individuals is reflective in the disproportionate rate of incarceration,
with Black men imprisoned at 5.8 times the rate of white men and Black women
imprisoned at 1.8 times the rate of white women, year-end 2018 (Carson, 2020).
These assumptions of criminality occur regardless of educational level, as African
American male college students have been found to experience a series of racial
microaggressions due to assumed criminal behaviour (Bennett et al., 2017).

As assumptions of criminality are not as pronounced for white individuals, job
market effects often differ. As found in a study by Pager (2003), race significantly
affected the rate of call-backs for a job interview when comparing Black and

white male applicants with and without a criminal history. White men with a criminal history received a callback rate of 17% as compared to 34% for those without, whereas the callback rates for Black men with a criminal history was only 5% and without 14%. The assumption of criminality based on race aligns with a recent study that suggests policies such as Ban the Box, which is intended to assist individuals with a criminal history, may result in some employers making assumptions about the existence of a criminal history on the basis of other characteristics (Doleac & Hansen, 2020). In short, race continues to play a pivotal role in the perception and interpretation criminality and employment.

Gender/Sex. 'Invisibility is a fact of life for women in prison. All too often when we envision an inmate behind bars, we see a male face'. (Zaitzow, 2006, p. 4). Despite the exponential growth of women in prison (Tonkin et al., 2004), employers may experience cognitive dissonance when encountering a woman with a criminal history. The theoretical model of Young and Powell (2015) builds upon this notion as it proposes that gender has an effect on the perception and interpretation of criminal history within the context of hiring. Research suggests that while most individuals exiting prison face similar challenges upon release, the re-entry experiences for women are vastly different (see Lartey, 2016; Smith, 2005; Williams, 2016). Justice-involved women are disproportionately low-income, women of colour, undereducated and under skilled (Bloom et al., 2003). With approximately two-thirds of incarcerated women unemployed at their initial time of arrest, the trend continues upon return, as they typically experience sporadic, low- or entry-level occupations with limited opportunities for advancement (Bloom et al., 2003).

Access to employment-related training is also of concern, as prior to incarceration, women are less likely to have received vocational training than their male counterparts (Bloom et al., 2003). While incarcerated, the employment training available in correctional facilities and work-release programmes may be geared towards male-dominated industries (see Young et al., 2019). Male-dominated industries, which often include more manual, blue-collar industries (i.e. construction, manufacturing), also tend to be more willing to hire individuals with a criminal record (Holzer et al., 2003). Considering stereotypical gender roles, women who do not conform to these expectations, and those that embody the physical representations of incarceration, women may be at a further disadvantage (Moran, 2012). Thus, by way of their gender and gendered experiences, women may believe their employment opportunities are limited.

While some women have expressed interest in employment opportunities in male-dominated spaces (e.g. construction; Delveaux et al., 2005), many may continue to be attracted to occupations that predominantly employ women (e.g. administration, cosmetology, nursing; U.S. Bureau of Labor Statistics, 2021). Despite a feeling that employment options may be limited, a study of formerly incarcerated women in Canada found them to be employed in various industries such as sales and service, and business, finance and administration (Delveaux et al., 2005). In short, the employment experiences for women with a criminal history may be quite nuanced.

Age. Ageing is especially challenging for those who spend extended periods of time in a correctional facility (see Shantz & Frigon, 2009). Ageing in prison involves more than just getting older, as it features symbolic and actual intrusions of physical privacy and freedoms, which translate to consistent reminders of who one was, where one is and what one has become (Wahidin, 2002). Many correctional facilities are unprepared or underprepared to treat a variety of chronic health conditions that affect individuals while incarcerated (Williams et al., 2012).Thus, incarcerated individuals tend to physiologically age faster in prison, such that an individual at age 50 may have similar concerns as a non-incarcerated elderly individual (Aday, 2006).

Within the realm of employment, appearing older than your age can result in a multitude of issues. Age, and specifically, those who appear older, can result in employment discrimination, which has consistently accounted for at least 20% of the charges filed against employers in the United States since 2000 (U.S. Equal Employment Opportunity Commission, 2020b). Second, while age and work experience are generally positively correlated (Ng & Feldman, 2009), this relationship may not exist for those with a criminal history. Many individuals with a criminal history have limited work experience or a noticeable gap in their employment history (Holzer et al., 2003). Thus, a hiring manager may experience cognitive dissonance as they try to reconcile how or why an older applicant may have limited work experience. Cognitive dissonance may also exist for an older applicant with a criminal history upon the realisation that despite their age, they may only be qualified to obtain an entry-level position.

Inscription. The body can be described as a site of 'textual inscription' that influences individual identity, as well as interactions and relationships with others (see Moran, 2012). Individuals who have been incarcerated may bear physical markers of imprisonment such as poor dental hygiene, numerous tattoos or other marks representative of their criminal activity or incarceration (Shantz & Frigon, 2010). While tattoos have become increasingly common, these inscriptions have often been followed by negative judgements and preconceived notions around culture, social status or criminality (Buss & Hodges, 2017). These mixed views have resulted in the persistence of perceptions between tattoos and deviance (Broussard & Harton, 2018; Fisher, 2002). Individuals who are tattooed, pierced or otherwise inscribed (or 'modified') tend to experience prejudice and stigma in employment, which can affect their self-esteem, performance and other work-related outcomes (Ellis, 2015).

Moreover, because numerous work environments require a professional appearance (Rima, 2018), the workplace context can inform and even dictate appearance standards. Thus, an applicant or employee who appears counter to organisational preferences may be least preferred (Cavico et al., 2012; Corbett, 2007; Ellis, 2015). Indeed, 'the perception of outsiders to employees and potential employees is of paramount concern to organizations' (Ellis, 2015, p. 107), and perhaps even more so if apparent indicators, such as inscriptions, are interpreted to be reflective of one's criminal past.

Structural Barriers That Increase the Appearance of Criminal History

Even if individuals do not proactively share their criminal history information, it can be easily uncovered as information is readily accessible through online searches and informal digital platforms (see Anazodo et al., 2020). Beyond this, structural barriers and biases continue to negatively affect the employment of those with a criminal history long after their conviction or period of incarceration. Possessing a criminal history generally results in a plethora of collateral consequences including a lack of access to housing, occupational licences and education (National Inventory of Collateral Consequences, 2022). While these consequences may be invisible to hiring managers and colleagues, they may further exacerbate employment gaps in a résumé, limit access to a bank account or negatively affect a credit history (Bonanni et al., 2011). Taken together, these factors may further highlight the appearance of a criminal history and negatively affect individuals in the employment context.

The Résumé Gap. A gap on a résumé is common for those with a criminal history. To navigate around this, individuals are often given advice such as to create a functional résumé (see Prison Fellowship, 2020; Minnesota State CareerWise, 2020), which can emphasise skills and abilities, rather than the time frame a particular job was held. While this format may be advantageous for those with a criminal history, because a chronological résumé format is still largely preferred by employers (Ross & Young, 2005; Schullery et al., 2009), applicants may still need to explain the presence of a gap or employers will attempt to ascertain why the gap exists (Smith et al., 2005). As Smith et al. (2005) suggest these gaps may be grouped into two categories of fault – fault on part of the individual (e.g. unsatisfactory work) or external factors (e.g. recession). As employers will likely utilise a combination of available information to make this assessment, an assumption of a criminal history is likely to be met with negative employment outcomes.

Credit History Information. During latter stages of the employment process, some employers may request additional information about applicants, such as a credit history report. Considering the limited opportunity to establish credit while incarcerated, credit history information may be particularly detrimental for individuals with a criminal history, and especially for those who have served a period of incarceration (Kuhn, 2020). While applicants must grant permission for potential employers to gain access to their credit report (Federal Trade Commission, 2018), hiring managers have the right to *interpret* information, which is subject to individual-level biases. Similarly here, hiring managers can determine whether a negative credit report was due to the fault of the individual (i.e. applicant is responsible for their credit) or society (i.e. structural factors affected credit) (Kiviat, 2019). Considering this document in conjunction with other factors (e.g. prior work history) may result in an assumption of criminal history and decrease the likelihood to hire.

Restrictions on occupational licences. Forfeiture or restrictions on obtaining occupational licences significantly and negatively affects individuals with a criminal history from re-entering or entering employment in a variety of fields (National Inventory of Collateral Consequences, 2022). One of the underlying purposes of occupational licencing is to keep barriers to entry high (Kleiner & Krueger, 2013), which maintains the number of professionals in an industry (Kleiner, 2000). Despite the invisibility of justice involvement, this can have a disproportionately negative effect on assessments of individuals who possess a criminal history (Rodriguez & Avery, 2016; Slivinski, 2016), which may further limit career mobility and wage growth (Western, 2002).

Community supervision guidelines. Community supervision, such as probation and parole, is a supervised release following, or in lieu of, a period of incarceration (Maruschak & Bonczar, 2013). Community supervision guidelines are often restrictive and frequently limit the type of work or work hours that individuals can maintain. In some cases, individuals are prohibited from associating with others who have prior convictions (Harding, 2003), which may limit the work spaces where individuals can seek employment. Further, conditions to community supervision often mean that individuals can expect an in-person visit from their assigned probation officer '...at any time at your home or elsewhere...' (United States Courts, 2022). These visits serve as a constant visual reminder and can enable other employees or customers to learn of an individual's criminal history. In short, an individual's criminal history may appear at various junctures of the employment process and to various individuals beyond just the hiring manager.

Moving Forward

As we consider the appearance of a highly stigmatised characteristic such as criminal history, it is important to rethink visibility, interpretation and related implications. First, we need to consider the implications of appearance as pertains to a devalued or stigmatised characteristic. We encourage researchers to continue delving deeper into truly understanding the experiences of individuals should their invisible, stigmatised characteristic appear within the workplace context. Moreover, gaining additional perspective from the vantage point of the individual may enable organisations to be more inclusive towards individuals who possess a variety of characteristics.

Second, we encourage employers and researchers to consider how the appearance of criminal history may perpetuate or mitigate the stigma of this population within the workplace. Biased assumptions towards criminality may negatively affect those who are disproportionally affected by the carceral system (i.e. young, Black men). While implicit bias training provides an opportunity for individuals to evaluate their individual interactions, this is an opportune time to review organisational policies and processes and consider embedded, structural bias and inequity. As individuals *without* a criminal history are also often negatively affected by many of these policies and practices, it is likely that these broader changes will be relevant beyond just those who possess a criminal history.

Third, appearance of a criminal record is an opportunity to consciously advocate for the inclusion of individuals with a criminal history in various workplaces and industries. Studies have found manufacturing, construction, trade, mining and retail industries to be more supportive of hiring individuals with a criminal history, likely due to the assumed low level of customer interaction (Lichtenberger, 2006). However, as noted by Griffith and Young (2017), some hiring managers in industries beyond the aforementioned hold favourable perspectives about hiring individuals with a criminal history. One recent example is J.P. Morgan Chase, a large financial services firm, which has adopted a 'Second Chance Hiring' strategy that hires individuals with a criminal history into 'in roles that do not impact the financial system' (J.P. Morgan Chase, 2021). J.P. Morgan Chase has openly adopted this strategy and promotes doing so because it recognises the 'significant barriers to employment' that individuals encounter once they have a criminal history. While some organisations may think that hiring employees with a criminal history would be detrimental to their reputation, this assumption may not align with consumer perspectives. In a study by Young and Keech (2022), consumers were surveyed about their perceptions of organisations that hire individuals with a criminal history. Consumers were no more or less likely to do business with service organisations that hired, and in the scenario where there was some hesitation, this difference was mitigated when the organisation provided an explanation of why this hiring practice was adopted. In this context, increasing the visibility of criminal history may help to simultaneously advocate and decrease the stigma attached to individuals who possess a criminal history.

This proactive and transparent communication to consumers may align well with organisations that value the social dimension of corporate social responsibility, which emphasises the relationship between the organisation and society (Dahlsrud, 2008). Research suggests that communities may benefit from providing resources that empower individuals with a criminal history to successfully transition back into their communities as valuable, productive and contributing members of society (Andress et al., 2004). The majority of the public is generally supportive of these efforts (Rade et al., 2018a, 2018b). Thus, it is an opportune time for organisations to move beyond the question of 'how does this benefit our specific organization?', and instead push forward on various initiatives that can simultaneously benefit the organisation and society.

As organisations and employment decision-makers wrestle with the meaning of the appearance of criminal history, we encourage them to also consider how this information may emerge, how they may interpret it and why they may consider it relevant. It is the answer to these questions that may provide us with the greatest insight about the likelihood that negative outcomes due to the appearance of criminal history will occur, and enable us to work towards more equitable access to employment for all.

References

Aday, R. H. (2006). Aging prisoners' concerns toward dying in prison. *Omega: The Journal of Death and Dying, 52*(3), 199–216.

Anazodo, K., Ricciardelli, R., & Chan, C. (2019). Employment after incarceration: Managing a socially stigmatized identity. *Equality, Diversity and Inclusion, 38*(5), 564–582.

Anazodo, K. S., Young, N. C. J., & Ricciardelli, R. (2020). Challenging the status quo: Exploring organizational deviations from discriminatory norms towards criminal history. *The Annual Review of Interdisciplinary Justice Research (IJR), 9*, 206–236.

Andress, D., Wildes, T., Rechtine, D., & Moritsugu, K. P. (2004). Jails, prisons, and your community's health. *Journal of Law Medicine & Ethics, 32*(4), 50–51.

Avery, B. (2019). *Ban the box: U.S. cities, counties, and states adopt fair hiring policies.* National Employment Law Project. https://www.nelp.org/publication/ban-the-box-fair-chance-hiring-state-and-local-guide/

Bennett, L. M., McIntosh, E., & Henson, F. O. (2017). African American college students and racial microaggressions: Assumptions of criminality. *Journal of Psychology, 5*(2), 14–20.

Bloom, B., Owen, B. A., & Covington, S. (2003). *Gender-responsive strategies: Research, practice, and guiding principles for women offenders.* U.S. Department of Justice: National Institute of Corrections. https://s3.amazonaws.com/static.nicic.gov/Library/018017.pdf

Bonanni, C., Drysdale, D., Hughes, A., & Doyle, P. (2011). Employee background verification: The cross-referencing effect. *International Business & Economics Research Journal, 5*(11), 1–7.

Broussard, K. A., & Harton, H. C. (2018). Tattoo or taboo? Tattoo stigma and negative attitudes toward tattooed individuals. *The Journal of Social Psychology, 158*(5), 521–540.

Buss, L., & Hodges, K. (2017). Marked: Tattoo as an expression of psyche. *Psychological Perspectives, 60*(1), 4–38.

Campbell, C., & Deacon, H. (2006). Unravelling the contexts of stigma: From internalisation to resistance to change. *Journal of Community & Applied Social Psychology, 16*(6), 411–417.

Carson, E. A. (2020). *Prisoners in 2018.* U.S. Department of Justice. https://www.bjs.gov/content/pub/pdf/p18.pdf

Cavico, F. J., Muffler, S. C., & Mujtaba, B. G. (2012). Appearance discrimination, lookism and lookphobia in the workplace. *Journal of Applied Business Research, 28*(5), 791–802.

Chaudoir, S. R., & Fisher, J. D. (2010). The disclosure processes model: Understanding disclosure decision making and postdisclosure outcomes among people living with a concealable stigmatized identity. *Psychological Bulletin, 136*, 236–256.

Conscious Company. (2018). *The Conscious Company glossary – Open hiring.* Conscious Company. https://consciouscompanymedia.com/glossary/open-hiring/#:~:text=Conscious%20Company%20Glossary-,Open%20Hiring%E2%84%A2,background%20checks%20or%20interview%20process

Corbett, W. R. (2007). The ugly truth about appearance discrimination and the beauty of our employment discrimination law. *Duke Journal of Gender Law & Policy, 14*, 153–183.

Corrigan, P. W., & Shapiro, J. R. (2010). Measuring the impact of programs that challenge the public stigma of mental illness. *Clinical Psychology Review, 30*(8), 907–922.

Corrigan, P. W., Watson, A. C., & Barr, L. (2006). The self–stigma of mental illness: Implications for self–esteem and self–efficacy. *Journal of Social and Clinical Psychology, 25*(8), 875–884.

Couloute, L., & Kopf, D. (2018). Out of prison & out of work: Unemployment among formerly incarcerated people. *Prison Policy Initiative.* https://www.prisonpolicy.org/reports/outofwork.html

Dahlsrud, A. (2008). How corporate social responsibility is defined: An analysis of 37 definitions. *Corporate Social Responsibility and Environmental Management, 15*(1), 1–13.

Delveaux, K., Blanchette, K., & Wickett, J. M. (2005). *Employment needs, interests, and programming for women offenders.* Research Branch, Correctional Service of Canada.

Doleac, J. L., & Hansen, B. (2020). The unintended consequences of "ban the box": Statistical discrimination and employment outcomes when criminal histories are hidden. *Journal of Labor Economics, 38*(2), 321–374.

Ellis, A. D. (2015). A picture is worth one thousand words: Body art in the workplace. *Employee Responsibilities and Rights Journal, 27*(2), 101–113.

Federal Trade Commission. (2018). Background checks. https://www.consumer.ftc.gov/articles/0157-background-checks

Fisher, J. A. (2002). Tattooing the body, marking culture. *Body & Society, 8*(4), 91–107.

Graffam, J., Shinkfield, A. J., & Hardcastle, L. (2008). The perceived employability of ex-prisoners and offenders. *International Journal of Offender Therapy and Comparative Criminology, 52*(6), 673–685.

Green, E. (2003). Suiting ourselves: Women professors using clothes to signal authority, belonging, and personal style. In A. Guy, E. Green, & M. Banim (Eds.), *Through the wardrobe: Women's relationships with their clothes* (2nd ed., pp. 97–116). Berg.

Griffiths, C. T., Dandurand, Y., & Murdoch, D. (2007). *The social reintegration of offenders and crime prevention* (Vol. 4). National Crime Prevention Centre.

Griffith, J., & Young, N. C. J. (2017). Hiring ex-offenders? The case of ban the box. *Equality, Diversity and Inclusion: An International Journal, 36*(6), 501–518.

Harding, D. J. (2003). Jean Valjean's dilemma: The management of ex-convict identity in the search for employment. *Deviant Behavior, 24*(6), 571–595.

Holzer, H. J., Raphael, S., & Stoll, M. A. (2003). *Employment barriers facing ex-offenders* (pp. 1–23). Urban Institute Reentry Roundtable.

Holzer, H. J., Raphael, S., & Stoll, M. A. (2006). Perceived criminality, criminal background checks, and the racial hiring practices of employers. *The Journal of Law and Economics, 49*(2), 451–480.

Hughes, T., & Wilson, D. J. (2020). *Reentry trends in the U.S.: Inmates returning to the community after serving time in prison.* Bureau of Justice Statistics. https://www.bjs.gov/content/reentry/reentry.cfm

Kaiser, S., Chandler, J., & Hammidi, T. (2003). Minding appearances in female academic culture. In A. Guy, E. Green, & M. Banim (Eds.), *Through the wardrobe: Women's relationships with their clothes* (2nd ed., pp. 117–136). Berg.

Kimle, P. A., & Damhorst, M. L. (1997). A grounded theory model of the ideal business image for women. *Symbolic Interaction, 20*(1), 45–68.

Kiviat, B. (2019). The art of deciding with data: Evidence from how employers translate credit reports into hiring decisions. *Socio-Economic Review*, *17*(2), 283–309.

Kleiner, M. M. (2000). Occupational licensing. *The Journal of Economic Perspectives*, *14*(4), 189–202.

Kleiner, M. M., & Krueger, A. B. (2013). Analyzing the extent and influence of occupational licensing on the labor market. *Journal of Labor Economics*, *31*(S1), S173–S202.

Kluckow, R., & Zeng, Z. (2022). *Correctional populations in the United States, 2020.* https://bjs.ojp.gov/content/pub/pdf/cpus20st.pdf

Kuhn, K. M. (2020). The why and when of background checks: Situational factors moderate effects of criminal and financial stigma. *International Journal of Selection and Assessment*, *00*, 1–14.

Lartey, J. (2016). Women in jails are the fastest growing prison population. *The Guardian.* https://www.theguardian.com/us-news/2016/aug/17/women-incarceration-rates-growth-study

Lichtenberger, E. (2006). Where do ex-offenders find jobs? An industrial profile of the employers of ex-offenders in Virginia. *Journal of Correctional Education*, 297–311.

MacLin, M. K., & Herrera, V. (2006). The criminal stereotype. *North American Journal of Psychology*, *8*(2), 197–208.

Maruschak, L. M., & Bonczar, T. P. (2013). *Probation and parole in the United States, 2012* (No. NCJ 243826). Bureau of Justice Statistics, US Department of Justice.

Minnesota State CareerWise. (2020). Career planning for people with a criminal conviction: Resume writing tips. *Minnesota State CAREERwise.* https://careerwise.minnstate.edu/exoffenders/find-job/resume-tips.html

Moore, K., Stuewig, J., & Tangney, J. (2013). Jail inmates' perceived and anticipated stigma: Implications for post-release functioning. *Self and Identity*, *12*, 527–547.

Moran, D. (2012). Prisoner reintegration and the stigma of prison time inscribed on the body. *Punishment & Society*, *14*(5), 564–583.

Morgan Chase, J. P. (2021). Second chance agenda. https://www.jpmorganchase.com/impact/our-approach/policy-center/second-chance-agenda

National Inventory of Collateral Consequences. (2022). About. *Justice Center: The Council of State Governments.* https://niccc.csgjusticecenter.org/about/

Ng, T. W., & Feldman, D. C. (2009). Age, work experience, and the psychological contract. *Journal of Organizational Behavior*, *30*(8), 1053–1075.

Pager, D. (2003). The mark of a criminal record. *American Journal of Sociology*, *108*, 937–975.

Prison Fellowship. (2020). How to write a resume when you have a criminal record. *Prison Fellowship.* https://www.prisonfellowship.org/resources/support-friends-family-of-prisoners/supporting-successful-prisoner-reentry/write-resume-criminal-record/

Rade, C. B., Desmarais, S. L., & Burnette, J. L. (2018a). An integrative theoretical model of public support for ex-offender reentry. *International Journal of Offender Therapy and Comparative Criminology*, *62*(8), 2131–2152.

Rade, C. B., Desmarais, S. L., & Burnette, J. L. (2018b). Implicit theories of criminal behavior: Fostering public support for ex-offender community reentry. *Applied Psychology in Criminal Justice*, *14*(1), 14–36.

Rafaeli, A., Dutton, J., Harquail, C. V., & Mackie-Lewis, S. (1997). Navigating by attire: The use of dress by female administrative employees. *Academy of Management Journal, 40*(1), 9–45.

Rima, W. (2018). The human body: The canvas for tattoos; the public workplace: An exhibit for new form of art. *Drake Law Review, 66*(3), 705–732.

Rodriguez, M. N., & Avery, B. (2016). *Unlicensed and untapped: Removing barriers to state occupational licenses for people with records.* National Employment Law Project. http://nelp.org/content/uploads/Unlicensed-Untapped-Removing-Barriers-State-Occupational-Licenses.pdf. Accessed on July 21, 2021.

Ross, C. M., & Young, S. J. (2005). Resume preferences: Is it really "business as usual". *Journal of Career Development, 32*(2), 153–164.

Ruddell, R., & Winfree, L. T., Jr. (2006). Setting aside criminal convictions in Canada: A successful approach to offender reintegration. *The Prison Journal, 86*(4), 452–469.

Schullery, N. M., Ickes, L., & Schullery, S. E. (2009). Employer preferences for résumés and cover letters. *Business Communication Quarterly, 72*(2), 163–176.

Shantz, L., & Frigon, S. (2009). Aging, women and health: From the pains of imprisonment to the pains of reintegration. *International Journal of Prisoner Health, 5*(1), 3–15.

Shantz, L., & Frigon, S. (2010). Home free? The (after) effects of imprisonment on women's bodies, physical and mental health and identity. *Aporia, 2*(1), 6–17.

Slivinski, S. (2016). *Turning shackles into bootstraps: Why occupational licensing reform is the mising piece of criminal justice reform* (Policy Report No. 2016-01). Center for the Study of Economic Liberty, Arizona State University. https://research.wpcarey.asu.edu/economic-liberty/wp-content/uploads/2016/11/CSEL-Policy-Report-2016-01-Turning-Shackles-into-Bootstraps.pdf

Smith, B. V. (2005). Sexual abuse of women in United States prisons: A modern corollary of slavery. *Fordham Urban Law Journal, 33*, 101–136.

Smith, F. L., Tabak, F., Showail, S., Parks, J. M., & Kleist, J. S. (2005). The name game: Employability evaluations of prototypical applicants with stereotypical feminine and masculine first names. *Sex Roles, 52*(1), 63–82.

Society for Human Resource Management and Charles Koch Institute. (2018). *Workers with criminal records.* https://www.shrm.org/hr-today/trends-and-forecasting/research-and-surveys/Documents/SHRM-CKI%20Workers%20with%20Criminal%20Records%20Issue%20Brief%202018-05-17.pdf

Tedeschi, J. T. (2013). *Impression management theory and social psychological research.* Academic Press.

Tonkin, P., Dickie, J., Alemagno, S., & Grove, W. (2004). Women in jail: "Soft Skills" and barriers to employment. *Journal of Offender Rehabilitation, 38*(4), 51–71.

United States Courts. (2022). Chapter 2. Visits by probation officer (Probation and supervised release conditions). https://www.uscourts.gov/services-forms/visits-probation-officer-probation-supervised-release-conditions

U.S. Bureau of Labor Statistics. (2021). Labor force statistics from current population survey. https://www.bls.gov/cps/cpsaat11.htm

U.S. Equal Employment Opportunity Commission. (2020a). Who is protected from employment discrimination? https://www.eeoc.gov/employers/smallbusiness/faq/who_is_protected.cfm

U.S. Equal Employment Opportunity Commission. (2020b). Charge statistics (Charges filed with EEOC) FY 1997 Through FY 2019. https://www.eeoc.gov/enforcement/charge-statistics-charges-filed-eeoc-fy-1997-through-fy-2019

Valla, J. M., Ceci, S. J., & Williams, W. M. (2011). The accuracy of inferences about criminality based on facial appearance. *Journal of Social, Evolutionary, and Cultural Psychology*, 5(1), 66–91.

Visher, C. A., Debus-Sherrill, S. A., & Yahner, J. (2011). Employment after prison: A longitudinal study of former prisoners. *Justice Quarterly*, 28(5), 698–718.

Wahidin, A. (2002). Reconfiguring older bodies in the prison time machine. *Journal of Ageing and Society*, 7(3), 177–193.

Walmsley, R. (2018). World Prison population list. https://www.prisonstudies.org/sites/default/files/resources/downloads/wppl_12.pdf. Accessed on July 15, 2021.

Welch, K. (2007). Black criminal stereotypes and racial profiling. *Journal of Contemporary Criminal Justice*, 23(3), 276–288.

Western, B. (2002). The impact of incarceration on wage mobility and inequality. *American Sociological Review*, 526–546.

Williams, T. (2016). Number of women in jail has grown far faster than that of men, study says. https://www.nytimes.com/2016/08/18/us/number-of-women-in-jail-has-grown-far-faster-than-that-of-men-study-says.html?_r=0

Williams, B. A., Stern, M. F., Mellow, J., Safer, M., & Greifinger, R. B. (2012). Aging in correctional custody: Setting a policy agenda for older prisoner health care. *American Journal of Public Health*, 102(8), 1475–1481.

Wilson, M. (2002). Six views of embodied cognition. *Psychological Bulletin and Review*, 9(4), 625–636.

Young, N. C. J., & Anazodo, K. S. (2020). Exploring the overlooked: Women, work, & criminal history. *Gender in Management: An International Journal*, 35(6), 505–528.

Young, N. C. J., Griffith, J. N., & Anazodo, K. S. (2019). Exploring the impact of training on equitable access to employment: A gendered perspective of work release programs. *Journal of Human Resource Management*, 22(2), 70–86.

Young, N. C. J., & Keech, J. (2022). Second chance hiring: Exploring consumer perception of employers who hire individuals with criminal histories. *Management Decision*, 60(9), 2389–2408.

Young, N. C. J., & Powell, G. N. (2015). Hiring ex-offenders: A theoretical model. *Human Resource Management Review*, 25(3), 298–312.

Zaitzow, B. H. (2006). Empowerment not entrapment: Providing opportunities for incarcerated women to move beyond "doing time". *Justice Policy Journal*, 3(1), 1–24.

Zaitzow, B. H. (2011). Challenges and opportunities for incarcerated women to overcome reentry barriers. In I. O. Ekunwe & R. S. Jones (Eds.), *Global perspectives on re-entry* (pp. 225–256). Tampere University Press.

Ziemke, T. (2003). What's that thing called embodiment? *Proceedings of the Annual Meeting of the Cognitive Science Society*, 25(25), 1305–1310.

Chapter 17

The Impact of Workers' Tattoos and Piercings on Employment: Suggestions for Pragmatic Career Planning

Leonidas Efthymiou, Yianna Orphanidou and Achilleas Karayiannis

Abstract

What is the impact of workers' tattoos and piercings on hospitality work? While body-art is prohibited in some hotels, it is encouraged in others. Also, an even more ambiguous situation arises when body-art is neither accepted nor prohibited, depending on labour market conditions and managers' individualistic preferences. In this chapter, we explore how this ambiguity imposes challenges on employment and career planning. We first seek to understand how managers' perceptions and decisions concerning worker body-art change in different hotel categories. To do so, we draw on interviews with 25 General and Human Resource Managers in 18 upper market hotels, three lifestyle boutique-hotels and four luxury hotels. Then, we offer pragmatic suggestions on career planning.

Keywords: Tattoos; piercings; body-art; career planning; hotels; hospitality

Introduction

It feels that tattoos and piercings are everywhere these days – on nearly every football player, famous TV chefs, Instagram influencers and everyday people around us. Their increasing popularity is attributed to changing societal perceptions and attitudes about body-art in the last two decades or so (Atkinson, 2003; Kang & Jones, 2007; Sanders & Vail, 2008; Timming, 2015, 2017). It does not go unnoticed, of course, that when employees bring their body-art at the workplace, established work processes and aesthetic policies are challenged, causing employment tensions (Nath et al., 2016). Tattoos are perceived by managers negatively, they carry a stigma (Timming, 2015) and are linked to increased

The Emerald Handbook of Appearance in the Workplace, 301–316
doi:10.1108/978-1-80071-174-720230018

worker deviance (Tews & Stafford, 2019), resulting in managerial prejudice, negative evaluations and reduced employment chances (Bekhor et al., 1995; Brallier et al., 2011; Swanger, 2006). Such studies are situated in the broader literature of impression management, where visible characteristics, like tattoos, cause visual disturbance, negative customer perceptions, workplace fragmentation and stigma (Belkin, 2021).

Recent studies, nevertheless, contradict the widely held perception that visible body-art reduces the chances of obtaining employment (Sexton et al., 2023). It seems that body-art has a mixed effect across different organisations, contexts and cultures (Dean, 2010; Timming, 2017). French et al. (2018), for example, found no empirical evidence of employment, wage or earnings discrimination against people with various types of tattoos. Also, while restricted in a particular context, such as a restaurant, tattoos and piercings may be desired in another, just as in a nightclub (Timming, 2017). Thus, body-art increases the chances of employment in a nightclub and decreases one's chances of employment in the context of a fine dining restaurant. In addition, Pinto et al. (2019) found that pierced receptionists are better rated than non-pierced receptionists, especially female ones. This is because pierced receptionists, in certain contexts, express warmth and confidence, which influence customers positively.

In some workplaces, moreover, the acceptance or prohibition of workers' body-art is not so clear cut. Drawing from a study in high-end hotels, Efthymiou (2018) explains how the scarcity of available labour, along with prolonged understaffing, induces managers to soften up their aesthetic standards and accept workers with visible and non-visible tattoos. In other words, managers are forced by labour market conditions to hire employees they wouldn't have accepted otherwise – an indirect form of discrimination for workers' careers. In the same hotels, workers' lifestyles are appropriated by management as hotel employees are encouraged to make their tattoos and piercings visible for certain events, such as disco events.

These findings point to a vagueness that lies in the heart of hospitality employment. While body-art is prohibited in some workplaces, it is encouraged in others. Also, an even more ambiguous situation arises when body-art is neither accepted nor prohibited, depending on labour market conditions and managers' individualistic preferences. In this chapter, we explore how this ambiguity imposes further challenges on employment and career planning. We first seek to understand how managers' perceptions and decisions concerning worker body-art change in different hotel categories. Then, we offer pragmatic suggestions on career planning. To do so, we broadened our sample to include several hotel categories, and, thus, a wider range of managerial perceptions. We draw on interviews with 25 General and Human Resource (HR) Managers in 18 upper market hotels, three lifestyle boutique-hotels and four luxury hotels. The interested audience of this chapter includes students in the field of hospitality, recent graduates, trade unions, as well as current and future employees.

The study is undertaken within the theoretical body of 'aesthetic labour' (Warhurst et al., 2000), which is a tool capable of opening up fields of analysis and re-problematising systematic worker embodiment at work. Given that body-art has a different effect across contexts and cultures, it is worth mentioning that the Cypriot hotel sector, as with other parts of Europe (Nickson et al., 2003), is characterised by irregular working hours, low wages, limited opportunities for advancement, fewer benefits and sharp seasonal fluctuations, resulting to labour-market shortages, especially in the peak summer season. On top of that, ever increasing numbers of tourist arrivals (Hadjioannou, 2019) worsen the shortage of labour even further.

Theory and Concepts

The increasing adoption of tattoos, piercings and other forms of body-art is the result of changing perceptions and attitudes in the society (Atkinson, 2003; Kang & Jones, 2007; Sanders & Vail, 2008; Timming, 2015, 2017). From a form of deviance and marker of criminality, that is traced all the way back to ancient Greece (Belden, 2016), tattoos have evolved to a voluntary form of self-expression, a symbol of individuality, self-mastery and construction of the self (Jefferys, 2000; Pitts, 2003). Body-art also infiltrates the workplace, causing employment tensions (Nath et al., 2016).

The impact of worker body-art in interactive service workplaces is an ongoing inquiry in 'aesthetic labour' (Warhurst et al., 2000), which is a significant and enduring body of literature, exploring systematic worker embodiment at work. Aesthetic labour includes using worker appearance and demeanour in forming organisational core competencies and/or developing a competitive advantage. In doing so, some workplaces prescribe (implicitly or explicitly, in writing or not), restrict and shape aesthetic elements, such as worker hairstyles, jewellery, nails, make-up (Edwards, 2003), attractiveness, weight, ethnicity-related characteristics and body odour (Wu et al., 2019). The appearance of worker tattoos, moreover, raises much broader questions about employment and future career management.

Let us first consider what we already know about the impact of body-art in interactive service workplaces. We have known for some time that managers perceive worker body-art negatively while the employment chances of tattooed and pierced employees are reduced. Swanger (2006), for instance, suggests that 87% of human resource managers perceived visible tattoos and body piercings negatively. We know, following the work of Timming (2015), that while being rooted in prejudice, body-art carries a stigma that results in negative evaluations, and, therefore, lower hireability. Another study depicts that less than 30% out of 242 employers would hire an applicant with visible tattoos in hotels, restaurants and quick-service restaurant chains (Bekhor et al., 1995). Likewise, through a study among 192 restaurant managers, Brallier et al. (2011) reaffirm that hiring decisions are influenced negatively by visible body modifications, as 87.8% of managers would rather hire a non-tattooed individual. Also, worker body-art has been linked to workplace resistance, misbehaviour and deviance. Workers with visible tattoos may be resistant to organisational authority, whereas, a greater 'number' of tattoos are associated with greater organisational deviance (Tews & Stafford, 2019). Organisational deviance is also linked to 'darker' tattoos, including gothic images, science fiction, symbols reflecting death or violence, and are likely to evoke negative emotions. Therefore, workers' decisions about career should not be unrelated to decisions concerning their number and genre of tattoos. Overall, these studies confirm the widely held perception that the presence of visible tattoos and piercings significantly reduce the chance of obtaining employment.

Furthermore, what else do we already know about body-art at the workplace? That, recent studies contradict the findings presented in the previous paragraph. For instance, French et al. (2018) found no empirical evidence of employment, wage or earnings discrimination against people with various types of tattoos. Also, while restricted in a particular context, tattoos and piercings may be desired in another (Timming, 2017). Although the presence of visible tattoos is a significant liability in a fine dining restaurant, it is a significant asset in a nightclub and a pub. As such, visible body-art increases the chances of employment in a nightclub and decreases one's chances of employment in the context of a fine dining restaurant.

It has also been recorded that hiring managers in hotels are often induced to bypass or soften up their aesthetic standards to accept both visible and non-visible tattoos. More specifically, Efthymiou (2018) reports that the scarcity of available labour results to upper market hotels being understaffed during peak season. As a consequence, aesthetic requirements and body-art restrictions for front-of-house workers are informally altered. The same applies for quick-service restaurants like McDonalds-Cyprus, which has changed its 'no-tattooed workers' policy due to labour shortage (Andreou, 2021, General Manager, McDonald's Cyprus, Personal discussion). In the US coffee retailing, Starbucks changed its aesthetic standards too. A petition campaign was created by a Starbucks' employee, who claimed that the company's Mission Statement (*Our mission is to inspire and nurture the human spirit*) does not align with the way it treats tattooed employees (Williams, 2014, 'Let us have visible tattoos!!!' https://www.coworker.org/petitions/let-us-have-visible-tattoos). Societal response to the petition was overwhelming and, within a short period of time, Starbucks changed its dress code to allow visible tattoos. Such findings reveal that, changing perceptions and values about tattoos among the society have an impact on organisations and their processes. They make some of the traditional hiring policies look outdated and ethically wrong, generating conflicts, societal response and resulting to worker discrimination lawsuits (Elzweig & Peeples, 2011). Visible body-art, thus, can be said to have a differing and ambiguous effect across different organisations and contexts globally (Dean, 2010; Timming, 2017).

It is also known that employees' appearance is an effective means through which to convey a particular 'branded' image (Timming, 2017) and, together with other aesthetic merits, the actual product itself (Bitner, 1990; Crang, 1997; Witz et al., 2003). Employees' appearance can be a major determinant of customer satisfaction (Adelman et al., 1994) whereby customer preferences are shaped by various elements, including age, gender, ethnic, race differences and tattoos (Baumann et al., 2016). Worker appearance, such as piercings, has also been matched to behavioural characteristics such as warmth and confidence (Pinto et al., 2019).

Additionally, it is well known that aesthetic attributes and worker lifestyles are often captured and used by management (Fleming & Spicer, 2007) through the 'just be yourself' corporate philosophy (Fleming & Sturdy, 2009, 2011) and the realm of 'lifestyle organisations' (Fleming, 2015). The example of Radisson Hotel Group (RHG) is quite enlightening in terms of differing aesthetic standards, even within a single hotel group. According to Efthymiou (2018), unlike the Radisson Blu, where visible tattoos are unwelcomed, the Radisson Red category encourages workers' artistic expressions, including fashionable hair designs, tattoos and piercings. Radisson Red and similar types of hotels, divert away from conventional approaches to hospitality service, as they target a specific type of customer. Located in urban central locations, they adopt an artistic, music and fashion mindset, where visitors and workers are encouraged to keep their everyday lifestyle. When employees can authentically 'be themselves' they are more likely to voluntarily enact the 'buzz of life' in tasks that increasingly require interpersonal virtuosity and authenticity, especially in the service sector.

Lastly, reporting from upper market hotels, Efthymiou (2018) explains how employees are encouraged to make their tattoos and piercings visible for certain events, such as disco nights and themed parties. It's a form of appropriation, where workers' aesthetic characteristics become part of the show. Unlike the lifestyle hotels described earlier, the process in upper market hotels is a form of 'staged authenticity' (Efthymiou, 2022). As soon as the performance is completed, workers will have to remove their piercings, change their hairstyle and cover up their tattoos with long sleeves.

Departing from these observations, this chapter explores employment tensions and career planning in hospitality. The data drawn upon in this chapter were collected through 25 qualitative in-depth interviews with general and HR managers, in the same number of hotels. The sample is comprised by luxury, upper market and lifestyle hotels. Prior to conducting interviews, cover letters were sent to all managers, in 2018. Also, the fieldwork adopted a snowball method where the first managers introduced researchers to their colleagues. During fieldwork, the researchers applied a two-cycle coding to categorise findings under key themes (Gioia et al., 2013; Saldaña, 2015). This process enabled the development of sentences and paragraphs for the analysis. The collection of findings ended in 2020, when much of the information appeared to be repetitive under each hotel category. The repetitiveness of findings and commonality of themes expressed by managers was considered as a sign of saturation, a point at which gathering more data no longer reveals new properties about a particular phenomenon (Bryant & Charmaz, 2019). The next section presents the findings of the study, along with implications for practice and career management recommendations.

Findings

The findings of the study reconfirm that hotels find it increasingly difficult to staff their premises adequately. 'The local hospitality industry suffers by chronic labour shortage, which is attributed to mobility patterns among the local society (Efthymiou et al., 2020, p. 294). Paradoxically, hotel vacancies and high national unemployment exist simultaneously, whereas, more luxury, upper market, boutique and casino hotels are relentlessly being built throughout the island (Theopoulou, 2019). Also, stemming from our findings, it seems that there is an ongoing change regarding aesthetic policies and politics at the workplace. Change manifests itself differently in each context, influencing the way individual hotels operate. Below we present three main hotel types with different approaches to worker body-art, namely: upper market hotels, lifestyle hotels and luxury hotels.

Playful Twist of Aesthetic Labour in Upper Market Hotels: 'We Changed Our Policies, but Not Our Standards'

The term 'upper market hotels', also known as 'high-end' or 'upscale full service hotels' in the Mediterranean region refers to deluxe, four- and five-star hotels, catering predominantly to a package holiday market (Efthymiou, 2018). It seems that two interview questions and two sets of answers describe the current employment situation in the upper market hotels we visited:

- Question 1: *do you hire workers with visible tattoos?*
- Response 1: 'yes'.
- Question 2: *do you think it's appropriate to have workers with visible tattoos at the workplace?*
- Response 2: 'no'.

Managers in all 18 hotels responded to these questions in the same manner. What these answers reflect is a workplace reality that coexists with contradicting, yet formal aesthetic standards. All 'upper market' hotels participating in the sample have individuals with body-art on their payroll, with some of the art being visible and some not. Sixteen out of eighteen managers would certainly hire an inked worker, unless the tattoo is excessive (e.g. on face and neck). Four hotels make it compulsory to keep tattoos hidden, especially those on the neck, arms and hands. Eleven hotels require workers to remove their facial piercings during the shift. In the remaining nine hotels piercings are accepted as long as they are not excessive.

However, if managers had a choice, they wouldn't accept visible body-art among the workforce. None of the managers we interviewed was keen to divert away from the enduring legacy of aesthetic labour; and the need to project a professional and appropriate image to guests. An interesting statement by a manager is indicative of this attitude: 'although I have two tattoos, don't even think of adopting a tattoo' – meaning that, although the manager was inked, he wouldn't suggest tattoos to anyone interested in a career in hospitality. He further explained, 'I inked myself when I was young and tattoos were not that popular. I kept them hidden day and night. They may be popular but in our sector are still unwelcomed'.

The question is, if they don't want this situation, why do they allow it? Their consent is attributed to considerable labour shortages in the hospitality sector, in combination with high labour turnover, the ever increasing rates of tourist arrivals and the growing popularity of body-art among customers and employees. 'Until a year ago, visible tattoos were by no means tolerated. Now, we relax our aesthetic policies too. Not because we want to promote inclusivity, but simply because labour during summer is scarce', a manager mentioned. Another manager added, 'we had to re-examine our appearance standards, accepting that tattoos is a way to broaden our recruitment pool during peak season'. In a four-star hotel, a general manager admitted: '[w]e hire them but we ask them to cover up'. Another interesting statement was 'we changed our policies but not our standards', meaning that visible tattoos are accepted with a heavy heart, only because they have to cope with labour market shortages. Softening up their aesthetic policies started as a conditional acceptance that gradually became a norm. These findings resonate with previous studies, suggesting that 'unless somebody has a completely bizarre face tattoo or piercing then, as long as they fit other emotional and aesthetic labour criteria, they will get a job because of the lack of available labour' (Efthymiou, 2018, p. 105).

In some hotels, moreover, managers expressed themselves positively about tattoos. Four managers were inked and another two expressed an intention of adopting a tattoo. Another manager mentioned, 'I like to see tattoos on people. Some of them are nice'. *A small cute tattoo may be acceptable*, a female manager said. 'I would love to have a couple of tattoos. But my wife decided negatively on my behalf', a manager mentioned while laughing. *I know fellow General Managers with tattoos*, she added. But, despite their gravitation towards body-art, their professional mentality, opinion and workplace politics regarding aesthetic policies remain unchanged. They all agreed that if they had a choice, they would rather not hire employees with visible tattoos whereas hair shall be neatly groomed; female workers' piercings should not be excessive; and male piercings at the workplace should be avoided (except where authority has been granted otherwise, which is the case in four of the hotels we interviewed).

When asked about the number of tattooed workers on their payroll, 17 managers could only offer estimations. There was only one hotel with a tattoo-related question being part of its hiring process. Its manager claimed: *[m]ost of our hiring interviews take place in winter where applicants wear long-sleeve clothes. To avoid unpleasant surprises in the summer, we tend to ask. Based on our records, at least one third of our employees are tattooed. You need to be able to judge during the interview.* Although not precisely, the remaining managers seemed to know a lot about inked personnel. Possibly, because employees often arrive to work with Bermuda shorts and short-sleeve shirts for a shift in the pool bar, breakfast restaurant or other parts of the hotel. Also, employees are asked to make their body-work visible and self-fashioning part of the product for specific events in the hotels. As a manager said, 'in pop music events and pirate nights, we ask them to reveal all those tattoos that we normally ask them to hide'. Another manager explained how employees are expected to arrive 20 minutes earlier to get ready. They often help each other while trying to fix their extreme hairstyles. In a 5-star hotel, these kind of events are 'male employees' opportunity to put on their piercings'. Similarly, '[e]verything can be accepted if it suits the club's theme, our Hawaiian themed beach-parties and Latin dancing Fridays', a manager claimed. When asked a question on recruitment and selection, a manager laughed and said, '[y]es, in these instances, tattoos and piercings are considered to be an additional qualification'.

Additionally, all managers agreed that men should not wear a beard. They claimed reasons of hygiene and appearance. 12 out of 18 hotels prefer male employees without a ponytail; 6 hotels accept it if neatly groomed. All managers agreed that no negative feedback has been received by guests regarding body-art so far. Three multinational chain hotels use typified hiring techniques to measure

Table 1. Hotel Categories: Characteristics and Responses to Worker Body-Art.

Upper Market Hotels

Predominantly informal hiring processes; subject to each manager's judgement; hiring rules not necessarily consulted during the selection process.

Hotels forced to employ inked workers (both visible and non-visible) due to labour shortage, which entails a form of indirect discrimination.

Workers' aesthetic choices/identity expressions (e.g. tattoos, piercings, hairstyles) appropriated by management for certain events, such as disco-nights and themed nights.

Conditional body-art acceptance gradually became a norm.

Lifestyle Hotels

Informal and relaxed hiring processes.

Body-art culture encouraged among guests and customers.

Workers' appearance tie with hotels' aesthetic philosophy.

Visible body-art a qualification rather than a liability.

Lifestyle hotels part of cultural clusters.

Luxury Hotels

Formal, standardised hiring processes in all hotels.

Emphasis on culture that excludes worker body-art.

Meticulous appearance regulation, linked to performance appraisal.

Stereotyping and discrimination on the base that tattooed workers cannot conform with hotel culture and aesthetic philosophy.

emotional capacity and appropriateness. All the rest rely on informal hiring, where managers evaluate workers' appropriateness during meetings.

Overall, as presented in Table 1, tattoos in upper market hotels are neither prohibited, nor embraced. Remarkably, behaviour that was deemed unacceptable in the past is gradually becoming part of hotels' standard work processes due to employment shortages. Actions that would normally count as a major aesthetic sin and automatically be condemned by management, such as workers adopting a visible tattoo, are now somehow accepted. Likewise, employees who would secretly maintain a hidden tattoo may now be asked to make it visible, in themed events and disco nights. Our findings reconfirm the changing aesthetic landscape in certain service workplaces (e.g. Efthymiou, 2018; Timming, 2017). However, as we explain in the next section, each hotel category responds differently to societal change.

Emerging Lifestyle Hotel Categories: Body Art is Part of the Setting

Having presented the findings collected in upper market hotels, we now turn to the second category comprising our sample: 'lifestyle hotels'. Usually a sub-category of boutique hotels, lifestyle establishments include a range of stylish, funky and fashionable establishments, which reinforce self-identity and consumers' lifestyle. As such, they are considered to be more customer-centric than traditional hotel brands (Jones et al., 2013). For the purpose of this study, we visited three establishments whereby two of them were self-identified as purposely friendly to customers with non-standard body-art. As a manager in the first hotel explained:

> [a]lthough not all customers are inked or pierced, many of them celebrate their lifestyle, which is very much related to body-art and appearance. They arrive from all over the world to combine sun, sea and tattoo conventions. They have certain expectations and know how to share their story online [positive or negative] with other body-art enthusiasts. If they are happy, they keep coming back. We offer them special rates near the annual convention season. We also approach social media reviewers acting as body-art influencers with complimentary offers.

Lifestyle hotels offer guests the opportunity to network with other body-art enthusiasts, tattoo artists and keep updated on new trends. Guests are connected by common lifestyle characteristics, whereas many of them are part of a large and growing market of Millennials. To these travellers, body-art is becoming an essential component in deciding in which hotel to stay. Their choices are guided by social media and body-art influencer reviews. It also seems that lifestyle hotels are strategically located in areas formulating body-art clusters. They are located near tattoos studios, contemporary art galleries, street festivals and clubs that organise dedicated body-art activities. In one of the hotels, the manager explained that body-art enthusiasts seek sites where they can hang out, meet and socialise with fellow enthusiasts. Lifestyle establishments do that – they enable guests to experience and reproduce this kind of culture.

Workers too, however, have a role to play in the development of memorable and authentic aesthetic experiences. Employees in lifestyle hotels are encouraged to display their self-identity and personalities. Their tattoos and piercings are not antithetical to the hotel's overall workplace setting. On the contrary, managers too seem to embrace wider social trends. In one of the hotels, we had the opportunity to sit and discuss with two managers simultaneously. The first manager said 'I love tattoos, it's social energy. You can't stop the urban energy that comes with it. . . tattoos are part of the setting and an inseparable part of our philosophy'. Along the same lines, the second manager mentioned rather seriously: 'here, body-art is not simply acceptable, but rather desired. If you don't have tattoos, possibly you are not appropriate for the job'. 'Our employees share similar lifestyles with guests', she continued, while we were getting served by a male waiter, tattoo-collector with black nail polish.

Much of the guest influx is often attributed to workers inasmuch as their body-art, which is part of the hotels' artistic design, attracts customers with similar likes and preferences. These findings (also presented in Table 1), resonate with some of the studies presented earlier (e.g. Timming, 2017), explaining how companies project a brand-congruent physical appearance through body-art. Adding to those studies, we also found that workers are more likely to apply for work to body-art friendly establishments, such as boutique and lifestyle hotels, rather than upper market and luxury hotels. This is an important finding, which is directly linked to the labour market structure and how it evolves in the light of social changes. As one of the managers explained, 'at a time where labour is scarce, our approach attracts a lot of good workers. Some of them are heavily tattooed, individuals with great skills and character'. The second manager said: 'we keep the door open to heavily tattooed people, both guests and employees. Some of our guests right now are here for the 6th Cyprus International Tattoo Convention. They are studio employees, tattoo artists and piercers from all over the world who love getting served by waiters sharing the same passion'. In a country where hospitality employees are scarce during the peak season, lifestyle hotels seem to have adequate job applicants and low labour turnover. Recruiting and selecting inked and pierced employees helps them solve the hiring difficulties that are common in other hotel categories, as explained below.

Normative Control and Zero-Tolerance to Body-Art in Multinational Luxury Hotels

In total, we managed to conduct four interviews in luxury establishments, with two of them being domestic and the other two being part of multinational chain corporations (MNCs). As presented in Table 1, their recruitment and selection practices are formal and standardised. Aesthetic regulation and personality filtering is also important inasmuch as workers' commitment to service is key.

As with previous observations in the literature, the luxury hotels we visited are highly aestheticised workplaces, characterised by an emphasis on culture, status and perceived elegance. Their guests enjoy luxurious moments (Sherman, 2007) and engage with employees in classy interactions (Warhurst & Nickson, 2007). This experience and interactions are regulated through close aesthetic monitoring, which rejects any form of visible tattoos or other excessive body art expressions. All managers expressed a clear disagreement to all visible forms of body-art. This disagreement is characterised by a blend of brand management, cultural management and stereotyping. Some of the responses are indicative:

- Hotel 1: 'Our aesthetic and behavioural policies are standardized throughout the world'.
- Hotel 2: 'Tattoos do not align with our culture of respect, it's against the "can do" philosophy and culture we have around here. To align with our hotel's philosophy, all employees, anywhere in the hotel, should be tolerant and considerate. Tattoos are against the hotel's philosophy and culture'.
- Hotel 3: 'tattoos express people who are uncompromised. They carry messages of noncompliance. In the hotel, we support, respect, tolerance, friendliness and compliance as part of our brand value proposition. Individuals with tattoos are against the hotel's philosophy of respect and the principles of our value proposition. A tattoo signals in the opposite direction, it runs counter to good organizational citizenship, it's a rebellious act'.
- Hotel 4: 'Tattoos harm yourself; they also carry messages of deviance'.

Based on our findings, the hiring possibilities of tattooed workers in luxury hotels are highly reduced. This is because tattoos are associated with deviance and unconformity – a status that contradicts the 'image management' of luxurious settings. This is not new of course. Our findings resonate with previous literature, focusing on how corporations strive to project a brand-congruent physical appearance (Hall & van den Broek, 2011; Timming, 2017). The main principle of image management does not seem to be very different between luxury hotels and other categories, such as lifestyle hotels. Managers set standards and work towards their implementation while trying to provide guests with authentic experiences. To do so, they match workers' appearance to the hotel's aesthetic philosophy and staged surroundings (Efthymiou et al., 2020). However, what is different in luxury hotels concerning body-art is the perception of managers. Not only they disapprove tattoos at the workplace, but they also reject their usefulness in the wider society. They perceive tattoos as unnecessary, harmful modifications, which can cause health damage. Managers' responses remind us that tattooed and pierced individuals can be stigmatised and become subjects of prejudice. Such findings convey implications concerning career planning for students and recent graduates, whose decisions regarding body art should not be disconnected from their future career intentions.

Managers were also asked if they would lay off an existing employee who decides to adopt a visible tattoo. Two managers responded positively, another one skipped the question and the fourth manager responded: *I wouldn't fire the employee, the organization culture and climate will do so. At this level, (s)he will be expelled by the organisation's culture. She/he will become a foreign body.*

Finally, much of workers' labour, both aesthetic and emotional, is monitored and measured. Although hotels in all three categories are subject to digital customer ratings and feedback, which is collected and evaluated by managers through internal software systems, luxury hotels offered descriptions of a far more holistic approach. A manager described how they conduct internal surveys with customers on a daily basis – about 15–20 personal interviews with customers everyday through schemes that are known as 'Climate Surveys'. The survey results aim at cross-checking employee performance with customer perceived brand value and expectations. Then, employees are invited to interviews as part of a triangulation process. Also, all four hotels, domestic and MNCs, assign their 'mystery shoppers' programmes to consultancy companies like Ernst & Young and Deloitte. These findings reveal the increasing role of public customer reviews and ratings as part of a wider measurability realm, which expands to incorporate several work aspects, including aesthetic performance.

The normative control, together with digitised and physical surveillance of aesthetic expectations, reveal the restrictions that tattooed and pierced individuals are likely to face in this hotel category. To assist future career decisions and appearance choices, we present a list of recommendations in the next section.

Discussion and Recommendations for Career Planning

In this chapter, we contribute to an ongoing discussion in the field of aesthetic labour by presenting approaches to body-art in three hotel categories, namely: (a) upper market hotels; (b) fashionable lifestyle establishments; and (c) luxury hotels. In each of these categories, the approaches and responses to worker body-art differ. This contradiction reveals that we have just started forming an understanding of the way body-art is dealt with in different industries, sectors, job roles or organisations. We know even less about workers' changing lifestyle decisions, and whether they are forced to leave an industry or choose alternative employment. Based on the findings, we offer the following recommendations on career planning in the hospitality sector:

- Students and young professionals are advised to cultivate skills and appearance qualifications that are relevant to future organisations' needs. Based on the findings we presented earlier, adopting visible tattoos excludes an applicant from a luxury hotel and increases hireablity in a lifestyle hotel. But, in essence, the principle of image management is not very different between lifestyle and luxury hotels. Managers in both categories set standards to match workers' appearance to the hotel's aesthetic philosophy, surroundings and clientele. Likewise, workers' career progression can be planned careful, by taking into consideration personal preferences and each category's specifics.

- When it comes to managing a career, workers are in charge. This happens when workers discover their interests and values. Only then a worker is able to make the right career decisions. Matching personal interests with right career choices may help the individual to use the aesthetic standards in the organisation to his/her advantage and enjoy positive effects on self-esteem, which is likely to result to a successful career (Nath et al., 2016).
- Set goals and tracked accomplishments should take into consideration possible aesthetic and personality expectations. Likewise, becoming a tattoo collector does not guarantee employment in a lifestyle hotel. Personality plays an equal role and applicants are encouraged to consider developing a 'personal brand'.
- Workers are encouraged to forge relationships within the company and industry. An employee who maintains an open communication channel with his/her managers, and a steady, long-lasting work performance, will be able to discuss intentions of adopting visible body-art and match future career plans with identity expressions.

While planning, choosing or managing a career, students or employees may also consider the following questions:

- Does this career allow me to adopt the appearance characteristics and modifications that are important to me?
- Likewise, do these appearance modifications allow me to follow the career that is most interesting to me?
- What kind of body-art would be the costliest – in professional regrets and missed opportunities – if adopted? Likewise, what career goals are likely to result to personal lifestyle regrets? Is it possible to strike a balance between the two? As explained earlier, while body-art may be considered as a qualification in one establishment, it is unconditionally restricted in another. Is it worth sacrificing certain personal or career goals?
- If there are discrepancies between what is important to an individual in terms of employment and body-art choices, it may be worth asking: How am I feeling in each domain of my life: work, home, community and self? Based on this evaluation, an employee may take serious steps towards changing a workplace (without necessarily withdrawing from the industry).

Finally, work is an important activity. It is a social process we are all invited to participate in (Efthymiou, 2010). However, workplaces often become settings of antagonistic and dialectic power interplay (Efthymiou & Michael, 2016). Candidates may be judged based on their appearance, either positively (e.g. in lifestyle hotels) or negatively (e.g. in luxury hotels). Workers' career progression may be subject to prejudicial managerial attitudes. Also, individuals may have to deal with potentially discriminatory aesthetic practices of hiring and promotion. Therefore, students and young professionals should consider personal aesthetic preferences as part of their career planning.

References

Adelman, M. B., Ahuvia, A., & Goodwin, C. (1994). Beyond smiling: Social support and service quality. *Service Quality: New Directions in Theory and Practice*, 139–171.

Antreou, R. (2021). General Manager of McDonald's Cyprus. Personal discussion at McDonald's Cyprus Headquarters, Larnaca, Cyprus. 12 January 2021.

Atkinson, M. (2003). The civilizing of resistance: Straightedge tattooing. *Deviant Behavior*, *24*(3), 197–220.

Baumann, C., Timming, A. R., & Gollan, P. J. (2016). Taboo tattoos? A study of the gendered effects of body art on consumers' attitudes toward visibly tattooed front line staff. *Journal of Retailing and Consumer Services*, *29*, 31–39.

Bekhor, P. S., Bekhor, L., & Gandrabur, M. (1995). Employer attitudes toward persons with visible tattoos. *Australasian Journal of Dermatology*, *36*(2), 75–77.

Belden, E. (2016). Tattoo's dark days – Ancient Greece & Rome. Tattoo.com. https://www.tattoo.com/blog/tattoos-dark-days-ancient-greece-rome/. Accessed on Jan 7, 2020.

Belkin, S. (2021). *Your co-worker undressed: Tattoos, identity, and stigma in the American white collar workplace*. University of Leicester. Thesis. https://doi.org/10.25392/leicester.data.14762049.v1

Bitner, M. J. (1990). Evaluating service encounters: The effects of physical surroundings and employee responses. *Journal of Marketing*, *54*, 69–82.

Brallier, S. A., Maguire, K. A., Smith, D., & Palm, L. J. (2011). Visible tattoos and employment in the restaurant service industry. *International Journal of Business and Social Science*, *2*(6), 72–76.

Bryant, A., & Charmaz, K. (Eds.). (2019). *The SAGE handbook of current developments in grounded theory*. Sage.

Crang, P. (1997). Performing the tourist product. In C. Rojek & J. Urry (Eds.), *Touring Cultures: Transformation of Travel and Theory*. Routledge.

Dean, D. H. (2010). Consumer perceptions of visible tattoos on service personnel. *Managing Service Quality*, *20*(3), 294–308.

Edwards, J. (2003, October 16). Saving face. *Brandweek*, 16.

Efthymiou, L. (2010). *Workplace control and resistance from below: An ethnographic study in a Cypriot luxury hotel*. Unpublished PhD Thesis. https://leicester.figshare.com/articles/thesis/Workplace_Control_and_Resistance_from_Below_An_Ethnographic_Study_in_a_Cypriot_Luxury_Hotel/10103318/1. Accessed on March 25, 2019.

Efthymiou, L. (2018). Worker body-art in upper-market hotels: Neither accepted, nor prohibited. *International Journal of Hospitality Management*, *74*, 99–108.

Efthymiou, L. (2022). Staged Authenticity. In D. Buhalis (Ed.), *Encyclopedia of tourism management and marketing*. Edward Elgar Publishing. https://doi.org/10.4337/9781800377486.staged.authenticity

Efthymiou, L., & Michael, S. (2016). The Cyprus cash crash: A case of collective punishment. In B. Batiz-Lazo & L. Efthymiou (Eds.), *The book of payments: Historical and contemporary views on the cashless economy*. Palgrave McMillan.

Efthymiou, L., Orphanidou, Y., & Panayiotou, G. (2020). Delineating the changing frontstage and backstage segregation in high-end and luxury hotels. *Hospitality & Society*, *10*(3), 287–312. https://doi.org/10.1386/hosp_00025_1

Elzweig, B., & Peeples, D. K. (2011). Tattoos and piercings: Issues of body modification and the workplace. *SAM Advanced Management Journal, 76*(1), 13–23.

Fleming, P. (2015). *Resisting work: The corporatization of life and its discontents.* Temple University Press.

Fleming, P., & Spicer, A. (2007). *Contesting the corporation: Struggle, power and resistance in organizations.* Cambridge University Press.

Fleming, P., & Sturdy, A. (2009). "Just be yourself!": Towards neo-normative control in organisations? *Employee Relations, 31*(6), 569–583. https://doi.org/10.1108/01425450910991730

Fleming, P., & Sturdy, A. (2011). 'Being yourself ' in the electronic sweatshop: New forms of normative control. *Human Relations, 64*(2), 177–200. https://doi.org/10.1177/0018726710375481

French, M., Mortensen, K., & Timming, A. (2018). Are tattoos associated with employment and wage discrimination? Analyzing the relationships between body art and labor market outcomes. *Human Relations, 72*(5), 962–987.

Gioia, D. A., Corley, K. G., & Hamilton, A. L. (2013). Seeking qualitative rigor in inductive research: Notes on the Gioia methodology. *Organizational Research Methods, 16*(1), 15–31. https://doi.org/10.1177/1094428112452151

Hadjioannou, B. (2019). Cystat: July tourist arrivals set record. https://in-cyprus.com/cystat-july-tourist-arrivals-set-record/. Accessed on Jan 5, 2020.

Hall, R., & van den Broek, D. (2011). Aestheticising retail workers: Orientations of aesthetic labour in Australian fashion retail. *Economic and Industrial Democracy, 33*(1), 85–102.

Jefferys, S. (2000). Body art and social status: Cutting, tattooing, and piercing from a feminist prospective. *Feminism & Psychology, 10*, 409–429.

Jones, D., Day, J., & Quadri-Felitti, D. (2013). Emerging definitions of boutique and lifestyle hotels: A Delphi study. *Journal of Travel & Tourism Marketing, 30*(7), 715–731.

Kang, M., & Jones, K. (2007). Why do people get tattoos? *Contexts, 6*(1), 42–47.

Nath, V., Bach, S., & Lockwood, G. (2016). Dress codes and appearance at work: Body supplements, body modification and aesthetic labour. https://archive.acas.org.uk/media/4649/Dress-codes-and-appearance-at-work-Body-supplements-body-modification-and-aesthetic-labour/pdf/Acas_Dress_codes_and_appearance_at_work.pdf. Accessed on December 20, 2019.

Nickson, D., Warhurst, C., Cullen, A. M., & Watt, A. (2003). Bringing in the excluded? Aesthetic labour, skills, and training in the 'new' economy. *Journal of Education and Work, 16*(2), 185–203.

Pinto, L., Vieira, B., & Fernandes, T. (2019). 'Service with a piercing': Does it (really) influence guests' perceptions of attraction, confidence and competence of hospitality receptionists? *International Journal of Hospitality Management, 86*, 102365.

Pitts, V. (2003). *In the flesh: The cultural politics of body modification.* Palgrave Macmillan.

Saldaña, J. (2015). *The coding manual for qualitative researchers.* Sage.

Sanders, C. R., & Vail, D. A. (2008). *Customising the body.* Temple University Press.

Sexton, M. C., Friedly, E., & Carter, J. (2023). Professionalism and body modifications: Considerations of library leadership. *Journal of Library Administration.* https://doi.org/10.1080/01930826.2022.2159241

Sherman, R. (2007). *Class acts: Service and inequality in luxury hotels.* University of California Press.

Swanger, N. (2006). Visible body modification (VBM): Evidence from human resource managers and recruiters and the effects on employment. *International Journal of Hospitality Management, 25*(1), 154–158.

Tews, M., & Stafford, K. (2019). The relationship between tattoos and employee workplace deviance. *Journal of Hospitality & Tourism Research, 43*(7), 1025–1043.

Theopoulou, T. (2019, August 13). Four new 5-star hotels in Cyprus within four years. *Cyprus.* https://in-cyprus.philenews.com/four-new-5-starhotels-in-cyprus-within-four-years/. Accessed on June 5, 2020.

Timming, A. R. (2015). Visible tattoos in the service sector: A new challenge to recruitment and selection. *Work, Employment & Society, 29*(1), 60–78.

Timming, A. R. (2017). Body art as branded labour: At the intersection of employee selection and relationship marketing. *Human Relations, 70*(9), 1041–1063.

Warhurst, C., & Nickson, D. (2007). A new labour aristocracy? Aesthetic labour and routine interactive service. *Work, Employment & Society, 21*(4), 785–798.

Warhurst, C., Nickson, D., Witz, A., & Cullen, A. M. (2000). Aesthetic labour in interactive service work: Some case study evidence from the 'New' Glasgow. *Service Industries Journal, 20*(3), 1–18.

Williams, T. (2014). *Let us have visible tattoos!!!.* https://www.coworker.org/petitions/let-us-have-visible-tattoos

Witz, A., Warhurst, C., & Nickson, D. (2003). The labour of aesthetics and the aesthetics of organization. *Organization, 10*(1), 33–54.

Wu, L., King, C., Lu, L., & Guchait, P. (2019). Hospitality aesthetic labor management: Consumers' and prospective employees' perspectives of hospitality brands. *International Journal of Hospitality Management, 87*(May). https://doi.org/10.1016/j.ijhm.2019.102373

Chapter 18

A Tattooed Workforce – Still a Liability?

Beth Wood and Adelina Broadbridge

Abstract

This chapter investigates the issue of tattoos and examines whether the presence of visible tattoos still influences front line workers' employment chances. It finds that irrespective of a general societal shift towards greater tattoo acceptance and integration into modern society, negative stereotypes about tattoos still exist. Acceptance of tattoos in the workplace was dependent on the nature, size and location of the tattoo, as well as the occupation in question, and individual customer characteristics. Respondents were generally more accepting of tattoos on people nowadays. However, there was concern that employees with visible tattoos may still face stigma in the workplace. The findings revealed that most people will cover up a tattoo during an interview out of fear of negative discrimination by the interviewer.

Keywords: Visible tattoos; stigma; acceptance; discrimination; perceptions; customers; workplace

Introduction

One's appearance can be regarded as very important in the workplace (Karl et al., 2013) and can have a very real impact on how employees are perceived (Peluchette et al., 2006; Timming et al., 2017; Yates et al., 2016). Yorke (2004, p. 410) defined employability as a 'set of skills, understandings, achievements and personal attributes that allows an individual to gain employment'. Recent work has shown how appearance can be an important component of the personal attributes required for employability, and is an area of increasing concern for individuals in search of a job (Carbery & Cross, 2015).

Simultaneously, there has been some recent controversy over whether visible tattoos are still regarded as offensive in the workplace, and whether this is an outdated view given their ubiquity in modern day society. With 26% of the British

The Emerald Handbook of Appearance in the Workplace, 317–330
Copyright © 2024 by Emerald Publishing Limited
All rights of reproduction in any form reserved
doi:10.1108/978-1-80071-174-720230019

public now having tattoos, including 11% having visible tattoos (Kirk, 2022), now is an apposite time to explore this topic further. Previous research shows evidence that tattoos render people less employable or present significant barriers to their employment (Arndt et al., 2016, 2017; Brallier et al., 2011; Nickson et al., 2005; Salary.com, 2018; Swanger, 2006; Timming, 2015; Timming et al., 2017; Thomas et al., 2010). Others suggest this is not always the case (French et al., 2016, 2019; Hopf, 2018; Robin, 2018), while others have found mixed evidence (Bennington, 2019; Dillingh et al., 2016; Efthymiou, 2018; Thomas, 2019; Timming, 2017). More recently, researchers are questioning whether tattoos are indeed seen as offensive in the workplace. For example, Hopf (2018) indicated that within the hospitality industry, some hotels and cafes are more open minded to the appearance of their employees nowadays, a finding also borne out by Efthymiou et al. (chapter 17). On the other hand, Botz-Bornstein (2013) argues there has only been a gradual shift in levels of acceptability of tattoos. Nickson et al. (2001) highlighted that workers' personal characteristics and appearance were linked to their suitability for a specific role, particularly in service organisations where there is face-to-face interaction between customer and employee. Relating the work on aesthetic labour to the stigma, stereotyping and prejudice existent towards tattoos, we might consider that having visible tattoos could affect the employability of an individual (Timming et al., 2017).

In this chapter, we examine the general literature on tattoos and their effect on workplace employment. We then illustrate some recent findings from a study undertaken on whether the presence of visible tattoos still influences front line workers' employment chances/employability.

Literature Review

Historically, tattoos held negative connotations, being associated with marginalised groups such as gangs, prisoners, bikers, sailors, soldiers and certain blue-collar occupations (French et al., 2016; Zestcott et al., 2017). Tattoos therefore signalised 'group-affiliation' and solidarity (Miller et al., 2009) and were associated with deviance and negative or risk taking behaviours (Heywood et al., 2012; Laumann & Derick, 2006; Lipscomb et al., 2008; Zestcott et al., 2017). This led to many tattooed people being stigmatised. Goffman (1963) maintained that stigma is an attribute, behaviour or reputation which is socially discrediting in a particular way, causing an individual to be classified by others as undesirable in some way rather than in an accepted, 'normal' one. Timming (2015) claims that stigma can result from a 'surface-level' characteristic, meaning that it depends on the physical and aesthetic appearance of an individual, which is easily judged in an interview setting. By dividing society into two distinguished groups, the 'stigmatised' and the 'normals', (tattooed and the non-tattooed people), Goffman's framework can be useful to analyse the interactions between the two actors, the 'normal' interviewer and 'stigmatised' tattooed worker during a 'mixed-interaction' – the interview (Heatherton, 2003). Hence, Goffman's theory is useful in detailing how stigma occurs, explaining how quickly a tattooed individual can be stigmatised in an interview or other workplace situation. So stigma encompasses stereotypes, prejudice, discrimination and power differentials (Benbow & Jolley, 2012), and being stigmatised has the potential to negatively affect an individual's employment chances (Timming et al., 2017). This includes having a visible tattoo (Herek, 2002), and tattooed individuals may face negative consequences from employers and customers in relation to their tattoos. Ellis (2015) even found fellow workers classified tattooed individuals as less qualified and less professional than non-tattooed peers. Furthermore, stigmatisation can result in decreased network ties, increased vulnerability and lowered self-esteem (Falk, 2001), all of which may negatively affect employment chances.

Associations of Tattoos

While not a protected category, appearance is a real issue with regards to discrimination and has surfaced terms like 'lookism' (Cavico et al., 2012; Warhurst et al., 2012), 'branded labour' (Pettinger, 2004; Timming, 2017), 'looks based appearance' (Bruton, 2015) and 'aesthetic labour' (Warhurst et al., 2000) where employees are recruited on the basis of their looks in a range of occupations and organisations, particularly within the service sector. Some say that this has resulted from the increased sovereignty of the customer in the service sector, especially in jobs involving face-to-face interaction (Nickson et al., 2001; Warhurst et al., 2000). The work on aesthetic labour has introduced a marketing perspective, shedding light on how important an employee's physical appearance is when trying to get a job in the service-sector. Due to the face-to-face interactions that workers will have with the customer, self-presentation that is aligned with the organisation's brand is paramount in representing the company's intended image.

Within the employment context, various studies have shown the negative associations of tattoos especially when considering customer facing roles (c.f. Arndt et al., 2016, 2017; Baumann et al., 2016; Bekhor et al., 1995; Dean, 2010, 2011; Doleac & Stein, 2013; French et al., 2016; Karl et al., 2016; Schultz et al., 2015; Timming, 2015). Employees represent the brand image of the company. (Karl et al., 2013; Nickson & Baum, 2017; Pettinger, 2004; Warhurst & Nickson, 2020; Williams & Connell, 2010). Customers perceive the image of the company through the contact they have with the workforce, thus making employee appearance important to some companies in their efforts to market the right image to their clientele, and therefore to provide commercial benefit for the organisation (Nickson et al., 2003; Witz et al., 2003). The traditional negative association with tattoos means that this brand image could be tarnished in some way, leading to transference of any negative biases held by the customers about tattoos onto the company (Arndt et al., 2017). French et al. (2016) contend that visible tattoos may reduce an employee's ability to effectively interact with customers because their body-art may offend or intimidate customers. This has a resultant outcome on perceived customer service and thus business success. Hence employers may be dissuaded from hiring a tattooed person for fear of the potential risky associations they convey for the business.

Timming (2015) showed that when recruiting tattooed workers, managers felt constrained by the broader societal judgements and customer viewpoints when making hiring decisions. Arndt et al. (2017) discovered similar findings – dentists made assumptions about their customers' perceptions of dental hygienists having tattoos when making recruitment decisions. Managers in both situations were not swayed by their own personal opinions, rather it was their customers' potentially negative perceptions that they based their decisions upon.

Factors Affecting Customer Perceptions of Tattoos

Extant literature has shown the factors that may alter customer perceptions of tattoos, and these can be split into three different segments: customer vs non-customer facing roles, different types of customer-facing service roles and the content, size and location of tattoo. Timming (2015) argued recruiters are less prejudicial when hiring for non-customer facing roles.

Some types of job roles may be regarded as less appropriate to have tattoos than others. Dean (2010) showed that visible tattoos on white-collar workers are deemed more inappropriate than similar tattoos on blue-collar personnel. He also found older consumers regard tattooed workers as less intelligent and less honest. This highlights that important job roles with more responsibilities require better customer perceptions in order to instil trust in the worker and the service being provided. Likewise, various researches have revealed that tattoos on employees in the health care sector can attract negative attention. For example, Winfield (2014) noted that tattoos are still taboo in healthcare and may lead to patients questioning a Doctor's personal hygiene, while Foster (2016) found that older patients view tattoos as 'untidy appearance' which gives the impression of poor hygiene standards and low professional competence. Moreover, Arndt et al. (2017) and Verissimo et al. (2016) revealed tattoos on workers in healthcare professions, specifically dentists, are viewed as inappropriate, lowering their perceived professionalism and potentially inhibiting whether a patient returns to their care. Tattoos in the hospitality and food industry have also been restricted due to beliefs that they compromise hygiene (Mengual et al., 2016; Swanger, 2006).

Tattoo genre is another feature that may affect perceptions of tattoos by the public, and certain images can reinforce prejudice and may offend certain people. Whereas innocuous tattoos such as flowers and butterflies are more widely accepted, those that portray violence, death, drug abuse or political views are more likely to offend people (Timming, 2015).

Location of the tattoo also influences customers' prejudicial views and consequently employment chances (French et al., 2016; Timming, 2015); with those displayed on the hands, neck or face considered as particular threatening. Arndt et al. (2017) state that not all tattoos are equally stigmatised because they vary greatly in size, location and meaning. They suggest that smaller tattoos are easier to cover up, while larger tattoos are open to more stigmatisation in service settings. In relation to career development, Baumann et al. (2016) acknowledge that employees need to consider their visible tattoos carefully and understand the size and type of tattoos may hinder their career opportunities.

Arndt and Glassman (2012) studied the varying opinions of tattoos, focusing on gender differences and how they affect perceptions. Their study suggested that masculine tattoos are more negatively rated than feminine tattoos on women and that feminine tattoos on males are not considered appropriate either. This demonstrates the power of people's perceptions in the requirement to conform to expected societal norms and stereotypes.

Of course, another factor that may influence how a customer perceives a tattooed worker is whether or not they have a tattoo themselves. Hawkes et al.'s (2004) study showed there was significant difference between the opinions of individuals with tattoos than those without them, and typically people without tattoos viewed them more negatively than tattooed individuals do.

The above points highlight that customer perceptions of tattoos can vary considerably and be somewhat subjective.

Shifting Attitudes Towards Tattoos?

Organisations are free to formulate policies against tattoos if they feel they are inappropriate for the specific job-role or do not fit with the company's brand image. Some researchers however, have identified that this may be misguided owing to the upsurge of tattoos in modern society and their wider acceptability (Elzweig & Peeples, 2011; Timming et al., 2017). These shifting attitudes have seen their increased popularity from the marginalised sectors of society to wider demographic, cultural and generational groups (French et al., 2016). Tattoos have emerged in present-day culture and are now associated with popular icons and celebrities, revealing a movement towards self-expression and increasing acceptance. Many negative connotations with them have declined (Larsen et al., 2014), signifying their detachment with outcast social groups (Miller et al., 2009; Roberts, 2012; Swanger, 2006).

While French et al. (2016) acknowledge their mounting social acceptability, policies about tattoos in the workplace tend to be more conservative. Timming et al. (2017), however, argue that HR policies need to be revisited so they remain up-to-date and reflective of the world outside the workplace. This indicates the reason why some organisations may choose to be lenient with tattoos in their HR policy. This clemency may however jar with how customers feel about being served by tattooed workers, as visible tattoos in service-roles still sometimes get attention and provoke negativity (Baumann et al., 2016).

In contrast to the negative research, tattoos can be seen as an asset to particular organisations if they are consistent with the organisation's overall brand personality. This work introduces the term 'branded-labour', which deals with employee appearance on the consumption side, by focusing on customer perceptions of the front-line workers' (Pettinger, 2004). If an organisation is targeting a younger, more 'edgier' demographic, then having front-line workers with tattoos may be more coherent with their branding strategy (Timming, 2017). Arndt et al. (2017) comments on the positive stereotypes associated with tattoos, such as creativity and freedom, meaning it is possible for these traits to transfer to their organisational image as well. A shift from the stigmatised negative viewpoint of tattoos to a wider acceptance into mainstream society has been described as a 'tattoo-renaissance' (Kosut, 2006) which also helps to explain why some organisations may see tattoos on an employee as a strength; positively contributing towards their brand and enhancing the relationship marketing with the customer.

Methodology

A mixed methods approach was adopted for this research to enable a more holistic view of the subject matter by gathering different perspectives and different types of data (Matthews & Ross, 2014). The aim was to gauge public opinion on visible tattoos generally and within the workplace specifically. The objectives therefore were to ascertain:

- customer attitudes towards employees with visible tattoos across different job-roles;
- whether customer perceptions are affected by their own personal characteristics and the presence of tattoos themselves;
- businesses reactions to visible tattoos on employees and whether they affect employment decisions.

A non-probability convenience sample using social media sites such as Facebook and Twitter was used to distribute an online survey to UK adults over the age of 18. The questionnaire examined how respondents depicted a tattooed person, the associations they assigned to them and any stereotypes that surfaced surrounding them.

A major question in the survey aimed to find out how appropriate respondents rated tattoos on workers in different job roles/professions. It explored respondents' thoughts regarding the appropriateness of tattoos in 18 various workplace settings, particularly in face-to-face service encounters. The jobs were categorised into low to medium skilled jobs and high-skilled. Some jobs included a hygiene element which enabled a further check to determine whether job roles that require cleanliness, a tidy uniform and good hygiene had any effect on the views of respondents (see Table 1).

The questionnaire went on to enquire whether visible tattoos should be covered up in the workplace and in interview situations. Two open-ended questions were included in order to explore in more depth how tattoos are viewed in the workplace and interview situations. Certain demographic data were collected from the respondents including whether they themselves had a tattoo. The questionnaire, which was analysed using SPSS, yielded 403 responses comprising 71.5% women; 73% under the age of 40; 50.5% of respondents having a tattoo themselves.

Table 1. Different Job Categories.

Low to Medium Skill/Low Hygiene	*High Skill/Low Hygiene*
• Retail sales assistant	• Bank teller
• Office or hotel receptionist	• Lawyer
• Tradesman	• Lecturer or school teacher
• Beautician or hairdresser	• Police
Low to Medium Skill/High Hygiene	*High Skill/High Hygiene*
• Waiter(ess}	• Dentist
• Fast food server	• Doctor
• Maid	• Nurse
• Bar worker	• Tattoo artist
• Air hostess/cabin crew	
• Childcare assistant	

Given that type of employment may have an influence on whether tattoos are regarded as acceptable in the employment setting (Arndt et al., 2017: Dean, 2010; Mengual et al., 2016; Swanger, 2006; Timming, 2015; Verissimo et al., 2016; Winfield, 2014), the survey was followed up with four in-depth interviews across four different service sectors, all of which involved face-to-face transactions with their customers. The interviews were with an owner and manager of a beauty therapy salon, an owner and director of a private nursery and afterschool care provider, a senior police chief involved in recruitment and a human resource manager for a leading bank. The questions were designed to gauge how much managerial control each employer had over the appearance of their employees, and also to discover the personal opinions each had on tattoos in the workplace, and in general.

Limitations

We are aware of potential limitations of the study. As a non-probability sampling technique was used, any generalisations made about the population must be treated with caution. The survey was confined to participants residing in the United Kingdom, thus the findings may not be appropriate globally. The survey did not use visual stimuli, e.g. pictures of tattooed individuals which meant respondents had to imagine the tattooed people. A final limitation is that the achieved sample demographics were skewed towards women and those under the age of 40.

Findings and Discussion

Customer Attitudes

The research highlighted there are different factors at play affecting the opinions of tattoos, making the investigation of tattoos in the workplace more complicated. When the survey asked how important the personal appearance of an employee is when the respondent was conducting a business transaction, 19.4% said it was crucial while another 55.8% said it was somewhat important. Just 13.1% said it was of little or no importance to them, demonstrating the influence that customer perceptions might have on appearance policies in the workplace.

With regard to visible tattoos, all findings (the survey and interviews) revealed that tattoo characteristics had an impact on the opinions of respondents (who are also deemed as customers). Some survey responses suggested opinions that tattoos are unprofessional, distracting and inappropriate for a business setting, as well as being trashy and unattractive, thus giving off a bad image to customers. Many claimed that employers should have a right to not employ someone based on their tattoo.

Nonetheless, the descriptive statistics revealed that across the 18 job types, survey respondents in general were more accepting of employees having visible tattoos than not. Over half the respondents believed that visible tattoos were acceptable in all the job types listed. In line with previous research (Arndt et al., 2017; Verissimo et al., 2016; Winfield, 2014), professions such as lawyers, doctors, nurses, dentists and teachers were more likely to attract a more negative association, with around two fifths considering these occupations to be inappropriate to display visible tattoos. Occupations particularly considered more appropriate for visible tattoos included tattoo artist, tradesmen, bar workers, fast food workers and sales assistants.

So, similar to Dean (2010), the research revealed respondents rated tattoos on workers in low to medium skill jobs as significantly more appropriate than on workers in high-skilled jobs ($t = 15.057$, $df = 3.99$, $p < 0.001$ [2-tailed]). It also indicated that people in jobs that required high levels of hygiene (dentist, doctor, nurse or childcare assistant) were rated more inappropriately than people in jobs with a low required hygiene. The interviews with the nursery owner and the human resource bank manager confirmed this, with both declaring they would not expect or want to see visible tattoos on people in specific professions such as, e.g. the Police, Doctors or Nurses. These results indicated that there remain differences in how visible tattoos are viewed on people in different professions, and signalled that people hold higher appearance standards for more professional roles.

Respondent Demographics

Further analysis of the data revealed differences between the opinions of male and female respondents, with men rating visible tattoos in every profession as significantly less appropriate than women did. Moreover, people aged 18–39 viewed visible tattoos significantly more positively for every job category than those over 40. While Dean (2011) found 18–24-year olds do not view tattoos as appropriate in the appearance of tax-providers, the current findings appear to indicate that opinions of younger people are changing and they are becoming more accepting of visible tattoos in the workplace. Nevertheless, while there might be generational differences in the opinions of visible tattoos, those under 40 may not always be the decision-makers in identifying career opportunities. As the in-depth interviews confirmed, employers are still aware of the stereotypes that prospective and existing customers may hold, and so be reluctant to be so accommodating. Finally, for each of the job categories, tattooed respondents rated tattooed workers significantly more positively than those without tattoos, which is congruent with Hawkes et al.'s (2004) study two decades ago, and perhaps not that surprising.

Covering Tattoos

Despite a view that tattoos are more appropriate in the workplace, less than a quarter (24.1%) of survey respondents believed that front line employees should *not* have to cover up their tattoos. Just 7% believed all visible tattoos should be covered while the rest said it depended on the subject of the tattoo (65%), the type of job (39.2%), the location of the tattoo (28.3%) or its size (16.1%). The in-depth interviews confirmed that discrimination and covering up a tattoo during a service encounter would depend on the above factors.

When asked 'Hypothetically, if you had a tattoo would you cover it up in an interview situation or a recruitment assessment centre?' 58% of respondents (the majority of whom were under the age of 40) said 'yes' against 27% who said 'no' (15% were undecided). By far the most respondents mentioned how important first impressions were during an interview. Reasons respondents gave for covering up a tattoo related to the view that employers may still hold traditional opinions, with the respondent fearing they would be judged, stigmatised and discriminated against, thus jeopardising their chances of gaining that job.

The survey respondents who were unprepared to cover up tattoos during the interview process, regarding them to be part of their identity, character and self-expression. These respondents also professed they would not want to work for a business that discriminated based on tattoos. They commented that tattoos do not define a person's ability, have no relevance to work, and that their performance during an interview matters more than their appearance. To what extent these thoughts are misguided given the continued importance of customer expectations and representing a corporate image requires more research attention.

Business Attitudes

The four in-depth interviewees all acknowledged how important good appearance is in their specific job-roles. They alluded to the issues of employees representing the company they worked for and putting across a 'brand image'. The beautician and bank manager agreed that tattoos should not be visible during business transactions wherever possible, because of the negative connotations they may attract, although they relented that non-offensive, small ones may be tolerable. The findings, in line with Timming (2015) and Baumann et al. (2016), suggested that customers and managers concur that offensive tattoos (such as political, religious, sexist or homophobic) are higher risk in altering customer perceptions, and that they should not be visible during service transactions at any cost. All four business personnel believed that offensive tattoos must be covered up at work.

The question of whether the presence of a tattoo would dissuade the managers from hiring someone was also posed in the in-depth interviews. The beautician stated she would not let a tattoo block someone's chances of employment, but that it would be best if they were covered up where possible, as beauty therapy requires a neat and tidy appearance. The human resource bank manager argued that tattoos should be covered up as much as possible, due to the level of professionalism expected in banking. Although their policy had changed, the police chief stood firm that employees must not have visible tattoos that could cause offence. The nursery owner herself had no qualms about tattoos and emphasised the freedom of expression and individuality that it teaches its children. Therefore, she considered that stopping its employees from having tattoos would go against this culture, unless the tattoo carried an offensive meaning. Nevertheless, she acknowledged that customers might be more negative in their views. The appearance of staff was considered important across all four organisations, and while personal attitudes may be more relaxed, respondents tended to be more conservative in their policies of covering up visible tattoos for fear of customer reprisal and organisational professionalism. This is consistent with the findings of Arndt et al. (2017) and Timming (2015).

Despite, all four in-depth interview personnel recognising the negative stereotypes visible tattoos can bring at work, the nursery owner and human resource bank manager both agreed they think people are moving away from the 'preconceived perceptions' about tattooed individuals and that they are now more fashionable and accepted in society. The police chief also acknowledged that different sections of the community might now hold differing views on tattoos, mentioning younger people being more relaxed about them than older people, which confirmed the survey findings. In response, the police have recently modernised their policy on tattoos to allow more tattooed people into their workforce. Nowadays the Police only forbid facial tattoos whereas before any visible tattoos were prohibited.

Conclusion

There is no clear consensus on the display of tattoos in the workplace. Attitudes towards tattoos have shifted in recent years as they have become more prevalent in society. In some jobs and workplaces they may be embraced, upholding the culture of the company. In many other cases, however, concern continues to be raised about their appropriateness in the organisation, and the impact this has on brand image and thus the bottom line. The general view from both the quantitative and qualitative research was that irrespective of the fact that there has been a definite shift towards greater tattoo acceptance and integration into modern society, negative stereotypes about tattoos still exist. Several variables, such as the nature, size and location of the tattoo, the occupation in question, as well as individual customer characteristics can affect the acceptance of visible tattoos on employees by customers.

From a business perspective, organisations are critically aware of their profit margins and need for commercial gain. Like Timming et al. (2017) and Arndt et al. (2017), this study proposes that organisations remain constrained by societal judgements and customer perceptions. Employees with visible tattoos may still face stigma from others. This shows how traditional stereotypes can overpower contemporary youthful attitudes, and how established organisation principles can be perpetuated. There remains a fear that allowing visible tattoos in the workplace may blemish the reputation of the organisation and offend or intimidate their customers.

While Timming et al. (2017) argued that policies about tattoos need overhauling in light of modern society, the solution is not so clear. We argue that tattoos continue to pose a liability in employment terms. Prospective employees need to be aware of the potential views of their employing organisation regarding visible tattoos and take appropriate action. Tattooed employees may continue to be affected in their chances of attaining a job depending on the type and location of tattoo(s) and kind of job. Validation of this was confirmed in the research showing that most people will cover up a tattoo during an interview out of fear of negative discrimination by the interviewer.

Rather than impose a blanket approach to all employees regarding company policies towards tattoos, perhaps HR managers need to consider the appropriateness of employees with visible tattoos on a case by case basis and be given some discretion over their recommendations.

References

Arndt, A. D., & Glassman, M. (2012). What tattoos tell customers about salespeople: The role of gender norms. *Marketing Management Journal, 22*(1), 50–65.

Arndt, A. D., Karande, K., & Guthrie, J. P. (2016). How context interferes with similarity-attraction between customers and service providers. *Journal of Retailing and Consumer Services, 31*(July), 294–303.

Arndt, A. D., McCombs, G., Tolle, S. L., & Cox, C. (2017). Why are health care managers biased against hiring service providers with tattoos? *Services Marketing Quarterly, 38*(2), 88–99.

Baumann, C., Timming, A. R., & Gollan, P. J. (2016). Taboo tattoos? A study of the gendered effects of body art on consumers' attitudes toward visibly tattooed front line staff. *Journal of Retailing and Consumer Services, 29*(March), 31–39.

Bekhor, P., Bekhor, L., & Gandrabur, M. (1995). Employer attitudes toward persons with visible tattoos. *Australasian Journal of Dermatology, 36*(2), 75–77. https://doi.org/10.1111/j.1440-0960.1995.tb00936.x

Benbow, S. M., & Jolley, D. (2012). Dementia: Stigma and its effects. *Neurodegenerative Disease Management, 2*(2), 165–172. https://www.futuremedicine.com/doi/abs/10.2217/nmt.12.7. Accessed on June 19, 2019.

Bennington, L. (2019). *The debate: Will a tattoo affect my employability?* Careers Service at the Univeristy of Essex. https://employabilityandcareersattheuniversityofessex.wordpress.com/2019/04/24/the-debate-will-a-tattoo-affect-my-employability/

Botz-Bornstein, T. (2013). From stigmatized tattoo to the graffitied body: Femininity in the tattoo renaissance. *Gender, Place & Culture, 20*(2), 236–252.

Brallier, S. A., Maguire, K. A., Smith, D. A., & Palm, L. J. (2011). Visible tattoos and employment in the restaurant service industry. *International Journal of Business and Social Science, 2*(6), 72–76.

Bruton, S. (2015). Looks-based hiring and wrongful discrimination. *Business and Society Review, 120*(4), 607–635.

Carbery, R., & Cross, C. (2015). *Human resource development.* Palgrave Macmillan.

Cavico, F. J., Muffler, S. C., & Mujtaba, B. G. (2012). Appearance discrimination, "lookism" and "lookphobia" in the work-place. *Journal of Applied Business Research (JABR), 28*(5), 791–802.

Dean, D. H. (2010). Consumer perceptions of visible tattoos on service personnel. Managing Service Quality. *An International Journal, 20*(3), 294–308.

Dean, D. H. (2011). Young adult perception of visible tattoos on a white-collar service provider. *Young Consumers, 12*(3), 254–264.

Dillingh, R., Kooreman, P., & Potters, J. (2016). *Tattoos, life style and the labor market.* IZA Discussion paper 9675. http://ftp.iza.org/dp9675.pdf. Accessed on September 24, 2019.

Doleac, J. L., & Stein, L. D. (2013). The visible hand: Race and online market outcomes. *The Economic Journal, 123*(672), F469–F492.

Efthymiou, L. (2018). Worker body-art in upper-market hotels: Neither accepted, nor prohibited. *International Journal of Hospitality Management, 74*, 99–108.

Ellis, A. (2015). A Picture is worth one thousand words: Body art in the workplace. *Employee Responsibilities and Rights Journal, 27*(2), 101–113.

Elzweig, B., & Peeples, D. K. (2011). Tattoos and piercings: Issues of body modification and the workplace. *SAM Advanced Management Journal, 76*(1), 13–23.

Falk, G. (2001). *Stigma: How we treat outsiders.* Prometheus Books.

Foster, S. (2016). Like it or not, the way we look matters. *British Journal of Nursing, 25*(6), 941.

French, M. T., Maclean, J. C., Robins, P. K., Sayed, B., & Shiferaw, L. (2016). Tattoos, employment, and labor market earnings: Is there a link in the ink? *Southern Economic Journal, 82*(4), 1212–1246.

French, M. T., Mortensen, K., & Timming, A. R. (2019). Are tattoos associated with employment and wage discrimination? Analysing the relationships between body art and labor market outcomes. *Human Relations, 72*(5), 962–987.

Goffman, E. (1963). *Stigma: Notes on the management of spoiled identity.* Prentice-Hall.

Hawkes, D., Senn, C., & Thorn, C. (2004). Factors that influence attitudes toward women with tattoos. *Sex Roles, 50*(9/10), 593–604.

Heatherton, T. (2003). *The social psychology of stigma.* Guilford Press.

Herek, G. M. (2002). Thinking about AIDS and stigma: A psychologist's perspective. *Journal of Law, Medicine & Ethics, 30*(4), 594–607.

Heywood, W., Patrick, K., Smith, A., Simpson, J., Pitts, M., Richters, J., & Shelley, J. (2012). Who gets tattoos? Demographic and behavioral correlates of ever being tattooed in a representative sample of men and women. *Annals of Epidemiology, 22*(1), 51–56.

Hopf, V. (2018). Does the body modified appearance of front-line employees matter to hotel guests? *Research in Hospitality Management, 8*(1), 67–71.

Karl, K., Hall, L. M., & Peluchette, J. (2013). City employee perceptions of the impact of dress and appearance: You are what you wear. *Public Personnel Management, 42*(3), 452–470.

Karl, K., Peluchette, J. V. E., & Hall, L. M. (2016). Employee beliefs regarding the impact of unconventional appearance on customers in Mexico and Turkey. *Employee Relations, 38*(2), 161–181.

Kirk, I. (2022). Should visible tattoos be allowed in the workplace? https://yougov.co.uk/topics/society/articles-reports/2022/08/05/should-visible-tattoos-be-allowed-workplace. Accessed on November 09, 2022.

Kosut, M. (2006). An ironic fad: The commodification and consumption of tattoos. *Journal of Popular Culture, 39*(6), 1035–1048.

Larsen, G., Patterson, M., & Markham, L. (2014). A Deviant Art: Tattoo-related stigma in an era of commodification. *Psychology and Marketing, 31*(8), 670–681.

Laumann, A., & Derick, A. (2006). Tattoos and body piercings in the United States: A national data set. *Journal of the American Academy of Dermatology, 55*(3), 413–421.

Lipscomb, T. J., Jones, M. A., & Totten, J. W. (2008). Body art: Prevalence, search and evaluation among university business students. *Services Marketing Quarterly, 29*(4), 42–65.

Matthews, B., & Ross, L. (2014). *Research methods: A practical guide for social sciences* (1st. ed.). Longman.

Mengual, L. M., Gamez, N. M., Carcedo, I., Lopez, M. A., & Alava, J. I. (2016). Accessorries of food handlers and restaurant staff as a source for food contaminiation. *Journal of Food Microbiology Safety Hygiene, 1*(1), 1–5.

Miller, B., McGlashan Nicols, K., & Eure, J. (2009). Body art in the workplace: Piercing the prejudice? *Personnel Review, 38*(6), 621–640.

Nickson, D., & Baum, T. (2017). Young at heart, but what about my body? Age and aesthetic labour in the hospitality and retail industries. In E. Parry & J. McCarthy (Eds.), *The Palgrave handbook of age diversity and work* (pp. 539–559). Palgrave Macmillan Ltd.

Nickson, D., Warhurst, C., Cullen, A., & Watt, A. (2003). Bringing in the excluded? Aesthetic labour, skills and training in the 'new' economy. *Journal of Education and Work, 16*(2), 185–203.

Nickson, D., Warhurst, C., & Dutton, E. (2005). The importance of attitude and appearance in the service encounter in retail and hospitality. *Managing Service Quality, 15*(2), 195.

Nickson, D. P., Warhurst, C., Witz, A., & Cullen, A. M. (2001). The importance of being aesthetic: Work, employment and service organization. In A. Sturdy, I. Grugulis, & H. Wilmott (Eds.), *Customer service*. Palgrave.

Peluchette, J., Karl, K., & Rust, K. (2006). Dressing to impress: Beliefs and attitudes regarding workplace attire. *Journal of Business and Psychology, 21*(1), 45–63.

Pettinger, L. (2004). Brand culture and branded workers: Service work and aesthetic labour in fashion retail. *Consumption, Markets and Culture, 7*(2), 165–184.

Roberts, D. (2012). Secret ink: Tattoo's place in contemporary American culture. *The Journal of American Culture, 35*(2), 153–165.

Robin, M. (2018). Tattoos may actually *help* you get hired for a job, so feel free to rub that in your judgy relative's face. https://www.allure.com/story/how-tattoos-affect-employment-study. Accessed on October 01, 2019.

Salary.com. (2018). Tattoos hurt your chances of getting a job. https://www.salary.com/articles/tattoos-hurt-chances-getting-job/. Accessed on October 01, 2019.

Schultz, M., Harvey, D., & Bosco, S. (2015). Tattoos and body piercings in the workforce. In *Proceedings for the Northeast Region Decision Sciences Institute (NEDSI)* (pp. 1–10). Accessed on November 1, 2020.

Swanger, N. (2006). Visible body modification (VBM): Evidence from human resource managers and recruiters and the effects on employment. *International Journal of Hospitality Management, 25*(1), 154–158.

Thomas, D. (2019) Tattoos at work: Are they still an issue? BBC News. https://www.bbc.co.uk/news/business-48620528

Thomas, C. M., Ehret, A., Ellis, B., Colon-Shoop, S., Linton, J., Schultz, M., Harvey, D., Bosco, S., & Metz, S. (2010). Tattoos and body piercings in the workforce Perception of nurse caring, skills, and knowledge based on appearance. *Journal of Nursing Administration, 40*(11), 489–497.

Timming, A. R. (2015). Visible tattoos in the service sector: A new challenge to recruitment and selection. *Work, Employment & Society, 29*(1), 60–78.

Timming, A. (2017). Body art as branded labour: At the intersection of employee selection and relationship marketing. *Human Relations, 70*(9), 1041–1063.

Timming, A. R., Nickson, D., Re, D., & Perrett, D. (2017). What do you think of my ink? Assessing the effects of body art on employment chances. *Human Resource Management, 56*(1), 133–149.

Verissimo, A., Tolle, S. L., McCombs, G., & Arndt, A. (2016). Assessing dental clients' perceptions of dental hygienists with visible tattoos. *Canadian Journal of Dental Hygiene, 50*(3), 109–115.

Warhurst, C., & Nickson, D. (2020). *Aesthetic Labour.* Sage. https://doi.org/10.4135/9781529702002

Warhurst, C., Nickson, D., Witz, A., & Cullen, A. M. (2000). Aesthetic labour in interactive service work: Some case study evidence from the 'New' Glasgow. *The Service Industries Journal, 20*(3), 1–18.

Warhurst, C., van den Broek, D., Nickson, D., & Hall, R. (2012). Great expectations: Gender, looks and lookism at work. *International Journal of Work Organisation and Emotion, 5*(1), 72–90.

Williams, C. L., & Connell, C. (2010). "Looking good and sound right": Aesthetic labor and social inequality in the retail industry. *Work and Occupations, 37*(3), 349–377.

Winfield, S. (2014). Body art is still taboo in health care. *British Medical Journal.* https://www.bmj.com/content/349/bmj.g6259

Witz, A., Warhurst, C., & Nickson, D. (2003). The Labour of aesthetics and the aesthetics of organization. *Organization, 10*(1), 33–54.

Yates, J., Hooley, T., & Bagri, K. K. (2016). Good looks and good practice: The attitudes of career practitioners to attractiveness and appearance. *British Journal of Guidance & Counselling, 45*(5), 547–561.

Yorke, M. (2004). *Employability in higher education: What it is – What it is not.* Higher Education Academy/ESECT.

Zestcott, C. A., Tompkins, T. L., Kozak Williams, M., Livesay, K., & Chan, K. L. (2017). What do you think about ink? An examination of implicit and explicit attitudes toward tattooed individuals. *The Journal of Social Psychology, 158*(1), 7–22.

Chapter 19

Tattoos and the Social Psychology of Stigma: Implications for Career Development

Terence Chia and Andrew R. Timming

Abstract

Diversity and inclusion initiatives are normally centred on legally protected traits such as race and gender. As the legal framework expands to ensure that underrepresented workers are protected, there exists a subset of the workforce who have diversity characteristics that are legally unprotected. For example, individuals who have visible tattoos can face employment discrimination when they are looking for work or looking to progress their careers. To add to the challenge, the perception of stigma is fluid and expectations related to the appearance of employees are determined by managers' perceptions of consumers' preferences. Drawing theoretically from self-categorisation theory and information processing theory, we discuss how the creation of a marketing and brand proposition framework can help to build an organisational identity that can benefit consumers and the organisation simultaneously. We also discuss the practical implications and strategies that organisations can consider to reduce such workplace discrimination.

Keywords: Body art; careers; discrimination; diversity; tattoos; stigma

Introduction

Academic debates surrounding equality, diversity and inclusion have traditionally centred around job applicants' and employees' legally protected characteristics such as gender (Triana et al., 2019), race and ethnicity (Guillaume et al., 2017), migrant status (Pio, 2005), age (North, 2019), disability (Santuzzi & Waltz, 2016), LGBTQ status (Webster et al., 2018) and religion (Hèliot et al., 2019), among others. Diversity management in the workplace gained traction in the 1960s when

The Emerald Handbook of Appearance in the Workplace, 331–342
doi:10.1108/978-1-80071-174-720230020

advocates for equality championed for an anti-discriminatory approach to the hiring, retention and the promotion of minority employees after the race riots in the USA and discrimination against women (Ferner et al., 2005). This resulted in the equal employment opportunity and affirmative action policies that proliferated in US-based organisations and multinational firms, and this nascent phase of diversity management was effective in advancing the representation of minority workers (Crosby et al., 2006).

By the 1980s, the tide began to turn as demographic based initiatives were confronted with legal challenges such as reverse discrimination and, as a result, such initiatives started to decline (Shore et al., 2009). To justify diversity initiatives and circumvent legal challenges, diversity practitioners have recently sought to reframe diversity management initiatives as a business case to justify it as an organisational diversity management effort and policy (Litvin, 2006). This promoted diversity practitioners and scholars to explore and investigate how diversity management policies benefit employees and organisations (van Dijk et al., 2012). While there was a shift from equal employment opportunity and affirmative action policies to the organisation-based business case approach, the diversity management strategy has largely remained the same – policies and initiatives enacted are mostly reactive approaches to address the current inequality situation within the firm. These reactive demographic-based approaches to diversity management have largely characterised diversity management research over the past 40 years (Shore et al., 2009). Although reactive approaches help to address historical and current issues surrounding discriminatory practices in organisations, by and large, they have not produced positive outcomes for organisations because they paint a lens where diversity is perceived as a problematic issue that needs to be 'managed' or 'dealt with' (Shore et al., 2011). There is a need to ensure that diversity management strategies stretch beyond reactive initiatives to focus on proactive and sustainable directions beyond legally protected categories such as individual traits, beliefs, and identities.

Thus, without debasing the importance of continued research into these legally protected categories, we argue that employment discrimination extends far and wide beyond these characteristics and into individual traits that are much more difficult, if not impossible, for governments to regulate. The chapters in this book provide critical examples of what might be referred to as legally *un*protected diversity characteristics, including, but not limited to, dress codes, hair style, attractiveness and body weight (see also Nickson et al., 2016) – though it should be noted that the latter may well qualify for legal protection if it meets the criteria of a physical disability (Puhl & Brownell, 2001). Although many organisations have 'appearance policies' that seek to regulate the aesthetic presentation of employees (Bandsuch, 2008), litigants would be very hard pressed to win a discrimination claim in an employment tribunal unless they can clearly demonstrate that the employer discriminated on the basis of a legally protected category.

Elsewhere in this book, Efthymiou (Chapter 17) demonstrates that the increased prevalence in Western societies of visible body art presents new diversity-related challenges to hospitality management in multinational luxury hotels. Tattoos are generally legally *un*protected traits (Elzweig & Peeples, 2011), with possible exceptions being for those specific images that have cultural or religious significance (Timming & Perrett, 2016). On the whole, it would be difficult for any government to legally regulate tattoos because each image is a unique artistic signifier (Timming & Perrett, 2017). As a result, employers are generally free to discriminate against visibly tattooed employees and job applicants (Bekhor et al., 1995; Timming, 2015; Timming et al., 2017). Although tattoos can and still do present as a potential stigma (Dickson et al., 2014; Swami & Furnham, 2007) in the workplace, thereby at times inhibiting employability, it is increasingly recognised that body art, among other forms of visible stigma, can also present as an asset in the labour market (Timming, 2017). Whereas Efthymiou's chapter points to the mismatch between tattoos and luxury multinational hotels, our chapter, in contrast, further examines the circumstances in which visible body art on front-line employees might be aligned with the 'brand personality' of the employing organisation (Aaker, 1997).

Drawing from the diversity management literature, we argue that the appearance of front-line employees, especially in the interactive services sector, is determined not so much by managers' tastes and preferences, but rather by managers' perceptions of consumers' tastes and preferences. Insofar as tattoos are aligned with consumers' expectations as well as their social identities (Baumann et al., 2016), body art is likely to be not only tolerated in the workplace, but perhaps even encouraged as a positive cue, or signal, to potential customers. The key implication of this argument is that stigma (Goffman, 2009; Link & Phelan, 2001) is a fundamentally *fluid* social category: the same individual may well be stigmatised in one context and celebrated in another (Shih, 2004), depending on consumer dispositions towards the trait.

Theory and Concepts

The two most common explanations for the effects of diversity management are self-categorisation theory and information processing theory (see Mayo et al., 2017 for a review). Self-categorisation theory (Turner et al., 1987) highlights similarities and differences between employees, which often draw out in-group and out-group distinctions like demographic variables as sources of conflict within and between workgroups (Reynolds et al., 2003). Self-categorisation theory suggests that a diverse workgroup might perform less effectively because employees might co-operate only with others who share similar attributes, resulting in conflict with members from the out-group.

In contrast, the information processing theory (Williams & O'Reilly, 1998) focuses on the advantages derived from diverse views stemming from the different sources of knowledge represented in the workgroup. This viewpoint supports the idea that a diverse workgroup, especially when a group includes members from the minority group, is more likely to have access to a broader range of knowledge, skills and abilities, which coincide with the social categories that differ among members (Bell et al., 2011; Klein & Harrison, 2007; Simons et al., 1999). Homogenous groups (e.g. teams with low nationality diversity) may benefit from better workgroup cohesion and communication, but they may be less creative (Homan et al., 2015). Cha and Roberts (2019) found that that organisations can gain advantages in their firm's performance by hiring employees who are from minority groups such as those who are underrepresented in society. Organisations with a diversity climate that allows for engagement of diversity for the purpose to both inform and improve work processes (Hajro et al., 2017) can allow employees from the minority group to use their unique perspectives to contribute to the team. In addition, these unique perspectives can be a key to allow the organisation to reach out to minority stakeholders in the community and widen their customer base (Cha & Roberts, 2019).

Following the same, or very similar, logic, organisations may well seek to employ front-line staff with visible tattoos in order to attract that particular demographic of customer. Whether a job applicant's visible tattoos are viewed by hiring managers as an asset or as a liability ultimately depends on the 'brand personality' (Aaker, 1997) of the organisation and the corresponding target demographic of customer it is seeking to reach. As illustrated in Efthymiou's chapter, the clientele of a luxury multinational hotel might tend towards a particular customer based that is perhaps culturally conservative and therefore averse to the presence of visible body art. Thus, older, wealthier clientele are more apt to view tattoos in a negative light compared to their younger counterparts (Lin, 2002). On the other hand, organisations with a 'young', 'exciting', 'creative', and/or 'rebellious' brand personality are likely to view visible body art in a positive light. Examples of companies that might welcome visible body art in the workplace include, but are not limited to: technology firms like Apple and Google, marketing firms like WPP and Omnicom, clothing and apparel firms like H&M and Vans, and any number of small and medium-sized enterprises including bars, nightclubs, and retail shops offering heavily appearance-based goods. In the public sector, an argument could be even made that police officers and prison guards may well benefit from displaying visible tattoos that allow them to connect on an emotional level with their 'clients' as well.

The key theoretical purchase of this argument is that it challenges as too overly simplistic the prevailing social psychological theories of stigma (Kusow, 2004). Arguably the most prominent theory of stigma over the last century is offered by Goffman (2009). In it, he points out that the English word 'stigma' derives from the Greek word meaning 'tattoo'. Goffman divides the social world into two groups: 'the stigmatised' are those in society who are either already discredited or otherwise discreditable; 'normals' are everyone else. Many of the examples of stigma he gives are visual and aesthetic: e.g., facial disfigurements, physical dis-abilities, or general unattractiveness to the opposite sex. Other examples are latent, including sexual orientation, criminal history, or mental illness. Regardless of whether a stigma is manifest or latent, Goffman argues that the stigmatised are shamed, ostracised, excluded, and devalued by 'normals'. For this reason, the former often seek to conceal their stigma in social interaction, with much of Goffman's book dedicated to investigating those stigma concealment strategies. While this general argument may hold water in the context of employment in Efthymiou's luxury multinational hotel chain, it ultimately presents itself as much less convincing when the 'brand personality' (Aaker, 1997) of the organisation is accounted for.

Extant social psychological theories of stigma (e.g. Goffman, 2009; Link & Phelan, 2001), therefore, must recognised the dual nature of these so-called 'undesirable' qualities. Given that all knowledge is, in the final analysis, socially constructed and constituted (Berger & Luckmann, 1991), it logically follows that group membership 'colours' all social signals emitted by an individual in the course of social interaction. This *fluidity* of social meaning is really at the heart of all critiques of stereotypes and their lack of universal accuracy (Ryan, 2003). What may be viewed through the lens of negativity by members of one group may be viewed through the lens of positivity by members of another. Thus, visibly tattooed job applicants may do well to steer clear of organisations targeting an older, more conservative demographic of customer, but they may use their body art to their advantage in organisations that are targeting a younger, more liberal demographic of customer. This context dependency may explain why, contrary to popular belief, stigma is not associated with reduced self-esteem (Crocker & Major, 1989). Stigma, it would thus seem, is always in the eye of the beholder.

Practical Implications and Recommendations

The discussion up to this point has important practical and theoretical import. The key practical implications have relevance to employees, employers, and policy-makers, while the theoretical implications have relevance to extant academic debates that cross the diverse fields of social psychology, services marketing and human resource management. The aim of this section is to tease out these implications and to provide future researchers with some directions for future research.

The fluidity of social meaning and its influence on the perception of stigma can lead to bias, both positive and negative, vis-à-vis visibly tattooed individuals in their job applications and career development. To add clarity and aid potential employees in their decision to determine if they are a good fit with a prospective organisation, potential employees can assess this fit by evaluating if the image of a firm aligns with their values and beliefs as well as appearance. To strengthen how a brand is perceived, the hiring firm can engage in a strategic marketing plan such as designing and executing a personalised chain of marketing productivity (Rust et al., 2004). Based on the marketing productivity framework, firms should set up promotion and product strategies that drive tactical actions such as advertising campaigns or service improvements. Organisations need to put emphasis on designing purposeful tactical actions which can build a brand personality (Aaker, 1997) so that it can authentically showcase the firm's ethos and values.

Building these characteristics can set off a chain of impact that can have a sequential flow on effect – customer impact, market impact and financial impact. When the organisation takes action to shape customer impact, employers should consider the impact it can have on customers' attitudes and satisfaction towards its brand. This targeted outcome on customers' perspectives can also be applied to potential employees because job applicants can adopt a customer lens and seek out organisations they can resonate with. Take, for example, Vans, an American manufacturer of skateboarding shoes. The company has built a brand personality of a 'rebellious' organisation (Aaker, 1997) by designing its core product and marketing campaign appeal to a targeted demographic of skateboarders and customers subscribed to the skateboarding culture. Vans positions its brand in alignment with the skateboarding and punk subculture, which has a fashion and language of its own. To further strengthen this brand personality, Vans sponsors rock music festivals and other extreme sports like snowboarding, BMX and motocross teams (Vans, 2020). In return, customers aligned with these interests subscribe themselves with the values and identity that Vans have created, and at the same time, job seekers looking to work for Vans can align their own brand personality to that of Vans. This is an effective strategy as the creation of a clear and targeted brand personality can shape customers' and job applicants' perceptions towards the organisation (Wilden et al., 2010). It can also play a role in the retention of current employees (Wheeler et al., 2006). In this specific example, individuals who are visibly tattooed are part of the skateboarding culture, so hiring job applicants who are visibly inked allows the organisation's identity to authentically resonate with skateboarding, extreme sports, street and punk culture.

Expanding this discussion on marketing strategies and tactics that firms can undertake, organisational behaviour scholars have recently explored how firms can utilise anthropomorphism, the act of applying human qualities to inanimate objects, to enhance social connection with their employees and customer base (Ashforth et al., 2020). Anthropomorphism allows employees to understand 'who' rather than 'what' an organisation is and what exactly it represents. There are numerous benefits as an outcome of anthropomorphising organisations. The process of prescribing human qualities to the organisational identity facilitates sensemaking and promotes social connection. The approach primes accountability and emotional attachment and strengthens the psychological contract (a perceived informal mutual obligation, see Rousseau, 1995) between the worker and the firm (Ashforth et al., 2020). At the industry level, when the perception of a firm is anthropomorphised, it allows the organisation to be easily recognised and stand out from competitors. Cutting through the noise from the rest of the industry is a position that brands aspire to achieve. When firms are able to articulate their brand proposition in personified manners, customers not only recall the brand more easily, but also identify with it in an emotionally attached manner equivalent to consumers perceiving the firm as a relationship partner (Aggarwal, 2004). This relationship, in turn, influences the way the consumer behaves towards the brand and guides how the consumer should evaluate product releases or actions that the firm undertakes (Aggarwal & McGill, 2012). In this fashion, when visibly tattooed job applicants consider employment prospect with such personified organisations, they will be able to ascertain if their visible tattoos 'fit in' with the firm's image or if they have to dress appropriately for their job.

Let's take a hypothetical situation as an example, a visibly tattooed job applicant who takes an interest with Volvo, a luxury car brand associated with safety, would be more likely to dress conservatively when interviewing for a sales job with the firm, and when hired as a sales person, the tattooed employee will likely be dressed in more formal attire to sell to customers who prioritise safety, the traditional targeted demographic of the brand. However, due to a recent marketing strategy to reposition itself as a brand that also caters to a younger generation, Volvo has a new ambition to be a more 'progressive' premium brand within the automobile industry (Volvo, 2018). The tattooed job applicant or employee can thus have the potential to connect the brand's traditional image with the younger generation.

In addition to organisational strategies for establishing an authentic brand personality, firms can revisit their policies for recruitment and selection, and employee retention and development programs, paying attention especially to those who are underrepresented or stigmatised. As mentioned above, the fluidity of social meaning and the prescription of stigma are in the eye of the beholder. In a similar vein, when discrimination occurs during the recruitment and selection process, it usually falls back to the stereotypes and biases held by the recruiter or hiring manager, where interviewers seek a typical ideal worker that they have in mind for the role (Davison & Burke, 2000). van Dijk et al. (2012) proposed that a recruitment and selection process based on virtue ethics can minimise the discrimination and benefit both minority and underrepresented groups, and the organisation. Instead of being influenced by a preconceived idea of an ideal type of worker for the role, the selection panel should work out the virtues that the ideal candidate should possess so that biases and stereotypes from different stakeholders can be discussed and clarified before the hiring process takes place. Further to the recruitment and selection processes, van Dijk et al. (2012) also proposed to apply the 'virtue ethic' approach to performance management to reduce discrimination and biases since it might be more likely that standards lean towards majority members rather than minority groups. Similar to the hiring process, the authors proposed the identification of virtues for each organisational position and then create performance measures to evaluate if an employee has the prescribed virtues and correctly applies them at work.

Take, for example, the role of a primary school teacher. When hiring or promoting a candidate, the school principal and members of the selection or promotion panel should discuss teaching relevant virtues such as perseverance, leadership and fairness (Arthur et al., 2015), that the candidate must possess for the role. The mark of a tattoo can be perceived as a mark of insolence in many traditional societies, and children and adolescents can associate tattooed individuals with negative attributes (Durkin & Houghton, 2000). These biases can be an implicit barrier for gaining employment or career progression for the visibly tattooed school primary teacher who is passionate about teaching. Therefore, when recruitment and selection, and performance management processes are consciously shaped by virtues and ethics, this can help minimise bias and discrimination. Engaging in this action can benefit both employees and organisations by ensuring the best candidate securing the role and the organisation benefits from the commitment and accomplishments from the employee. The school can also compromise by letting a teacher dress in formal attire to cover up tattoos when on the job. Alternatively, management can allow the teacher to display non-offensive or non-divisive tattoos in class to help break down the negative perception towards individuals with tattoos.

Future cross-disciplinary research integrating marketing, social psychology, organisational behaviour and human resources management can explore the topic of how firms can create an inclusive culture of hiring, retaining and developing employees who are historically underrepresented and socially stigmatised due to invisible and visible traits. This is especially important because while legal reforms from decades of anti-discrimination activism have helped shape the current workplace landscape to be more tolerant and inclusive of minorities, indirect and subtle forms of discrimination (e.g. casual racism, Deitch et al., 2003) and unconscious bias during the hiring process such as discrimination due to visible body tattoo continue (Timming et al., 2017).

Conclusions

Diversity management will remain a key focus for organisations that value productivity as more firms appreciate the financial return of investment from managing diversity well in the workplace (Smulowitz et al., 2019). Yet, as we shift to an organisation-based business case approach, diversity initiatives mostly involve reactive approaches, which have produced mixed results (Williams & O'Reilly, 1998). Adding to the challenge, employment discrimination extends far and wide beyond legally protected characteristics, such as visible body art. This becomes even more challenging when we acknowledge that the perception of stigma is fluid.

Acknowledging the benefits of diversity in the workplace for both organisation and the workforce, we want to highlight some strategies organisations can undertake to reduce implicit and subtle forms of discrimination, especially towards visibly tattooed job applicants or employees. When firms engage in branding strategies that communicate a brand personality or a campaign that anthropomorphises the firm, an obvious benefit is standing out from its competitors and building brand loyalty with consumers and increasing emotional attachment to the firm. Another benefit is the added clarity in how the organisation is perceived by the firm's stakeholders such as its consumers and (potential) workforce. This can attract employees who are aligned to the firm's values and allow for individuals with visible social stigma to make an informed decision by assessing if they fit in to the culture of the firm. Past research has shown the hiring and performance management process to be open to bias and discrimination, especially against non-legally protected traits like visible tattoos. To reduce discrimination in these processes, decision-makers should evaluate the suitability or performance of a job candidate by the virtues and ethics relevant to the job position (van Dijk et al., 2012) and not be influenced by preconceived notions of a job candidate's appearance.

In conclusion, to reduce stigma and create a workplace that takes proactive initiatives, employers must create an inclusive environment (Hajro et al., 2017) that authentically engages everyone's contributions and uniqueness to achieve optimal outcomes. Only then can we accept the differences that exist and learn about the uniqueness from one another to benefit from diversity.

References

Aaker, J. L. (1997). Dimensions of brand personality. *Journal of Marketing Research, 34*(3), 347–356.

Aggarwal, P. (2004). The effects of brand relationship norms on consumer attitudes and behavior. *Journal of Consumer Research, 31*, 87–101.

Aggarwal, P., & McGill, A. L. (2012). When brands seem human, do humans act like brands? Automatic behavioral priming effects of brand anthropomorphism. *Journal of Consumer Research, 39*(2), 307–323.

Arthur, J., Kristjansson, K., Cook, S., Brown, E., & Carr, D. (2015). *The good teacher: Understanding virtues in practice (research report)*. Jubilee Centre for Character and Virtues.

Ashforth, B. E., Schinoff, B. S., & Brickson, S. L. (2020). "My company is friendly," "Mine's a Rebel": Anthropomorphism and shifting organizational identity from "What" to "Who. *Academy of Management Review, 45*(1), 29–57.

Bandsuch, M. R. (2008). Dressing up Title VII's analysis of workplace appearance policies. *Columbia Human Rights Law Review, 40*, 287.

Baumann, C., Timming, A. R., & Gollan, P. J. (2016). Taboo tattoos? A study of the gendered effects of body art on consumers' attitudes toward visibly tattooed front line staff. *Journal of Retailing and Consumer Services, 29*, 31–39.

Bekhor, P. S., Bekhor, L., & Gandrabur, M. (1995). Employer attitudes toward persons with visible tattoos. *Australasian Journal of Dermatology, 36*(2), 75–77.

Bell, S. T., Villado, A. J., Lukasik, M. A., Belau, L., & Briggs, A. L. (2011). Getting specific about demographic diversity variable and team performance relationships: A meta-analysis. *Journal of Management, 37*(3), 709–743.

Berger, P. L., & Luckmann, T. (1991). *The social construction of reality: A treatise in the sociology of knowledge* (No. 10). Penguin Books.

Cha, S. E., & Roberts, L. M. (2019). Leveraging minority identities at work: An individual-level framework of the identity mobilization process. *Organization Science, 30*(4), 735–760.

Crocker, J., & Major, B. (1989). Social stigma and self-esteem: The self-protective properties of stigma. *Psychological Review, 96*(4), 608.

Crosby, F. J., Iyer, A., & Sincharoen, S. (2006). Understanding affirmative action. *Annual Review of Psychology, 57*, 585–611.

Davison, H. K., & Burke, M. J. (2000). Sex discrimination in simulated employment contexts: A meta-analytic investigation. *Journal of Vocational Behavior, 56*, 225–248.

Deitch, E. A., Barsky, A., Butz, R. M., Chan, S., Brief, A. P., & Bradley, J. C. (2003). Subtle yet significant: The existence and impact of everyday racial discrimination in the workplace. *Human Relations, 56*, 1299–1324.

Dickson, L., Dukes, R., Smith, H., & Strapko, N. (2014). Stigma of ink: Tattoo attitudes among college students. *The Social Science Journal, 51*(2), 268–276.

van Dijk, H., van Engen, M., & Paauwe, J. (2012). Reframing the business case for diversity: A values and virtues perspective. *Journal of Business Ethics, 111*, 73–84.

Durkin, K., & Houghton, S. (2000). Children'and adolescents' stereotypes of tattooed people as delinquent. *Legal and Criminological Psychology, 5*, 153–164.

Elzweig, B., & Peeples, D. K. (2011). Tattoos and piercings: Issues of body modification and the workplace. *SAM Advanced Management Journal, 76*(1), 13.

Ferner, A., Almond, P., & Colling, T. (2005). US multinationals, competitive advantage and the diffusion of HR policy: The case of workforce diversity. *Journal of International Business Studies, 36*, 304–321.

Goffman, E. (2009). *Stigma: Notes on the management of spoiled identity*. Simon and Schuster.

Guillaume, Y. R., Dawson, J. F., Otaye-Ebede, L., Woods, S. A., & West, M. A. (2017). Harnessing demographic differences in organizations: What moderates the effects of workplace diversity? *Journal of Organizational Behavior, 38*(2), 276–303.

Hajro, A., Gibson, C. B., & Pudelko, M. (2017). Knowledge exchange processes in multicultural teams: Linking organizational diversity climates to teams' effectiveness. *Academy of Management Journal, 60*(1), 345–372.

Héliot, Y., Gleibs, I. H., Coyle, A., Rousseau, D. M., & Rojon, C. (2019). Religious identity in the workplace: A systematic review, research agenda, and practical implications. *Human Resource Management*. https://doi.org/10.1002/hrm.21983

Homan, A. C., Buengeler, C., Eckhoff, R. A., van Ginkel, W. P., & Voelpel, S. C. (2015). The interplay of diversity training and diversity beliefs on team creativity in nationality diverse teams. *Journal of Applied Psychology, 100*, 1456–1467.

Klein, K. J., & Harrison, D. A. (2007). On the diversity of diversity: Tidy logic, messier realities. *Academy of Management Perspectives, 21*(4), 26–33.

Kusow, A. M. (2004). Contesting stigma: On Goffman's assumptions of normative order. *Symbolic Interaction, 27*(2), 179–197.

Lin, Y. (2002). Age, sex, education, religion, and perception of tattoos. *Psychological Reports, 90*(2), 654–658.

Link, B. G., & Phelan, J. C. (2001). Conceptualizing stigma. *Annual Review of Sociology, 27*(1), 363–385.

Litvin, D. R. (2006). Diversity: Making space for a better case. In A. M. Konrad, P. Prasad, & J. K. Pringle (Eds.), *Handbook of workplace diversity* (pp. 75–94). SAGE.

Mayo, M., Kakarika, M., Mainemelis, C., & Deuschel, N. T. (2017). A metatheoretical framework of diversity in teams. *Human Relations, 70*, 911–939.

Nickson, D., Timming, A. R., Re, D., & Perrett, D. (2016). Subtle increases in BMI within a healthy weight range still reduce women's employment chances in the service sector. *PLoS One, 11*(9), 1–14.

North, M. S. (2019). A GATE to understanding "older" workers: Generation, age, tenure, experience. *The Academy of Management Annals, 13*, 414–443.

Pio, E. (2005). Knotted strands: Working lives of Indian women migrants in New Zealand. *Human Relations, 58*, 1277–1299.

Puhl, R., & Brownell, K. D. (2001). Bias, discrimination, and obesity. *Obesity Research, 9*(12), 788–805.

Reynolds, K. J., Turner, J. C., & Haslam, S. A. (2003). Social identity and self-categorization theories' contribution to understanding identification, salience and diversity in teams and organizations. In *Identity issues in groups* (pp. 279–304). Emerald Publishing Limited.

Rousseau, D. M. (1995). *Psychological contracts in organizations: Understanding written and unwritten agreements.* Sage.

Rust, R. T., Ambler, T., Carpenter, G. S., Kumar, V., & Srivastava, R. K. (2004). Measuring marketing productivity: Current knowledge and future directions. *Journal of Marketing, 68,* 76–89.

Ryan, C. (2003). Stereotype accuracy. *European Review of Social Psychology, 13*(1), 75–109.

Santuzzi, A. M., & Waltz, P. R. (2016). Disability in the workplace: A unique and variable identity. *Journal of Management, 42,* 1111–1135.

Shih, M. (2004). Positive stigma: Examining resilience and empowerment in overcoming stigma. *The Annals of the American Academy of Political and Social Science, 591*(1), 175–185.

Shore, L. M., Chung-Herrera, B. G., Dean, M. A., Ehrhart, K. H., Jung, D. I., Randel, A. E., & Singh, G. (2009). Diversity in organizations: Where are we now and where are we going? *Human Resource Management Review, 19,* 117–133.

Shore, L. M., Randel, A. E., Chung, B. G., Dean, M. A., Ehrhart, K. H., & Singh, G. (2011). Inclusion and diversity in work groups: A review and model for future research. *Journal of Management, 37,* 1262–1289.

Simons, T., Pelled, L. H., & Smith, K. A. (1999). Making use of difference: Diversity, debate, and decision comprehensiveness in top management teams. *Academy of Management Journal, 42,* 662–673.

Smulowitz, S., Becerra, M., & Mayo, M. (2019). Racial diversity and its asymmetry within and across hierarchical levels: The effects on financial performance. *Human Relations, 72,* 1671–1696.

Swami, V., & Furnham, A. (2007). Unattractive, promiscuous and heavy drinkers: Perceptions of women with tattoos. *Body Image, 4*(4), 343–352.

Timming, A. R. (2015). Visible tattoos in the service sector: A new challenge to recruitment and selection. *Work, Employment & Society, 29*(1), 60–78.

Timming, A. R. (2017). Body art as branded labour: At the intersection of employee selection and relationship marketing. *Human Relations, 70*(9), 1041–1063.

Timming, A. R., Nickson, D., Re, D., & Perrett, D. (2017). What do you think of my ink? Assessing the effects of body art on employment chances. *Human Resource Management, 56*(1), 133–149.

Timming, A. R., & Perrett, D. (2016). Trust and mixed signals: A study of religion, tattoos and cognitive dissonance. *Personality and Individual Differences, 97,* 234–238.

Timming, A. R., & Perrett, D. I. (2017). An experimental study of the effects of tattoo genre on perceived trustworthiness: Not all tattoos are created equal. *Journal of Trust Research, 7*(2), 115–128.

Triana, M. D. C., Jayasinghe, M., Pieper, J. R., Delgado, D. M., & Li, M. (2019). Perceived workplace gender discrimination and employee consequences: A meta-analysis and complementary studies considering country context. *Journal of Management, 45,* 2419–2447.

Turner, J. C., Hogg, M. A., Oakes, P. J., Reicher, S. D., & Wetherell, M. S. (1987). *Rediscovering the social group: A self-categorization theory.* Basil Blackwell.

Vans. (2020, January 01). A brief history of Vans: "Off the wall" since '66. https://www.vans.com/history/

Volvo. (2018, February 18). New-generation customers. https://www.volvocars.com/au/about/australia/i-roll-enewsletter/2018/february/new-generation-customers

Webster, J. R., Adams, G. A., Maranto, C. L., Sawyer, K., & Thoroughgood, C. (2018). Workplace contextual supports for LGBT employees: A review, meta-analysis, and agenda for future research. *Human Resource Management*, *57*(1), 193–210.

Wheeler, A. R., Richey, R. G., Tokkman, M., & Sablynski, C. J. (2006). Retaining employees for service competency: The role of corporate brand identity. *Journal of Brand Management*, *14*, 96–113.

Wilden, R., Gudergan, S., & Lings, I. (2010). Employer branding: Strategic implications for staff recruitment. *Journal of Marketing Management*, *26*, 56–73.

Williams, K., & O'Reilly, C. A. (1998). Demography and diversity in organizations: A review of 40 years of research. In B. M. Staw & L. L. Cummings (Eds.), *Research in organizational behavior* (Vol. 20, pp. 77–140). JAI Press.

Conclusions

Adelina Broadbridge

Introduction

Appearance is an expression of ourselves. As individuals, we can say a lot about our identity and values through our appearance – the clothes we wear, the way we present our bodies, our demeanour and manner of speech and the embellishments we might adopt to emphasise (or minimise) our identities. Yet the appearance and clothing we select not only communicates our identity in wider society, but also can affect how individuals engage at work and conveys particular meanings in the workplace (McInnis & Medvedev, 2021). Within the context of workplace employment appearance is an important resource, although some employees might be oblivious of its significant standing regarding their employment chances and/or progression.

In this handbook, we have presented 19 chapters that draw on a variety of authors and topics in the field and have shown how different factors, situations and norms regulate how appearance is regarded in the workplace. Each chapter has examined a particular aspect of appearance and considered its impact in employment terms. The chapters adopt a critical stance of physical appearance and exposed various tensions that require reconciliation. The issues raised in these chapters refer to various characteristics people possess in addition to how people may deliberately manipulate their appearance, and how these impact employment opportunities. The findings indicate the complexity of appearance and how it can be considered an asset or a drawback for employment purposes. It can either support the acquisition of a job and progression through the employment process, else it can lessen a person's chances in the workplace.

So how far have we come with appearance matters in the workplace? In this concluding chapter, we use evidence from contemporary research to argue that it would seem like not a great deal has progressed in terms of the possession of physical characteristics and appearance issues at work. Despite various protected characterises being legislated for, individuals' appearance can still be open to discrimination, albeit sometimes subtly. There is an expectation for everyone to appear appropriately, yet dress and appearance are tied in with hegemonic management (Haynes, 2012), and so in a male dominated culture, women and minorities particularly suffer owing to their deviation from the male standard

The Emerald Handbook of Appearance in the Workplace, 343–360
Copyright © 2024 by Emerald Publishing Limited
All rights of reproduction in any form reserved
doi:10.1108/978-1-80071-174-720230021

norm. There is a pressure to conform to idealised norms created by society and this is espoused by employers. Employees might be expected to present themselves in a way that meets organisational expectations and cultural norms, but not necessarily their own personal values or identities. Anyone not fitting the ideal image of what an employee should look like needs to consider altering their appearance in some way else remain vulnerable to discrimination and stereotyping at work. All of this can affect career chances, as well as leading to personal tensions of how to self-present.

Theoretical Underpinnings

Various theoretical lenses have been espoused in this handbook to understand and explain issues surrounding workplace appearance. These include inter alia stereotyping, facades of conformity, stigma, impression management, embodiment, cognitive dissonance and labelling theory. Many of these theories are derivatives of seminal philosophers such as Goffman (1959) and his work on stigma, performance and impression management, and Bourdieu (1984) and his concepts of cultural capital where physical appearance can be considered as an independent form of capital. Drawing on both Goffman (1959) and Bourdieu (1984), Witz et al. (2003) claimed that workers are moulded via training to embody the look of an organisation.

So some chapters align with the work of Goffman where employees' bodies, clothing and appearance have been controlled and form part of the performance and communication of an organisation's brand image. This appearance is not only confined to their dress but also by their mannerisms and scripted conversations with customers. Other chapters have roots in Bourdieu's (1984) theory of capital. For Bourdieu (1984), the body conveys symbolic power and is a form of physical capital (Haynes, 2012). Identifying physical appearance as a form of capital enables an understanding of how it can be transformed into the three basic forms of capital identified by Bourdieu (economic, social and cultural). The use and strategic manipulation of physical appearance can bring various benefits to the workplace in the form of these economic, social and cultural resources and assets.

Warhurst et al. (2000) drew on Hochschild's (1983) term aesthetic labour, which they defined as 'a supply of embodied capacities and attributes possessed by workers at the point of entry into employment...' (2000, p. 1). Employers then use these to ensure employees offer a particular style of service encounter. Özbilgin et al. (chapter 1) noted how carnal capital includes changes in the body which may be natural, involuntary and voluntary. They highlight the social dimension of appearance and how physical qualities are interpreted, rated and judged, and attributed varied meanings and values across different settings. This explains is how some people may experience positive experiences while others negative.

The Possession of Appearance Characteristics

Organisational standards, certainly in positions of power and influence, are generally based around a male norm; a norm which also tends to encompass Eurocentric, white, able bodied, cisgendered, well educated and middle class. Against these norms, various aspects of personal characteristics (e.g. gender, age, disability, race, class, sexuality) are connected with systemic forms of stereotyping, inequalities and power. Negative stereotypes about a specific group based on a common attribute such as appearance leads to communications prejudice and overt discrimination towards that group (Powroznik, 2017). Prejudice is the negative evaluation of a social group, and discrimination is the unfair and unequal treatment of that group. Minority groups are viewed as atypical and outsiders, and so are susceptible to being 'othered' thereby threatening their workplace and career chances.

As well as gender identity and age (discussed below), characteristics that employees may possess that can cause stigma in the workplace include fatness (Gruys, 2012; Powroznik, 2017; Roehling et al., 2018), accents (Carlson & McHenry, 2006; Timming, 2017), race (Johnson et al., 2017) and criminal history (Goffman, 1959; Young & Keech, 2022). Brower (2013) identified that appearance/dress codes punish anyone who is an outlier by reason of gender, sexuality, race, religion, or culture. Appearance based on various characteristics people possess has been shown to be problematic in various chapters of this book and have indicated that such stigmas, stereotypes and discrimination still exist (e.g. chapters Ferdous, chapter 6; Grant, Mizzi & O'Loghen, chapter 4; Karl, Peluchette & Dawson, chapter 3; Peluchette & Karl, chapter 2; Hurd, chapter 5).

An abundance of negative signifiers was used to describe curly hair and black women's hair (Peluchette & Karl; Karl et al., chapters 2 & 3). The same is true for overweight (Grant et al., chapter 4) and older people (Hurd, chapter 5). These all point away from the archetypal body ideals that seem to be so important in the western world. If a person is not deemed to conform with the organisational criteria, this can lead to their marginalisation and stigmatisation. This clearly makes appearance issues even more difficult for anyone who does not meet with the desired organisational standards. Watson et al. (2020) also concluded that physical characteristics such as body traits and clothing continue to influence the employment decisions of managers. Ferdous (chapter 6) demonstrated how Muslim women are 'othered' and suffer discriminatory treatment in the workforce. They are marked out by gender, race and religion, which is accentuated by their appearance. Wearing a hijab or veil forms part of this 'othering' process and them being regarded as less desirable and an outsider. From an employment perspective, Ferdous noted these women had the highest unemployment rates or were more likely to be working in the informal economy.

Gender

With regard to the possession of appearance characteristics, men face less predicaments by strict aesthetic standards than do women (Kuipers, 2015). Several chapters in this book relate specifically to gender (e.g. Ferdous, chapter 6, Grandy et al., chapter 8; Grant et al., chapter 4; Jyrkinen et al., chapter 11; Karl et al., chapter 3; Peluchette & Karl, chapter 2; Sanghvi and Hodges, chapter 9). They serve to demonstrate that women continue to face certain dilemmas in their appearance and presentation as part of their attempts to fit the ideal mould of acceptability in organisations.

Leading authors have problematised the issue of gender and conforming to managerial and professional expectations at work (e.g. Fitzgerald, 2018; Haynes, 2008, 2012; Mavin & Grandy, 2012). Masculinity and power are intertwined so that men represent the institutional norm and dominate. Drawing on Bourdieu's concepts of capital, Haynes (2008, 2012) explored how physical capital is connected with the process of socialisation, subordination and control, and how presentation and appearance is significant in the construction of the personal and professional self for displaying conformity (Haynes, 2008). Her work on women's careers in professional service firms (a sector where masculine professional embodiment is embedded in the culture of the profession and seen as natural and rewarded) found that in order to demonstrate professional identity, women needed to learn from others how to fit this dominant masculine model of performance or success. She found some women deliberately played the game as a way to succeed by endorsing masculine norms and using their dress and self-presentation as a means to support their credibility and authority. Haynes (2012), however, acknowledged how women face a professional dilemma in their demeanour and appearance according to traditional stereotypes. If they complied with the traditional masculine norms of behaviour, this was seen as converse to their femininity and so attracted negative descriptions. This led Haynes (2012) to conclude that 'Women have to tread a fine line between hiding negatively constructed aspects of femininity while displaying positively construed masculine forms of embodiment in order to be taken seriously' (Haynes, 2012, p. 504). Women are under pressure to look professional yet feminine enough. The work of Mavin and Grandy (2012, 2016a, 2016b), Fitzgerald (2018) and Tsaousi (2020) confirms this. Mavin and Grandy (2016a, 2016b) show that some women assume a tough and masculine management style in their attempt to blend in with the male management stereotype yet, they claim, they are simultaneously being given the message that they are different. Women who exhibit agentic behaviours in their demeanour associated with masculinity may therefore be open to reprimand and may be maligned by both men and women.

Fitzgerald's (2018) research confirmed that physical appearance, clothing, gestures and behaviours remain central to the practice of leadership, and also highlighted the contradictions women face. She found women moderated their dress so that they were not rejected as too feminine by their male colleagues yet not perceived as too masculine by their female peers. Women were expected to dress in understated ways so as not to draw attention to their physical presence or femininity or their credibility was at stake: 'Careful posture, neat unrestrained clothing (not too much colour), minimal make-up, and conservative hairstyles are deemed appropriately feminine and professional attire. These are the gendered signs of self-management and self-control that is overt, permissible and public'

(Fitzgerald, 2018, p. 4). Not doing so could result in recrimination and constraint. She argues 'women mask and monitor their feminine and "out of place" bodies through their dress and physical appearance in order to be seamlessly woven into the organizational fabric and not be marked by their bodily difference to their male colleagues' (Fitzgerald, 2018, p. 2). So, Fitzgerald argued, women leaders partake in self-regulatory practices to minimise their 'otherness' from their male colleagues and be perceived more positively. In Chapter 8, Grandy et al., declare that dress and appearance is tied to power relations and considerations of occupational prestige, gender, sexuality, class, race and culture. Through body, appearance and other performative aspects, women leaders in academia are simultaneously required to negotiate an inherently masculine culture (doing gender differently) yet at the same time are expected to exercise a degree of femininity (doing gender well).

The work of these authors illustrates how women's appearance is far more problematic to negotiate in organisations than men's and how dress codes are primarily gendered practices. The fact that women's bodies are more gendered and sexualised mean they face more challenges in their dress than men (Tsaousi, 2020) and they can be subjected to unrealistic standards of ideal appearance (McInnis & Medvedev, 2021).

Much work on gender and appearance assumes gender as a binary division. Brower (chapter 11) contests this. He explains gender expression as how one performs gender through clothing and other attire as well as behaviours and tone of voice. In the past decade we have seen the growth of Millennials and Generation Z identifying as gender expansive, gender fluid and non-binary more so than previous generations and so there are calls for organisations to take this into consideration when devising any dress code policy (Jones, 2018; Wilson & Meyer, 2021). However, Brower identified how transgender appearances might 'offend' customer expectations, thereby disrupting the overall brand image, so whether organisations take these issues seriously remains to be seen. Interestingly, Middlemiss (2018) reported a survey where 89% of employers with dress codes claim they took steps to ensure that their policy does not did not discriminate. Moreover, these companies stated they had only received 2.6% complaints that their code was discriminatory. Nonetheless, Middlemiss insists that discriminatory dress codes continue to disadvantage women and transgender employees.

Age

The issue of age is also an important demographic possession when considering the physical appearance of people in the workplace. It is of particular note given that retirement ages are rising across the western world, and Hurd (chapter 5) and Jyrkinen et al. (chapter 11) illustrate how appearance-based ageism in the workplace, especially for women, continues to be deeply engrained. The process of managing one's appearance starts early. From a young age, appearance is instilled into people's minds when applying for a job/entering the employment market. This was borne out by Yates (chapter 15), and Wood and Broadbridge (chapter 18). In the early stages of one's career pressures are placed on employees to be convincing and professional, and this necessitates wearing safe and conservative clothing. Work by Cutts et al. (2015) found that students viewed clothing and appearance as an important aspect of their transition to the workplace, believing that appearance could help them be taken more seriously and enable them to 'fit in' and meet the expectations of employers. Hird-Saunders (2022) also found this to be the case with young women lawyers in the early stages of their career. For both studies, it was perceived that women and men are judged on their appearance although women were judged more critically than men. Wood and Broadbridge (chapter 18) also demonstrated that people were conscious of being judged for their appearance, claiming that they would cover up tattoos at an interview in fear of negative stereotyping and discrimination by prospective employers. This might be sage thinking on their behalf, but like Cutts et al. (2015), there was some recognition that this might be at the expense of their identity and values. These studies reveal how the younger generation continues to comply rather than challenge these organisational standards, hence establishing their conformity at an early age.

As people age, this may not overly change men's appearance, but it can impact more on women's appearance in several ways depending on the circumstances. Various chapters in the book have established that appearance is closely connected with aesthetic labour. Jyrkinen et al. (chapter 11) comment that aesthetic labour is highly aged as well as being gendered, racialised and classed. Older workers are regarded as no longer possessing the aesthetic labour qualities perceived important by customers (Warhurst & Nickson, 2007), and companies may implicitly or explicitly make clear preference for younger workers to fit their brand image (Nickson & Baum, 2017). While many men are traditionally associated with becoming more distinguished and wise as they age, ageing for a woman is another story. Jyrkinen (2014) discussed how the symptoms of menopause visibly ages women. With this they start experiencing the effects of lookism, and so the process of disguising one's age might be employed in order to appeal more aesthetically. Others' evaluations can have an influence on women's efforts to look young, well groomed and slim, and, as indicated by Jyrkinen et al. (chapter 11), the female gaze is also not necessarily gentle or supportive. Moreover, Hurd (chapter 5) highlighted that women are likely to suffer more harshly than men from financial insecurities and pensions as they age, and so economic necessity can also result in their transformations (McInnis & Medvedev, 2021) to maintain their looks.

Another point of interest is that as one gets older and more senior in the workplace so one may feel more established in themselves. In professional and managerial posts, having spent time blending in, here could be older women's chance to stand out and be a little more rebellious in their appearance. Fitzgerald (2018) found some women leaders exercised some resistance with their appearance, such as adding a colourful scarf to a conservative suit, leading Fitzgerald (2018) to argue that while mainly conforming, they also deliberately marked themselves out as different. Similarly, Hird-Saunders (2022) found older established women lawyers to dare to expose themselves more by adding colour to their attire. Their position in their profession had conferred more confidence and enabled them to exercise more defiance to traditional norms and stereotypes. This was markedly different from the junior women lawyers who felt the need to conform fully with traditionally valued appearance norms, and not deviate in any way from them (Hird-Saunders, 2022). In fact, the older women were found to caution younger and more junior women to be more conservative in their appearance. This was possibly to ensure that younger women 'blended in' rather than 'stood out' for the wrong reasons thus potentially damaging their career opportunities. So, as Fitzgerald's and Hird-Saunder's research signified, it might be argued that there is a need for younger and/or junior women to fit in or fake it until they make it. Only then can they loosen the reins of traditional norms and legitimately stand apart, thereby demonstrating their seniority, sense of empowerment and authority.

Other Possessions

Eagly et al. (1991) referred to the physical attractiveness stereotype and how beauty is considered positively and advantageous because people associate it with other desirable traits. Beauty is consequently regarded as commercially beneficial by employers and customers (Anderson et al., 2010; Hamermesh, 2011; James, 2008; Warhurst & Nickson, 2009). Overall, a person's beauty and attractiveness poses more of an advantage than disadvantage in the workplace (e.g. see chapter 10 by Frevert et al.). Mujtaba et al. (chapter 12) argue that appearance affects first impressions and attractive candidates benefit from this 'unearned privilege'. Frevert et al. (chapter 10) also argue that attractive candidates were perceived more competent or a better fit for the job. They show the link of attractiveness to the selection process, in interactions with others, impression management and also for leadership positions. Frevert et al. assert that 'certain facial characteristics are ascribed status values that act as proxy indicators of leaders' perceived competence'. This chapter verifies how one looks can affect the recruitment and career progression decisions of employers.

Conversely, and drawing out the gender dynamics, Jyrkinen et al. (chapter 11) commented that young women could be regarded as *too* good looking to be taken seriously enough, arguing that they were evaluated first as a woman not a manager. This adds another complexity into the equation of how one appears in the workplace. It can be associated with the incongruity of the roles ascribed to women and the masculine construct of management and leadership (Eagly & Karau, 2002; Haynes, 2008, 2012; Mavin & Grandy, 2012). Furthermore, it can also lead to issues with the objectification and sexualisation of women, a topic that has received less attention in this book.

A different kind of possessed characteristic is criminal history, and this is an often stigmatised characteristic (Goffman, 1956). This was the subject of examination by Jones Young and Anazodo (chapter 16). They talk about the 'bleak' experience of ex-offenders trying to return to the workplace and show how gender, race and appearance can all interact to impact on their employment chances. Slightly encouraging however, despite many organisations being concerned about customer perceptions of employees, Young and Keech (2022) found evidence from a survey to suggest that organisations should not assume consumers will respond negatively to them employing ex-offenders.

The Manipulation of Appearance Characteristics

There can be an incongruity between the 'real' and 'presented self' in the workplace for individuals who do not meet organisational criteria. They are vulnerable to being exposed by their appearance else may need to decide what aspects of their identity they reveal. This draws on Goffman's theory where the actor suppresses aspects of their self or conceals information in order to create or maintain a self-representation that accords with the audience. Particular personal characteristics such as race may not be changeable but employees may decide to conceal or disguise other aspects of their personal characteristics such as age, forms of disabilities, sexuality and class. So, women conform to masculine standards of dress; LGBTQI+ do not disclose their true selves via their appearance; disabled people may hide their disability; older people try to look younger. One question that needs to be addressed is at what price does hiding various characteristics have on one's true identity? Consider the stress and strain these individuals experience in having to hide certain aspects of themselves in order to conform to company policies. Jyrkinen et al. (chapter 11) draw attention to some of these tensions between individuals trying to fit in with the organisational codes and being true to themselves. Thus, we see how in a working environment pressure can be placed on people to engineer their appearance in order to 'blend in' or 'fit in' and conform with organisational norms and practices. Failure to meet these norms, customs and expectations can result in their abilities and authority being questioned (see Barry, 2018) and them being marginalised (Haynes, 2008, 2012).

Identity is performative in the sense that individuals make decisions about how to present themselves to others. The way work continues to largely be organised can be related to the 'facades of conformity' noted by Hewlin (2003) where people behave in a way that is consistent to the organisation thereby masking their true self and raising issues of dissonance. This led van den Berg and Arts (2019) to argue that the pressure to conform and look a certain way has become an occupational necessity. Hird-Saunders (2022) confirmed how women lawyers used dress to construct their professional identity and how they engineered their appearance to present themselves differently according to their situation and/or audiences/clients. This was also found to be the case with women academics Tsaousi (2020) and reinforced in the chapter by Grandy et al. (chapter 8).

So we see that some employees intentionally present themselves differently in different settings (Clarke & Turner, 2007), and according to the workplace culture and expected behaviours (Brower, 2013). Here, appearance is used strategically to manage the impression of others, and alter an individual's body image (Frith & Gleeson, 2008; Haynes, 2012). Various chapters (e.g. Hurd, chapter 5; Karl et al., chapter 3; Wood & Broadbridge, chapter 18) have shown that numerous employees manipulate their appearances at work in order to conform and adhere to organisational rules of dress and appearance.

Other chapters have indicated the tensions produced between conforming to workplace dress codes and showing one's self-expression; they either resist appearance codes or deny their own self-expression (e.g. Brower, chapter 7; Wood and Broadbridge, chapter 18; Efthymiou, Orphanidou & Karayiannis, chapter 17; Chia & Timming, chapter 19). By conforming, individuals are compromising part of their appearance and identity to meet these organisational expectations. This then raises questions about the degree of choice involved in this process. Do people readily choose how they appear in the workplace to impress others or are they coerced to conform to organisational norms in order to secure or protect their employment? If the latter, surely this serves to ratify the persistence of discrimination and stereotypes associated with appearance. As seen earlier, this also can be associated to the stage in one's career. Those in earlier stages of their career may feel under more obligation to conform than those at later stages or in more senior roles where they feel more established.

The issue of lookism and aesthetic labour draws on Brannon's (1993) perspectives of appearance management: a self-system (where we draw on ourselves and find strategies to conceal or reveal ourselves through dress and self-presentation), and a behavioural system which concerns the social implications of dress and helps determine our strategies for social interactions via impression management techniques. Looking and sounding 'the part' continues to be an important feature of many contemporary workplaces and can be crucial to career success (see Sanghvi & Hodges, chapter 9; Warhurst et al., chapter 13). Mujtaba et al. (chapter 12) illustrate how appearance continues to affect customer perceptions of the brand value of the organisation, and can subsequently affect appearance based hiring. Efthymiou et al. (chapter 17) emphasise how brand management can be accomplished by matching the appearance of employees to a hotel's aesthetic philosophy and target guest market. In some kind of hotels, tattoos and piercings are embraced, while in others they are forbidden; it all depends on the culture of the organisation. Thus, customer perceptions remain extremely important, and employees are judged according to their appearance as also seen in the chapters by Chia and Timming (chapter 19); Jones Young and Anazodo (chapter 16); Mujtaba et al. (chapter 12). While some attempts have been made to oppose appearance-based discrimination, Waring (chapter 14) shows how contradictions remain, particularly where aesthetic labour is used for commercial gain. Timming (2017) argues that in customer facing jobs there remains evidence of prejudice and discrimination on the basis of 'physical capital' and this was also uncovered in the chapters by Ferdous (chapter 6), Grant et al. (chapter 4), Hurd (chapter 5) and Karl et al. (chapter 3).

Perpetuation of Trends or Is There a Way Forward?

The above observations are discouraging, and we might question whether the circumstances are likely to be perpetuated. The ageing population is of concern given that engrained appearance based ageism in the workplace continues to exist (Hurd, chapter 5). At the other end of the age spectrum, despite Generations

Y and Z valuing independence, personal integrity and authenticity (Broadbridge et al., 2007; Burke, 2019; Twenge & Campbell, 2008), indications are that they can still be swayed by stereotypical views and are prepared to conform in the workplace whether this be voluntary or involuntarily (see for example Karl et al., chapter 3; Peluchette & Dawson, chapter 2; Wood & Broadbridge, chapter 18).

Over the last decade, there has been an increasing attention on people who identify as gender nonconforming, gender expansive or transgender. This gives rise to appearance issues in work as these people are less likely to be catered for in dress codes. These staff are open to customer and co-worker abuse because of how they look and present themselves (Bowie, 2019). Recently, Hadjisolomou (2021) found transgender retail employees were stigmatised because of their appearance through a series of micro aggressions from customers, and these were often ignored by management. This is of considerable concern as this dismissal by management emphasises their disregard to such matters in favour of customer opinion. This completely serves to perpetuate and sanction discriminatory behaviour towards employees who do not conform to idealised appearance stereotypes. Without a critical examination of organisational cultures, minimal change is likely for the near future.

With the growing obesity epidemic over the last couple of decades and its associated health problems, we might speculate that employers in future might be even *more* discerning in their employment practices of overweight people. This serves to intensify negative stereotypes and stigmatisation on the grounds of appearance. For several years prospective employees' profiles on social media sites such as LinkedIn and Facebook have been used by potential employers to take decisions about hiring right from the very start of the employment process. The use of social media in the recruitment process was referred to by Frevert et al. (chapter 10) and mentioned as becoming *more* common, corroborating the findings of Watson et al. (2020). Moreover, the advent of social media has intensified the fixation with appearance. We are surrounded by a plethora of aesthetically pleasing bodies and images, many of which have been enhanced to display specific notions of beauty. Younger people (especially women) are adopting invasive and non-invasive cosmetic procedures in an aim to transform their looks. This does nothing to overthrow the concepts of beauty in society and can even heighten them. The consequences include damage to self-image and self-esteem, and can result in mental health difficulties (Well, 2023). It also poses physical health issues and negative practices such as the consumption of illegal drugs and weight loss pills (Butler & Harris, 2015). Further health issues including death are increasingly reported by the media. Nevertheless, the global cosmetic surgery industry is predicted to rise almost 30% between 2022 and 2029 which is undoubtedly associated with the importance of aesthetics in our lives (Fortune Business Insights, 2022). Thus, we may see even more importance attached with appearance than previously. This not only impacts on individuals' physical and mental health generally but might become all embracing in their employment prospects as well.

Societal pressures to adopt Eurocentric standards of beauty remain (Dawson & Karl, 2018). Consider the amount of East Asian women who are transforming their bodies to look more European through for example, their facial features and skin tones. Recent research positions Eurocentric hair as the ideal at work (Johnson et al., 2017), and natural hair on Black women encompasses negative connotations for workplace employment and continued stereotyping and discrimination (see Karl et al. chapter 3; Bagalini, 2021; Gougeon, 2021; Lee, 2020). However, of some consolation is that several laws are now being taken/appropriated in the US and UK regarding the wearing of natural hair and calls for afro hair to be made a protected characteristic which is somewhat encouraging (Karl et al., chapter 3; CBBC, 2021).

The issue of body art is one that is interesting to reflect upon and has witnessed more leniency of late as tattoos and piercings have become more accepted in society and more people have acquired them. Wood and Broadbridge (chapter 18), as well as findings by Kirk (2022) proposed that visible tattoos are generally acceptable in various work environments as long as they are not offensive or on the face, neck or hands. Nonetheless, they can still be considered a taboo subject when it comes to employment. Tattoos are not a protected characteristic, meaning that employers can refuse to hire or legally dismiss a person having a tattoo. A tattooist reported by Kirk (2022) explained she alerted her clients to the possible negative consequences relating to hand and neck tattoos for their future employment. This tended to deter the majority of people from proceeding with the tattoo, yet it does continue to perpetuate appearance assumptions in the workplace. Nevertheless, several sources have found that labour market conditions (as well as recruiters'/managers' own proclivities) can impact on whether appearance is deemed tolerable in the workplace (e.g. Efthymiou et al., chapter 17; Rylah, 2022). Efthymiou et al. argued managers are forced by labour market conditions to hire employees they wouldn't have otherwise hired, thus pointing to economic conditions being the driving force rather than any relaxation of social considerations. Labour market conditions might also explain how some company appearance codes are ambiguous. These codes can leave employees bemused regarding what is acceptable and unacceptable appearance at work (see Mujtaba et al., chapter 12 and Warhurst & van den Broek, chapter 13). Middlemiss (2018) specified that even if there is no explicit reference to clothing in the employment contract, employees are still under an implied duty to observe their employer's reasonable and lawful instructions regarding expected standards, including their clothing and appearance.

In the United Kingdom, it is illegal to discriminate against people with protected characteristics (e.g. gender, age, disability, sexuality, race, religion), yet we have seen through various chapters that in practice, these people continue to be discriminated against on the basis of their appearance. Current legislation regarding appearance at work seems to be sporadic and unhelpful. Warhurst et al. (chapter 13) showed how legislation in Victoria, NSW prohibits discrimination against workers on the basis of height, weight or other bodily characteristics. Nevertheless, it can be difficult to prove discrimination on the basis of appearance, and Chia and Timming (chapter 19) argue that complainants would struggle to win a discrimination case. Middlemiss also acknowledged the lack of effective legal basis for challenging employer dress codes in the UK workplace. Courts mainly rule in favour of the employers and claim that it does not constitute discrimination (Dawson & Karl, 2018). As such, legal cases often support the employers' managerial prerogative to impose dress restrictions, which tend to adhere to traditional stereotypes (Dawson & Karl, 2018). The power of legislation therefore seems to be largely ineffectual when applied to employees and their rights, which can help to perpetuate traditional stereotypes.

From the chapters in this book, we can deduce that there remains considerable discrimination and stereotyping based on appearance in the workplace. Very little of what has been reported differs from previous work on appearance. This begs the question as to how things might change and what recommendation can be made for the future. How do we stop treating people inequitably on the basis of their appearance, particularly when we know it is commercially lucrative?

Morally, we can argue that appearance-based discrimination is wrong. It has nothing (or rarely) to do with the capabilities of somebody to undertake the job. However, it continues to flourish, and so building a business case for examining appearance policies may be the solution if we are to revolutionise future approaches towards organisational appearance policies. Employers need to re-evaluate their appearance policies and consider how their workplace culture and employment practices can be altered in harmony with broader diversity and inclusion (D&I) issues, so that differentiating employees on their appearance ends. So, for example, in line with gender expansion, organisational dress codes should be revisited, so that they take into consideration gender fluidity and represent gender neutrality (Fütty et al., 2020; Middlemiss, 2018). Brower (chapter 7) recognises that gender-neutral dress codes mitigate some aspects of a gender-differentiated policy but is not a panacea. However, another question is the extent to which D&I initiatives are truly incorporated into an organisation's strategic plan or are they a mere public relations activity, as Waring (chapter 14) suspected of CSR initiatives? Unless the senior management in organisations genuinely commits to changing company culture and takes D&I initiatives seriously, little is likely to change. Companies need to sincerely close the gap between their espoused and enacted values, otherwise appearance policies will remain to be paid lip service. To help this change, several authors recommended raising awareness of appearance issues in the workplace via activities such as unconscious bias training and holding employee resource groups. These would help to educate staff in the understanding that discrimination on the basis of appearance for whatever reason is deemed inexcusable. Acknowledging the many differences in people and aligning appearance policies with a more diverse customer group can help to overcome some appearance issues in the workplace, and should contribute not only morally but also economically.

Overall Summary

The chapters in this book have revealed the importance appearance continues to have in the workplace, and how this may impact on individuals' chances for employment. Appearance can be a critical factor in contributing to an organisation's financial performance. It meets these economic needs by prescribing certain employee appearance code expectations that will satisfy the needs of customers, while promoting an aspired to brand image. This commercial viability was alluded to in various chapters (see for example, the chapters by Chia & Timming, chapter 19; Grant et al., chapter 4; Mutjaba et al., chapter 12; Warhurst & van den Broek, chapter 13), and explains why specific organisations may have differing appearance guidelines in their attempts to match the target customer profile (see Efthymiou et al., chapter 17).

The pressure to conform to idealised norms created by society is endorsed in many organisations. We have seen how appearance is socially constructed in the workplace, and dress codes and norms follow a predominantly male model. People not fitting the idealised norms are 'othered', and this can create significant barriers to their labour market integration and result in their poorer outcomes in employment terms. Discrimination occurs and inevitably affects those who are in the minority in society, i.e. those who conform least to the standardised idealised norms. Any deviation of an employee in appearance terms can be subject to persecution. The chapters have shown how negative attributes are still associated with certain looks (e.g. race, age, weight, religion). Idealised norms have led to the growth in terms such as 'lookism' and 'aesthetic labour' as companies seek to employ certain types of persons for their organisation. Attractiveness serves as a social status and can be associated with positive benefits in employment chances (Frevert et al., chapter 10).

Gender and appearance was the focus of several chapters (Grandy et al., chapter 8; Peluchette & Karl, chapter 2; Sanghvi & Hodges, chapter 9) because their deviation from the male standard norm illustrates how organisations continue to be highly gendered. These chapters show how women can be 'othered' and suffer from negative stereotypes and biases. Further, employers may capitalise on women's sexuality in order to attract customers (Mutjaba et al., chapter 12). Yet, much stereotyping and discrimination in appearance terms can be extended to, and also intersect with, other protected characteristics (see for example chapters by Brower, chapter 7; Ferdous, chapter 6; Hurd, chapter 5; Jrykinnen et al., chapter 11; Karl et al., chapter 3).

We have seen how some people will attempt to 'blend in' with the stereotyped norm and use their appearance strategically as a form of impression management. However, blending in can lead to supplementary problems. As Karl et al. (chapter 3) showed, when women blend in, they are emphasising their similarities with members of the more positively regarded social identity. This is the same for other minority groups. By doing so, are they compromising or suppressing their own identities in the quest for employment opportunities? Are they merely helping to anchor and perpetuate these idealised norms? Yet, contravening the idealised norms is difficult (especially when you are in a minority) and can jeopardise employment prospects. In this sense, we can view appearance as a currency, investment or resource. Several participants in Peluchette & Karl 's (chapter 2) and Wood and Broadridge's (chapter 18) chapters said they would not want to work for a company that required them to change their appearance. This is commendable morally, yet it is interesting to reflect on the reality of this when confronted with the opportunity of a job, especially when labour market conditions are adverse. As Sarpila and Erola (2016) noted, as jobs become more scarce so focussing on one's physical appearance may become *more* of an occupational necessity. Many will end up compromising their appearance in their endeavour to secure some employment as Wood and Broadbridge, chapter 18 discovered. This perpetuates the appearance norms already in place and preserves notions of the 'right' appearance in the workplace. Yet ignoring appearance norms may lead to a candidate not gaining a job because of their mismatch with the standards of the organisations they are applying to. Yates illustrated this dilemma in chapter 15 when discussing the challenges career advisors face in advising clients whether to adhere to appearance matters. Her suggestion to raise appearance issues through a handbook or via the website rather than raising the issue to clients directly arguably serves to maintain traditional viewpoints and presents a genuine dilemma for advisors.

It seems that only when one gets to a certain level, can they resist appearance norms and defy certain conventions. Rather than blending in, this enables them to stand out but this time for the right reasons, demonstrating their self-assurance and authority. Power lies in the hands of the employers; employees have little control - they either accept how they should appear in the workplace else run the risk of discrimination or leave. As Chia and Timing (chapter 19) argued, few employees are likely to win any legal battle over appearance issues in the workplace.

The contributions of this book show how appearance in the workplace is possessed and manipulated in different respects. Not everyone experiences the benefits of appearance equally. Some who do not possess the right characteristics expected by organisational norms and cultures are open to discrimination and face fewer employment chances.

There are limitations and areas for further research uncovered by this book. Some authors had to withdraw their participation in the book because of the consequences of Covid. Their contributions could have brought a different approach to the topic area and uncovered fresh areas of interest. The chapters are predominantly referring to western countries. Efforts were made to include more worldwide perspectives regarding appearance in the workplace but this was not possible. The influence of cultural differences on workplace appearance is important to research further. Another area requiring more research is that of employees who identify as non binary or gender expansive. This issue generates considerable negativity generally in society. It can be extremely alienating in employment where the employee is never sure how an employer, fellow employee, manager or customer will react to them. Understanding their concerns and how to best address these is imperative. Another issue that did not constitute much attention in the book yet is worthy to unpick in more depth is that of sexualisation. Sexual harassment is a very real issue in organisations and can be influenced by appearance policies, especially those that emphasise sexual attraction, and lead to adverse consequences for employment opportunities.

More voice should be given directly to minority workers and those with protected characteristics so their stories of appearance experiences and discrimination can be heard, e.g. LGBTQI+, race, ethnicity, pregnant, disabled. It is important to understand their lived experiences associated with appearance in the workplace. How do they fare if they have to conceal parts of their identities? Is the suppressing of their individualism leading to other negative concerns? How do appearance issues faced by people affect their self-esteem and self-confidence, and how might this affect their relative work-based experiences and performance?

I hope the issues raised in this book have provoked curiosity among its readership and encourages researchers to continue exploring this fascinating and highly relevant area of research.

References

Anderson, T. L., Grunert, C., Katz, A., & Lovascio, S. (2010). Aesthetic capital: A research review on beauty perks and penalties. *Sociology Compass, 4*(8), 564–575. https://doi.org/10.1111/j.1751-9020.2010.00312.x

Bagalini, A. (2021). How wearing natural hairstyles harms the prospects of Black women. https://www.weforum.org/agenda/2021/02/natural-hair-black-women-job-discrimination/

Barry, B. (2018). (Re)fashioning masculinity: Social identity and context in men's hybrid masculinities through dress. *Gender & Society, 32*(5), 638–662.

van den Berg, M., & Arts, J. (2019). The aesthetics of work-readiness: Aesthetic judgements and pedagogies for conditional welfare and post-Fordist labour markets. *Work, Employment & Society, 33*(2), 298–313. https://doi.org/10.1177/0950017018758196

Bourdieu, P. (1984). *Distinction: A social critique of the judgement of taste.* Harvard University Press.

Bowie, S. (2019). *An evaluation on trans-issues within the workplace of Company A and whether Trans-inclusive initiatives can effectively influence employee perception on transgenderism.* Unpublsihed dissertation. University of Stirling.

Brannon, E. L. (1993). Affect and cognition in appearance management: A review. In S. J. Lennon & L. D. Burns (Eds.), *Social science aspects of dress: New directions* (pp. 82–92). Monument: International Textiles and Apparel Association.

Broadbridge, A., Maxwell, G., & Ogden, S. (2007). 13_2_30: Expectations, perceptions and experiences of retail employment for Generation Y. *Career Development International, 12*(6), 523–544.

Brower, T. (2013). What's in the closet: Dress and appearance codes and lessons from sexual orientation. *Equality, Diversity and Inclusion: An International Journal, 32*(5), 491–502. https://doi.org/10.1108/EDI-02-2013-0006

Burke, F. (2019, February 26). Gen Z is all about authenticity. https://medium.com/clyde-group/gen-z-is-all-about-authenticity-59d863b0bdcf. Accessed on June 29, 2022.

Butler, C., & Harris, J. (2015). Pills, ills and the ugly face of aesthetic labour: 'They should've discriminated against me'. *Work, Employment & Society*, *29*(3), 508–516.

Carlson, H. K., & McHenry, M. A. (2006). Effect of accent and dialect on employability. *Journal of Employment Counseling*, *43*(2), 70–81. https://doi.org/10.1002/j.2161-1920.2006.tb00008.x

CBBC Newsround. (2021). Afro hair discrimination should be treated as racism, say MPs and campaigners – CBBC Newsround.

Clarke, V., & Turner, K. (2007). Clothes maketh the queer? Dress, appearance and the construction of lesbian, gay and bisexual identities. *Feminism & Psychology*, *17*(2), 267–276.

Cutts, B., Hooley, T., & Yates, J. (2015). Fitting in or being yourself? How undergraduates plan to use hair, clothes and make-up to smooth their transition to the workplace. *Industry and Higher Education*, *29*(4), 271–282.

Dawson, G., & Karl, K. (2018). I am not my hair, or am I? Examining hair choices of Black female executives. *Journal of Business Diversity*, *18*, 46–56.

Eagly, A. H., Ashmore, R. D., Makhijani, M. G., & Longo, L. C. (1991). What is beautiful is good, but: Meta-analysis of the beauty is good stereotype literature. *Psychological Bulletin*, *110*, 109–128.

Eagly, A. H., & Karau, S. J. (2002). Role congruity theory of prejudice toward female leaders. *Psychological Review*, *109*(3), 573–598. https://doi.org/10.1037/0033-295x.109.3.573

Fitzgerald, T. (2018). Looking good and being good: Women leaders in Australian universities. *Education Sciences*, *8*(2), 54. https://doi.org/10.3390/educsci8020054

Fortune Business Insights. (2022). Cosmetic surgery market size, share, growth & trends [2029].https://www.fortunebusinessinsights.com/cosmetic-surgery-market-102628

Frith, H., & Gleeson, K. (2008). Dressing the body: The role of clothing in sustaining body pride and managing body distress. *Qualitative Research in Psychology*, 249–264.

Fütty, T. J., Höhne, M. S., & Caselles, E. L. (2020). *Gender diversity in employment and occupation. Employers' needs and options to implement anti-discrimination policies*. Federal Anti-Discrimination Agency.

Goffman, E. (1956). Embarrassment and social organization. *American Journal of Sociology*, *62*, 264–271.

Goffman, E. (1959). *The presentation of self in everyday life*. Doubleday Anchor Books.

Gougeon, R. (2021). Black hair' is never 'just hair': A closer look at Afro discrimination in the workplace. Law.Com. https://www.law.com/international-edition/2021/10/28/black-hair-is-never-just-hair-a-closer-look-at-afro-discrimination-in-the-workplace/?slreturn=20230228104805

Gruys, K. (2012). Does this make me look fat? Aesthetic labor and fat talk as emotional labor in a women's plus-size clothing store. *Social Problems*, *59*(4), 481–500.

Hadjisolomou, A. (2021). Doing and negotiating transgender on the front line: Customer abuse, transphobia and stigma in the food retail sector. *Work, Employment & Society*, *35*(5), 979–988.

Hamermesh, D. S. (2011). *Beauty pays: Why attractive people are more successful*. Princeton University Press.

Haynes, K. (2008). (Re)figuring accounting and maternal bodies: The gendered embodiment of accounting professionals. *Accounting, Organizations and Society, 33*(4–5), 328–348.

Haynes, K. (2012). Body beautiful? Gender, identity and the body in professional services firms, gender. *Work and Organization, 19*(5), 489–507.

Hewlin, P. (2003). And the award for best actor goes to. . .: Facades of conformity in organizational settings. *Academy of Management Review, 28*(4), 633–642. https://doi.org/10.5465/amr.2003.10899442

Hird-Saunders, S. A. (2022, July). *'An exploration of women lawyers' experiences of managing appearance at work.* Unpublished PhD thesis. The University of Stirling.

Hochschild, A. R. (1983). *The managed heart.* University of California Press.

James, H. R. (2008, Winter). If you are attractive and you know it, please apply: Appearance based discrimination and employer discretion. *Valparaiso University Law Review, 42*, 629–677.

Johnson, A., Godsil, R., MacFarlane, J., Tropp, L. R., & Goff, P. A. (2017, February). Explicit and implicit attitudes toward Black women's hair. https://perception.org/wp-content/uploads/2017/01/TheGood-HairStudyFindingsReport.pdf. Accessed on June 29, 2022.

Jones, E. M. (2018). The kids are queer: The rise of post-millennial American queer identification. In C. Stewart (Ed.), *Lesbian, gay, bisexual, and transgender Americans at risk: Problems and solutions.* Praeger.

Jyrkinen, M. (2014). Women managers, careers and gendered ageism. *Scandinavian Journal of Management, 30*(2), 175–185. https://doi.org/10.1016/j.scaman.2013.07.002

Kirk, I. (2022). Should visible tattoos be allowed in the workplace? https://yougov.co.uk/topics/society/articles-reports/2022/08/05/should-visible-tattoos-be-allowed-workplace. Accessed on November 11, 2022.

Kuipers, G. (2015). Beauty and distinction? The evaluation of appearance and cultural capital in five European countries. *Poetics, 53*, 38–51. https://doi.org/10.1016/j.poetic.2015.10.001

Lee, S. (2020). Bias against natural hair limits opportunities for Black women, study suggests, Verywell mind. https://www.verywellmind.com/bias-against-natural-hair-limits-opportunity-for-black-women-5077299

Mavin, S., & Grandy, G. (2012). Doing gender well and differently in management. *Gender in Management: An International Journal, 27*(4), 218–231.

Mavin, S., & Grandy, G. (2016a). A theory of abject appearance: Women elite leaders' intra-gender 'management' of bodies and appearance. *Human Relations, 69*(5), 1095–1120. https://doi.org/10.1177/0018726715609107

Mavin, S., & Grandy, G. (2016b). Women elite leaders doing respectable business femininity: How privilege is conferred, contested and defended through the body. *Gender, Work and Organization, 23*(4), 379–396.

McInnis, A., & Medvedev, K. (2021). Sartorial appearance management strategies of creative professional women over age 50 in the fashion industry. *Fashion Practice, 13*(1), 25–47.

Middlemiss, S. (2018). Not what to wear? Employers' liability for dress codes? *International Journal of Discrimination and the Law, 18*(1), 40–51. https://doi.org/10.1177/1358229118757867

Nickson, D., & Baum, T. (2017). Young at heart, but what about my body? Age and aesthetic labour in the hospitality and retail industries. In E. Parry & J. McCarthy

(Eds.), *The Palgrave handbook of age diversity and work*. Palgrave Macmillan Ltd. (pp. 539–559).

Powroznik, K. M. (2017). Healthism and weight-based discrimination: The unintended consequences of health promotion in the workplace. *Work and Occupations*, *44*(2), 139–170. https://doi.org/10.1177/0730888416682576

Roehling, P. V., Roehling, M. V., & Elluru, A. (2018). Size does matter: The impact of size on career. In A. M. Broadbridge & S. L. Fielden (Eds.), *Research handbook of diversity and careers*. Edward Elgar, Chapter 6.

Rylah, J. B. (2022). Second change hiring, explained. *The Hustle*. https://thehustle.co/10122022-second-chance-hiring/. Accessed on November 11, 2022.

Sarpila, O., & Erola, J. (2016). Physical attractiveness – Who believes it is a ticket to success? *Research on Finnish Society*, *9*, 5–14.

Timming, A. (2017). Body art as branded labour: At the intersection of employee selection and relationship marketing. *Human Relations*, *70*(9), 1041–1063.

Tsaousi, C. (2020). That's funny…you don't look like a lecturer! Dress and professional identity of female academics. *Studies in Higher Education*, *45*(9), 1809–1820. https://doi.org/10.1080/03075079.2019.1637839

Twenge, J., & Campbell, S. (2008). Generational differences in psychological traits and their impact in the workplace. *Journal of Managerial Psychology*, *23*(8), 862–877. https://doi.org/10.1108/02683940810904367

Warhurst, C., & Nickson, D. (2007). Employee experience of aesthetic labour in retail and hospitality. *Work, Employment & Society*, *21*(1), 103–120.

Warhurst, C., & Nickson, D. (2009). Who's got the look? Emotional, aesthetic and sexualised labour in interactive service's. *Gender, Work and Organization*, *16*(3), 385–404.

Warhurst, C., Nickson, D., Witz, A., & Cullen, A. (2000). Aesthetic labour in interactive service work: Some case study evidence from the 'new' Glasgow. *Service Industries Journal*, *20*(3), 1–18.

Watson, B. F., Griggs, T. L., & Szeman, M. (2020). When hair color influences job marketability: The impact of red hair color on perceived attributes and employment outcomes for Caucasian male and female job applicants. *Journal of Business, Industry and Economics*, *25*(spring), 33–63.

Well, T. (2023). The hidden danger of online beauty filters. *Psychology Today*, The Hidden Danger of Online Beauty Filters | Psychology Today United Kingdom.

Wilson, B. D. M., & Meyer, I. H. (2021). *Nonbinary LGBTQ Adults in the United States*. The Williams Institute. https://williamsinstitute.law.ucla.edu/wp-content/uploads/Nonbinary-LGBTQ-Adults-Jun-2021.pdf

Witz, A., Warhurst, C., & Nickson, D. (2003). The labour of aesthetics and the aesthetics of organization. *Organization*, *10*(1), 33–54.

Young, N. C. J., & Keech, J. (2022). Second chance hiring: Exploring consumer perception of employers who hire individuals with criminal histories. *Management Decision*, *60*(9), 2389–2408.

Index

Abject appearance, 157–158
Absenteeism, 33
Academia, 60, 156
  bodies of women in academia as
    barriers to advancement,
    158–160
Academic discipline, 63–65
Academic leaders, 156
Acceptance, 321
Acknowledgement/acknowledging,
    188–189
  of beauty, 188–189
  of sex, 188–189
Advocacy Academy, 30–31
Aesthetic labour, 2, 4, 8, 198, 234, 237,
    250, 302–303, 344
  data, 200
  professional women in
    low/no-hierarchy
    organisations, 204–208
  rebelling against aesthetic labour
    and lookism pressures,
    203–204
  recommendations, 208–209
  senior women managers,
    200–204
  theoretical framework, 198–200
Afrocentric hairstyles, 58, 66
Age, 292, 347, 349
Age Discrimination in Employment
    Act (ADEA), 219–221
Age-based discrimination, 102
Ageing, 102–103
Ageism, 104–105
  ageing, gender and older body,
    102–103
  ageism, appearance and workplace,
    104–105

  older workers' experiences of and
    responses to ageism in
    workplace, 105–107
  practical implications and
    recommendations, 107–108
Agency, religiosity as, 121–123
Ambiguity, 302
Americans With Disabilities Act
    (ADA), 221–222
Anthropomorphism, 336
Appearance, 1, 8, 19–21, 23, 104–105,
    155–156, 171, 175, 214, 250,
    273–274, 287–288, 317, 343
ADA, 221–222
ageing, gender and older body,
    102–103
ageism, appearance and workplace,
    104–105
appearance codes and aesthetic
    labour, 2–4
appearance-based ageism, 107–108
appearance-based discrimination,
    11
appearance-based inferences of
    criminality, 290–292
BFOQ Defence, 220–221
business necessity defence,
    219–220
civil rights laws, 215–221
diversity and inclusion and CSR,
    251–253
employer and employee analysis,
    226–227
ethical tensions, 274–276
expectations, 179
gender and, 6–7
implications and recommendations,
    227–229

importance of appearance at work,
    2–6
making impression and attracting
    attractive, 4–6
managing conversations, 276–282
manipulation of appearance
    characteristics, 350–351
matters, 178–180
methodology, 253–254
as national origin discrimination,
    219
older workers' experiences of and
    responses to ageism in
    workplace, 105–107
perpetuation of trends, 351–354
possession of appearance
    characteristics, 344–350
practical implications and
    recommendations, 107–108
as race or colour discrimination, 217
as religious discrimination, 217
as sex discrimination, 218–219
state and municipal civil rights laws,
    222–226
theoretical underpinnings, 344
Appearance management, 170–172
appearance and political marketing,
    172
appearance management and
    female politicians, 172–173
interpretation, 175–180
literature review, 170–173
method, 173–175
workwear, 175–176
Apple (Company), 2
Assigned Male At Birth (AMAB), 135
Assimilation, 59
Associate Dean, 162–163
Attorney General, 238
Attractiveness, 185
aspects, 185–186
biases, 187–188
effects, 186–187
as status characteristic, 186–187
at work, 187, 190, 192–193
Australia, 234

aesthetic labour, employee
    appearance and lookism,
    234–237
physical features discrimination and
    Equal Opportunity Act
    1995, 237–239
procedural and jurisdictional issues
    with physical features law,
    239–243
Australian Capital Territory (ACT),
    234
Autoethnographic approach,
    161

Beauty, 214
Behavioural-system theoretical
    orientation, 171
Bias, 57–58, 66
Binary gender, 139
Binary-identified transgender people,
    143–144
Biological sex, 134
Black, Asian and Minority Ethnic
    (BAME), 30
Black, 159–160
Black women in Academia, examining
    hair choices of
    academic discipline, 63–65
    level in organisational hierarchy,
        60–62
    limitations and directions for future
        research, 68
    method, 65
    results, 66
    theoretical framework and relevant
        literature, 58–60
    type of university, 62–63
Body art, 332–333, 353
Body Mass Index (BMI), 77
Body modifications, 170–171
Body weight, 185–186
    data extraction, 78–93
    evidence for weight discrimination
        against overweight women
        in customer-facing roles,
        94–95

literature search and screening
procedure, 76–94
obesity adversely affect women
more than men in customer-
facing roles, 95–96
practical implications and
recommendations, 96–97
theory and concepts, 77–94
Body work, 198–199
Body-art, 301–303, 309–310
Bodywork of women, 160–161
Bona Fide Occupational Qualification
Defence (BFOQ Defence),
220–221, 236
Brand, 215
management, 351
value, 215
Branded-labour, 321–322
British Muslim women's work and
career
embodied presence at work,
123–124
embodied racial identities and
ethnic belongning, 118–121
Muslim women, Islamic attires and
west, 115–118
religiosity as agency, 121–123
Burqa, 114, 121
Business attitudes, 325–326
Business necessity defence, 219–220
Business school dean
bodies of women in academia as
barriers to advancement,
158–160
literature review, 157–160
reflexive accounts by two women
business school deans,
160–164
stories, 161–162, 164
women's abjected bodies in
organisations, 157–158
Business schools, 159–160, 162

Call back rates, 96
Campaigns, 170, 178
Career development, 279–280, 335

practical implications and
recommendations, 335–338
theory and concepts, 333–335
Career Development Institute in
United Kingdom, 276
Career planning, 302
findings, 306–312
recommendations, 312–313
theory and concepts, 303–305
Careers, 170, 186–187
ensembles, 137–138
practitioners, 274–275
progression, 135–136
trajectory, 136
Carnal capital, 20–21, 24–26, 33
Carnal sociology, 24
Carnal theorising, 24
Civil Rights Act of 1964, 216
Civil rights laws, 215–221
Climate Surveys, 312
Clothing, 1
Commission's lack of enforcement
powers, 240–241
Community supervision guidelines, 294
Conformity, 48–49
facades of, 42–43
Consistency, 143
Conspicuous consumption concept, 29
Consumers, 181
Cooperation, 191
Corporate social responsibility (CSR),
11, 251, 253–255
Correct credentials, 2, 6
CostCo Wholesale, 256
Covering tattoos, 325
Creating a Respectful and Open World
for Natural Hair Act
(CROWN Act), 57–58
Credit history information, 293
Criminal history, 287–288
Curly hair
conformity, 48–49
data analysis, 44
data collection, 43–44
design and procedure, 44–45
facades of conformity, 42–43

labelling theory, 42, 45, 48
limitations and directions for future
    research, 52–54
method, 43–45
no curly hair bias, 49–50
results, 45–51
theoretical framework, 42
Customer attitudes, 323–324
Customer service, 77
Customer-facing roles, 76
    evidence for weight discrimination
        against overweight women
        in, 94–95
    obesity adversely affect women
        more than men in, 95–96
Customers, 318–319
Cybervetting, 96–97

Demographic analyses, 146
Disablism, 30
Discipline-based attire norms, 64–65
Discrimination, 147, 215, 318–319,
    331–332
    evidentiary issues associated with
        establishing, 242–243
    in recruitment, 241
District of Columbia (DC), 236–237
Diversity, 20, 28, 251, 253, 255, 257,
    331–332
Diversity and inclusion (D&I), 354
Doe court, 136
Doing gender differently, 160
Doing gender well, 160
Dress codes, 136–139
    disaggregating sex, gender identity,
        gender expression and
        sexual orientation, 133–136
    gender expansiveness and explicitly
        gender-differentiated dress
        codes, 139–141
    gender expansiveness and gender-
        neutral dress codes,
        141–144
    practical impacts, 144–146
    theory and concepts, 133–144

Elliott-Larsen Civil Rights Act of 1976,
    223
Embedded agency, 121–122
Embodied Intersectionality, 115–116
Embodied presence at work, 123–124
Embodied racial identities, 118–121
Embodiment, 289–290
Employability, 317
Employee analysis, 226–227
Employee appearance, 234–237
Employee resource groups (ERGs),
    256–257
Employees appearance, 304–305
Employer, 226–227
Employment, 287–288, 302, 323
    process, 2
    selection, 187–190
    settings, 76
Environmental, Social and
    Governance (ESG), 252
Equal employment opportunity (EEO),
    252–253
Equal Employment Opportunity
    Commission (EEOC),
    215–216
Equal Opportunity Act 1995, 234, 237,
    239
Ethnic belongning, 118–121
Ethnicity, 30
Eurocentric hairstyles, 65
Evidence, 41, 63–64
Evidentiary issues associated with
    establishing discrimination,
    242–243
Exalted masculinity, 103
Explicitly gender-differentiated dress
    codes, 139–141
ExxonMobil, 255

Facades of conformity theory, 48–49
Face Research Lab, 23
Facial Action Coding System (FACS),
    27
Facial attractiveness, 185–186
Facial symmetry, 185–186

Female politicians, appearance
    management and, 172–173
Female sexuality, 138
Financial service organisations, 28
Financial Times Stock Exchange
    (FTSE), 163
Firms, 215
Five-point Likert scale, 45
Front-line employees, 333
Funeral Home, The, 132–133

Gender, 5, 102–103, 114, 118, 157, 176,
    188–189, 345, 347
  and appearance, 6–7
  expansive people, 132
  expansiveness, 135, 139, 141, 144
  gender-based discrimination,
    199–200
  gender-differentiated policies, 137
  gender/sex, 291
  invalidation, 143–144
  non-binary individuals, 134–135
  non-binary workers, 145
  salience, 144
  violation, 143–144
Gender expression, 134
  disaggregating, 133–136
Gender identity, 133
  disaggregating, 133–136
'Gender Jihad', 116
'Gender neutral' colours, 159–160
Gender-neutral dress codes, 141–144
Gender-neutral policies, 137
Gendered dress codes, 138
Gendered environment in academia,
    158
Gendered expectations in political
    workplace, 177–178
Gendered presentability, 201–202
Genetic stigmata, 42
Global Reporting Initiative (GRI), 252
Golden ratio, 22
Governor Burns, 179
Greater Manchester study, The,
    123–124
Green Bonds, 252

Grounded theory approach, 44

Habitus, 20–21, 24–25, 28
Hair bias, 68
  in recruitment, 41
Hair care, 106
Hair manipulation, 45
Hair straightening, 41
Halo Code, 57–58
Halo Collective, 30–31
Hegemonic masculinity, 156
Hijab, 114
Historically Black College or
    University (HBCU), 60, 62
Hospitality, 302
Hotels, 307–308
Human Resource (HR), 302
  professionals, 145

Identity, 118, 350
  identity-management strategies, 144
Image, 170
Impression and attracting attractive,
    4–6
Impression management, 62
In vivo coding, 44
Inclusion, 251, 253, 255, 257, 294–295
Independent variables (IVs), 94–95
Information processing theory, 333
Inscription, 292
Integration, 60
Interactional power, 190–192
Internalisation, 289
Interpretation, 175–180
  gendered expectations in political
    workplace, 177–178
  long job interview, 176–177
  from national to local, 178–180
  workwear, 175–176
Intersectional approach, 118
  appearance, 21–23
  carnal capital and symbolic
    violence, 24–26
  intersectionality, carnal capital and
    symbolic violence, 26–33
Intersectionality, 26, 33, 118

theory of, 26
Involuntary change, 30
Islamic feminism, 115
Islamic feminists, 116–117
Islamic framings, 118

J.P. Morgan Chase, 294–295

Knowledge work, 198

Labelling, 45–48
    theory, 42, 54
Labour, 157
Labour market integration
    process, 124–125
    shaping of, 115–118
Laws, 140, 215–216
Leadership, 192–193
LGBTQ people, 136
Long job interview process, 176–178
Lookism, 3–5, 8, 10–11, 21–22, 105,
        107, 198, 222–223, 234, 237

Male politician's uniform,
        175–176
Masculine tattoos, 321
Masculinity, 346
'Me too' campaign, 2
Men in customer-facing roles, obesity
        affect, 95–96
Minority groups, 345
Mixed methods approach, 322
Mixed-Method Appraisal Tool
        (MMAT), 94
MONVA, 50–51
Multi-ethnic British society,
        114
Multinational chain corporations
        (MNCs), 310–311
Multinational luxury hotels, normative
        control and zero-tolerance
        to body-art in, 310–312
Municipal civil rights laws,
        222–226
Muslim feminism, 115
Muslim women, 114, 119, 345

Islamic attires and west, 115–118

National Women's Political Caucus,
        177
Negative customer perceptions,
        301–302
Negative stereotypes, 345
Neoliberal context, 157
Niqaab, 114
No curly hair bias, 49–50
Non-directive approach, 281–282
Non-directivity, 281–282
Non-Islamic feminist, 118
Non-probability sampling technique,
        323

Obesity, 185–186
    affect women in customer-facing
        roles, 95–96
Occupational licences, restrictions on,
        293–294
Occupational sorting, 146
Older adults, 101–102, 105–106
Older body, 102–103
Older workers, 106
    experiences of and responses to
        ageism in workplace,
        105–107
Organisational deviance, 303–304
Organisational standards, 345
Organisations, 333–334
    women's abjected bodies in,
        157–158
Othering process, 120
Outward appearance, 214
Overweight women in customer-facing
        roles, evidence for weight
        discrimination against,
        94–95

Passing, 140–141
Perceived work discrimination, 96
Perceptions, 320
Perpetuation of trends, 351–354
Phenomenological epistemology, 24
Physical appearance, 20

Physical attractiveness, 185
Physical body, 157
Physical features
    discrimination, 237–239
    legal definition, 241–242
Physicality of leadership, 157
Physiology, 26–27
Piercings, 301–303
Policies, 117–118
Political Action Committees (PAC),
    173
Political brands, 180
Political marketing
    appearance and, 172
    process, 170
    theory, 180
Political workplace, gendered
        expectations in, 177–178
Politics of respectability, 62–63
Positive distinctiveness strategies,
    59–60
Possessions, 349–350
Power, 186, 346
Practical disincentives for pursuing
        physical features
        discrimination claim, 243
Practices, 118
Predominantly White Institution
    (PWI), 60
Prejudice, 345
Prescription, 144–146
Primary school teacher,
    337–338
Professionals, 214–216, 273–274
    activities, 135
    habitus, 25
    image construction, 59
    programs, 64–65
    settings, 58
    women in low/no-hierarchy
        organisations, 204–208
Proscription, 144–146
Psychological theories, 275

Qualification in Career Development,
    276

Queer theory, 134

Race, 290
Racial segregation, 121
Radisson Hotel Group (RHG), 305
Reasonable factors other than age test
    (RFOA test), 219–220
Recognition process, 181
Reflexive accounts by two women
        business school deans,
        160–164
Reflexivity, 164
Relative obscurity of physical features
        discrimination jurisdiction,
        239–240
Religiosity as agency, 121–123
Research, 60–61
Research Questions (RQ), 76
Respectable business femininity
        process, 157–158
Respondent demographics, 324–325
Résumé gap, 293
Rule of the game, 20–21, 24–25
Rules of symmetry, 22

Search string, 77
Selection, 186–187
Self identity, 19–20
Self-categorisation theory, 333
Self-descriptive photo essays, 191–192
Self-system theoretical orientation, 171
Senior women managers, 200–204
Sens pratique, 24–25
Sex, disaggregating, 133–136
Sexism
    ageing, gender and older body,
        102–103
    ageism, appearance and workplace,
        104–105
    older workers' experiences of and
        responses to ageism in
        workplace, 105–107
    practical implications and
        recommendations, 107–108
Sexual harassment, 6–7
Sexual orientation, 135–136

disaggregating, 133–136
Social identity group membership, 59
Social identity–based impression
    management (SIM), 59
  framework, 66–68
  strategies, 61–62
Social integration process, 125
Social interactions, 191–192
Social media, 190
Social othering process, 121
Social recategorisation strategy of
    assimilation, 59
Socially responsible investment (SRI),
    252
Sociological approaches, 275
South Asian women, 123–124
Starbucks, 304
State level civil rights laws, 223
Status beliefs, 186
Status characteristic, 186–187
Status competition, 191
Stigma, 42, 288, 301–302, 318–319,
    334–335
Stigmatisation of curly hair, 42
Symbolic violence concept, 24–26, 33

Tattoos, 301–303, 311, 318–319,
    332–333
  associations, 319–320
  factors affecting customer
      perceptions, 320–321
  shifting attitudes, 321–322
Tengai, 27–28
Toothless tigers, 240
Traditional workplaces, 28
Transgender, 132, 135–136
  persons, 139
Transnational dynamics, 123–124

U.S. Equal Employment Opportunity
    Commission, 144
UK Equalities Act (2010), 139–140
Unconscious bias training (UBT), 256
Uniforms, 171
United Nation's Global Compact, 252
United States Supreme Court, 132

University, type of, 62–63
Upper market hotels, playful twist of
    aesthetic labour in,
    306–309
Urbana in Illinois, 236–237

Vans, 335–336
Verbal communication, 1
Victorian Civil and Administrative
    Tribunal (VCAT),
    239
Victorian Equal Opportunity
    Commission (EOC), 234
Virtue ethic' approach, 337
Visibility, 287–288
  appearance-based inferences of
      criminality, 290–292
  embodiment, 289–290
  structural barriers, 293–294
Visible tattoos, 304, 317–318, 353
  findings, 323–326
  literature review, 318–322
  methodology, 322–323
Visual disturbance,
    301–302
Volvo, 336–337

Weight discrimination against
    overweight women in
    customer-facing roles,
    evidence for, 94–95
Western society, 102
Wilson v. Southwest Airlines Company
    (1981), 220–221
Woman Dean of university business
    school, 161
Women, 41–42, 53, 155–156, 169–170,
    172–173
  abjected bodies in organisations,
      157–158
  bodies, 156
  bodies of women in academia as
      barriers to advancement,
      158–160
  career paths, 199
  leaders, 157

in management, 6
reflexive accounts by two women
   business school deans,
   160–164
Women academics, 158–159
   leaders, 156
Women Deans, 156, 164–165
   of business, 156
   of university business schools,
      155–156
Work
   embodied presence at, 123–124
   negotiating work choices and
      decisions, 121–123

Working relationship, 280
Workplaces, 104–105, 141–142,
   187–188, 317
   approach, 8–11
   employment, 343
   fragmentation, 301–302
   importance of appearance at work,
      2–6
   inspiration, 7–8
   older workers' experiences of and
      responses to ageism in,
      105–107

Younger generations, 2